D0225970

SOCIAL
POWER
and
POLITICAL
FREEDOM

Gene Sharp

SOCIAL
POWER
and
POLITICAL
FREEDOM

Introduction by
Senator Mark O. Hatfield

Extending Horizons Books
PORTER SARGENT PUBLISHERS, INC.
11 Beacon St., Boston, MA 02108

Copyright © 1980 by Gene Sharp
All rights reserved
Manufactured in the United States of America
Library of Congress Catalog Card Number: 80-81479
ISBN: 0-87558-091-2 (clothbound)
ISBN: 0-87558-093-9 (paperback)

Designed by Christopher Leonesio
Composed by Howard Kirshen Printing Corporation,
Boston, Massachusetts

Contents

JC
328.3
.S46

303.6
8h2.

Introduction
by Senator Mark O. Hatfield

Gene Sharp is a man of deep social insight and political intellect. His scholarly training and background are vast in their depth and focus in the fields of the social and political sciences. He is extremely well-prepared for the work he has undertaken in this volume, and his perceptions could prove revolutionary in their application in the international political arena.

The main thrust of his life's work has been centered on stressing the need to reexamine and redefine our political institutions and their sanctions, so that we might eliminate our historical dependency on the use of violent means in solving conflicts. He pointedly describes the violent methods to which we have traditionally resorted: war, dictatorship, genocide, and systems of social oppression, which have not solved our problems, but have only succeeded in destroying human life and suppressing political freedoms. The basis for the hope that Dr. Sharp offers is dependent on the ability and capacity of the human mind to comprehend and discover the requirements for the elimination of the use of these violent means in resolving conflicts.

His vision and apprehension of the criminal realities of centralized government are foremost in importance. In this work he pragmatically describes the resulting institutionalized violence that spews from centralized government, whether that government is ruled by self-appointed or elected officials — war, dictatorships, genocide, and systems of social oppression will always follow. This apprehension is expressed by James Madison in the Federalist Papers where he writes:

> The accumulation of all powers, legislative, executive, and judiciary, in the same hands, whether one, a few, or many, and whether hereditary, self-appointed, or elective, may justly be pronounced the very definition of tyranny.[1]

This is the kind of tyranny which demeans human life and political freedoms.

In his grasp of the true nature of the crisis, Gene Sharp points the way to the decentralization of political institutions and power, which must eventually be achieved if we are to avoid the recurring and senseless annihilation of human life, and the continued erosion of our personal freedoms. This is the only way to bring to government the political and practical reality of the words "we the people."

A person might say that this sounds like fine rhetoric, but how do we bring about this change without resorting to the use of violent means ourselves? Again, Dr. Sharp's faculty for seeing into the inner character of the underlying truth provides the solution. It is based on two fundamental principles: (1) that the power of any government is dependent on the cooperation of the people it governs, and that governmental power varies inversely with the noncooperation of the people; and, (2) that the people have the right to change that government if it fails to protect the inalienable rights of the governed. This prerogative is expressed in the Declaration of Independence in the following words:

> That to secure these rights, governments are instituted among men...that, whenever any form of government becomes destructive of these ends, it is the right of the people to alter or abolish it, and to institute new government....

Thus, Gene Sharp's genius provides the guidelines by which change can be rightfully wrought in government through the knowledgeable, organized, and disciplined use of nonviolent dissent and peaceful civil disobedience. This is not to say that nonviolent dissent is easy and will not require tremendous sacrifice, but as he describes in this work, the long-run benefits will ensure the desired results.

As I pointed out in my book, *Between a Rock and a Hard Place,*

> Our world is so deeply addicted to violence that it has lost all objectivity about its actual efficacy and value. Having developed such psychological and economic needs for their machines of war, nations are no more capable of exercising detached and wise judgments about the usefulness of violence as opposed to other nonviolent alternatives than a junky could render about heroin.[2]

Knowing this, Sharp is pleading for us to understand historically and strategically, as well as morally, what nonviolence can accomplish. His is the most persuasive case I have seen to this end. His works are landmarks. *The Politics of Nonviolent Action,* and now *Social Power and Political Freedom,* objectively present the success and shortcomings of nonviolent political action throughout history in such a way that even the most hardened realist can see how objectives sought by nations through war can also be sought by nonviolent means. The case he presents, which we have personally discussed, is not made on moral and theological truths; rather it rests on history, and on a profound understanding of what constitutes political power. Therefore, Sharp's case has relevance to all, no matter what their theological or moral persuasion.

While I depart little from the political and sociological application of Dr. Sharp's insights, I do believe that the primary requirement for solving our extremely grave problems does not merely rely on what the mind of man can do alone. My personal conviction concerning the primary requirement for solving these extremely grave problems in light of our current potential for human destruction is graphically portrayed by the words of General Omar N. Bradley:

> With the monstrous weapons man already has, humanity is in danger of being trapped in this world by its moral adolescence. Our knowledge of science has clearly outstripped our capacity to control it. We have too many men of science, too few men of God. We have grasped the mystery of the atom and rejected the Sermon on the Mount. Man is stumbling blindly through spiritual darkness while toying with the precarious secrets of life and death....
>
> ...The world has achieved brilliance without wisdom, power without conscience. Ours is a world of nuclear giants and ethical infants. We know more about war than we know about peace; more about killing, than we know about living.[3]

In my view, this describes the source to which we must look, and the foundation on which we must use our wisdom and brilliance to build. The foundations for the solutions to our gravest problems have always been there, it is just that the application of those principles has largely been ignored and unexplored. Dr. Sharp's intuitive grasp and understanding of the practical vehicles for just such an application of divine principles make this work monumental in its time. In this era, which cries out for such visionary alternatives, I urge the reader to give heed to its contents.

NOTES

1. Federalist Papers, no. 47.
2. Mark O. Hatfield, **Between a Rock and a Hard Place** (Waco, Texas: Word Books, 1976), p. 136.
3. Armistice Day Address, Boston, Massachusetts, 11 November 1948.

Preface

The unsolved major political problems of our time require us to rethink politics. As a consequence of that effort, we must explore not only how to preserve that from the past which is of merit, but also new possibilities. These include both new institutional forms in place of those which are inadequate or harmful, and also nonviolent means of applying pressures and waging conflicts in place of institutionalized political violence.

These chapters have been written, and this book prepared, on the conviction that we need to turn our minds to examination of our society's problems and to seek ways of resolving them, in harmony with the espoused ideals of our society and with the goal of meeting human needs more adequately.

Most of our problems have been created by human beings. Therefore, as human beings we can solve them. This requires that we discover the requirements for doing so, and that we make the needed efforts. These, in turn, are possible only if we face the problems and think about them in a new light. We must be willing to consider the possibility that prevalent insights, patterns of action, structures, and forms of sanctions are not the only possibilities. Alternatives to them may at times offer realistic hope for building a better future. In this, we must, of necessity, draw upon the past, but not be bound by it, in our quest to develop more accurate and complete perceptions of reality and to develop alternatives to existing policies.

The concept of replacing violent sanctions with nonviolent sanctions in a series of specific substitutions is not utopian. To a degree not generally recognized, this already occurs in various conflict situations, even on scales which affect our domestic society and international relations. Far from being utopian, nonviolent sanctions build upon crucial parts of our past and present reality. Past cases, however, are only the crude beginnings of alternative nonviolent sanctions. These could be refined and developed to increase their power potential, and adapted to meet society's genuine needs for sanctions. One of the major tasks before us is to learn better how nonviolent sanctions can be used more effectively in place of violent sanctions to preserve and defend societies.

Major efforts have been made to make this book as intelligible and readable as possible, in the conviction that writings in political philosophy and social science, as well as other fields, should to the maximum degree possible be readily accessible to the general educated public.

The chapters of this book vary in the degree to which they are popular-style explorations or are more strictly academic analyses. They also differ in the degree to which they deal with concrete problems or offer broader theoretical analyses of our problems and the nature of solutions to them. Although these chapters have been written over a twenty-year period (see Appendix H, "Origins of the Chapters"), they combine to explore in a generally unified way the central problems which have been selected for attention. Of the four chapters written especially for this book, "Rethinking Politics," "The Societal Imperative," and "Popular Empowerment" offer integrative analyses relevant to all the themes and topics of the book. One can, therefore, read this book from beginning to end, or one can read individual chapters of particular interest, and be led by the cross references back to other chapters tangential to the discussions.

The aim of this book is to provoke thought about the nature of our major problems and possible solutions to them. Therefore, full discussion, challenge, reasoned criticisms, and presentations of other new analyses are welcomed.

G.S.

Cambridge, Massachusetts
April 1980

Acknowledgements

This book has been made possible due to the assistance and kindness of many people over the years.

A variety of people have directly or indirectly helped in the original publication of the previously published articles or chapters from which eight of the chapters of this book have been prepared. In addition to persons specifically mentioned here, the editors and staff members of the publications and books in which those chapters were published merit acknowledgement. These publications are listed in Appendix H.

Several of the chapters draw, in varying degrees, on lectures which I have given to a variety of audiences, institutions, and universities in England and the United States. These are also listed in Appendix H. I am grateful to these bodies, and the persons who invited me to them, for the stimuli to continue to develop new thinking, the opportunity to share ideas with others, and for helpful comments, suggestions, and criticisms from persons I met there.

The chapters of this book were variously written while I have been affiliated with St. Catherine's College, Oxford; the Institute of Philosophy and the History of Ideas of the University of Oslo; the weekly *Peace News* (London); the Institute for Social Research, Oslo; Southeastern Massachusetts University; and the Center for International Affairs of Harvard University. I am grateful to their staffs, libraries, and the persons who made my affiliations with them possible and enjoyable.

The editing, revisions, and rewriting of this book have been done at the Center for International Affairs of Harvard University while I have been a Visiting Scholar, and while I have also been Professor of Political Science and Sociology at Southeastern Massachusetts University.

Without the financial support of various institutions and individuals, some of them too modest to encourage mention of their assistance, the original research and writing, and the very considerable revisions and editorial work in transforming the original essays into this book would have been impossible.

Agnes Brophy was my Assistant in the summer of 1978 when I

began seriously to explore editing various previously published articles and chapters into two books, which after many changes eventually became this book and *Gandhi as a Political Strategist*. She offered valuable advice on the original conception, consideration of what to include and exclude, evaluation of ideas for new chapters, criticisms of the content and editorial condition of various existing publications, newly drafted chapters, and many revisions of both. She also did most of the work on obtaining permissions to quote copyrighted material. Her help and advice at all stages were crucial in making this book possible.

When Ms. Brophy moved from Cambridge in October 1979 her position was filled by Jane Shorall. Although she stepped into this project as it was approaching completion, she, with amazing rapidity, continued most ably the tasks of offering criticisms and suggestions on current drafts of new chapters, consideration of whether to include or exclude individual appendices, and a variety of other editorial and production tasks. Julia Kittross ably assisted in the final editorial steps and in coordinating proofreading.

Nancy A. Tramontin spent months of work to help make this book as good as possible by identifying and helping to correct editorial and stylistic problems in her role as copy editor. She also stepped into the breach and informally served as a substantive editorial advisor, exploring with me the needs of the developing book as it began to take on a life of its own. This included the need, or lack of need, for certain chapters, and evaluation of the needs of early drafts of new chapters and sections of chapters written for this book. As the concept and substance of the book grew far beyond the original idea for an edited compilation of previous publications, and as I never seemed able to cease preparing new drafts of chapters, her work expanded considerably. Her assistance, friendly persistence, and valuable contributions have helped to transform the original plan into the present volume.

Extremely valuable comments, candid evaluations, and editorial suggestions for individual chapters have also been offered by several good friends. These are Stephanie Barry, Lisa Foley, Rabbi Everett Gendler, Charles Hamilton, Julia Kittross, Douglas Kruse, George Lakey, Charles Norchi III, David Toscano, William Vogele, James Young, and especially Christopher Moore. When on occasion I did not follow their advice, some special problem interfered, my perspective was different, or the poor judgment was mine. I have learned in recent years how valuable such assistance can be, whether from colleagues, friends, or undergraduate helpers.

I am extremely grateful to Senator Mark O. Hatfield for preparing his Introduction in the midst of his many other responsibilities. Senator Hatfield has long had a deep concern to find better means to resolve the problems of our world, including the problems of war and violence, and to find ways in which to implement moral principles in the practical political world.

The preparation of the index has been the responsibility of William Vogele. This type of index, which includes concepts and analyses of particular phenomena and ideas is exceptionally difficult to prepare. Mr. Vogele has done this in consultation with me with great perceptiveness and sensitivity to the ideas and shades of meaning, as well as with attention to the usual type of entries. His advice on other problems and strengths of proposed chapters, and on the book as a whole, have also been extremely helpful.

The title of Chapter Eleven, "The Societal Imperative," is taken from that of my 1976 lecture at Manhattan College (see Appendix H), and was originally suggested to me by Charles Norchi III, an undergraduate volunteer research assistant from Manhattan College the summer of 1976, while I was at Harvard University's Program for Science and International Affairs.

I would also like to thank everyone at Porter Sargent Publishers who assisted in the publishing of this book.

Copyrights are acknowledged separately in Appendix G.

1

Rethinking Politics

We have, to a large degree, lost the confidence, and even the hope, that we can solve our most serious domestic and international problems. This loss alone must be placed high on the list of the tragedies of the twentieth century.

Only a few decades ago, Americans, Europeans, and others who shared the Western intellectual heritage, viewed the future very differently. The world was perceived as becoming progressively better. It was believed that advances in the physical sciences, medicine, and technology were already being paralleled by improvements in society, economics, politics, and international relations. Human progress was believed to be inevitable. By one path or another — there were differences of opinion about the means — social justice, economic plenty, political freedom, respect for human dignity, and international peace would, before long, be established. In the foreseeable future, oppression, inhumanities, war, and injustice would be eradicated. Many people believed that by individual or group action they could control their own lives, build the type of society they wanted, and shape their own destinies. This was to a significant degree true even of oppressed people. Somehow — by their own efforts, the spread of education, social evolution, or the destined change of social systems — their own lot, or at least the lot of their posterity, would be improved and their oppression ended in a re-formed society.

That hope, that sense of power, that confidence in our ability to control and to shape the future, are now largely gone. They have been destroyed by the tragedies that have devastated the twentieth century. Almost everywhere, people sense that they have been overwhelmed, and still remain threatened, by a series of grave problems, disasters, and powerful forces which they feel are far beyond their control. Hence, a sense of helplessness, loss of hope, and finally fatalism has spread.

We must face the reality that, with all of our achievements, we have failed to solve some of the most grave problems of our time — dictatorship, genocide, war, and social oppression.

The people of our century have experienced the most extreme dictatorships in human history. Our imperfect and often feeble efforts to achieve freedom have frequently been forced into retreat, and our limited accomplishments toward freedom have at times been abolished under diverse attacks. Even in the constitutional democracies which survive, many people sense that they are powerless to improve their society in any significant way — powerless even to maintain their basic civil liberties against gradual erosion.

Once again in human history, deliberate genocide — an attempt to exterminate a whole people — has been committed in the attacks against Armenians, Jews, Gypsies, certain African peoples, and others. Indeed, genocide is technologically far more possible now than it was in 1940. Other mass killings have occurred in Cambodia, Bengal, and elsewhere. Bigotry and racism have survived and sometimes even intensified, including in societies in which they were believed to be disappearing. Anticipating future famine, we are already discussing triage — whom to allow to starve.

Changes in the nature and technology of war initiated during the

First World War have accelerated. They have vastly expanded its destructiveness, and deliberately targeted civilians. Because of all this, the possibility of effective defense (traditionally defined as protection, preservation, and warding off of danger) has been abolished. Now, action intended as resistance to perceived evil conducted in the name of defense of people and principles can result in vast annihilation.

We have also failed to create societies able to meet human needs. Serious efforts in the past to abolish injustice, oppression, and exploitation have been too few, have met with vigorous opposition, and have had only limited effectiveness. Instead of achieving those goals, the results of these efforts have often included depersonalization, bureaucratization, centralization of power, and dependency. On occasion, the results have been extreme dictatorship and terror. Today terror tactics are widely used domestically both by those who seek to maintain established systems, and also by those who claim to take seriously the words of justice and humanity.

The list of tragedies could be continued.

This is not the entire story of this century, however. We also have made some positive gains. We now concern ourselves with some problems which previously we did not fully recognize, such as the extermination of other species, violation of the environment, manipulation of people's minds, destruction of other cultures, and the existence of widespread hunger and starvation. We have even begun to respond to them with limited successes. We have also made some important attempts to meet more adequately basic human needs, and to oppose one type of oppression or another. At times we have tried to learn how to struggle more effectively against perceived evils and how to build better institutions. These efforts and limited gains must be acknowledged and appreciated.

Yet, concerning the four grave problems on which we are focusing in this book — dictatorship, genocide, war, and social oppression — we have made little progress. In important ways they have even been exacerbated. Despite many attempts grounded in established political assumptions and existing policies to solve these problems, we have lost ground. These problems have become more grave as the institutional and technical capacities for imposing dictatorship, perpetrating genocide, waging war, and inflicting social oppression have increased.

As the perception that we can shape our own future and improve our societies recedes, individuals and whole populations increasingly see their major problems to be insoluble and themselves to be power-less. Many people stop trying. Their resulting inaction is misperceived as apathy.

RESPONSES TO OUR PROBLEMS

Despite all this, some people have retained both a sensitivity to the seriousness of our problems and a commitment to try to solve them. These people have responded to our problems in several different ways.* First, some people espouse "solutions" which they see as pure and complete, spiritually or politically, but which are essentially millennial. That is, the solutions depend on some extraordinary intervention into human affairs of a force which is beyond the control of human consciousness and action. Second, other people appalled by the problems of our time have abandoned rationality and systematic efforts to achieve change. They deny the importance of intellectual analysis, planning, or consideration of how change is to be effected before they act. Instead, they have stressed emotions, spontaneity, and unpredictability, believing that if they and others act as they "feel," significant changes will occur in ways which they cannot predict. Third, most people who still attempt to improve society and resolve its problems pursue one of the "solutions" handed down to us from the past which maintain that human societies are controllable by human beings, that rationality and systematic efforts to achieve change are important, and that by some type of action and programs using mild or extreme measures we can solve our problems.

---

*These people usually adhere to one of various social, religious, or political world-views which offer both explanations for the world's ills and prescriptions to correct them. These world-views and the groups espousing and seeking to apply them are diverse; their beliefs, group characteristics, and types of action may differ widely. Despite this, their explanations and recommended solutions often share important major characteristics with others even when they differ widely in specifics. We will here and later focus solely on those main outlines of their world-views in order to enable us to see them in stark relief in comparison to very different types of views. If one is familiar with such world-views and groups, one may recognize how the details of their specific beliefs and activities relate to the very broad characteristics on which we are focusing.

This repudiation of the millenarian approach in favor of the postulate of human capacity to control human societies, and of the antirational emotional response in favor of rationality and of careful consideration of how to effect change, remain valid and highly important points of departure if we are to face and resolve our grave problems. The traditional, broadly political, approaches have not been at fault on these points. They have, however, not succeeded in eradicating our gravest problems, and are at present inadequate.

To date, all the existing political doctrines and programs have fallen short of implementing our avowed principles, achieving our goals, meeting our needs, and resolving the four grave problems we have discussed. Therefore, we must not presume the full validity and adequacy of traditional conservative, liberal, radical, Marxist, anarchist, pacifist, or any other doctrine or comprehensive program. However, we of course need to understand these past approaches, without becoming entrapped in their assumptions and their internal "logic." We need to examine them all carefully, to see both their positive lessons as well as their fallacies and inadequacies. We need to pay particular attention to those approaches which have aimed to achieve significant social change.

THREE APPROACHES TO CHANGE

Most of the major existing approaches to social change can be grouped under three general perspectives: the utopian, reformist, and dictatorial schools of change. Let us discuss briefly the outlines of each of these approaches.

Utopians are often especially sensitive to the evils of the world and, craving certainty, purity, and completeness, firmly reject the evils as totally as possible, wishing to avoid any compromises with them. Instead, utopians assert an alternative vision of the world which they would like to come into being. Their visionary belief may be labeled "religious" or "political" — it matters little for this discussion. They await a "new world" which is to come into being by an act of God, by a change in the human spirit, by autonomous changes in economic conditions, or by a deep spontaneous social upheaval — all beyond deliberate human control. These believers are primarily concerned with espousing the "true" understanding of the evil and the principles by which people should live, gaining converts, living with the least possible compromise until the great change arrives. They may deliberately seek to establish ways of living and communities which exemplify their principles and which may inspire others to do likewise.

The most serious weakness of this response to the problems of this world is not the broad vision, or the commitment of the people who believe in it. The weakness is that these believers have no effective way to reach the society of their dreams. Condemnation of social evil, espousal of an alternative order of life, a deep personal commitment, and an effort to live according to it, are all good and necessary, but unfortunately alone they do not transform human society and institutions. To do that, an instrumentally effective program of achievable steps for dealing with the evils of existing society and for creating an improved social order is required.

Reformists, on the other hand, are highly concerned with being effective in making changes in the world as it is, with all its powerful groups supporting the status quo and its other limitations impeding major transformation. Therefore, they concentrate almost solely on minor specific changes in the established policies, practices, and institutions, even though these remain fundamentally unaltered. After much hard work and a great deal of time, these specific changes are sometimes accomplished. They are, however, won at a price, often including heavy personal costs and ethical compromises. The changes won can be very important in relieving particular expressions of injustices and in improving specific conditions. However, the most serious political cost of the reformist approach is acceptance of one's incapacity to change the most grave political evils of the society and the accepted postulates upon which they rest. At best, only relatively minor steps may be taken with this approach, while the great problems cited above remain untouched. No program for systemic change is formulated, much less initiated. So those problems continue, their bases intact, the influences contributing to their perpetuation and even to their growth still operative.

A third group of people impatiently perceive the incapacity of the above two approaches to accomplish fundamental change. Believing that the whole structure of society requires change, they adopt a more daring and rigorous course. These people are determined neither to become politically irrelevant, nor to settle for political trivia. They conclude that to avoid the dangers of the previous two approaches, they must enter into "real politics." If minor changes are but sops to prevent basic change, these people determine that they should tackle the structure of society. Real politics, they believe, means full use of the most important single political institution of their society: the State* apparatus, with its bureaucracy, police and prison system, and permanent military forces. In order to achieve their goals, this group believes that control of the State must not only be taken away from those who have used it to support the existing system, but also be placed in the hands of those who are committed to radical structural change and who "know" how to achieve it. In their view, the full utilization of State power is required to achieve the goal of structural change.

In their eyes, "ordinary" people are weak, unreliable, short-sighted, and are preoccupied with immediate pleasures, economic needs, and day-to-day life — especially the people who are most oppressed and stultified by the old system. Therefore, in the opinion of these exponents of fundamental change, ordinary people cannot do what is required to transform society.† The general populace cannot be relied upon to save themselves, nor to take control of the State to bring in a new order of society. This task, therefore, is seen to shift from the people to the self-chosen elite. Members of that elite, usually a Party, but sometimes a military clique, believe that they alone know what is required, and that they alone are able to take the needed action. Therefore, they believe, they have the right, and even the duty, to seize control of the State, and to use its full resources, including its bureaucracy and apparatus of violence, to effect the

---

*The State in this volume refers to the most prevalent form of government in the modern world, characterized by a permanent bureaucracy, a permanent police force and penal system, and a permanent military system. The State claims for itself the legal monopoly within the society of the use of violence as a domestic and international sanction, and also frequently claims the highest loyalty of its citizens. The State is also discussed in several later chapters, especially Chapter Two, "Social Power and Political Freedom," Chapter Eight, "The Problem of Political Technique in Radical Politics," and Chapter Twelve, "Popular Empowerment."

†This is clearly the view of Leninists. See, for example, V. I. Lenin, "What Is To Be Done? Burning Questions of Our Movement," in V. I. Lenin, *Selected Works in Three Volumes* (New York: International Publishers, 1967, and Moscow: Progress Publishers, 1967), vol. I, pp. 97-256; and Joseph Stalin, "The Foundations of Leninism," in Arthur P. Mendel, ed., *Essential Works of Marxism* (New York: Bantam Books, 1965), pp. 209-296.

revolution. Thereby, they believe, they will be able to eradicate the old order and to construct a new structure.

With the ownership of the underlying economic structure shifted to the State in the name of the people, given the necessary time for the society to mature, oppression would cease, these advocates believe. Some of them maintain that the State itself would finally no longer be needed and would dissolve. The new society would then exist to meet human needs and enable people to fulfill their potential, while the old evils of oppression, injustice, war, and tyranny are left safely back in the earlier period of human history, or "prehistory."

Whatever the appeal of this third approach to change, the results of its application in the real world have not been simply inadequate; they have been alarming. The anticipated ideal society in fact has never arrived, and has even ceased to be a goal which is really expected in the foreseeable future. Instead, a refined dictatorship, more thorough, extensive, and ruthless, has replaced the old cruel, but relatively incompetent, one. The new bureaucracy has grown far larger than the original. The previous economic and political class domination has been replaced by a new, more rigorous, political class domination, and that class itself is controlled by a very small super elite. The old forms of cruelty and repression have been superseded by massive secret police, and sometimes concentration camps and killings on a scale rarely attempted earlier. The old army has become a massive military machine of both domestic and international danger. The elite in command of the State apparatus and the Party has been able sharply to change policies and shift doctrines at will. Perhaps most tragic of all in terms of the early revolutionary dreams is that the people themselves remain as excluded and powerless as ever — despite the rhetoric and slogans.

Why has this third route to social change failed? It appears that a fundamentally different society cannot be created by deliberately building it on the foundation of a refined application of the most dubious characteristics of the old society: elite domination, centralization, political violence, and manipulation of the supposedly incompetent "masses."

Major variations, of course, exist within each of these three general responses to the need for change. Those variations are important, but not sufficient to correct the basic weaknesses and errors of these approaches, nor to enable them to solve the important problems of our society. Are these three general approaches to change the best of which we are capable?

ROOTS OF OUR FAILURE

Some people dismiss their responsibility for trying to create a better society by passing off the problems and tragedies of our society as inevitable consequences of human aggressiveness or "human nature." This response has its own appeal and is comforting: "We can't help it." That outlook is not valid, however, for it ignores much psychological knowledge and especially the almost endless variations in cultures, outlooks, personalities, and institutions revealed by cultural anthropologists. No single such factor as "aggressiveness" immutably shapes all present and future societies beyond human control. While human beings are capable of great cruelty and evil, we are also capable of kindness and goodness. Our "human nature" permits vast beneficial changes. We are not doomed to be aggressive killing beings, excusing ourselves by slanderously blaming our behavior on our supposed inheritance from the far more innocent animals.

As people who say we believe in the worth of human beings, freedom, justice, economic well-being, peace, and related principles, we have a responsibility to try to implement those principles in the world in which we now live, and to build a society closer to those ideals for the people who will come after us. Sometimes we need to preserve as best we can parts of our present society which actualize those principles. At other times, we need to seek to achieve fundamental changes of other parts of our society which violate those principles. In any case, we must carefully choose courses of action which will positively contribute to achieving our goals.

It is always tempting for people who feel deeply about society's ills to choose courses of action which are emotionally satisfying, and to assume that the action will achieve the goals, that is, be "instrumental." However desirable that might be, we cannot assume that all action which is emotionally satisfying will also be instrumental. The prime problem for advocates of change is to formulate courses of action, programs, and policies which can instrumentally contribute to producing the kind of society which we wish to achieve. That requires that we first understand well our present problems, and both the alternative means of struggle and ways to build better institutions which are available to us. Then we must be able to choose wisely the particular means of action by which we will be able to move from our present position toward our goal. The initial problem, therefore, is conceptual, analytical, and strategic. It will also be important to deal with and to satisfy our emotions, but emotional release alone can lead to wasted activities on naive projects, or to counterproductive release of frustrations and hatreds in hostilities and violence. If our efforts and their costs are really to contribute to achieving our aims, we need first to think, then develop instrumental strategies of change, and finally channel our emotions and energy into positive action.

If we wish to implement the ideals we espouse, resolve the grave problems of our society, and achieve basic social change to meet human needs more adequately, the prime task before us is not to be pure, nor just to assert ideals, nor to describe in detail the desired ultimate society. The task is not even simply to live personally by our ideals, nor to develop a doctrine of dissent or resistance. Nor is the most important task before us to get a new law enacted this year, nor a certain political party or persons elected to governmental positions soon. Much less is our task to install as our dictator some Leader, doctrinal Party, or military clique which promises to save us.

The prime task before us is first to formulate the next major steps to move toward a fundamentally better society. The task is then to make major changes in our imperfect society, leading to additional improvements, moving progressively toward the kind of society which most of us wish to see ultimately: a society based upon the widely espoused but often ignored principles of human dignity and worth, social justice, political freedom, and world peace. Our responsibility, therefore, is not to dissent from dictatorships but to prevent and disintegrate them, not to denounce genocide but to make it impossible, not to renounce war individually but to remove war from society, not to repudiate particular social oppression but to construct a very different society with justice. All this requires that we begin by thinking about our problems, developing better solutions to them, and initiating viable steps to achieve responsible and acceptable social change.

Our past and present failures to reach such a society are largely rooted in our assumption that we already are on the right path, or that the path exists and as soon as enough people find and follow it, all will be well. Both of these assumptions may be false. People still argue about which existing political doctrine, dogma, or program is right, when all of them may be inadequate or worse. Pursuit of them, with whatever commitment, determination, and sacrifice, is likely to lead to no better results than have been achieved in the past.

THE NEED TO RETHINK

If in this situation we keep searching for the one true political doctrine, we are like the man, described by Sir John Maynard in 1689, who was lost in the wilderness and stood crying, "Where is the king's highway? I shall walk nowhere but on the king's highway." In our political wilderness no established dogmas and programs exist which can lead to the society we seek, whether they espouse conservation from the past, moderate social change, or fundamental social revolution. Indeed, they, and our continued confidence in them, are now often a hindrance to the needed rethinking of politics and the charting of a viable course toward the society we seek. We need to look beyond *all* of them — not in indifference to what positively may be gained from them, but without acceptance of the limitations imposed by the inadequacies of their assumptions and thought.

The future is not hopeless. Most of our problems are human problems, created by human beings. We can, therefore, with sufficient long-term thought, analysis, planning, hard work, and action, solve them. We can, as human beings, change human institutions. We are the helpless victims of hostile forces only if we believe that we are, and if we do not do what is necessary to save ourselves. Significant roles exist for human will and for the human intellect and reason in understanding our problems and in charting new paths toward solutions. Certainly a role also exists for courageous action. We have the capacities to make the future better, if we come to understand the nature of our problems, if we choose our means and programs wisely, and if we apply them well.

This requires, however, that we stop to think, that we use our minds consciously and actively to find the answers to our society's problems. We need deliberately to by-pass the old asusmptions, programs, and alignments, unless after careful reexamination we have determined them to be valid. No one can provide us with ready-made answers.

The reasons for our inability thus far to solve our most serious problems may go to the roots of our conception of the nature of politics. If our basic postulates about politics have been erroneous, it is no wonder that our policies have been ineffective, or that they have produced the opposite of what we intended to achieve. If we are required to rethink the nature and practice of politics fundamentally, the answer to our present needs cannot be the unthinking adoption of a sweeping new political doctrine which purports to explain all evil and to offer political salvation better than the old doctrines. Nor will the required rethinking be accomplished easily and quickly, and then be laid out in full, ready simply to be believed and applied. Only some ideas toward the needed rethinking can be offered here. Rethinking is itself only a step toward the needed reshaping of politics.

How is this rethinking to happen? Clearly our response to this need cannot be another utopian trap in which we simply assert our full ideas or glorify the desired society but lack the ability to develop and implement attainable steps toward its creation. Obviously, too, we must abandon repetition of our sweeping sloganized "solutions" — such as "nationalization," "education," "disarmament," "legislation," "revolution," "spontaneity of the masses," and "world government" — which we recite without thinking in face of our problems, as though they were incantations able to ward off evil political spirits, until and unless new anlaysis fills these with new substance and relevance.

In addition, on an elementary basis, we must abandon unexamined acceptance of such assumptions as these: (1) that we already know the answers; (2) that some doctrine or ideology can supply the needed answers; (3) that some special group can "save" humanity; (4) that violence is required for realistic politics; (5) that centralization in politics and economics is desirable; and (6) even that we are as yet able to ask all the necessary questions.

If we are to avoid the limitations and mistakes of past efforts to deal with society's problems and to build a better order, our *first* task is to attempt to rethink politics. Our first task is not the denunciation of particular institutions or of violence if we do not wish to be relegated to the simple role of dissent of those who are unable to help to shape our society. Rethinking is required if we are to be able to deal with various institutions and violence in a new way, more effectively than has been done in the past.

Ideals and ultimate goals are usually less of a problem in politics than has sometimes been assumed. Most individuals and political groups would say that they desire a society which practices the principles of human dignity, freedom, justice, respect for life, and peace. When we speak these words we must be careful to give real meaning to them, in order that they do not become mere clichés without content. It is not our ideals, but rather our understanding of the nature of our problems, and of the means by which we can achieve a society which practices those ideals, which is weak. We need to reexamine our past understanding of those aspects, and to think freshly about present conditions, and ways to build a better society.* How can we begin to "rethink politics?"

QUESTIONING THE OBVIOUS

We usually take the familiar for granted, and do not really "see" it. We often fail to ponder that which is unmistakably before us, to give it our close attention, and to ask simple but fundamental questions about it, as we would if it appeared before us for the first time. We may assume its innocence because it seems to be the only possibil-

---

*One way to begin is to ask questions, often very simple ones, about our problems. We need to choose our questions carefully to ensure that they can open the way to new insights. Among the simple questions which might, if explored in depth under appropriate conditions, be helpful in stimulating new thinking are:

What is really the nature of the problem? Have we understood it correctly or fully? Do new perspectives on the nature of the problem exist, or can they be developed, which might lead us to fresh insights into its nature, and therefore into the needed means for its resolution?

What are the several alternative hypotheses which exist, or could be developed, to explain why a given problem or phenomenon exists? When these alternative hypotheses are examined rigorously, concerning their assumptions, reasoning, and validity, which of them merit further examination? Do other hypotheses now occur to us which should be considered?

Can the problem be solved in isolation from other problems or conditions? What are its interrelationships with other problems? Are they incidental, accidental, or casual? Or, are they substantive? If the problem is causally interconnected with other problems or conditions, how can we locate the points at which to begin to make changes? What means can be used which would be instrumentally effective?

ity. Our unexamined assumptions may interfere with our perception
and reaction; we may "know" that a given phenomenon is necessary,
could not cause a problem, or in any case is inevitable. We may not
ask what the phenomenon means, what causes it, or what it may
cause. It may not occur to us to question its significance or to explore
whether alternatives to it exist. Our familiarity with our world often
stifles our curiosity about it, and thereby limits our control over our
future.

If we try, we could lift this limitation on our understanding of
our world and our problems. We could ask simple questions as
though they were being asked for the first time in an effort to gain
fresh insights into the nature of our problems and the means to
resolve them.

The story told about Isaac Newton and the apple illustrates the
point. Apples had been falling from trees as long as apple trees had
existed, and presumably many people who had been under them at
the right moment had also been hit by the falling apples long before
Newton. But only Newton is reputed to have asked, "Why?" Could
there be some reason, not only for *this* apple falling, and for *apples* in
general falling, but for *all* things falling? This led him to seek an
answer to that question, until he finally developed the Law of Gravity
which enlarged our understanding of the physical world and had
beneficial practical consequences.

In order to find solutions to our most grave and persistent
problems, we also may need, as one of various tools, to resort to such
simple questions as: Why do dictatorship, genocide, war, social
oppression, and our other problems happen? What makes them
possible? When do they occur? Are the problems universal and
inevitable? Are better answers to our problems possible than we have
been given already? Do alternatives to them and means of resolving
them exist, or could they be developed?

What different questions can we ask about some of our most
serious problems which might give us new insights into them, or
might lead us to other helpful questions, facts, or interrelationships?

While studying dictatorships, their strengths and means of control, we might ask what may be their weaknesses and limitations. If
we located significant weaknesses, we could ask whether those might
be subject to deliberate aggravation in order to limit, or even to
disintegrate, dictatorial systems without an internal violent upheaval

or an international war. Instead of simply describing how dictator-ships come into being, we might ask how we could prevent their development, and how to bar dictatorial groups from seizing control in the first place. Instead of merely recording and bemoaning the diminution of human freedom, we could ask what actions and struc-tures may be required to ensure that substantive freedom survives and grows.

While investigating past attempts at genocide, we could also look at the limits and failures of such attempts, and ask how future attempts to commit genocide could be prevented and defeated.

Instead of only describing the spread of terrorism, analyzing it as a response to the helplessness of an alienated group, or recording its tendency to induce in the attacked society authoritarian controls, we could ask different questions: In what situations has terrorism failed or been rejected and why? What other means of action can empower excluded and oppressed groups? What responses to terrorist attacks other than authoritarian controls and violent suppression have been or can be effective?

Instead of lamenting the dangers of modern war, recording its escalation in military hardware, or pursuing only the proposed reme-dies which demonstrably have not succeeded, we might reexamine the problem of war, reasons for our failure to solve it, and the popular perception that a capacity to wage wars is needed. We might ask whether other means of defense and open struggle exist or could be developed which might provide a political equivalent of war.

Instead of concentrating solely on analyses of the nature and origins of particular social injustices, and recounting existing mea-sures to correct them, we could ask whether any general causes or prerequisites of the conditions we call social injustices exist, whether any general preconditions are required for their development or maintenance, and what means, if any, could make it possible to increase social justice without resorting to dictatorship and violence.

REEXAMINING "FACTS" AND ASSUMPTIONS

Neither must we take for granted without questioning and exa-mining alternatives our standard assumptions about the nature of society and politics and what has happened in history. Have phenomena existed which we have assumed were not possible? Have events happened which we have not previously noticed? Have major changes been caused by the factors we have been told or by different ones? If reality is not what we have assumed, if the problem is different from what we have thought, if the potentialities are other than we have supposed, we may have fewer, more, or different options than we have believed. Sometimes minor corrections in our view of reality and the historical record may make little difference in our ability to deal with problems and to shape our future, but if the corrections are major, then this may make an important difference.

Are the explanations of the causes of certain phenomena and problems which we have been given really accurate? Are the remedies and program which we have received from others for dealing with our problems really based on valid analyses, and capable of resolving the problems? Careful reexamination of the explanations, remedies, and programs from the past, in terms of their assumptions, facts, reasoning, and adequacy may shed important light on the means by which we may be able to resolve those problems.

Special attention must be given to assumptions about the nature of society and politics which we have accepted, and to the diagnoses of our problems which we have assumed to be obviously true. It is possible that neither the assumptions nor the diagnoses may be accurate. By deliberate attention to locating and examining both, we may be better able to determine their validity, and to examine or develop alternative assumptions and diagnoses. Implicit or hidden assumptions and axiomatically accepted remedies are particularly in need of identification and critical examination.

RECOGNIZING OUR POLITICAL POSTULATES

The operating postulates of our political society are rarely critically examined. These are the assumptions about the ways in which politics needs to operate to be realistic and effective, as distinct from the ideals espoused in the society. The operating postulates are the "obviously true" points of departure for political activities and structures. These postulates are so often simply taken for granted as bases of political reality that we frequently could not even name them, and rarely do we give them our careful attention. We can find them, however, if we look carefully. We ought to do so, for they appear to be integrally associated with our most serious problems.

These operating postulates include the beliefs that centralization is necessary and preferable to decentralization, that elite controls are required in institutions, especially political ones, that largeness of size in most institutions and other areas is desirable, efficient, and otherwise to be preferred to smallness, that political violence* is required as the ultimate sanction of realistic politics, and that State power is required both to maintain social order and to improve the society in any substantial way. These are prominent among the common operating postulates of the politics of Western civilization and history.

We act upon these operating postulates, assuming that increasing centralization, control by one elite or another, the concept of "bigger is better," certain types of political violence, and State power placed in the hands of the "good guys" are necessary evils, positive goods, or at least inevitable. "That is the way the world is."

We have developed elaborate, reputedly accurate, and sophisticated explanations and rationales to back up the views that these operating postulates are correct, and that when applied by the right people, they are relatively innocent, and certainly useful. We repudiate, discredit, or label with rude names the rare dissidents who suggest that at least certain of these operating postulates may be false and harmful, and that alternatives to them exist.

Instead, most of us, espousing various points of political view, have regarded these operating postulates as necessary for realistic politics. These postulates are applied in action to shape the institutions and sanctions of the political society. These postulates are assumed to be needed for dealing with our problems, for improving our societies, and for providing protection against internal dangers and foreign attacks. These postulates are rarely questioned.

We hold to these operating postulates despite rare and fleeting notice of contrary evidence. These postulates are especially clearly applied by those particular regimes whose practices we commonly most deplore, and are intimately associated with dictatorship, genocide, war, and systems of social oppression. When we do note associations between applications of these postulates and our serious

---

*Political violence** in this book means physical violence or the threat of it used to further political objectives whether by the State or by non-State groups, or by individuals. The term includes: imprisonment of political opponents, police and military action against a political opposition, assassination, rioting, coup d'état, guerrilla war, civil war, conventional war, and nuclear war.

problems, we assume that the problem could not possibly be those postulates themselves. We often do not really "see" the relationship. Nor do we ask if the postulates may be contributing to the existence and seriousness of those problems. Instead, we may simply assume that there is little or no causal relationship; the problem is only the application of those operating postulates by *certain* groups, or in *certain* ways, or is simply the failure to abide by or to apply certain restrictions. New legislation or a constitutional change is usually regarded as all that is needed to correct an "abuse" or "excess." At most that institution (the centralization, the State, the controls) and the sanctions (political violence), based on the operating postulates, are at the moment in the wrong hands. However, these same institutions and sanctions will, it is usually assumed, be most useful when we ourselves, or our political friends, are able to take charge and to use them for our own better purposes.

We seldom reexamine seriously those operating postulates about political reality to see if they are in fact true and necessary. We need, however, to question the adequacy of these long accepted assumptions about how to structure our institutions, how to act in political societies, and how to wield sanctions. We need to examine possible relationships between our operating postulates and our most serious problems. Are those postulates really valid? Must the assumption of their validity be the basis of realistic politics?

Where alternative institutions and sanctions — instead of centralization, elite controls, political violence, and State power — have occurred, we usually ignore those parts of social and political reality. They could, however, tell us something important if only we would notice them and ask fundamental questions about them. Such experience and practice might give us insights into society and politics, and reveal additional options which we could evaluate and possibly choose and develop. Such reexamination could make it possible for us to forge new paths for resolving the problems which threaten us and imperil our future.

REEXAMINING ASSUMPTIONS AND ALTERNATIVES

What alternative operating postulates and political options exist or could be developed? Is a realistic system of politics based on different starting points possible which would not lead to our present grave problems?

Both in the area of institutions and that of sanctions, we need to explore what alternatives may be offered to present practices. Instead of assuming that centralization in politics and economics is inevitable and beneficial, and that its costs are necessary, we might ask if centralization is really necessary, and what alternatives to it exist or can be developed. We might ask whether elite controls of various types are really required or inevitable, and what alternatives exist to expansion of State power and dependency-inducing governmental action might be developed. Are there realistic ways by which people acting independently could resolve their own problems and meet their own needs?

We usually assume that violence is the ultimate force necessary for politics and therefore that we require the capacity to apply it adequately (while we often lament its use, and design means to control it). Instead, we might ask whether there exist alternatives to political violence, nonviolent sanctions (including forms of struggle) in politics, and whether those alternatives could be deliberately developed to meet the society's legitimate needs for sanctions.

We need to think anew about the nature of political power. We have commonly assumed that power is the property of rulers alone, that it originates in violence, or that it is a durable "thing" which is passed from one commanding elite in control of the State apparatus to another, while none who is not among the rulers, who lacks the capacity for major violence, or who is outside the State can wield it. Demonstrably, even on the basis of current events in our society and the world, that view is highly questionable. What then *is* power in politics? Where does it originate? What are its sources? What are the prerequisites for its presence, and how does it change in the course of its development and application?* What determines whether power will be effective when applied against power from other bodies? What does all this mean for the kind of politics we now have and which we might develop?

The relationships between social and political structures and sanctions may be far more significant than we have realized, and indeed may be intimately related to some of our most serious problems.†

*See Chapter Two, "Social Power and Political Freedom."

†See Chapter Eleven, "The Societal Imperative," and Chapter Twelve, "Popular Empowerment."

We also need to think again about the nature of freedom. What is it? How can it be achieved? Does it have prerequisites? How, under present and anticipated future conditions, can it be extended, or perhaps even created?

What role is there for the human will in politics? Is it real, or is it simply a myth? Do our present institutions and sanctions help it to be expressed, or must we find new types of institutions, and new empowering forms of action and struggle to make it real?

To what degree must we challenge other axioms of our society in order to assert control over our lives and to have the chance to shape our present and future society? Are there assumptions about the requirements of society and politics which need to be discarded? What about sovereignty? Should there be *any* person, group, or position in a society which has the ultimate right of command? Or, as Hannah Arendt suggested, is sovereignty intrinsically dangerous for substantive freedom?*

The search for answers to these and other questions challenging our political assumptions and outlooks may lead us to fresh insights and new possibilities for improving our political society and resolving the grave problems which still confront us.

We need to develop new approaches to politics and new programs of social change — in short, to create a new kind of politics. In this search, we must face real dangers squarely, and take nothing for granted. We must develop concrete steps which will, stage by stage, make significant progress toward a more humane society and world. Basic to this effort is that we think.

---

*See Chapter Six, "Freedom and Revolution. A Review of Hannah Arendt's *On Revolution.*"

2

Social Power
and
Political Freedom

SEEKING CONTROLS
OVER GOVERNMENTS

One of the most urgent general problems in politics today is how to control the actions of modern governments. Their uncontrolled power threatens us in various ways — most blatantly in the forms of modern tyranny and war. The traditional means of controlling rulers — constitutional limitations, elections, self-restraint in the rulers themselves, and violent revolution — have been demonstrated to have significant limitations and disadvantages, regardless of their

21

other contributions. In extreme situations in which control is most needed, we can no longer rely upon those traditional means as our only options. If we are not to become helpless political automatons, or to be annihilated, we must find and implement effective means of control over the power of rulers.

If we are to discover, develop, and implement such means of control we must *think* about this problem. To do this, we need to go back to a much more basic level of discussion of political power than is usual these days in discussions of the problems of war, tyranny, and oppression. We need to locate and consider the various elements of the problem of uncontrolled political power and examine their interrelationships. In doing this we must be careful not to accept unconsciously the commonly held views about political power. These views will impose limits on our thinking which may prevent us from successfully developing effective means of control. Instead, as we seek to understand and examine the social and political realities related to political power, we need consciously to try to go beyond the conceptual boundaries imposed by automatic acceptance of traditional assumptions. We need to explore whether other means of controlling rulers may exist or be developed in addition to the means of control relied upon in the past.

Before we can even begin to think about ways to control political power in extreme situations, we must look at political power itself. What is it, and what is its nature? These questions are basic to considerations of the means which can be used to control political power when its wielders do not wish to be controlled. Different views of political power and its nature will lead to corresponding perceptions of the options which may be available to those who wish to apply controls.

It is often assumed that the power of a "ruler" (including, of course, not only chief executives but also ruling groups and all bodies in command of the State structure) is rather like a granite mountain: solid, monolithic, long-lasting, or virtually permanent. From that perspective, such power is in extremities subject only to certain possible means of control. One might exercise some control by changing the "ownership" or "management" of the State structure. This could be done legally (as through elections) or illegally (as through coup d'état). Both ways would usually leave the structure and available power to the "owner" or "manager" virtually intact. Or, one might threaten or implement a direct explosive attack of great magnitude (as a violent revolution or an international war) intended to destroy at least part of the mighty structure. It has been widely assumed that against a ruler unwilling to accept limits or to abdicate voluntarily only such destructive means are capable of weakening or abolishing the power of the regime.

THE SOURCES OF THE POWER OF RULERS CAN BE SEVERED

An alternative view of the nature of the power of rulers is almost the opposite. The political power of a ruler is perceived to be nothing like a granite mountain requiring explosive capacity for control. According to this other theory, the ruler (or ruling group) is a human being (or group of human beings). The ruler has in his own person no more power than any other human being. This insight is so elementary that it is often never noticed. Recognition of it, however, leads to new insights and options. If the ruler has in his own body and mind no more power than has any other individual, then his power to rule must come from outside of his person. That power must therefore have sources in the society, and these can be located. These sources include the acceptance of the ruler's right to rule ("authority"), economic resources, manpower, military capacity, knowledge, skills, administration, police, prisons, courts, and the like. Each of these sources is in turn closely related to, or directly dependent upon, the degree of cooperation, submission, obedience, and assistance that the ruler is able to obtain from his subjects. These include both the general population and his paid "helpers" and agents. That dependence makes it possible, under certain circumstances, for the subjects to reduce the availability of these sources of power, or to withdraw them completely, by reducing or withdrawing their necessary cooperation and obedience.

If the acceptance, submission, and assistance of the paid "helpers" and agents and also of the general population are withdrawn partially or completely, the sources of power are consequently restricted, and therefore the ruler's effective power is weakened. That weakening will be roughly in proportion to the degree to which the availability of the necessary sources of power is restricted. If the withdrawal of acceptance, submission, and help can be maintained in face of the ruler's punishments for disobedience ("sanctions"), then an end of the regime is in sight. Thus, all rulers are dependent for their positions and political power upon the obedience, submission, and cooperation of their subjects. This is an extremely condensed summary of a much longer (and somewhat less simple) analysis.[1] It should be sufficient, however, to suggest that the ruler's power not only is not monolithic or permanent, but instead is always based upon an intricate and fragile structure of human and institutional relationships. The implications of this insight are obvious, although immense practical problems in implementing withdrawal of support as a means of control still require serious attention.

This principle of withdrawing sources of power from rulers, when practically applied, could supply the needed effective means of struggle to impose control over rulers who do not wish to be controlled. Means of struggle against that type of ruler are obviously among the most crucial components in the general capacity of a society to control its rulers.

THE SOCIETY'S STRUCTURE AFFECTS THE POSSIBILITIES OF CONTROL

Another highly important component in such a capacity is the institutional or structural condition of the society. This refers to the existence or absence of various institutions, their numbers, the degree of their centralization or decentralization, their internal decision-making processes, and the degree of their internal strength and vitality. One extreme condition would be a society in which every institution was either a part of the centralized State structure or effectively subordinated to it and controlled by it. The other extreme would be a society in which all of its needs were met by a great variety of independent institutions and in which forms of government were present but the centralized State was not. ("State" here refers to a particular form of government which possesses, among other elements, a permanent bureaucracy, a permanent military system, and a permanent police force utilizing violent means of control, backed by a prison system.) Those extreme structural conditions of high centralization or decentralization rarely or never exist, however. Virtually all political societies have a structure somewhere between those extremities. The *degree* of concentration or diffusion of effective power capacity in the society, the *degree* to which that capacity is centralized in the State or decentralized among the independent institutions of the society, is the important question.

The structural condition of the society affects the capacity of the society to control the power of rulers in two ways. If power is highly decentralized among strong and vital independent institutions, that condition will be of great assistance in emergencies in which struggle is required to control a ruler. It will greatly strengthen the capacity of the subjects and their institutions to withdraw the sources of the ruler's power in order to impose such control. Also, the structural condition will set the broad boundaries of a ruler's potential power beyond which he may not go without structural changes or deliberately increased active assistance from the subjects and their institutions.

Any particular ruler occupying the position of command of the State structure will not necessarily extend his exercised power, domination, and control over the society as far or deep as the structural condition may permit. Lack of motivation, respect for constitutionally determined limits, moral or religious convictions, or adherence to certain theories or philosophies of politics may cause the ruler deliberately to refrain from utilizing the full power potential which the structural condition of the society makes available to him. However, if the ruler's views change, if conditions appear to him to require more extreme actions, if personality needs cause him to become more power hungry, or if a new person or group by usurpation seizes the position of ruler, then the ruler may push his exercise of power potential fully to the boundaries determined by the structural condition of the society. The ruler may even seek to undermine or attack the institutions which by their strength set those limits.

This all suggests, therefore, that a technique of struggle to control rulers who do not wish to be controlled and also a structural condition of the society which sets effective boundaries on the power potential of rulers are both needed over and above constitutional arrangements and self-imposed limits of the ruler himself in order to establish effective control over the power of modern rulers.

A technique of struggle exists which is based upon the above view of the nature of power (that it has sources which may be restricted by withdrawal of cooperation and obedience). This is called "nonviolent action." It includes nonviolent symbolic protest; economic, social, and political noncooperation; and nonviolent intervention in psychological, physical, social, economic, and political forms.[2] This technique when refined, developed, and implemented in a multitude of specific situations, may constitute the heart of the solution to the need for a technique of struggle to control the power of rulers who are unwilling to accept voluntarily limits to their power. A great deal of research, analysis, policy studies, and development are needed on the nature and potential of that technique of control.

This chapter, however, is primarily focused on the role of the underlying social structure in determining the boundaries of the power potential of the ruler. Central to this discussion is consideration of the long-term consequences of the relative concentration of the society's power potential in the State, as compared to the long-term consequences of the relative diffusion of power among the non-State institutions of the society as a whole.

At times, though not often, individuals can significantly influence the course of social and political events by their personal power of persuasion, their connections with persons in key positions in the structure, and their capacity to use particular types of nonviolent action. Some of Mohandas K. Gandhi's individual acts illustrate this latter capacity. However, those instances are rare, especially against rulers who are determined to rule as they wish without limitations. In those cases their power may only be seriously curtailed or dissolved by restriction of their sources of power. Such restriction, however, cannot be produced by isolated individuals. The sources of the ruler's power are normally only threatened significantly when assistance, cooperation, and obedience are withheld by large numbers of subjects at the same time, that is, by social groups and institutions. The ability of such bodies to withhold the sources they supply is then pivotal. That ability will be influenced by various factors, including the subjects' skill in applying the technique of struggle, and also the ruler's relative need for the sources of power which they may provide. Important, too, is the degree to which these groups possess the capacity to act independently against the ruler.

Two broad possibilities exist at that point. Power may be so concentrated in the State, and the subjects so atomized, that no significant social groups or institutions exist which are capable of withholding the sources of the ruler's power, and therefore controlling the actions of the ruler. On the other hand, if such groups capable of independent action, and therefore control, do exist to a significant degree in the society, their presence and strength will significantly increase the chances of success in a struggle to control the ruler's power. Such groups and institutions capable of independent action are called "*loci* (or places) of power."

"Power" here obviously refers to political power, a sub-type of social power. Political power here is defined as the totality of means, influences, and pressures — including authority, rewards, and sanctions — available for use to achieve the objectives of the power-holder, especially the institutions of government, the State, and groups opposing either of them. Political power may be measured by the ability to *control* the situation, people, or institutions, or to *mobilize* people and institutions for some activity. Power may be used to enable a group to achieve a goal, to implement or change policies, to induce others to behave as the wielders of power wish, to engage in opposition, to maintain the established system, policies, and relationships, or to alter, destroy, or replace the prior power relationships. Sanctions — which may be either violent or nonviolent — are usually a key element in power. It is not always necessary to apply the capacity to wield sanctions in order for it to be effective. The mere ability to apply sanctions and to utilize other components of power may be sufficient to achieve the objective. In such cases power is no less present than when it is applied with direct infliction of sanctions.[3]

THE ROLE OF DIFFUSED *LOCI* OF POWER IN THE CONTROL OF POLITICAL POWER

The precise form and nature of *loci* of power (or places in which power is located, converges, or is expressed) vary from society to society and from situation to situation. However, they are likely to include such social groups and institutions as families, social classes, religious groups, cultural and nationality groups, occupational groups, economic groups, villages, towns, cities, provinces and regions, smaller governmental bodies, voluntary organizations, and political parties. Most often they are traditional, established, formal social groups and institutions. Sometimes, however, *loci* of power may be less formally organized, and may even be recently created or revitalized in the process of achieving some objective or of opposing the ruler (as the workers' councils during the 1956 Hungarian Revolution). Their status as *loci* will be determined by their capacity to act independently, to wield effective power, and to regulate the effective power of others, such as the ruler, or of some other *locus* or *loci* of power.

The capacity of these *loci* to control the ruler's actions, then, will be influenced by (1) the extent of the existence of such *loci*, (2) the degree of their independence of action, (3) the sources of power which they control, (4) the amount of social power which they can independently wield or control, and (5) sometimes other factors. If all of these factors are extensively present, the *loci* may make freely available the sources of power needed by the ruler, or instead they may elect to restrict or sever those sources which the ruler requires.

LOCI OF POWER SET LIMITS TO THE RULER'S POWER CAPACITY

The power structure of the society as a whole includes both the relationships among these *loci* of power and between those and the ruler. The society's power structure, that is, these relationships, in the long run determines the spheres and the strength of the ruler's maximum effective power.[4] When power is effectively diffused throughout the society among such *loci,* the ruler's power is most likely to be subjected to controls and limits. This condition is associated with political "freedom." When, on the other hand, such *loci* have been seriously weakened, effectively destroyed, or have had their independent existence and autonomy of action destroyed by some type of superimposed controls, the ruler's power is most likely to be uncontrolled. This condition is associated with "tyranny." "When a man sees and feels one human authority only is the condition furthest removed from liberty," Bertrand de Jouvenel has written.[5]

When the *loci* of power are too numerous and strong to permit the ruler to exercise unlimited control or to destroy them, it may still be possible for the ruler to obtain from them the sources of power which he needs. In order to do so, however, the ruler must keep such social groups and institutions sufficiently sympathetic to him, his policies and measures, and his regime as a whole, so that they are willing to submit, cooperate, and make available the sources of power. To achieve this, the ruler must adjust his behavior and policies in order to keep the goodwill and cooperation of the people who constitute the groups and institutions of the society. This is one type of indirect control which these *loci* of power exercise over a ruler. If such an adjustment is not attempted or is unsuccessful, and the ruler offends the population he would rule, then the society's strong *loci* of power may, in open conflict, withhold the sources of power which they control and which the ruler requires. In this way the population acting through their groups and institutions may impose control over an ambitious antidemocratic ruler or even disintegrate the regime and dissolve the ruler's power.

The reverse is also true. When these social groups and institutions lose their capacity for independent decision and action, their control of the sources of power, or are themselves drastically weakened or destroyed, such loss will contribute significantly to making the ruler's power unlimited and uncontrollable. Under conditions in which such *loci* of power do not significantly exist and the subjects are a mass of atomized individuals incapable of effective group action, the ruler's power will be the least controllable by the subjects.

DELIBERATE ATTACKS AND UNINTENDED EFFECTS MAY WEAKEN THE *LOCI* OF POWER

Quite different causes may weaken or destroy the society's *loci* of power. Deliberate policies of the ruler to attack their independence, undermine their strength, or even destroy them are only one possibility. Similar results may follow as a secondary unintended effect of the operation of other social, economic, or political policies or forces.

Where the attack is deliberate, it may be launched because the ruler perceives such groups and institutions as rivals, and recognizes that they impose limits to his power and ambition to be omnipotent.

The ruler may then deliberately seek to destroy their independence and even to dissolve the body itself. The German sociologist Georg Simmel argued that the desire of the rulers to "equalize" their subjects was not due to a moral preference for equality, but was instead due to a desire to weaken those groups capable of limiting the power of the rulers.[6] The particular body may disappear from the ranks of the society's social groups and institutions, especially if it is incapable of effective resistance to the ruler's efforts. More likely, however, the group or institution will formally continue to exist, but will be deprived of the qualities which gave it independence and ability to control a source of power. Less extremely, the group may continue to exist with its independence and power drastically reduced but not eradicated. The ruler who seeks unlimited and unchallenged power may attempt to replace an independent *locus* with an institution firmly controlled by his system.

When such attacks on the society's *loci* of power are recognized as attempts to achieve an egoistic power aggrandizement for the ruler, to impose a dictatorial regime, or to extend control by an already oppressive regime, then those attacks may be widely viewed as alarming. This is not always the case, however. When the particular group or institution under attack has itself been widely seen to have been oppressive, exploitative, or antisocial, or was otherwise in disfavor, an attack upon it by the ruler who can apply the resources of the more powerful State is often widely approved and seen to be progressive and even liberating. This does not in any way refute the above view that a weakening or destruction of *loci* of power will enhance the power potential of the ruler in command of the State.

The attacked *loci* may have operated to the detriment or to the welfare of the society as a whole; in either case they will also have restricted the power capacity of the ruler. This in no way means that groups and institutions which operate to harm the general population or sections of it should be passively accepted and permitted to continue their past practices. It is not control over such bodies, or even their abolition, which itself creates the problem. It is the specific *way* the control or abolition is achieved which may enhance the capacity of the ruler to be dictatorial and oppressive. The problem is created when the control or abolition is carried out by the State apparatus and without the creation of new *loci* of power, or the strengthening of the power of other existing *loci* which are at least equally outside the control of the ruler as was the attacked *locus*. On this particular point it matters little whether the old *locus* has been brought to subjection by liberal democratic legislation, by decree of an autocrat, or by edict of a revolutionary leadership. Under a variety of systems the effect is broadly the same. The effect is both to increase the size and capacities of the State apparatus and also to weaken or remove a group or institution which was capable of resisting and limiting the power capacity of the ruler who is in command of the State structure.

So long as the *locus* of power has been drastically weakened or destroyed *without a balancing increase in power by existing groups and institutions or the creation of new ones independent of the State,* the result is in one sense essentially the same: an increase in the power of the ruler and a reduced capacity of the subjects to limit or to control that power. This does not only apply to the present ruler immediately in control of the State. Such a ruler may in fact have humanitarian aims and no desire to become dictatorial. The result applies also to those future rulers who inherit the State's expanded power potential, who may be far less humanitarian than their predecessors, and who may in fact have seized control of the State apparatus by usurpation, as a coup d'état. The same general process operated in the very different situations in the destruction of the nobility and feudal lords in revolutionary France and in the destruction of independent trade unions and political parties in both Communist Russia under Lenin and Stalin, and also Nazi Germany under Hitler. The result in these cases was increased centralization of power in the society, expansion of the power capacity of the State, and a reduction of the de facto limitations and popular controls on the ruler's effective power capacity.

OTHER FACTORS MAY INFLUENCE RULERS BUT NOT CONTROL THEM

This does not mean that a strict mathematical relationship will exist between the degree to which power is diffused among these *loci* or is concentrated in the State, and the degree to which the ruler's power is either controllable or autocratic. As previously indicated, other factors may also influence the actual behavior of a given ruler, including any self-imposed limitations he may accept on the exercise of his power and any limitations set by established institutional procedures, such as elections, constitutional provisions, and judicial decisions, *provided that the ruler is willing to abide by them.*

This analysis does mean, however, that the relative strength and internal condition of such *loci* will set the rough boundaries within which the ruler may exercise his power. He may not go beyond them in virtual indifference to the opinions of the subjects. Those limits may under those conditions only be exceeded with the willing consent and assistance of the society's social groups and institutions, and not against their demonstrated opposition. *The condition of the society's* loci *of power will in large degree determine the long-run capacity of the society to control the ruler's power.* A society in which groups and institutions exist which possess significant social power and are capable of independent action is more capable of controlling the ruler's power, and thus of resisting tyranny, than a society in which the subjects are all equally impotent.

INSTITUTIONAL FORMS SECONDARY TO THE ACTUAL DISTRIBUTION OF POWER

The formal institutional framework and procedures of government remain important in the context of this insight, but the underlying structural condition is in the long run dominant over the formal political arrangements. *It is the distribution of power throughout the society's structure as a whole which determines the de facto power of the ruler, regardless of the principles which are avowed for the system or its institutional forms.*

Even though the formal political structure of the government may be highly dictatorial, if significant effective power is diffused among various social groups and institutions, the society will probably be internally strong enough to maintain a relatively "free" political system and to limit and control the ruler's effective power. Even a formally "autocratic" regime may be thereby subjected to strict limits and controls. Conversely, where *loci* of power are weak, the society is likely to be unable to prevent domination by a despotic regime, whether of internal or external origin. A society which possesses a democratic constitution but which lacks strong *loci* of power is thus especially vulnerable to a would-be dictator, while a constitutionally "democratic" regime may have virtually unlimited and uncontrolled power. Allowing for a time lag, the degree of actual diffusion or concentration of power throughout the society is likely to be reflected at some point in the formal political arrangements of the society.

STRONG *LOCI* OF POWER MAY CONTROL TYRANTS

Examples from the French and Russian feudal monarchies will illustrate how the power of rulers which is theoretically unlimited may be controlled when power is diffused among various *loci* throughout the society.

The important early nineteenth century French political analyst Alexis de Tocqueville suggested that among the "barriers which formerly arrested the aggressions of tyranny"[7] were these three: (1) religion, which once helped both rulers and ruled to "define the natural limits of despotism,"[8] (2) respect for the rulers, the absence of which, once it was destroyed by revolutions, allowed the rulers to fall back unashamed upon "the seductions of arbitrary power,"[9] and — the one with which we are here concerned — (3) the existence of *loci* of effective power throughout the society, such as the provinces, towns, nobles, and families.[10]

Prior to the French Revolution, under the *ancien régime,* at the very time when "the laws and the consent of the people had invested princes with an almost unlimited authority,"[11] the "power of a part of his subjects was an insurmountable barrier to the tyranny of the prince...."[12] Among the sources of this limiting power, Tocqueville continued , were "the prerogatives of the nobility,...the authority of the supreme courts of justice,...provincial privileges, which served to break the blows of the sovereign authority, and to maintain a spirit of resistance in the nation."[13] In that age people were closely bound to their fellow citizens; if one was being unjustly assailed, one's associates would offer assistance.[14] The provinces and towns were relatively independent, and "each of them had a will of its own, which was opposed to the general will of subjection...."[15] The nobles possessed considerable power, and even after that power was lost they continued to wield considerable influence. They "dared to cope single-handed with the efforts of the public authority."[16] When family feeling was strong, the "antagonist of oppression was never alone" but could find support among relatives, hereditary friends, and clients.[17] Even when these were weak, one gained confidence from one's ancestry and hope for one's posterity.[18] These and other influences of the independent *loci* of power in the society served to limit the de facto political power of the theoretically omnipotent ruler.

The contemporary French political philosopher Bertrand de Jouvenel has described this condition in similar terms. In seventeenth century France, while theoretically the sovereign was all powerful, his political power was, in fact, sharply limited. This limitation was effected in ways which cannot be attributed simply to variations in technology between that time and our own.

> It was. . .everywhere denied that it lay with the sovereign will to lay down rules as it pleased; it was not believed that its wishes, whatever they happened to be, had power to bind. Everyone knew that the ordinance of a temporal power was not morally binding in virtue of its form, if its adherence did not satisfy certain conditions.
>
> In a word, the sovereign, or his spokesman, were less free under the *ancien régime* than they are at present, and command was less arbitrary.[19]

Similarly, the twentieth century Italian political sociologist Gaetano Mosca argued:

> The head of a feudal state will be able to wrong any one of his barons, but he will never be absolute master of them all. They have at their disposal a certain amount of public force. . . .and will always be able to exercise *de facto* a right of resistance. . . .The individual barons, in their turn, find that there is a limit to the tyranny which they can exercise over the masses of their subjects. Unreasonableness on their part may provoke a desperate unrest which may easily become rebellion. So it turns out that in all truly federal countries the rule of the masters may be violent and arbitrary by fits and starts, but on the whole it is considerably limited by customs.[20]

Although the constitution was itself despotic under feudalism, the combined power of social groups and institutions throughout the society, and the influence of less tangible limitations on the power of the ruler, operated to restrain effectively the power of the kings. "Princes had the right, but they had neither the means nor the desire of doing whatever they pleased," wrote Tocqueville.[21] Some of these groups, such as the nobility, might have been opposed to personal liberty. Nevertheless their independence and power generally served, he argued, to keep alive the love and condition of freedom.[22] The very existence of multiple authorities and claimants to the subject's loyalty — instead of a single one — allowed the subject a certain degree of choice and ability to maneuver. In such a situation, Simmel maintained, the person "gains a certain independence in respect to each of them and, as far as his intimate feelings are concerned, even, perhaps, in respect to their totality."[23]

A comparable situation existed in the Russian Empire under the nineteenth century tsarist system. The respected historian of that society and its revolutionary movements, Franco Venturi, wrote: "...the extraordinary power held by Nicholas I, the most despotic of contemporary European sovereigns, was in fact extremely limited when it came to tampering with the foundations of Russia's social structure."[24] For example, when the Tsar, prior to the emancipation of the serfs, sought means to improve the lot of the peasants, he faced opposition from the various groups and classes whose support or acquiescence he required to make the changes he wished.[25] The State was in fact unable to intervene in the relations between the peasants and the nobles. This was "only one more proof of the weakness of Nicholas I's despotism; strong only when it remained static, and weak as soon as it tried to take action."[26]

The potentially active opposition to the Tsar's schemes arose from both the peasants and the nobles. The peasants on private estates almost universally believed that although *they* belonged to the nobles and landlords, the *land* belonged to the serfs themselves. They therefore rejected any attempt to "free" them personally while giving the land to the nobility. Such an attempt could have led to revolution with the serfs attempting to hold their land and also claiming complete liberation from taxation.[27] That prospect was serious because the peasants possessed their own organizations of self-administration, the *obshchina* and *mir* — that is, effective *loci* of power. They were experienced in meeting, discussing, making decisions, and acting together, capacities which had a long history, Venturi reported:

> The State brought into being by Peter the Great's reforms had never succeeded in striking roots throughout the country. Parallel to it, there survived a system of local self-administration dating from medieval times with its organized groups of peasants and merchants.[28]

"It was through these organizations, the only ones at its disposal, that peasant society defended itself."[29] Therefore, the Tsar's government sought control over the *obshchina*.[30]

While the opposition of the nobles to reform has been exaggerated in the West, it was still significant. Their opposition, Venturi wrote, placed the Tsar in a "weak position."[31] The nobles, too, feared a peasant revolution, and their opposition was intensified by the perception that the Tsar was more desirous for reform than was the case. "The resistance of the nobles was proportionate to the weakness of the autocracy...."[32] The nobles, individually and also as a group, were obviously too powerful for the Tsar to ignore or crush.

The peasants feared dispossession from their land, and the nobles feared dispossession from their serfs. Both groups possessed the capacity for corporate action and constituted significant *loci* of power which could not be ignored. These *loci* of power thus effectively limited and controlled the power of the theoretically omnipotent Tsar.

These French and Russian examples are simply illustrations of the general capacity of *loci* of power of any type, if sufficiently strong and independent, to restrain the power of a ruler no matter how omnipotent he theoretically is supposed to be. The examples should by no means be interpreted as apologies for feudalism. Although Tocqueville has been accused of being an apologist for feudalism, he was quite clear in his own mind that control exercised by *loci* of power in France under the *ancien régime* was not the result of the aristocratic system per se. Instead, the capacity for control came from the effective diffusion of power throughout the society, which in this particular case was a quality of the aristocratic system. Such diffusion of power among the society's groups and institutions could also operate under different systems, and result in similar control over the ruler. The capacity for control is made possible by diffusion of power.

Tocqueville perceived that the impact of diffused power over the power of rulers extended beyond internal politics. It also potentially included the ruler's ability to wage foreign wars without the support of the subjects, and even the capacity of an invading ruler to conquer a country with a diffused power structure.

> A great aristocratic people cannot either conquer its neighbours, or be conquered by them, without great difficulty. It cannot conquer them, because all its forces can never be collected and held together

for a considerable period: it cannot be conquered, because an enemy meets at every step small centres of resistance by which invasion is arrested. War against an aristocracy may be compared to war in a mountainous country; the defeated party has constant opportunities of rallying its forces to make a stand in a new position.[33]

While effective *loci* of power may impose limits and controls over a ruler's power, if they are weak, absent, or destroyed the ruler's power will to that degree be uncontrolled.

THE DESTRUCTION OF *LOCI* OF POWER MAY ASSIST TYRANNY

In the absence of significant power-wielding social groups and institutions it will be much more difficult to exercise effective control over a ruler by regulating the availability of the necessary sources of his power. This applies to any system, whatever its avowed nature or doctrine. If the ruler — whether a king, representatives of an economic oligarchy, or a group of avowed revolutionaries — deliberately weakens or destroys *loci* of power without creating others at least as strong as the old ones, the result will be a weakening of the limits on the power of the ruler. This applies whatever the espoused political philosophy or constitutional arrangements may be.

Tocqueville argued that this is what happened during the destruction of the *ancien régime* in France. Previously, the provinces and towns were able to resist the ruler. The revolution, however, destroyed their immunities, customs, traditions, and even names, and subjected them all to the same laws. Consequently, "it is not more difficult to oppress them collectively than it was formerly to oppress them singly."[34] Whereas family feeling previously supported the individual in opposing the ruler, the drastic weakening or destruction of family feeling left the individual alone in a constantly changing society.[35] Formerly the nobility could challenge and restrain the king. With the destruction of that class their power became concentrated in the new occupants of the position of ruler.[36]

> I perceive that we have destroyed those independent beings which were able to cope with tyranny single-handed; but it is the Government that has inherited the privileges of which families, corpora-

tions, and individuals have been deprived; the weakness of the whole community has therefore succeeded that influence of a small body of citizens, which, if it was sometimes oppressive, was often conservative.[37]

Thus, said Tocqueville, the French Revolution overthrew both the "despotic power and the checks to its abuses...its tendency was at once to overthrow and centralise."[38] The destruction of the nobility and the upper middle class made possible the centralization of power under Napoleon.[39] Jouvenel similarly pointed to the post-revolutionary concentration of power and the destruction of significant *loci* of power as acts which laid the foundation for the monolithic State.[40] Specifically, he pointed to the destruction of the middle class as "the proximate cause of modern despotisms,"[41] and argued in some detail that revolution in the past has generally contributed to an increase in the power at the disposal of the central government.[42]

It should be emphasized that it is not simply the abolition of the oppressing classes or the establishment of approximate equality which leads to centralization. It is, rather, as Tocqueville wrote, "the manner in which this equality has been established."[43] ("Equality" is used here in a highly relative sense, of course.) Usually this "equality" is achieved by the destruction of the existing *loci* of power (such as the French nobility) *without the creation of new social groups and institutions with sufficient independence and power to resist the central ruler.* Further, as we shall see, the violent means of struggle and violent State sanctions relied upon to produce such "equality" have frequently contributed to increased concentration of power in the State. It is these particular types of changes in the name of a movement toward equality which constitute a significant contribution to the modern forms of tyranny.

When the diffused *loci* of social power are destroyed without the creation of new ones of at least equal importance and strength, the result tends to be a society composed of relatively equal, but atomized, helpless individuals.

Those individuals will then be without groups and institutions with whose members they can consult, from whom they can receive support, and with whom they can combine for action. Atomized individuals, unable to act together, cannot unite to make significant protest, to withhold by their noncooperation the ruler's needed sources of power, and, in some cases, to intervene to disrupt the status quo. Those individuals are therefore unable to limit or control the political power wielded by the present ruler, or by any new one who may seize control of the State apparatus and place himself at its pinnacle of command.

This process of weakening and destroying those groups and institutions capable of resisting the State, with the resulting weakness of the society and powerlessness of the individual citizens, was clearly recognized by Tocqueville in the early stages of its development. He pointed out that while the citizen of a democratic country may feel pride in being the equal of any one of the other fellow citizens, that is not the entire picture. When the person compares himself as an individual to the huge number of citizens, "he is instantly over-whelmed by the sense of his own insignificance and weakness."[44] The individual tends to "disappear in the throng and is easily lost in the midst of a common obscurity...."[45] No longer a part of a group which is capable of genuine independence of action and of opposition to the ruler, the individual subject becomes but one of a multitude of equally weak and equally dependent citizens. Each has only "his personal impotence to oppose to the organised force of the Govern-ment."[46] Under such conditions, "every man naturally stands alone...and he is trampled on with impunity."[47] In democratic countries, therefore, the power of the State is "naturally much stronger" than elsewhere.[48] Whatever the constitutional arrange-ments, the capacity of that society to maintain genuine freedom is weak once the State machinery has been captured, whether by elec-tion, executive usurpation, coup d'état, or invasion by a would-be tyrant. "What resistance can be afforded to tyranny in a country where every private individual is impotent, and where the citizens are united by no common tie?"[49] How far this actually exists will of course vary with the degree to which that process has extended. The condition will not be so severe if groups and institutions with some autonomy have survived, been revitalized, or newly created. Also, people may in certain more limited aspects of their lives retain a capacity to influence events, while concerning the larger issues affect-ing the society as a whole and the policies of the Government, they may see themselves as incapable of exerting any effective control. The feeling of impotence of ordinary people, even in constitutional democracies, to influence the actual course of political events is perhaps much more widely and deeply felt today than it was in Tocqueville's time.[50]

This condition has been called to our attention by both Karen Horney and Erich Fromm, among others. A basic conflict exists, Horney wrote, "between the alleged freedom of the individual and all his factual limitations. . . . The result for the individual is a wavering between a feeling of boundless power in determining his own fate and a feeling of entire helplessness."[51] Fromm similarly warned: ". . . in our own society we are faced with the same phenomenon that is fertile soil for the rise of Fascism anywhere: the insignificance and power-lessness of the individual."[52] "In spite of a veneer of optimism and initiative, modern man is overcome by a profound feeling of power-lessness which makes him gaze towards approaching catastrophes as though he were paralyzed."[53]

The reasons offered by various analysts to explain this condition vary. In political terms, however, they all relate to the weak power position of the isolated individual who faces a powerful ruler, of whatever type. The individual does not feel a part of social groups and institutions with sufficient power and independence of action to resist effectively and together to control the ruler's power, because society's independent social groups and institutions are weak, have been brought under control, or do not exist. In modern political societies a relative atomization of the subjects has occurred. The degree to which this has happened, and the stage of its development, vary with the country, the political system, and the forces operating to produce or prevent that process. These variations are important, often highly so. Also, at times the process of atomization may be reversed, either as an unintended consequence of changes in the society's structure or of deliberate changes to create or strengthen independent institutions. In Western constitutional democracies, the relative independence and power of social groups and institutions outside of State control are significantly greater than under totalitar-ian systems in which atomization reached its zenith to that point in history. At the time of Stalin's purges, for example, "no one could trust his fellow or feel secure in the protection of any institution or individual on whom he had hitherto relied," Leonard Schapiro has written. "The 'atomization' of society, which some have seen as the most characteristic feature of totalitarian rule, was completed in the years of terror."[54]

Such deliberate atomization results from measures of the ruler to weaken or destroy the significant *loci* of power which are structurally situated between the individual and the ruler. A ruler who wishes to make his regime all powerful may deliberately initiate measures to achieve that objective. This was true in both Nazi Germany[55] and the Soviet Union.[56] "Despotism. . .is never more secure of continuance," Tocqueville wrote, "than when it can keep men asunder; and all its influence is commonly exerted for that purpose."[57] Or, the ruler may seek to maintain dominance not by destroying *loci* of power but by modifying their strengths so as to keep himself on top. Simmel suggested that a ruler may encourage "the efforts of the lower classes which are directed toward legal equality with those intermediate powers."[58] This will produce a new *locus* of power strong enough to balance the influence of the "intermediate powers" on the ruler, thereby creating a relative leveling, and thereby assisting the ruler in maintaining his domination over the whole.[59]

The relative atomization of the subjects may also follow as an unintended result of other policies or social changes, designed neither to atomize the population nor to contribute to unlimited power for the ruler. This is especially likely to occur where reformers and revolutionaries use the State apparatus to control certain social and economic groups, such as the nobility, landlords, or capitalists, and where the State is used as the primary instrument for controlling the economic and political development of the country. The concentration of power in the State may successfully control the particular group against whom the measures were instituted. However, other long-term consequences follow from that concentration of power for that control or development. Reliance on the State to achieve those objectives not only utilizes the existing concentration of power in the State, but also contributes to its growth both absolutely and in comparison to the other institutions of the society. Further, that reliance on the State not only does not strengthen the population and its independent institutions, but is likely to weaken them both absolutely and relatively. For example, the establishment of State control over the economy may provide the present or a future ruler with the means by which to "hold in closer dependence the population which they govern," as Tocqueville put it.[60] State ownership of the economy has, for example, provided Communist regimes with the capacity to apply a massive blacklist against political dissidents. This capacity far exceeds that of earlier capitalists, who used such lists far less efficiently to keep trade union organizers from obtaining jobs.

The concentration of effective power in the State not only provides a ruler with means of direct control over the population. That concentration will also tend to exert a variety of psychological pressures and influences on the people which will not only reduce their ability to control the ruler, but even there desire to do so. The individual is subject to the extreme influence of the mass and is under pressure to accept opinions without the opportunity for reasoned consideration,[61] especially pressure in the form of pleas of morality, ideology, patriotism, and expertise. Those who attempt to act together to change the society, or to challenge the ruler's omnipotence are regarded as dangerous and antisocial.[62] The population accepts more and more that it is the right, and even the duty, of the ruler "to guide as well as govern each private citizen."[63] That doctrine is dangerous for freedom, and for the maintenance and development of controls over the ruler's political power.

Whatever the apparent short-term benefits, the long-term results of reliance on concentrated State power to deal with the society's problems may be disastrous for the society's political future.

THE ACTUAL DISTRIBUTION OF POWER MAY INFLUENCE THE GOVERNMENT'S INSTITUTIONAL FORMS

The actual power structure of the society is likely in the long run to help determine the formal institutional form of government. A diffused power structure in the society as a whole with multiple *loci* of effective power will tend to produce a more democratic form. On the other hand, a society of atomized individuals and concentrated power in the hands of the State will facilitate a despotic form of government. "What we call the constitution is only the crowning story of the social structure; and where the lower stages are utterly different the uppermost stages must also differ," wrote F.C. Montague.[64] Similarly, Mosca argued that the de facto limits on the ruler's power, or the absence of them, may lead to their later formal recognition in the constitution and the law.[65] The *loci* of diffused power may be so strong that the ruler must officially recognize his dependence on them by institutional changes. "The meeting of parliament had, then, from the start this essential characteristic," wrote Jouvenel, "that it was the convocation of authorities, great and small, to which the king could not give orders and with which he had to parley."[66] Conversely, where such social groups and institutions are relatively absent or weak, unable to resist the central ruler and unable to control the sources of his power, the formal political structure may change from nominally democratic and become openly highly centralized and despotic.

Changes in the formal framework of government to reflect the actual distribution of power and structural condition of the society as a whole are usually made only after a time gap. It may be a lengthy one under appropriate conditions. The outward forms of one political system may continue long after the distribution of power in the society, which originally helped to produce those governmental forms, has significantly altered. The formal machinery of constitutional democracy may continue for some time after the effective diffusion of power among groups and institutions of the society has been replaced by effective concentration of power in the hands of the ruler. If so, the power potential of the ruler may be as uncontrolled in practice as if the constitution were frankly autocratic. Although the old constitution may continue long after the conditions which produced it have changed, this situation is potentially highly unstable. In a society in which the social groups and non-State institutions are weak, already controlled by the ruler, or otherwise incapable of independent action and resistance to the ruler, and the population either does not wish to resist usurpations or feels powerless to do so, a frankly autocratic form of government may be easily accepted. This may be introduced as a "temporary" arrangement to meet a particular need or emergency, or as a permanent change. In the latter case, the change may emerge from gradual constitutional changes, shifts in practice, judicial decisions, legislation, and the like. Alternatively, the change may follow an executive usurpation, coups d'état, or foreign invasion. Sometimes the change may follow directly from the "requirements" for conducting an effective foreign or internal war.

The reverse situation may also occur. A formally dictatorial type of government which originated much earlier may continue to exist for some time after the society's social groups and non-State institutions, which have continued under that system, have grown in strength and in their capacity for independent action, and perhaps after quite new ones with those qualities have come into existence. In such a case, while the formal constitution is still dictatorial, in practice those *loci* of power would exert a significant degree of control over the ruler. That is, the society in practice would have become more democratic than indicated by the surviving formal governmental form. In this case as well, the altered power relationships and the new structural condition would tend in time to be formally recognized by a constitutional change.

In both cases, the structural condition of the society and the actual distribution of effective power are likely in practice to modify the operation of the ruler's exercise of power away from the formal constitutional provisions and governmental structure.

At times the incongruence between the society's structural condition and the formal governmental structure may exist when a ruler — especially in the form of an ideologically oriented political party — seizes control of the State to impose a dictatorship aimed at remolding the society's underlying structure. The success or failure of that effort would then be significantly influenced by the society's structural condition: whether the social groups and institutions were strong enough to resist that dictatorship's efforts, were too weak to succeed or even to try, or whether they willingly assisted in their own demise in favor of the ruler's objective.

CONTROL OF POLITICAL POWER AS A RESULT OF INTERNAL STRENGTH

The degree, then, to which a ruler's power can be controlled by the subjects depends primarily upon the internal strength of the social order and of the subjects themselves. This view is contrary to the currently favored explanations of the ways to control power. It is common today to place nearly complete reliance on the formal constitution, legislation, and judicial decisions to establish and preserve political freedom. It is also common to assume that only the intentions, acts, and policies of a dictator or oppressor (whether an individual or a group) are responsible for the existence of a dictatorship or oppression. In addition, it is also commonly assumed that the removal of a dictator or oppressor will itself bring about a condition of freedom. In light of this analysis, however, those views are all erroneous. Worse, they are likely to lead to policies which are incapable of producing the desired results.

The view that a ruler's power is ultimately the consequence of the condition of the society itself is neither original nor new. This view has been argued by a variety of political theorists and observers over the centuries.

William Godwin, a late eighteenth century English political thinker, for example, was of the opinion that the character of political institutions is largely determined by the state of the people's social and political understanding. If that understanding is limited, then to that degree the institutions will be imperfect. If their understanding is great, then the accepted institutions will be improved, and those institutions which are rejected will lapse through lack of support.[67] Changes in the opinion of the public therefore necessarily precede social and political changes, if the changes are to last.[68] The degree of immaturity or maturity of the populace will be reflected in the political system, Godwin wrote, producing a dictatorial regime or a condition of freedom. Internal weakness makes a people easy prey to a conquerer, while the effort to hold down a people prepared for freedom is likely to be short-lived.[69]

Niccolo Machiavelli, the sixteenth century Italian "realist" thinker and advisor to princes, pointed to the inability of people unaccustomed to responsible self-rule to maintain liberty.[70] It was, he wrote, a situation comparable to that of an animal brought up in captivity which when set free is unable to fend for itself. It becomes the prey of the first person seeking to restore it to the former condition.[71] "For it was neither the name nor the rank of dictator that made Rome servile, but the loss of authority of which the citizens were deprived by the length of his rule."[72] The degree of accustomed passive obedience under a former prince, or instead the degree of the vitality and participation of the subjects in a republic, is significant, Machiavelli argued, in determining the relative ease or difficulty which a new ruler will encounter in attempting to establish himself.[73]

Baron de Montesquieu, the French eighteenth century political philosopher noted for his views on the importance of a division of powers within government, also contributed to the understanding of the relationship between a society's internal strength and the type of government which it has. Montesquieu emphasized the importance of "virtue" (defined as love of country and of equality) in the maintenance of freedom and popular government.[74] He added: "The customs of an enslaved people are a part of their servitude, those of a free people are a part of their liberty."[75] Mosca cited, among the factors which are necessary to make resistance to, and control over, the ruler possible, the presence of "organized social forces" not controlled by the ruler.[76] Tocqueville argued that the "passion and the habit of freedom" contribute to the preservation of liberty. On the other hand, he wrote, "I can conceive nothing better prepared for subjection, in case of defeat, than a democratic people without free institutions."[77] Jouvenel associated the condition of liberty with the active vigilance of the citizens,[78] and asserted that when the qualities of liberty exist to a high degree, it comes from "a man's own assertion of his own rights...."[79]

Significantly, the views of Mohandas K. Gandhi, nonviolent strategist and leader in the Indian nationalist movement, are fully compatible with these theorists on this view of the relation between social power and political freedom. Gandhi repeatedly argued that genuine self-rule *(swaraj)* was not simply a matter of the governmental arrangements and the identity of the ruler. Instead, democracy was based upon the inner strength of the society.[80] He attributed the Indian subjection to English rule to the weak condition of India herself.[81] Because "after all a people has the government which it deserves," self-government could "only come through self-effort."[82] Before self-rule could be established, the people had to rid themselves of "the feeling of helplessness"; they could not act to change the political structure without self-confidence.[83] "A perfect constitution super-imposed upon a rotten internal condition will be like a whitened sepulchre."[84] Therefore, a nonviolent revolution was not a program of seizure of power, but one of "a transformation of relationships ending in a peaceful transfer of power."[85] An internally strengthened, self-supporting, self-reliant India would be secure from foreign powers even without armaments, Gandhi argued.[86]

IMPLICATIONS OF THIS ANALYSIS FOR THE CONTROL OF POLITICAL POWER

At least three conclusions can be drawn from this discussion about the means by which political power may be controlled:

1. Societies in which strong *loci* of power are not present and in which the subjects are relatively atomized are, despite formal constitutions, highly susceptible to tyranny and other forms of uncontrolled political power.

2. Under those circumstances, simple replacement of the person, or group, which occupies the position of ruler is inadequate to establish effective control over the power of whoever occupies that position.

3. In order for effective control over the ruler's power to be possible in the long run, power must be effectively devolved and diffused among various social groups and institutions throughout the society.

Let us now consider each of these in more detail.

CONSTITUTIONS ARE INSUFFICIENT TO CONTROL A RULER'S POWER

We have seen that in the effort to control a ruler's power, the institutional forms of government are secondary in importance to the actual distribution of power throughout the society. Also, the weakening or destruction of *loci* of power is likely to increase signficantly the difficulties of the subjects in controlling their ruler.

Not even a democratic constitution, which sets limits on the legitimated powers of the government, which establishes regular procedures for the conduct of government and for the choice of ruler, and which guarantees certain liberties and rights to the subjects, is sufficient to reverse this tendency. Where the society is weak and the democratic ruler powerful, traditional or written constitutional limits to the powers of government and barriers to the prerogatives of the ruler will not be able to prevent seizure of the reins of government by an antidemocratic regime, as by coup d'état or invasion. Nor in that same condition in which the society is structurally weak will the subjects be able even to prevent rulers chosen by constitutional means from gradually extending their power beyond its legitimated limits, or from imposing an executive usurpation. When a powerful group is willing to violate the "rules" in a democracy, the clauses of the constitution and laws cannot by themselves prevent the usurpation.

However, a structurally strong society with effective power capacity diffused among the society's groups and institutions has the potential to regulate the ruler's sources of power and to struggle effectively to maintain or restore a democratic governmental system.

This insight into the structural requirements of constitutional democratic systems is today inadequately recognized even by ardent opponents of dictatorship and advocates of freedom. Instead, democrats of several varieties see a constitution outlining the structure and proper scope of government to operate the State to be the key to the establishment and preservation of a democratic political society. Despite such constitutions, however, a large number of constitutional democracies have been displaced by authoritarian or dictatorial regimes of domestic or foreign origin. This should demonstrate that when a powerful group is unwilling to abide by such a constitution, its provisions and restrictions by themselves are insufficient to control a ruler's powers. The society needs also the capacity to control rulers who are unwilling to conform voluntarily to the limits and procedures established by the constitition.

In a society which is internally weak with power concentrated in the State, constitutional barriers cannot prevent an antidemocratic seizure of power. Under those conditions the subjects will also be incapable of preventing a constitutionally chosen ruler from engaging in gradual illegitimate extensions of his power, or from suspending the constitution itself — perhaps by pleading a national crisis. What do the subjects do, for example, if their elected president, backed by the military forces, declares an Emergency to deal with a supposed crisis, disbands the legislature, cancels elections, arrests opposition leaders, and applies controls on newspapers, radio, and television?

To meet such situations, the subjects must be able to counter the usurper's power with their own power. To do so, they must be able to struggle effectively. That requires possession of effective *loci* of power throughout the social structure.

That necessary condition may not be present, however. The non-State institutions of the society may be weak and already subject to governmental controls. No group relevant to defeating the usurpation may have retained or developed the capacity for independent action and resistance to the ruler. The normal workings of the whole society may be inextricably bound to the State apparatus. Large portions of the population may be directly or indirectly dependent for their economic livelihood on that same apparatus. People may have become accustomed to passing their problems to "the government" instead of dealing with them themselves. If this condition exists then the chances of resistance to the usurpation — much less successful resistance — are very small. The society's structure and distribution of effective power capacity in normal times, and how it deals with its social and economic problems, will very strongly influence and even determine its ability to resist efforts to impose a dictatorship.

In that situation, the motives of those whose policies and acts have weakened the society's *loci* of power and enhanced the power of the State apparatus are irrelevant. Usurpers will not find their task more difficult simply because those changes were implemented by a government sincerely seeking to correct injustices, to promote welfare, or to provide effective military and administrative capacity to deter and defeat international military threats, or internal terrorist or guerrilla attacks.

In constititional democracies, diverse groups have constantly tended to give the State greater responsibilities for the society as a whole, and greater power over it. Almost all groups have relied upon the State's military capacity to deal with foreign dangers. Social reformers and revolutionaries of various types have relied upon the State to effect the changes they desired and to deal with the groups which they saw as responsible for social evils or which opposed the desired changes. This reliance on the State has been justified in democratic terms by claims that the legislature or other policy-determining bodies were exercising democratic control for the benefit of the whole society. In those cases, such social groups and institutions as the family, trade unions, religious groups, and industrial corporations have continued to exist outside of the State. However, their *relative* independence and power have almost always been significantly reduced in comparison with the power of such *loci* in earlier periods to control the ruler. Sometimes, the independence and strength of such groups and institutions have been undermined for less noble motives. While the consequences of such undermining and subjection for whatever motive will differ with the case, in this one respect they are always the same: the power potential of the ruler is increased at the expense of the society.

When the *loci* are weakened and the ruler's power potential expanded, the possibility of a change in the constitution and form of government toward dictatorship has been created. An immediate change will not necessarily occur, and is often unlikely. At least a semblance — and often some of the reality — of popular control over government has usually been maintained for some time. When this happens the control usually depends on the ruler's own willingness to conform to certain standards or limits required by the constitution, laws, tradition, or moral code. However, even an elected ruler may be unwilling to adhere to such limits. Or, the ruler's power may be extended gradually in a series of small or apparently innocent ways, so that no one seems to notice or be disturbed by it. Or, the reins of government may be abruptly seized from a ruler who has deliberately behaved with self-restraint by a group eager to utilize more fully the power potential of the position. In such cases as these, the ruler once in control of the State apparatus will have at his disposal the full governmental machinery and system of controls over the subjects and their institutions which have been forged in "normal" times,[87] albeit for very different motives. The populace will then be weak in comparison to the ruler and less capable of effective resistance than they would have been had not the social institutions been weakened and the power of the State increased.[88]

On the basis of his analysis of the political effects of the weakening of the independent *loci* of power in democratic societies, Tocqueville predicted that if absolute power were reestablished in such societies it would "assume a new form and appear under features unknown to our forefathers."[89] He made this prediction over a century before the rise of totalitarian systems in Stalinist Soviet Union and Nazi Germany.

Our experience with the demonstrated inadequacy of constitutional limits on the power of rulers and the severity of the threat of modern tyranny are both sufficiently grave to prod us to look beyond constitutional and legal provisions for additional means to control rulers who are unwilling to accept those limits.

In democratic theory, the right of the citizens to resort to violent revolution against tyrants has been recognized. Against foreign threats, constitutional democracies have relied upon the military forces. Grounds now exist to make us dissatisfied with the adequacy of those means of dealing with an emergency. Both violent mass revolution against tyrants and military resistance to invaders may face practical impediments to success. When unarmed subjects attempt a violent revolution against a well armed ruler, they are almost always at a severe disadvantage most likely to lead to their predictable defeat. Against a coup which has attacked the constitutional government, they are no better a match, for usually the military forces have initiated or supported the coup. In the case of a foreign invasion, the invading ruler of a foreign State will usually have determined that his regime has clear military superiority over the attacked country, so that defensive military resistance has severe odds against its success.

Guerrilla warfare is sometimes seen as a replacement for those means. However, it suffers from grave limitations due to the tendency toward immense casualties, the dubious propsects of success, the frequency of very long struggles, and the structural consequences. The regime under attack is immediately made still more dictatorial, and the regime which follows even a successful struggle also is more dictatorial due to the centralizing impact of the expanded military forces and to the weakening or destruction of the society's *loci* of power during the struggle.*

Thus, it is necessary to look beyond both the formal constitutional arrangements and such violent sanctions for means by which the population can in crises exercise effective control over rulers, domestic or foreign.

If at the time of such crises the society does not possess strong social groups and institutions capable of independent action, able to wield effective power, and capable of controlling the central ruler, then reliance on formal constitutional arrangements alone to set limits on the ruler may prove disastrous. Tocqueville warned of the plight in such a situation:

> ...democratic nations...easily bring their whole disposable force into the field, and when the nation is wealthy and populous it soon becomes victorious; but if ever it is conquered, and its territory invaded, it has few resources at command; and if the enemy takes the capital, the nation is lost. This may very well be explained: as

---

*For a fuller discussion of these problems with violent revolution, coup d'état, and guerrilla warfare, see Chapter Twelve, "Popular Empowerment," subchapter: Sanctions and Society.

each member of the community is individually isolated and extremely powerless, no one of the whole body can either defend himself or present a rallying point to others. Nothing is strong in a democratic country except the State; as the military strength of the State is destroyed by the destruction of the army, and its civil power paralysed by the capture of the chief city, all that remains is only a multitude without strength or government, unable to resist the organised power by which it is assailed. . . . [A]fter such a catastrophe, not only is the population unable to carry on hostilities, but it may be apprehended that they will not be inclined to attempt it.[90]

SIMPLE CHANGE OF RULERS IS ALSO INSUFFICIENT TO ESTABLISH LASTING CONTROL

By now it should be clear that the establishment of real and lasting control over the power of rulers is not to be achieved simply by exchanging one ruler for another to occupy the pinnacle of command. More basic changes are required. Yet, in constitutional democracies most of the political debate focuses on *who* should control the formal political structure. If we are concerned with implementation of democratic principles, the more fundamental question is instead this: what kind of a social and political order is in the long run desirable and capable of solving the problem of the control of political power?

The primary focus on personnel or faction rather than on structure has resulted in part from a lack of clear thinking. We have usually failed to distinguish between a specific tyrant and the condition and system of tyranny.[91] From this it has followed that whereas major efforts may have been made to remove the tyrant, little or no attention was given to changing the condition which made the tyranny possible. At those times when people have sought active means of struggle to combat a domestic or intruding foreign tyrant, little or no attention has been given to the conscious choice of means of struggle which would not only have the chance of immediate effectiveness but also would in the long run help to establish firm control capacity over the power of any ruler. In some cases, to the contrary, the means of combat used actually appear to have made long-term control more difficult.

We have also failed to distinguish between popular elections to choose the personnel or party to occupy the position of ruler and the condition in which people possess the opportunity for active participation in the political society.[92] As a result, major attention has been focused on periodic elections. However, little or no attention has been given to the need for diffused power among various social groups and institutions, nor to strengthening the capacity of the people to make important decisions for themselves and to maintain effective control over the ruler's power.

A change in the personnel or party occupying the position of ruler may or may not make a difference. Sometimes the difference will be significant, for better or for worse. Whether the change makes a difference, and if so what it is, appears to vary with such factors as these: (1) the degree of the ruler's self-control; (2) his social and political aims; and (3) the means used to obtain the position of ruler, to maintain that position, and to implement policies. If differences exist between a former and a new ruler, it is these three factors which are influential, not just a simple change in the personnel occupying the position of ruler, nor even in the capacity of the subjects to influence the choice of the new personnel. Neither such a change nor such influence necessarily demonstrate the capacity of the population to *control* their ruler if he is *unwilling* to be controlled. The political situations in which rulers do not wish to submit to restrictions and limitations on the exercise of their power are the most crucial and dangerous ones, and urgently require solutions.

Often the ability of the subjects to help to select their ruler, and to influence the political policies and practices of a ruler who is willing to be influenced, will be confused with the ability actually to *control* the exercise of power by a ruler who is determined to proceed without restrictions. That confusion is likely to create the illusion of greater democractic control than is in fact the case. This illusion may make it easier for the ruler to extend his control and power, while the subjects become more complacent and less interested in asserting control themselves and less willing to resist.[93] This confusion may also help to create the impression that there is greater difference between rivals for the position of ruler than is in fact the case. Tocqueville's insight is still valid: "Our contemporaries are therefore much less divided than is commonly supposed; they are constantly disputing as to the hands in which the supremacy is to be vested, but they readily agree upon the duties and the rights of that supremacy."[94]

Since the degree to which the ruler's capacity to wield power is actually exercised will vary with the factors listed above, a change of ruler may result in a short-term change in the extent and manner in which the ruler's power is applied. Very importantly, however, a change of personnel occupying the position of ruler does not itself reduce the *capacity* of whoever is ruler to wield power uncontrolled by the subjects. That change will only accompany the change of ruler if both the *loci* of power throughout the society and also the subjects' capacity to resist the ruler have been strengthened before the change in personnel, or during the efforts to achieve that change. Otherwise, no change in the potential for tyranny will have occurred. A growth of the society's capacity for freedom is therefore necessary if tyranny itself is to be ended as well as the regime of a particular tyrant.

> For a revolution formed by liberty becomes a confirmation of liberty [wrote Montesquieu]. A free nation may have a deliverer: a nation enslaved can have only another oppressor. For whoever is able to dethrone an absolute prince has a power sufficient to become absolute himself.[95]

Even when there appears to be some change in the outward form and constitution of the political system, the actual change may be more limited than it appears to be if the underlying power structure itself remains intact. The change from monarchy to a republic, said Jouvenel, maintained the whole monarchical State intact, while the position of the king was taken by "the representatives of the Nation."[96] ". . .[O]nce the principle of the unchecked and unbounded sovereignty of a human will is admitted, the resulting regime is in substance the same, to whatever person, real or fictive, this sovereign will is attributed."[97] Because of this, systems which appear most opposed, but which confer comparable uncontrolled power on the person or group occupying the position of ruler, have much in common.[98]

Under a system with a firm structure in which one group is superordinate and another subordinate, Simmel wrote, unless "a fundamental change in the social form" occurs, even "the liberation of the subordinates often does not entail general freedom . . . but only the rise of the subordinates into the ruling stratum."[99] Unless "the liberation of the subordinates" has been preceded or accompanied by the break-up of the concentration of effective power and its diffusion throughout the society and by the strengthening of the institutions of the society in comparison to the ruler, the simple change of persons in the position of ruler will not increase the subjects' capacity to control the ruler's power capacity. This is true whether the position of ruler continues to be occupied by the same personnel for a long time, or the personnel in that position are periodically changed while the society's power structure remains essentially unaltered.[100] If the political power of rulers is to be brought under control, clearly some more fundamental changes are required.

DEVOLUTION OF POWER IS ESSENTIAL FOR LASTING CONTROL

The establishment of a lasting capacity to exercise effective control over political power — especially in crises — requires strengthening the society at the expense of the ruler. That is to say, the establishment of such control requires significant devolution of effective power capacity among a variety of social groups and institutions. Those *loci* of power then will be able to play significant roles in the normal functioning of the society, and also be capable of wielding effective power, and of controlling the availability of the sources of power to the ruler.

It is not sufficient that these groups and institutions be permitted to make suggestions to the ruler, and to help administer his policies. They must be capable of making independent decisions and of carrying them out themselves. "How," asked Tocqueville, "can a populace unaccustomed to freedom in small concerns, learn to use it temperately in great affairs?"[101] Thus, the establishment of the capacity to wield effective control over the power of rulers requires social changes contrary to important trends in modern politics.

Where *loci* with such capacities still exist in a society, it would normally be important to preserve and improve them. Or, if they are for some reason unsuitable, it would be important to build up alternative groups and institutions. Where it is deemed necessary to weaken or remove certain existing groups and institutions which are themselves engaged in undesirable activities — say, oppressing other parts of the population — it would be important to do this by means which would not concentrate further power with the ruler and weaken relatively the general populace. In those cases it would be necessary to replace the old *loci* with new voluntary groups, associations, and institutions with effective independent power capacities. The new *loci* would then help to make the liberty of the individual subjects more secure while not diminishing their equality.[102] If freedom is to be preserved, each citizen must "combine with his fellow-citizens for the purpose of defending it...."[103]

Many — probably most — rulers are likely to discourage or actively oppose this devolution of power and strengthening of the society's voluntary groups and institutions. The idea itself may be regarded as subversive. However, at times a ruler may genuinely believe in democratic principles and may therefore even encourage and facilitate the process of devolution. The regime alone cannot carry out the process, however; it requires the active initiative, participation, and acceptance of responsibility by the groups, associations, and institutions of the society. In most other cases, the development and strengthening of such *loci* may be achieved quite independently by voluntary efforts alone, as Gandhi envisaged the development of a decentralized society through his constructive program.[104] Also, existing groups may contribute to such devolution by their struggles to achieve a relatively greater freedom of action, self-determination, or local control for neighborhoods, towns, and regions, and full autonomy for nationalities under external rule.

The means of struggle used in such situations and the type of ultimate sanction relied upon by the society and by the *loci* in crises will also be important in influencing the devolution or concentration of power in that political society, as we shall examine in more detail.

Other means of achieving devolution may be developed and old ones refined. But whatever may be the variety of means which are instrumental to that end, the devolution of effective power throughout the social structure as a whole is one of the requirements for a lasting capacity to prevent tyranny and other expressions of uncontrolled political power.*

For establishing effective control over rulers, both questions of social organization and of techniques of action (including ultimate sanctions) are relevant. In seeking to solve the problem of the control of political power, and in trying to find means to develop the kind of society which facilitates that control, we need to seek answers to these questions:

*This discussion of institutional devolution of power is developed more fully in Chapter Twelve, "Popular Empowerment," subchapter: Developing Strategies of Empowerment.

1. How can people organize a free society in ways that preserve and improve its capacity to remain free?

2. How can people produce social and political changes in ways which will both deal with the particular problem and also facilitate, not hinder, the long-term control of political power?

3. How can a society deal with particular instances of uncontrolled political power (as in oppression, tyranny, and war) by means which both help to solve the immediate problem and also help to control and diffuse — not concentrate — political power in the long run?

These and other such questions are closely related to the technique of action used to produce changes and the type of sanction relied upon to maintain the social system. This is because the nature of the sanctions applied in conflicts and for enforcement has a close causal connection to the degree of concentration or diffusion of power in the society. We need increased insight into that connection between sanctions and structure.

POLITICAL SANCTIONS AND THE DISTRIBUTION OF EFFECTIVE POWER

The two broad alternative types of sanctions may be called political violence[105] and nonviolent action. These two types are likely to have quite different effects on the future concentration of power in the society. Setting aside for the moment other questions related to violent and nonviolent action in politics, let us consider briefly how the choice of one or the other of these types of sanctions as the technique of control of a ruler or of an institution may significantly influence the long-term capacity of the subjects to control political power.

POLITICAL VIOLENCE CONTRIBUTES TO THE CONCENTRATION OF POWER

It has been widely recognized that violent revolutions and wars have been accompanied by and followed by increased centralization of power in the ruler. This recognition has by no means been limited to opponents of political violence and centralization. However, even when critics of the established social and political system — such as Karl Marx — have had this insight, they have rarely asked *why* centralized power was associated with political violence. Furthermore, they have rarely asked whether political violence was then compatible with the establishment of lasting effective control over the power of rulers. To the contrary, it has often happened that those persons sharply aware of the existing tendencies toward centralization have pressed for policies and measures which seem to have ensured that the centralization of power in the ruler and the difficulties of controlling that power would be *increased*. Both Karl Marx and Vladimir Lenin did so. Little attention has been paid to the very possible connection between the technique of action relied upon in struggle and the degree to which effective power is diffused among social groups and institutions or concentrated in the position of ruler.

Marx referred to the French State as "an immense bureaucratic and military organization" and as a "frightful parasitic body...." "All political upheavals" in France from the first French Revolution to the coup of Louis Napoleon "perfected this machine instead of smashing it. The parties that strove in turn for mastery regarded possession of this immense state edifice as the main booty for the victor."[106] Lenin — who intended to use this centralized State apparatus in Russia for his own ends — in 1917 referred to this passage from Marx as a "tremendous step forward" in Marxism: "...all revolutions which have taken place up to the present have helped to perfect the state machinery, whereas it must be shattered, broken to pieces." Lenin declared: "This conclusion is the chief and fundamental thesis in the Marxist theory of the State."[107] His basic Jacobin theory of revolution and his practice were, however, very different from that view, although he presented them as compatible.

Following a violent revolution in which a new group has seized control of the State, the new rulers have sometimes been regarded for a time as more humanitarian and less oppressive than the former regime. There has been no guarantee, however, that they would remain so. Lenin did not. Nor was any barrier established in his system to prevent others who somehow obtained the position of ruler after Lenin from behaving far more autocratically, as Stalin did.

The weakening of the society's groups, associations, and institutions, and the concentration of effective power capacity in the hands of the position of ruler consequently did not — could not — bring to the subjects increased ability to control the power of any future ruler who did not wish to be controlled. This process, argued Jouvenel, laid the foundation for the "monolithic State."[108]

Although the centralizing effect of war has been especially obvious in the twentieth century, the tendency had certainly been demonstrated earlier.[109] Technological changes and the near complete breakdown of the distinction between civilians and the military forces have accentuated this tendency. Effective mobilization of manpower and other resources into an efficient war machine, the necessity of centralized planning and direction, the disruptive effect of dissention and incomplete control, and the increase in the military might available to the ruler, all contribute to the strong tendency of modern war to concentrate more and more effective power in the hands of the ruler.

Other types of political violence may also contribute to this centralizing process. Modern developments in technology and political organization appear to be accentuating the tendencies of political violence toward centralization of effective power capacity.[110] Among these factors are the following:

1. Centralized direction and control of the preparations for and the waging of political violence is generally necessary if the violence is to be applied efficiently.

2. This requires centralized control of the weapons (and other material resources), the active combatants, and the groups and institutions on which these depend.

3. Such control (as in factors 1 and 2) means increased power during the struggle for those exercising that control, including the ability to apply physical violence to maintain it.

4. After a successful struggle by political violence, the group which controlled the conduct of the struggle is likely to retain the power capacity which it accumulated during the struggle. Or, if a coup d'état takes place, others, or a section of the original group, will obtain control of that institutionalized power capacity.*

5. The taking-over of the old State, strengthened by the newly accumulated additional power capacity, will mean an overall increase

*For an extended analysis of some of the consequences of institutionalized political violence, see Chapter Eleven, "The Societal Imperative," and Chapter Twelve, "Popular Empowerment."

in the effective power capacity of future rulers as compared to the old ones.

6. That power capacity is also likely to be increased by the destruction or weakening during the struggle of effective *loci* of power, with the result that the subjects are left relatively weakened vis-à-vis the ruler.

7. The new regime born out of violence will require reliance on violence, and therefore centralization, to defend itself from internal and external enemies.

8. In a society in which subjects and ruler alike regard violence as the only kind of effective power and the only real means of struggle, and in which the ruler has a vast capacity to wield political violence, the subjects are likely to feel helpless.

These factors and others help to reduce the capacity of subjects to control a ruler's power in a society which has relied upon political violence as its supreme sanction and means of struggle.

NONVIOLENT SANCTIONS CONTRIBUTE TO THE DIFFUSION OF POWER

Nonviolent action appears to have a quite different long-term effect on the distribution of power in the society. Not only does this technique not have the centralizing effects of political violence, but it appears to contribute significantly to the diffusion of effective power throughout the society. This, in turn, is likely to make it easier in the long run for the subjects to control their ruler's exercise of power. Widespread application of nonviolent action in place of political violence appears to diffuse power capacity among the subjects for these reasons:[111]

1. Although strong leadership may play an important role in initiating a nonviolent struggle movement, as the conflict develops and the original leadership is imprisoned or otherwise removed by the opponent, a continuing central leadership group frequently ceases to be necessary and, indeed, is often imposssible to maintain. In other cases in which leadership continues, participants still require a greater self-reliance. The movement as a whole thus tends to become self-reliant, and in extreme situations effectively leaderless. Especially under severe repression, efficiency in nonviolent action requires that the participants be able to act without dependence on a central leadership group.

2. The movement cannot be centrally controlled by the regulation of the distribution of weapons and ammunition to the combatants, because in nonviolent action there are no material weapons. Instead, the actionists depend on such qualities as their bravery, ability to maintain nonviolent discipline, and skill in applying the technique. These qualities and skills are more likely to develop with use. Thus, such practice helps to produce greater self-reliance than in the case of troops who rely on replenishment of equipment, ammunition, and orders from commanding officers.

3. The centralizing forces operating in political violence are not present in nonviolent action. The degree of dependence on the nonviolent leaders is reduced as the campaign proceeds. If they are to continue as leaders, it is only because of their voluntarily accepted moral authority and of people's perception of them as skillful leaders and strategists, not because of any capacity to enforce their will by threats or infliction of violence against the participants themselves.

4. Where the leaders do not accumulate in the course of the struggle the capacity to wield political violence, there are no such institutionalized means of repression ready to apply against their followers and others in the poststruggle period.

5. Where some of the leaders following the nonviolent struggle accept positions in the State, including that of ruler, as occurs following a national independence struggle, it is true that they will have at their disposal the police and military capacities of that State, but these will not have been increased by their own accumulated military forces and capacity to wage political violence.

6. The social groups and institutions throughout the society will not have been weakened or destroyed by political violence, or subordinated to its requirements. To the contrary, in nonviolent struggle these *loci* of power are likely to have been strengthened. The experience of working closely together in the struggle, demonstrating greater self-reliance, and gaining experience in means of asserting their ability to continue and to resist the opponent's repression and regimentation, are likely in a successful nonviolent struggle to have strengthened such *loci* appreciably. Gandhi often described a nonviolent action campaign as a means by which the people would generate the strength to enable them to advance toward achieving their political goals.[112]

7. A nonviolent campaign for a specific political objective cannot be expected to be followed immediately by the full rejection of violence by that political society in all situations. However, it is a step in that direction which may, or may not, be later followed by other substitutions of nonviolent sanctions for violent ones.

Changes won by political violence are likely to require continued political violence to defend them. Those changes "given" without effort can be as easily taken away. However, in the course of achieving changes by nonviolent struggle, the populace also generates the capacity to defend those changes nonviolently.[113] Changes achieved by nonviolent action are therefore likely to be more lasting. Such changes also contribute to freeing the society in that specific area from the "necessity" of relying on political violence to maintain the social structure.[114]

8. Whereas following a struggle with political violence, the subjects are likely to feel relatively helpless when they compare their own power capacity with that of the ruler, a quite different situation is likely to have developed during a successful nonviolent struggle. In the first place, they are likely to have experienced a transformation of their *potential* power into *effective* or real power by successful nonviolent action. Such experience will give them confidence, resources, and skill which will enhance their future ability to change their society and to control their ruler's effective power. This kind of training in "battle" helps to increase the subjects' capacity to apply the technique in future crises, contributes to the devolution of effective power and power capacity in the society,[115] and enhances the ability of that society as a whole to control rulers of domestic or foreign origin who would seek to impose their will against the will of the citizenry.

If valid, the discussion in this section has various important practical consequences. Even if we assume equal short-term effectiveness for the two types of sanctions, the choice of one or the other will have quite different long-term consequences for the society.*

---

*For further discussion of the long-term effects of violent and nonviolent sanctions, and of deliberate replacement of violent with nonviolent sanctions, see Chapter Twelve, "Popular Empowerment," subchapter: Sanctions and Society, and subchapter: Developing Strategies of Empowerment.

THE NEED TO THINK

This chapter has been an attempt to offer in broad outlines some thoughts about the relationship between the ruler's power capacity and the underlying distribution of power capacity throughout the social structure. The influence of alternative sanctions and means of struggle on the distribution of power capacity has also been explored.

The dangers of uncontrolled political power are so severe that solutions to that problem are imperative. However, not every proposal for dealing with a problem is likely to have the same results when put into action. Past proposals for controlling political power have had very limited success, have proven to be impotent, or have even been counterproductive. Even when "successful," the frequency with which past efforts appear to have contributed to reduced capacity for long-term control of power should stimulate us to seek more satisfactory solutions. That search requires that, among other things, we *think* about the nature of the problem and the requirments of a satisfactory solution.

Such attempts to think again about long-standing problems are at times unsettling. We are left often with a feeling of dissatisfaction. The adequacy of traditional "solutions" is thrown into doubt, while the alternative analysis of the nature of the problem and the alternative proposed "solution" both remain inadequately developed. Such unease may, however, be beneficial if it stimulates us to think, and ourselves to contribute to the effort to solve the problem before us.

NOTES

1. See Gene Sharp, **The Politics of Nonviolent Action** (Boston: Porter Sargent Publisher, 1973), Chapter One.
2. See ibid., Chapters Two-Fourteen for an analysis of the nature of nonviolent struggle.
3. For some related definitions of power, see Robert M. MacIver, **The Web of Government** (New York: Macmillan Co., 1947), pp. 82 and 87; Martin J. Hillenbrand, **Power and Morals** (New York: Columbia University Press, 1949), pp. 4-5; Jacques Maritain, **Man and the State** (London: Hollis & Carter, 1954), p. 114; and Harold D. Lasswell, **Power and Personality** (New York: W.W. Norton & Co., 1948), p. 12.
4. MacIver writes: "What power the government wields and to what ends it directs

this power depends on these other forces [*loci* of power], on the manner in which they are operatively adjusted to one another in the struggle and clash, the convergence and divergence, of power-possessing interests." (MacIver, **The Web of Government,** p. 91.)

5. Bertrand de Jouvenel, **Sovereignty: An Enquiry into the Public Good** (Chicago: University of Chicago Press, 1959, and Cambridge at the University Press, 1957), p. 71.

6. Georg Simmel writes: "The ruler's chief motive in equalizing hierarchical differences derives from the fact that relations of strong superordination and subordination among his subjects actually and psychologically compete with his own superordination. Besides, too great an oppression of certain classes by others is as dangerous to despotism as is the too great power of these oppressing classes." (Georg Simmel, **The Sociology of Georg Simmel** [Trans., ed., and with an Introduction by Kurt H. Wolff; Glencoe, Illinois: The Free Press, 1950], p. 198.)

7. Alexis de Tocqueville, **Democracy in America** [Trans. by Henry Reeve, C.B.; London: Longmans, Green and Co., 1889), vol. I, p. 332.

8. Ibid.

9. Ibid., p. 333.

10. Ibid.

11. Ibid., p. 332.

12. Ibid., p. 6.

13. Ibid., p. 332.

14. Ibid., vol. II, p. 296.

15. Ibid., vol. I, p. 333.

16. Ibid.

17. Ibid., p. 334.

18. Ibid.

19. Jouvenel, **Sovereignty,** p. 200.

20. Gaetano Mosca, **The Ruling Class** *(Elementi de Scienza Politica)* (Trans. by Hannah D. Kahn; ed. and rev. with an Introduction by Arthur Livingstone; New York and London: McGraw-Hill, 1939), p. 141.

21. Tocqueville, **Democracy in America,** vol. I, p. 332.

22. Ibid.

23. Simmel, **The Sociology of Georg Simmel,** p. 232.

24. Franco Venturi, **Roots of Revolution** (New York: Alfred A. Knopf, 1960, and London: Weidenfeld and Nicolson, 1960), p. 66.

25. See ibid.

26. Ibid., p. 67.

27. Ibid., pp. 68-69.

28. Ibid., p. 198.

29. Ibid., p. 70.

30. Ibid., p. 71.

31. See ibid., pp. 72-73.

32. Ibid., p. 72.

33. Tocqueville, **Democracy in America,** vol. II, p. 258.

34. Ibid., vol. I, p. 333.

35. Ibid., p. 334.

36. Ibid., p. 9.

37. Ibid.
38. Ibid., p. 93.
39. Ibid., vol. II, p. 271.
40. Bertrand de Jouvenel, **Power: Its Nature and the History of Its Growth** (Trans. by J. F. Huntington; Boston: Beacon Paperback, 1962, and London: Batchworth Press 1952 [1945]), pp. 244-246.
41. Ibid., p. 295.
42. See ibid., pp. 185-200.
43. Tocqueville, **Democracy in America,** vol. II., p. 272.
44. Ibid., p. 9; see also p. 47.
45. Ibid., vol. I, pp. 333-334.
46. Ibid., p. 334.
47. Ibid., vol. II, p. 296.
48. Ibid., p. 258.
49. Ibid., vol. I, p. 92.
50. See, for example, Karen Horney, **The Neurotic Personality of Our Time** (New York: W.W. Norton, 1937), p. 289; and Erich Fromm, **Escape From Freedom** (New York: Rinehart and Co., 1941), pp. 240 and 253-254. British ed.: **The Fear of Freedom** (London: Routledge and Kegan Paul, 1960), pp. 207 and 220.
51. Horney, **The Neurotic Personality of Our Time,** p. 289.
52. Fromm, **Escape From Freedom,** p. 240, and **The Fear of Freedom,** p. 207.
53. Fromm, **Escape From Freedom,** pp. 255-256 and **The Fear of Freedom,** p. 220.
54. Leonard Schapiro, **The Communist Party of the Soviet Union** (London: Eyre and Spottiswoode, 1960), p. 431.
55. On *Gleichschaltung* in Nazi Germany see Franz Neumann, **Behemoth: The Structure and Practice of National Socialism 1933-1944** (New York: Octagon Books, Inc., 1963); and Arthur Schweitzer, **Big Business in the Third Reich** (London: Eyre and Spottiswoode, 1964).
56. See Leonard Schapiro, **The Origins of the Communist Autocracy: Political Opposition in the Soviet State: First Phase 1917-1922** (London: G. Bell and Sons, Ltd., 1956), and Schapiro, **The Communist Party of the Soviet Union.**
57. Tocqueville, **Democracy in America,** vol. II, p. 93.
58. Simmel, **The Sociology of Georg Simmel,** p. 199.
59. See ibid., p. 198.
60. Tocqueville, **Democracy in America,** vol. II, p. 284.
61. Ibid., p. 9.
62. Ibid., p. 93.
63. Ibid., p. 265.
64. F.C. Montague, Introduction to Jeremy Bentham, **A Fragment on Government** (Ed. by F.C. Montague. London: Humphrey Milford, 1931 [1891]), p. 48.
65. Mosca, **The Ruling Class,** p. 141.
66. Jouvenel, **Power,** p. 206.
67. See William Godwin, **Enquiry Concerning Political Justice and Its Influence on Morals and Happiness** (Sec. ed.; London: G.G. and J. Robinson, 1796), vol. I, pp. 275-276.
68. See ibid., vol. I, pp. 257-261 and 304, and vol. II, pp. 221-222 and 244.
69. See ibid., vol. I, p. 108 and 254-255, and vol. II, p. 153.
70. Niccolo Machiavelli, **The Discourses of Niccolo Machiavelli** ("Discourses on the

First Ten Books of Titus Livy") (London: Routledge and Kegan Paul, 1950), vol. I, p. 252.

71. Ibid., pp. 252-253.
72. Ibid., p. 289.
73. Machiavelli, **The Prince** (London: J.M. Dent & Sons [Everyman Library], 1948), p. 38.
74. Baron de Montesquieu, **The Spirit of the Laws** (New York: Hafner Publishing Co., 1959), vol. I, pp. 20-23 and 34.
75. Ibid., p. 307.
76. Mosca, **The Ruling Class**, p. 134.
77. Tocqueville, **Democracy in America**, vol. II, p. 260.
78. Jouvenel, **Power**, p. 277.
79. Ibid., p. 293.
80. See M.K. Gandhi, **Non-violence in Peace and War** (Ahmedabad: Navajivan Publishing House, 1949), vol. II, pp. 187-188. Here he suggests that an India internally so weak as to be torn by riots would be easy prey to a new foreign ruler. See also N.K. Bose, **Studies in Gandhism** (Calcutta: Indian Associated Publishing Co., 1947), pp. 62-63.
81. See Gandhi, "Hind Swaraj or Indian Home Rule" (pamphlet, Ahmedabad: Navajivan, 1958), pp. 38-41, and Gene Sharp, "Gandhi on the Theory of Voluntary Servitude," in **Gandhi as a Political Strategist** (Boston: Porter Sargent Publishers, 1979).
82. Gandhi, **Non-violence in Peace and War** (Ahmedabad: Navajivan, 1948), vol. I, p. 36.
83. Ibid., p. 12.
84. Bose, **Selections from Gandhi** (Ahmedabad: Navajivan, 1948), p. 118. See also ibid. pp. 121 and 123; Gandhi, **Non-violence in Peace and War**, vol. I, p. 351; and Gandhi, **Satyagraha** (Ahmedabad: Navajivan, 1951), p. 283.
85. Gandhi, **Non-violence in Peace and War**, vol. II, p. 8.
86. See ibid., vol. I, pp. 103-104.
87. See Jouvenel, **Power**, pp. 22-23.
88. See Tocqueville, **Democracy in America**, vol. I, p. 93, and vol. II, p. 258.
89. Ibid., vol. I, p. 332, see also p. 334, and vol. II, pp. 288-290 and 294.
90. Tocqueville, **Democracy in America**, vol. II, p. 258.
91. See Montesquieu, **The Spirit of the Laws**, vol. I, p. 21.
92. Jouvenel, **Power**, p. 220, and Hannah Arendt, **On Revolution** (New York: Viking Press, 1963).
93. Montesquieu, **The Spirit of the Laws**, pp. 21-22.
94. Tocqueville, **Democracy in America**, vol. II, p. 266.
95. Montesquieu, **The Spirit of the Laws**, vol. I, p. 309.
96. Jouvenel, **Power**, p. 101.
97. Jouvenel, **Sovereignty**, p. 199.
98. Ibid.
99. Simmel, **The Sociology of Georg Simmel**, p. 274.
100. As in Pareto's theory of the circulation of the elites. See Vilfredo Pareto, **The Mind and Society** (New York: Harcourt Brace and Co., 1935), vol. IV, pp. 1787-1798.
101. Tocqueville, **Democracy in America**, vol. I, p. 92.

102. See ibid., vol. II, pp. 295-296.

103. Ibid., p. 97.

104. See Gene Sharp, "The Theory of Gandhi's Constructive Program," in **Gandhi as a Political Strategist,** Chapter Five.

105. Political violence here refers to physical violence or the threat of it used to further political objectives, whether by the State, non-State groups, or individuals, including imprisonment, execution, rioting, guerrilla war, conventional war, assassination, coup d'état, civil war, bombing, terrorism, and police and military action against opposition groups.

106. Karl Marx, **The Eighteenth Brumaire of Louis Bonapart,** pp. 238-239, in David Fernbach, ed., **Karl Marx: Political Writings,** vol. II, **Surveys from Exile** (New York: Vintage Books, Random House, 1974).

107. V.I. Lenin, **The State and the Revolution** (New York: International Publishers, 1974), p. 25.

108. See Jouvenel, **Power,** pp. 18-22 and 244-246.

109. See Quincy Wright, **A Study of War** (Chicago: University of Chicago Press, 1942), vol. I, pp. 232-242, 302, and esp. 311; Bronislaw Malinowski, "An Anthropological Analysis of War," **American Journal of Sociology,** vol. XLVI, no. 4, esp. p. 545; and Malinowski, **Freedom and Civilization** (New York: Roy Publishers, 1944), esp. pp. 265 and 305.

110. The following list of factors appears in similar form in Gene Sharp, **The Politics of Nonviolent Action,** pp. 800-802.

111. This list of factors also appears in similar form in ibid., pp. 802-806. See Part Three, "The Dynamics of Nonviolent Action" for analysis and data supporting these insights.

112. See Gandhi, **Satyagraha,** p. 356, and Gene Sharp, **Gandhi Wields the Weapon of Moral Power** (Ahmedabad: Navajivan, 1960), pp. 72 and 100.

113. See Sharp, **Gandhi Wields The Weapon of Moral Power,** p. 125, and Gandhi, **Non-violence in Peace and War,** vol. II, p. 340.

114. See Richard Gregg, **The Power of Non-violence** (Sec. rev. ed.: New York: Schocken, 1966, and London: James Clarke, 1960), p. 146.

115. Bose has written that experience in nonviolent action puts the people: "on their own legs. And when power comes with the revolution, it spreads evenly among the masses; for, under non-violence, any unarmed man, woman, or child can be effective provided the heart is stout. Under violence, this cannot be so; those who make the most effective use of violence gain the upper hand." (Bose, **Studies in Gandhism,** p. 148.)

3

The Lesson of Eichmann

A Review-Essay on Hannah Arendt's Eichmann in Jerusalem*

We do not yet understand the Holocaust, nor do we know how to respond adequately to it. The Nazis deliberately exterminated up to six million Jews, millions of Eastern Europeans, about a hundred thousand Gypsies, and many other people. We have the testimony of survivors, the photographs, the films, the Nazis' own records, scholarly studies, and television documentaries. But still, the numbers involved, the cruelty, even the elementary idea of killing off a whole unwanted population, are hard for us to comprehend in their depth and totality. This difficulty is itself a severe problem which continues to face us.

How should we respond adequately to that unspeakable

tragedy? This problem is at least equally important. The response which is least disturbing to ourselves is to try to ignore the Holocaust. When that is not really possible, we often refer to it only in passing. It is also easy and comforting for us simply to denounce the Nazis who perpetrated it, applying the standard phrases and clichés of condemnation, but with little thought or sense of our own responsibility for the future. For many persons — especially survivors , relatives and friends of victims, Jews, and others sensitive to these gross inhumanities — the response is and probably must be highly personal and emotional. Only very rarely does one find a response which faces squarely the reality of the Holocaust, and then attempts to react responsibly and rationally not only to the past, but also to the future danger of genocide.

Most people regard the Holocaust as an essentially unique occurrence in human history. This is not quite true. The Nazi extermination program indeed had its individual characteristics which set it off from earlier human tragedies. Genocide, however, did not originate in Hitler's mind, nor in the dynamics of the Nazi system. That observation is simple, but it is simultaneously devastating. The problem of genocide never was and cannot be delimited to the Nazi era. Genocide had happened before — in other circumstances, with fewer numbers, to different populations, by other perpetrators — but it had happened. That observation is not a simple correction of historical accuracy. That genocide had happened before means that it could happen again.

Even if one sees the Holocaust as unique in human history — which Hannah Arendt at times implies in *Eichmann in Jerusalem* — the fact that it occurred even once means that it could be attempted again. Simply punishing the perpetrators is insufficient. Whatever the punishment meted out to a criminal, it cannot prevent the commission of the same crime again, Arendt wrote. She believed that the trial and execution of Adolph Eichmann in Jerusalem for his actions as controller of the transportation system which carried the victims to the extermination camps were understandable and appropriate (despite certain legal problems); however, that action alone was, in her opinion, an inadequate response to the Holocaust.

---

*Hannah Arendt, *Eichmann in Jerusalem: A Report on the Banality of Evil*. New York: Viking Press, 1963, and London: Faber & Faber, 1963.

In her diverse books, Dr. Arendt approached significant social and political subjects from unusual perspectives, and probed important problems far more deeply than most writers. She tried to provoke us to think for ourselves about important questions and difficult problems. In all her books, Arendt constantly demanded that we *think*. Ironically, most politically-minded people ignore or rebel at the suggestion that they should think afresh about political problems, assuming either that they already do so, or that further thinking is unnecessary. That is, in my opinion, an erroneous and dangerous assumption which has significantly contributed to the failure of so much of modern politics.

Arendt in her books rigorously and rationally examined even exceedingly difficult and painful problems. In *Eichmann in Jerusalem* she attempted to examine in this same way the Holocaust, the most sensitive problem she ever tackled. This in part accounts for the widespread hostility with which many reviewers received the book on its publication in 1963. The book raised questions which she did not adequately answer, and which cannot be answered here; indeed they ought not to be, for here too she wanted to stimulate us to think for ourselves.

PREVENTING REPETITION

In *Eichmann in Jerusalem* she challenged us to examine the actual operation of the Nazi policy of genocide, including its most disturbing elements, so that we might become more able to prevent future genocide. It is not enough to denounce the evil; we must learn how to defeat it when it is next attempted. No one can be certain that such a crime against humanity will not be attempted again; therefore we must be prepared. "On the contrary...once a specific crime has appeared for the first time, its reappearance is more likely than its initial emergence could ever have been. The particular reasons that speak for the possibility of a repetition of the crimes committed by the Nazis are even more plausible": the modern population explosion; automation which makes large sections of the population "superfluous" even in terms of labor; and nuclear energy, which makes possible "instruments beside which Hitler's gassing installations look like an evil child's fumbling toys." This, Arendt wrote, "should be enough to make us tremble" (p. 250). Many reviewers who denounced the book appeared either not to have understood her purpose, or to have been unable to face her warning.

Eichmann in Jerusalem is a very unusual book; it is the report and commentary by one of the most important twentieth century political philosophers of the trial of Adolph Eichmann, following his sensational capture by Israeli agents in Argentina and kidnapping and transport to Israel. Arendt covered the trial for *The New Yorker,* in which her book was originally serialized. Despite her criticisms of the handling of the case by the Israeli Government and failures in the proceedings in the Jerusalem court, Arendt supported the trial and the execution of Eichmann. She did not stop there, however; that would be too easy, and it would enable us to rest too comfortably. It would also help us to ignore the most important single question: How can we prevent genocide and successfully resist any attempt to commit it in the future?

It would be comforting if anti-Semitism were only a German phenomenon, but this was clearly not true, Arendt reminded us. Both the Polish and Rumanian Governments had officially proclaimed their wish to be rid of their Jews. The Polish Government in 1937 explored (and found impractical) the possibility of shipping its nearly three million Jews to the large island of Madagascar in the Indian Ocean off southern Africa. In December 1938, the French Foreign Minister Georges Bonnet explored the possibility of sending France's *foreign* Jews (which numbered about 200,000) to Madagascar also, and even consulted with the German Foreign Minister Joachim von Ribbentrop on the idea. The Rumanian atrocities against the Jews during the war were so ruthless and cruel that the Germans intervened to stop them, preferring a more orderly evacuation to extermination camps. Even the prewar Netherlands Government had declared the 35,000 stateless Jews (primarily from Germany) in the country to be "undesirable," and many countries refused to accept as immigrants any considerable number of Jewish refugees at the time when emigration from Germany was permitted and many more could have been saved.

EICHMANN'S CONSCIENCE: THE SILENCE OF OTHERS

If Eichmann had been mentally insane, highly sadistic, or fanatically anti-Semitic, his role would be easier to understand. It would also be politically comforting, for if such identifiable people were kept out of bureaucracies the future dangers would be less serious. The evidence for these mental conditions in Eichmann, as revealed in the trial, is weak. In order better to understand how the genocide was conducted, Arendt tried to examine Adolph Eichmann as a human being, and not simply as the controller of the transportation system to the extermination camps, whose role had been so important in the deaths of millions. What kind of a person did this, and therefore what kind of a person might do such a job again?

This is the man she reveals: Eichmann was ambitious; he wanted to be someone important and to do something important. He needed a master and an idea to serve. He often "talked big" and exaggerated his own role. He could only speak and "think" in slogans and clichés.

Eichmann and his men decided how many Jews could or should be transported from any given area to the extermination camps, and organized their transport to specific destinations which had been selected by others. He knew that he was transporting millions to their deaths; yet when he viewed in person the killing and the horrors in the camps he became ill. Eichmann's conscience, as Arendt presents it, was a strange thing. Apparently, he had no personal hostility toward Jews, no insane hatred of them, and often behaved in a respectful manner to individual Jews with whom he consulted. However, he seemed unworried by his role in their extermination. He even explained at length to his Jewish police interrogator in Jerusalem that it was not *his* fault that he had been unable to attain a higher rank in the S.S. Eichmann seemed unperturbed by his contribution to the deaths of millions of Jews; but he was bothered by the memory that he had once slapped the face of Dr. Josef Löwenherz, the head of the Vienna Jewish Community. At his trial in Jerusalem, Eichmann became agitated only once, by the accusation (dismissed by the court) that he had personally beaten a Jewish boy to death.

Eichmann's conscience functioned briefly while he performed his job in the "Final Solution." He then became disturbed only by the killing of *German,* as distinct from East European, Jews, and had doubts about "such a bloody solution through violence" (p. 101). These doubts were, however, later dispelled. Eichmann lost his need to feel anything at all. He did his "duty," and obeyed orders and "the law." He did, however, try to avoid "unnecessary hardships" for the Jews on their way to the death camps (p. 87). Eichmann's conscience was sometimes aroused by other matters than human suffering.

Without Hitler's knowledge, Heinrich Himmler had in the spring of 1944 ordered that the extermination of the Jews be halted. Eichmann, motivated by "conscience" and "loyalty," sought nevertheless to nullify Himmler's order and to proceed with the transport of the Hungarian Jews to the gas chambers.

Yet, despite the post trial claims of the Israeli Attorney-General Gideon Hausner, Eichmann was certified by half a dozen psychiatrists to be "normal."

> The trouble with Eichmann was precisely that so many were like him, and that the many were neither perverted nor sadistic, that they were, terribly and terrifyingly normal. From the viewpoint of our legal institutions and our moral standards of judgment, this normality was much more terrifying than all the atrocities put together, for it implied...that this new type of criminal...commits his crimes under circumstances that make it well-nigh impossible for him to know or to feel that he is doing wrong [p. 253].

The judges could not believe that "an average 'normal' person ...could be perfectly incapable of telling right from wrong...and [thereby]," Arendt continued, "missed the greatest moral and even legal challenge of the whole case" (p. 23).

The problem with his conscience was not, however, exclusively psychological, but also social. "As Eichmann told it," Arendt reported, "the most potent factor in the soothing of his own conscience was the simple fact that [with one exception] he could see no-one...who actually was against the Final Solution" (p. 103). Only Dr. Rudolph Kasner asked him to stop "the death mills at Auschwitz" — the impression must have been deep, for Eichmann mentioned it several times (p. 103). Eichmann's conscience, Dr. Arendt wrote, "spoke with a 'respectable voice,' with the voice of a respectable society around him" — and that "respectable society" was silent, or sought simply to relieve *certain* sufferings, or to obtain exceptions for a *few* only, without challenging the policy itself. Many Germans who claimed to have been "inwardly opposed" to the Nazi regime took part in a so-called "inner emigration" in which they withdrew from participation in public life (p. 112). Yet their silence unknowingly supported Eichmann. Sometimes, also, to divert attention from their inner "disloyalty," they were knowingly outwardly even more ruthless than avowed Nazis.

One wonders what would have happened to Eichmann, to the

"inward emigrants," and to Germany, if the Jewish and anti-Nazi non-Jewish Germans had not permitted the killing to remain impersonally hidden in the extermination camps but had by their defiance forced the Nazis to commit their murders in the open streets of Germany's cities where all could see. The question is not one for mere idle speculation, but one which might enable us to learn how better to resist future attempts at genocide. Arendt offers us important clues.

IMPOSSIBLE WITHOUT COOPERATION

The politically most shattering — and to many people the most emotionally disturbing — insistence of Arendt in this book is that the extermination program would never have been possible if the Nazis had not received the cooperation of a multitude of diverse people who were never Nazis. These included non-Nazi German officials, military personnel, and civil servants. They included the general population of Germany and of the occupied countries, and the governments in those countries. And, most terrifyingly of all, they included the Jews themselves. Some Jews and non-Jews *did refuse* to cooperate and *did* resist; their actions saved many lives — often their own — and are very important for the future. That does not, however, remove the fact of widespread cooperation.

The Nazi officials were not certain that they would receive the cooperation which they knew they needed to carry out the program. Reinhardt Heydrich — Eichmann's superior, described by Gerald Reitlinger as "the real engineer of the Final Solution" — was apprehensive whether it would be possible to enlist the help of the undersecretaries and various experts in the mass murder program. Eichmann said that Heydrich " expected the greatest difficulties" (p. 100). Indeed, it appears that Heydrich deliberately undertook two experimental deportations of German Jews in 1940 to test whether the necessary cooperation would be forthcoming. On the night of 13 February 1940, 1,300 Germans Jews in Baden and the Saarpfalz were shipped to Unoccupied France. Both of these deportations were undertaken without the introduction of new laws which would have "legalized" such actions, deprived the deported German Jews of their citizenship, and the like. The deported Jews had therefore to sign a general waiver covering all their possessions.

Clearly, it was not the administrative apparatus that these first operations were supposed to test, [wrote Arendt]. The objective seems to have been a test of general political conditions — whether Jews could be made to walk to their doom. . . what the reaction of their neighbors would be. . . how foreign governments would react [when]. . . presented with thousands of Jewish "refugees." As far as the Nazis could see, everything turned out very satisfactorily [pp. 139-140].

German responsibility, Arendt indicated, was not limited to the staff of the special annihilation camps. Complicity stretched far beyond the Nazi Party. (Even the members of the anti-Hitler conspiracy of July 1944 were apparently much more bothered by Hitler being a "madman," his sacrificing "whole armies" against expert advice, and his concentration camps for political prisoners, than with the extermination camps which were "almost completely ignored" by them [p. 91].)

The "Final Solution. . . needed the active cooperation of all the Ministries and of the whole Civil Service" (p. 99). "Mere compliance would never have been enough to smooth out all the enormous difficulties of an operation that was soon to cover the whole of Nazi-occupied and Nazi-allied Europe or to soothe the consciences of the operators. . ." (p. 102). Extremely few defections occurred at the beginning of the extermination program. When they did happen, the motive was usually corruption rather than mercy. Occasionally, individuals did stand out, sometimes without penalty, sometimes at the cost of their lives. Members of execution squads were able to quit their jobs without serious difficulties for themselves. Occasionally religious leaders dissented, as the Protestant *Propst* Grüber and the Catholic *Dompropst* Lichtenberg who in different ways both sought to help the Jews. Both men themselves ended up in concentration camps; Lichtenberg died in one.

German military officers in Western occupied countries were "always reluctant to cooperate and to lend their troops to round up and seize Jews" (p. 135). The mass shootings of Jews and other civilians in Poland were apparently halted because of the protest of the army commanders, although other means of extermination were then used. Rarely an individual German soldier helped Jews at the price of his own execution. Anton Schmidt was one such soldier. When large numbers of German troops or their commanders became unreliable, the program for the "Final Solution" was put in grave jeopardy.

The cooperation of the civilian populations was also needed, as well as of the respective governments and puppet Governments. When Eichmann in 1944 went to Hungary to arrange for the deportation of the Jews to the extermination camps, "his worst fears concerned possible resistance on the part of the Hungarians with which he would have been unable to cope, because he lacked manpower and also lacked knowledge of local conditions. These fears proved quite unfounded" (p. 125).

Ironically and most tragically, the "Final Solution" also needed the cooperation and assistance of its victims. For the most part it received even that. This is not to say that other population groups faced with the same situation would have reacted differently. At the beginning many hoped that each repressive measure would be the last, and that "resettlement" was only that. Uncertainty, isolation, and fear took their toll. As Arendt pointed out, there are some fates worse than death, and the Nazis knew well how to inflict them. But sympathy for the victims in their suffering and death is an insufficient tribute to them. Our compassion for the victims of the "Final Solution" requires that we must learn how to prevent those unspeakable events from ever recurring. This effort to learn even from the behavior of the victims probably caused many of the emotional outbursts against Arendt's book. The purpose of *Eichmann In Jerusalem* (as is that of this chapter) was *not* to pass moral or personal judgement on the victims, but to stimulate us to think about ways to defeat attempted genocide in the future.

The extreme difficulties of the situation faced by the victims must be immediately admitted, both the dangers of resistance and the numbed state of mind the Nazis sought to induce in their victims. The victims were also almost completely unprepared, and certainly untrained, for conducting resistance to such a regime and policy. Nevertheless, there *were* acts of resistance by individuals and even collective opposition and struggle of various types, including both nonviolent and violent forms, even by groups of Jewish partisans. In proportion to the overall scene, however, these were decidedly the exception. In the early days people could always hope that the discrimination and attacks would not become worse, or would stop, that some kind of accommodation could be worked out. Later when the controls tightened, no line was drawn in most cases by the victims against further cooperation, even at their registration and the order to wear the yellow star. Some people cooperated in order to get exemption for special persons.

The cooperation of the Jews themselves was, however, absolutely needed by the Nazis for the implementation of their "Final Solution." Eichmann admitted under cross-examination that the Nazis regarded the cooperation of the *Judenrat* (Jewish Council) as "the very cornerstone" of their Jewish policy (p. 110). The Nazis were sometimes careful not to destroy that cooperation, as in their careful handling of the Jewish Council at Theresienstadt.

Jewish technicians built the gas chambers at Theresienstadt. In the camps the actual killing and salvage operations (as for gold teeth) were in the hands of Jewish commandos. The transport lists at Theresienstadt were drawn up — not by Eichmann himself as one witness maintained, but — by the camp's Jewish Council.

The cooperation of the victims was widespread. Arendt called this collaboration "undoubtedly the darkest chapter in the whole dark story." It took a wide variety of forms, she recounted:

> Wherever Jews lived there were recognized Jewish leaders, and this leadership, almost without exception, cooperated in one way or another, for one purpose or another, with the Nazis. The whole truth was that if the Jewish people had really been unorganized and leaderless there would have been chaos and plenty of misery, but the total number of victims would hardly have been between four and a half and six million people [p. 111].

> [Almost everywhere the] Jewish Councils of Elders were informed by Eichmann or his men of how many Jews were needed to fill each train, and they made out the list of deportees. The Jews registered, filled out innumerable forms, answered pages and pages of questionnaires regarding their property so that it could be seized the more easily, they then assembled at the collection points and boarded the trains. The few who tried to hide or to escape were rounded up by a special Jewish police force. As far as Eichmann could see, no one protested, no one refused to cooperate [p. 102].

> Without Jewish help in administrative and police work — the final rounding up of Jews in Berlin was...done entirely by Jewish police — there would have been either complete chaos or an impossibly severe drain on German manpower [p. 104].

It is important that we gain as much knowledge as possible about the Holocaust, that any historical errors which may have crept into

Arendt's account be corrected, that the deeds of both Jewish resisters and quiet heroes be recorded and remembered, and that we learn why people acted as they did. However, our responsibility to try to prevent future genocide also requires that we honestly examine the consequences of the behavior of everyone involved, even of its victims. For that purpose, the objective results of their action may be more important than the immediate reasons for their behavior.

NONCOOPERATION TO SAVE JEWS

Millions of men, women, and children were murdered. We must never forget that. But also many were saved. In some places it was only a few, in other places it was many, and occasionally very large numbers were saved. Perhaps much of the lesson we must learn concerning how to prevent the recurrence of a "Final Solution" lies in the actions which made it possible to save so many. We obviously need very detailed studies of what happened in every country. From the brief surveys of the events which Arendt offers, however, it is impossible to avoid the conclusion that where the Jews were saved in considerable numbers it was because of the refusal of cooperation by the Jews themselves, the general population, the Government, bureaucrats, or even the German officials — and sometimes a combination of these groups.

In Norway, for example, the efforts to arrest the country's 1,700 Jews led even to protest resignations by Quisling's own men in government posts. Sweden immediately offered asylum, and over half of the Jews were smuggled into Sweden to safety.

In Belgium, the police refused cooperation with the Germans, and railwaymen could not be trusted not to tamper with the deportation trains. As most of the Jewish leaders had fled the country, no Jewish Council existed to register Jews — "one of the most important prerequisites for their seizure" (p. 150). Not a single Belgian Jew was deported from the country and even half of the easily recognizable foreign Jews were saved. Eichmann's "adviser" in Belgium was apparently not very active in helping the program, and the German military administration had to conduct most of the operations.

In France, the Vichy Government and the French police cooperated in the deportations of foreign Jews in July, August, and September, 1942, when the French believed that the deported Jews were really being resettled in Eastern Europe. Later, when the Germans requested French Jews as well, and the French had learned that "resettlement" actually meant extermination, French cooperation ceased. Many Jews were allowed to flee to the safe Italian-occupied zone, and the French made so many difficulties for the Germans that the plans for further deportations were dropped. Over 80 percent of all the Jews in France were thus saved.

Italy, although allied with Germany, did not share anti-Semitism very seriously. The anti-Semitic legislation introduced under German pressure by Benito Mussolini in the late 1930s provided for such broad exceptions that the great majority of Jews were excluded by one clause or another. After the German occupation of parts of northern Italy following Italy's capitulation to the Allies, the Nazis made attempts to deport Italian Jews to the extermination camps. They rarely met a flat refusal, but usually a "subtly veiled resistance" with constantly repeated promises and constantly repeated failures to fulfill them (p. 159). Italian police, when acting under German orders, were not reliable, and Jews were often warned — frequently by long-time Fascists — in time to escape. Through trickery, some were eventually deported and killed, but well over 90 percent were saved.

In Denmark, "the enormous power potential inherent in nonviolent action and in resistance to an opponent possessing vastly superior means of violence" was demonstrated (p. 154). The Danes firmly opposed anti-Semitic measures as such and the Germans never succeeded in distinguishing between Danish and refugee Jews. In 1943 during a dockers' strike and a state of martial law, Himmler sought to speed up the anti-Jewish measures. He met not only with Danish resistance but also with unexpected German resistance. The German military commander refused to put troops at the disposal of the Reich plenipotentiary in Denmark (who could himself also no longer be trusted) and refused to order all Jews to report for "work." With the extermination policy confronted by Danish, Jewish, *and* German noncooperation, and also threatened by the unreliability of the ordinary German *Wehrmacht* troops stationed in Denmark, special troops were brought from Germany for a door-to-door search. The politically unreliable Reich plenipotentiary, however, told these troops that they could not break into apartments or fight with the Danes. After open warnings were issued by Jewish leaders in the synagogues, most Jews refused to open their doors to the German troops and escaped. The Jews were widely received in hiding among the rest of the Danes. Fewer than 500 Jews were seized and sent to Germany where, amazingly, they received special treatment and safety. The other 7,300 Jews were saved by secret evacuation at Danish expense to Sweden or by remaining in hiding.

The Bulgarians, in the Nazi view, had no "understanding of the Jewish problem" (p. 167). Jews from newly annexed territories were deported, probably without awareness of the consequences. Anti-Jewish legislation enacted under German pressure provided various exemptions and loopholes. Six months after the German request for "radical" measures, the yellow star was decreed — a very small one which most Jews refused to wear. The general population expressed widespread open sympathy to those who did. The decree was revoked. In response to additional German pressure Jews were expelled from Sofia to rural areas. Popular resistance then took place in Sofia and a demonstration was held before the police in an attempt to halt the expulsion. The dispersal of the Jews to the countryside actually made their collection more difficult. Despite the murder of the king (probably by the Nazis), the parliament and the population remained on the side of the Jews. The Jews themselves refused all collaboration. The German officials were not reliable. Not a single Bulgarian Jew was deported or was killed as part of the Nazi extermination program.

LEARNING HOW TO DEFEAT DESPOTISM

These events are important for the future. They demonstrate to a large degree that the will of a totalitarian regime can be thwarted by internal resistance. They refute the popular contention that only military action can be effective against such odds. The action described by Hannah Arendt was primarily noncooperation, and it was nonmilitary and nonviolent. These events also show the extreme importance of firm action, of "drawing the line" and of holding one's ground in face of ruthless opponents. The traditional means favored to deal with a totalitarian regime — coup d'état or war — are selected on the basis of a fallacious acceptance of the totalitarian's own claim that his regime is monolithic, which if true would drastically limit the possibilities for change. However, students of totalitarianism know that "the monolithic quality of this form of government is a myth" (p.

136). Totalitarian regimes, too, contain divisions and internal conflicts, a number of which are mentioned in Arendt's book. These
divisions facilitate a quite different means of dealing with such
tyrannies.*

It is often argued in excuse or explanation for the absence of
resistance to a totalitarian regime that martyrdom is a wasted effort;
in the words of a German army physician: "The totalitarian state lets
its opponents disappear in silent anonymity." Such sacrifice would
therefore be "in vain" and "practically useless" (p. 221). Hannah
Arendt's answer speaks for itself:

> It is true that totalitarian domination tried to establish these holes
> of oblivion into which all deeds, good and evil, would disappear,
> but just as the Nazis' feverish attempts...to erase all traces of the
> massacres...were doomed to failure, so all attempts to let their
> opponents "disappear in silent anonymity" were in vain. The holes
> of oblivion do not exist. Nothing human is that perfect, and there
> are simply too many people in the world to make oblivion possible.
> One man will always be left alive to tell the story. Hence, nothing
> can ever be "practically useless," at least, not in the long run....
>
> For the lesson of such stories [of resistance] is...that under
> conditions of terror most people will comply but *some people will
> not,* just as the lesson of the countries to which the Final Solution
> was proposed is that "it could happen" in most places but *it did not
> happen everywhere* [pp. 211-212].

The European experience with the "Final Solution" and with the
Nazi regime in general also shows that in many situations the Nazis
gained temporary advantage or made permanent "gains" because the
population with which they dealt was unprepared for such a situation
and did not know what to do, how to do it, nor when to do it. We
urgently need a major program of research, preparation, education,
and training if we are to ensure that the Nazi terrors will not be
repeated in new forms. We need a program of prevention and preparation to ensure that when confronted by new tyrannies and new
attempts at genocide, people will be able to disintegrate dictatorship
and defeat genocide.

The events of that era, and the insights which Dr. Arendt has
suggested into their meaning, require that many of our habitual
attitudes and "solutions" to political problems be reconsidered. We

*On this, see Chapter Four, "Facing Dictatorships With Confidence."

should not simply repeat familiar clichés of regret or denunciation, but should try to understand the nature of our problems and seek real solutions to them.

This throws us into the sphere of popular control of tyrants, of nonviolent struggle against political violence, of an acceptance of our human responsibility in face of a ruthlessness to describe which there exist no words. As Arendt would have told Eichmann, who claimed he had only followed orders: "...in politics obedience and support are the same" (p. 255). Disobedience and refusal of support by Jews and non-Jews saved the lives of many Jews and ensured their survival as a people. Will we and all people learn how to save ourselves from future despotism and attempted genocide? We desperately require major research, policy development, public education, and preparation to develop the capacity to prevent, to resist, and to defeat future attempts to commit genocide. We need to develop the capacity which will enable us to say with confidence: "Never again!"

WAR AND EXTERMINATION

Hannah Arendt did not seriously discuss in her book the connection between the war and the extermination program, except to say that the Führer's order to exterminate all Europe's Jews "had nothing to do with the war and never used military necessities as a pretext" (pp. 94-95). It is possible from that statement to draw the erroneous conclusion that there was no relationship between the two. That is clearly not accurate.

Even as a statement specifically limited to Hitler's order only, and not applicable to the general relationship between the war and the extermination program, Arendt's comment is more categorical than the facts justify. Reitlinger has reported that the "Führer Order" to executive "Jews, gipsies, racial inferiors, 'asocials,' and finally Soviet political commissars, was communicated to those responsible for its execution in stages." "The part of the Fuehrer Order concerning the execution of Jews was at any rate never put on paper and even those to whom it was passed were not all informed at the same time."[1] We do not, therefore, have a text of the Order concerning the Jews, much less a full document, the contents of which would establish whether in Hitler's view there was or was not a relationship between the war and the extermination. Even if such a document without a claim of military necessities existed, the question of the possible relationship between two of Nazi Germany's most important simultaneous endeavors would still be relevant. Arendt's failure to acknowledge the importance of such a question, and her simple unsupported assertion implying that there was no relationship, constitute a major weakness of the book. The question is relevant both for gaining accurate historical knowledge, and also for preventing future genocide.

Some people who are not well informed still share the illusion that the Second World War was fought to save the Jews, or at least that if it started for other reasons it did save Jews from extermination by the Nazis who otherwise would probably have succeeded in making Europe "Jew-free," in their hideous phrase. This illusion is shattered by an elementary look at certain facts. In the first place, the war did *not* save the Jews: between four-and-a-half and six million were exterminated, although it is true that many others already in the death camps were saved, either by Heinrich Himmler's anticipation of German defeat or by the event itself. Probably no one can be fully satisfied with the adequacy of the response of anyone to the reality of Nazism; our intent here is, therefore, not to praise or to cast blame, but to explore in an initial way a question which has not usually even been raised, despite some provocative circumstantial evidence: were the war and the extermination program independent or were they related?

"POSSIBILITIES...IN WARTIME"

As Arendt reminded us, the extermination program in the Eastern gas factories directed against Jews grew out of Hitler's euthanasia program, in which 50,000 to 70,000 mentally ill Germans were gassed between 1939 and 1941. (This program was then cancelled in face of widespread German protests.) The euthanasia program *was* clearly tied to war-time conditions. Hitler had told his Reich medical leader in 1935 that "if war came, he would take up and carry out this question of euthanasia, because it was easier to do so in war time" (p. 95).

Both Hitler himself and his propaganda chief Dr. Paul Josef Goebbels clearly connected the extermination of the Jews to war-time conditions. Hitler did this very early, well before the event itself and before other Nazi leaders argued the same point. In his 30 January 1939 speech to the Reichtag, Hitler declared:

> Today I want to be a prophet once more: If international-finance Jewry inside and outside of Europe should succeed once more in plunging nations into another world war, the consequence will not be the Bolshevization of the earth and thereby the victory of Jewry, but the annihilation [*Vernichtung*] of the Jewish race in Europe.[2]

Reitlinger reported that this was clearly no chance turn of the phrase in a moment of oratorical excitement, for Hitler publicly repeated the words verbatim on at least five later occasions (30 January 1942, 30 September 1942, 24 February 1943, 21 March 1943, and 9 November 1943).[3] In his diary, Goebbels later connected the extermination program to the on-going war. Writing 27 March 1942, Goebbels recalled Hitler's 1939 prediction. Goebbels wrote that the extermination of Jews in Poland, which had begun by March 1942, was being conducted "with considerable circumspection and according to a method that does not attract too much attention." This "barbaric" Nazi action was imperative, he wrote, continuing:

> Here, too, the Fuehrer is the undismayed champion of a radical solution necessitated by conditions and therefore inexorable. Fortunately a whole series of possibilities presents itself for us in wartime that would be denied us in peacetime. We shall have to profit by this.[4]

A year later, Goebbels returned to the same topic in his entry of 20 March 1943:

> The Fuehrer is happy over my report that the Jews have for the most part been evacuated from Berlin. He is right in saying that the war has made possible for us the solution of a whole series of problems that could never have been solved in normal times. The Jews will certainly be the losers in this war come what may.[5]

The Nuremberg Laws — the Reich Law of Citizenship published in 1935 and the ensuing supplementary decrees — were aimed at the expulsion of Jews from Germany permanently. Much effort was placed from 1938 through much of 1940 on various plans for deportation. Opinions differ as to whether the intent was really to deport, or whether the deportation plans were guises and transitional measures in preparation for extermination. Nevertheless, Hilberg reported, "The Jews were not killed before the emigration policy was literally exhausted."[6] (He referred, of course, to systematic executions.) Massive deportations, even from Germany alone, meant moving millions of people across oceans by ship, an undertaking that was probably only feasible under peacetime conditions, and even then would take some years. Nazi policies and other sources of antagonisms in Europe, however, made it obvious by late 1938 that war might break out before all the Jews had left the Third Reich. What, then, about the Jews who would remain? The S.S. newspaper *Schwarzekorps* published an article on 24 November 1938 with an answer: "the fate of such Jews as the outbreak of war should still find in Germany would be their final end, their annihilation *(Vernichtung)*."[7] The official policy, however, still remained emigration. On 24 January 1939, *Reichsmarschall* Hermann Goering established the Reich Central Office for Jewish Emigration, headed by Reinhard Heydrich. During the year serious anti-Jewish measures were taken in Germany and German-occupied territories.

EMIGRATION OR EXTERMINATION?

Negotiations took place in London and Berlin between representatives of the German Government and the Intergovernmental Refugee Committee from December 1938 to April 1939. They concerned possible arrangements for emigration from Germany of some 300,000 Jews, perhaps over a three to five year period. At times, Rhodesia and British Guiana were specifically discussed, and Hitler had in November 1938 considered Madagascar.[8]

In the spring of 1939 in announcing anti-Jewish measures, Goering declared: "If in the near future the German Reich should come into conflict with foreign Powers, it goes without saying that we in Germany would first of all let it come to a reckoning with the Jews."[9] Nevertheless, Reitlinger reported, as late as August and September 1939, "It does not seem that at this period systematic extermination of the Jews was considered."[10] An important distinction exists between random killings, pogroms, and even massacres, on the one hand, and a systematic effort to exterminate the entire Jewish population, on the other. The former is murder; the latter is genocide.

Germany invaded Poland on 1 September 1939 — after concluding a nonaggression pact with the Soviet Union which then seized eastern Poland. On 3 September Britain and France declared war on

Germany. Immediately on the invasion the Germans launched ruthless attacks on the civilian population of Poland, both non-Jewish
and Jewish, but particularly directed against Jews, with shootings,
arrests, burning of synagogues, and the like. By the end of December
1939 an estimated 250,000 Jews had died from shootings, starvation,
or disease produced by the invasion and occupation.[11]

The German policy to deal with the Jews, however, was still
emigration, and neither administrative nor technical facilities yet
existed which would make possible the deliberate extermination of
millions of people. In August 1940 Eichmann was commissioned to
prepare a plan for deportation of Jews to Madagascar; a year later on
15 August 1941 he submitted his plan to deport four million Jews to
Madagascar within a few years. The United States and Poland were
also discussed as recipients.[12]

By March 1941, however, it was reportedly known in high Nazi
Party circles that the Jews were to be exterminated.[13] This appears to
have followed a Führer Order, at least in part issued orally and in
stages, to those responsible for the implementation of its various
components.[14] Heydrich wrote to Ribbentrop, the Foreign Minister,
on 24 June 1941 that the whole problem of about three-and-a-half
million Jews then under German control could no longer be solved by
emigration; instead, Hilberg reported, Heydrich declared that a "territorial" final solution was required.[15] The next month, on 31 July
1941, Goering issued a formal written order to Heydrich, "to carry
out all preparations...for a total solution of the Jewish question in
those territories of Europe which are under German influence."[16]
Heydrich's *Einsatzgruppen* were already carrying out massacres in
the East, and, Levin reported, his Gestapo organization was already
preparing for Jews to be deported from West European countries.
Shortly after Goering's 31 July letter to Heydrich, Adolph Eichmann
was ordered to meet with Heydrich. At his Jerusalem trial, Eichmann
testified that Heydrich opened the interview with a short speech
which argued that emigration was impossible now that war with
Russia was underway. Heydrich then told him: "The Führer has
ordered the physical extermination of the Jews."[17]

DECEMBER 1941

Until the German invasion of the Soviet Union on 22 June 1941

the Germans were sensitive to Russian opinion, and until October
1941 when the first stage of the deportations ended, to American
opinion, reported Reitlinger. "Thus, while the conditions were invariably murderous, deliberate mass murder was not practiced."[18] It was
in December 1941 that Nazi policy in Poland became far more
extreme. At a conference of high German officials in Krakow, Hans
Frank, Governor-General of the section of former Poland then
known as *Generalgouvernement,* declared:

> Certainly, a major migration is about to start. But what is to
> happen to the Jews? Do you think they will actually be resettled in
> *Ostland* villages? We were told in Berlin: Why all this trouble
> [*Scherereien*]? We can't use them in the *Ostland* either; liquidate
> them yourselves! Gentlemen, I must ask you to arm yourself
> against all feelings of sympathy. We have to annihilate the Jews
> wherever we find them and wherever it is at all possible.[19]

This policy statement for Poland was connected with the war by
Reitlinger:

> It is significant that Frank used the words: "Liquidate them your-
> selves" nine days after Pearl Harbor and that the first gassings in
> Poland took place at the end of that year. It may even be doubted
> whether the "Fuehrer Order" to exterminate Russian Jewry would
> have spread west of the former Russian demarcation line, if the
> United States had not entered the war on December 7th, 1941.[20]

By the end of December 1941, Levin reported, the extermination of
Jews in Eastern Europe had become State policy.[21]

THE THRUST TO EXTERMINATE

Acting on Goering's order of 31 July 1941, Heydrich convened,
after weeks of postponement, the famous Gross-Wannsee Conference on 20 January 1942, attended by fifteen officials from various
ministries and the S.S. In roundabout language Heydrich made it
clear that "the slow murder of an entire race was intended," in
Reitlinger's words.[22] This meeting is recognized as the point at which
the German bureaucracy was directed to the task of genocide. The
next month, in February 1942, Franz Rademacher (of Project
Deutschland III in the Foreign Office) sent Foreign Office departments a new ruling:

The war with the Soviet Union has in the meantime created the possibility of disposing of other territories for the Final Solution. In consequence the Fuehrer has decided that the Jews should be evacuated not to Madagascar but to the East. Madagascar need no longer therefore be considered in connection with the Final Solution.[23]

As late as 7 March 1942, Goebbels still contemplated temporary isolation during the war to be followed by deportation, possibly to Madagascar, after the war. "In any case there can be no peace in Europe until the last Jews are eliminated from the continent."[24] During 1942 and 1943 discussions were still held among Hitler, Goebbels, Rosenberg, and others on Madagascar.[25]

However, the thrust of Nazi policy was clearly on the physical extermination of Europe's Jews. After Heydrich was killed on 29 May 1942 by a bomb thrown at his car near Lidice in Czechoslovakia, the pace of anti-Jewish measures increased.[26] During the summer of 1942 Himmler decided that Auschwitz should be the extermination center for Western European Jews.[27]

The dates of the significant actions, their sequence in terms of the important stages in the development of the Second World War, and the comments of Goebbels and Hitler which were never intended to be made public, all suggest that it is at least possible that the war created the necessary precondition for the perpetration of the Holocaust. The evidence is insufficient for final judgement, but we can no longer assume that there was no connection. Very careful historical research is merited into this relationship.

THE LESSON OF THE HOLOCAUST

The lesson not only of Eichmann, but also of the whole Holocaust, is that we need desperately to develop ways to prevent genocide, and to defeat attempts to exterminate peoples when they occur. We cannot smugly continue to assume that military preparations are the best way to do this. For clues to the solution to this problem we need to look to the brave men and women, Jews and Gentiles, who in various occupied countries and even Germany itself succeeded in saving the lives of many Jews who otherwise would have been killed. That start will need to be supplemented by critical examination of possible ways in which a situation in which genocide could occur can be prevented, and of points at which a genocide machine can be stopped. If we carry out these tasks, we will truly have honored the millions who died in the Holocaust.

NOTES

1. Gerald Reitlinger, **The Final Solution: The Attempt to Exterminate the Jews of Europe 1939-1945** (New York: A. S. Barnes & Co., 1961 [1953]), pp. 80-81.
2. Raul Hilberg, **The Destruction of the European Jews** (Chicago: Quadrangle Books, 1961, and London: W. H. Allen, 1961), p. 257.
3. Reitlinger, **The Final Solution**, pp. 22 and 543, n. 40.
4. Louis P. Lochner, ed. and trans., **The Goebbels Diaries 1942-1943** (Garden City, N. Y.: Doubleday & Co., 1948), p. 148.
5. Ibid., p. 314.
6. Hilberg, **The Destruction of the European Jews**, p. 258.
7. Reitlinger, **The Final Solution**, p. 8.
8. See ibid., pp. 20-21.
9. Ibid., p. 17.
10. Ibid., p. 34.
11. Nora Levin, **The Holocaust: The Destruction of European Jewry 1933-1945** (New York: Schocken Books, 1973), p. 150.
12. Reitlinger, **The Final Solution**, pp. 77-78.
13. Levin, **The Holocaust**, p. 291.
14. See Reitlinger, **The Final Solution**, pp. 80-81.
15. Hilberg, **The Destruction of the European Jews**, p. 262.
16. Reitlinger, **The Final Solution**, p. 82.
17. Levin, **The Holocaust**, pp. 290-291.
18. Reitlinger, **The Final Solution**, p. 51.
19. Hilberg, **The Destruction of the European Jews**, pp. 308-309.
20. Reitlinger, **The Final Solution**, p. 51.
21. Levin, **The Holocaust**, p. 293.
22. Reitlinger, **The Final Solution**, p. 98. For more details, see also Hilberg, **The Destruction of the European Jews**, pp. 264-265.
23. Quoted in Reitlinger, **The Final Solution**, p. 79.
24. Lochner, ed., **The Goebbels' Diaries**, p. 116.
25. Levin, **The Holocaust**, p. 202.
26. Reitlinger, **The Final Solution**, p. 100.
27. Ibid., p. 104.

4

Facing Dictatorships
With Confidence

The seriousness of the problem of dictatorships, the dangers they pose, and the need for effective means to deal with them have all increased since the First World War. Ordinary dictatorships — brutal though they have been for thousands of years — were superseded by the Hitler and Stalin regimes. With these developments totalitarianism became a far more formidable opponent. These totalitarian rulers attempted to engulf and control the whole life of each subject and every aspect of the society. The degree of control over individuals, transportation, communications, weapons, and entire social, economic, and political systems, increased dramatically over traditional dictatorships. Power became concentrated. Adolph Hitler and

91

Josef Stalin are now dead, the Nazi system is only a relic for historians, and the Soviet system is evolving. Nevertheless, the problem which dictatorships pose to people who believe in human dignity and freedom continues to grow.

The willingness of governments and political groups aiming to seize the State to deal ruthlessly with opposition and innocent people has not diminished. It may in fact have increased. Too often it is assumed that genocide was safely buried in 1945 under the rubble of Berlin. Various doctrines and ideologies, and fear of others, have provided political groups and regimes with a rationale and "justification" for policies and actions which otherwise would be seen as naked brutality. Recent technological advances in communication, transportation, data storage and retrieval, political organization, electronic surveillance, subliminal controls of populations, and the capacity to kill, have increased the capability of modern governments to establish and maintain effective dictatorships.

DANGERS OF NEW DICTATORSHIPS

Present liberal constitutional democracies are all imperfect, but remain clearly preferable to dictatorial regimes which are expanding in number. Yet severe problems within such democracies cast doubt on their durability. Internal imperfections, highly centralized controls, and decision-making by small elites often raise doubts about the vitality and effectiveness of democratic processes. This is true even in the countries which pride themselves in their democratic traditions and institutions. Many people feel powerless and unable to control their own lives and influence major political decisions. Direct attacks in a variety of forms continue to be made on democratic structures. The United States is not exempt; "Watergate" was an attempt to subvert the American constitutional processes of free elections. In various countries internal coups d'état by political and military groups, activities of police and foreign agents, political terrorism, and minority guerrilla wars continue to assault democratic systems, with the intent of replacing them with dictatorships. The groups using these means espouse diverse doctrines and wave various political flags. The growth in various countries and systems of powerful intelligence organizations, institutions of foreign agents, and central government police bodies creates the *potential* of those bodies, or some section of them, to defy and to attack the legal government, instead of serving its will.* Military forces have done this repeatedly in dozens of countries as they have launched coups d'état.

The underlying social conditions on which democratic structures rest have also changed. Social, economic, and political systems of all types have altered drastically since the advent of constitutional democracy in every country in which it has had a long history. The "grass roots" institutions of society, and even local and state or provincial governments, are increasingly subordinated to centralized administration. Powerful multinational corporations are taking control of the national economies outside of the countries themselves, and are using that control to manipulate governments in order to serve their own financial interests. All these conditions are inimical to freedom.

In the future, the tyrant will be able to use more subtle, yet no less diabolical, means of control through such methods as conditioning, psychological manipulation, and drugs provided by modern science to keep the subjects submissive and "happy." Aldous Huxley's *Brave New World* may not be far away; dictatorships using such psychological means may supersede totalitarianism. Other signs of future dangers also exist. The expanding breakdown and even active destruction of traditional societies and indigenous cultures in those parts of the world emerging from European colonialism are creating the condition of *anomie,* psychological, ethical, and personal confusion, and social disintegration. This condition, especially when combined with deep genuine grievances, nurtures various kinds of mass movements — social, religious, and political. They can presage a new political messiah or doctrine of salvation which leads directly to political enslavement.

If effective means are not soon found to destroy dictatorships, and to alter the conditions which make them possible, the task of preventing and resisting them will rapidly become yet more difficult. The future may thus be one in which the word "freedom" will have no meaning, or will be only the remnant of a forgotten dream.

Many cultures and countries have their own traditions of love of

*On the capacity of such bodies to be shifted to different purposes, see Chapter Eleven, "The Societal Imperative."

freedom and opposition to all tyranny, even though the practice does not always live up to the ideal. Opposition to political dictatorship was a basic American principle well before the adoption of the Constitution. The creation of new political structures on this continent, the colonial struggles against perceived tyranny, and the drafting of the basic frameworks for new governments were all motivated by belief in human freedom, whatever additional motives may have been present. The colonial fathers believed in a moral and political imperative to oppose existing dictatorships and to prevent the establishment of new tyrannies. (They were simultaneously, of course, often blind to their own imposition of tyrannical conditions on the Native Americans from whom they seized the land, and the Africans whom they enslaved, as well as the oppression of their own women.)

Since the time that the European settlers gained independence, American government policies and foreign alliances have not always followed that commitment to freedom and opposition to tyranny. However, the belief has remained fundamental for many Americans. The compromises that were made in practical policies were often perceived as necessary in face of a larger dictatorial threat. The First World War was fought, it was said, "to make the world safe for democracy." The Second World War was waged, most people were convinced, to defeat three dictatorial expansionist regimes, liberate conquered peoples, and, specifically, defeat the Nazi system — one of the most extreme forms of dictatorship yet known. The Cold War has been officially aimed at halting the expansion of Communist forms of dictatorship. Even the most interventionist United States activities in recent decades have been excused by their advocates as required to combat still more serious dictatorial threats. Although critics may at times, with justification, point to other motives, we still must confront the real dangers to freedom posed by all types of dictatorships.

INADEQUACIES OF THE TRADITIONAL ANSWERS

No easy answer to the problem of dictatorship exists. There are no effortless, safe ways by which people living under dictatorships can liberate themselves, or by which other people can defend themselves from future dangers. Nor do we have a simple way by which we can prevent the development of new tyrannies. Passivity in the face of such threats is clearly no guarantee of safety. In fact it is often the opposite. In any case, passivity is neither an effective nor a democratic response to this challenge. Every possible course of action in support of liberation and in defense of freedom will involve risks, and potential suffering, and take time to operate. Nor can *any* means of action ensure success in every situation.

How, then, are we to deal with dictatorships? The spontaneous answer most people who believe in freedom give is that you must fight and destroy them. If your country is the victim of a dictatorial regime, native or foreign, you fight against it. If your country is attacked by a dictatorial State, you resist that attack. If the subjects of a tyrant are in rebellion, you provide help. If a chance exists that your country might be attacked by a dictatorship, you prepare in advance to repel it, hoping that if you become strong enough you will deter attack. These are the common answers of most people who believe in freedom and oppose tyranny throughout the world. While these broad answers may in principle still be as valid as ever, the changes in military technology and political organization now make it necessary — whatever was true before — to implement them in quite different ways than were usual in previous times.

To enable us to confront the dangers of dictatorships, we have created massive military systems with hitherto unthinkable destructive capacities. We have organized ourselves to conduct many of the same antidemocratic activities against dictatorial forces as they themselves have done. We have supported one dictatorial group against another. And we have lamented the erosions of freedoms and democratic processes in other countries and in our own.

Despite these measures, few signs exist that the antidemocratic trends of this century are being slowed, let alone being contained or reversed. In fact, our policies may even have facilitated consolidation of old dictatorships and the emergence of new ones. The problem is not how to achieve "peaceful coexistence" with extreme dictatorships. The problem is how to reassert popular control over them, even over totalitarian systems: how to defeat and disintegrate them.

Ironically, at the very moment in history when the greatest need exists for effective means of struggle against tyranny, the traditional means of last resort in international conflicts — war — has, because of modern technology, become a highly dangerous option. Yet, if effective alternative ways are not found to replace war in such conflicts, people will persist in threatening and using war despite its dangers.* Similarly, very serious internal dangers also exist in attempts to revolt against domestic dictatorships. These are related to the concentration and destructiveness of military weaponry, the extreme costliness of civil wars generally, and guerrilla wars particularly, in casualties and social destruction, and the structural consequences of such violence.† Past means have often been inadequate even when they destroyed a specific dictatorship, for they allowed others to continue, facilitated their growth, or contributed to the development of new ones. The inadequacies of present means for dealing with dictatorships are so serious that we ought to consider how to develop alternative means. We require new policies, courses of action, and conceptions of liberation and defense in order to face the dangers of modern dictatorships and to deal with them. The view that one must choose between massively destructive war and passive submission to tyranny is false.

Our past understanding of the nature of the problem of modern dictatorships, totalitarian movements, genocide, and political usurpation has been inadequate. Similarly, our understanding of the possible means of struggle against them, and of preventing their development has been incomplete. With inadequate understanding as the foundation of our policies, it is no wonder that they have proven ineffective.

Other options must, of course, be evaluated fairly. For example, in weighing alternative policies it is important to compare the worst possible results of each, as well as the best, and not (as happens) simply the best of one with the worst of the other. Also, one must consider not only the odds for or against certain results of optional policies occurring; attention is also required to the nature of those results, including possible corrective and remedial measures to counteract them. Inadequacies in present policies and in proposed new policies will need full examination, as will claims of strengths and effectiveness of each. By using such means of comparison, a fair evaluation becomes possible.

---

*See Chapter Ten, "Seeking a Solution to the Problem of War."

†See Chapter Twelve, "Popular Empowerment," subchapter: Sanctions and Society.

LESS THAN OMNIPOTENT

Our capacity to discover and to develop new ways of preventing dictatorships in the first place, and of destroying them once they exist, may be increased if we can locate characteristics of such systems which already constitute problems for the dictators, hindering their efforts to hold their systems together, or hindering implementation of their will. Remarkably, while great attention has been given to the means of police repression and to the military capacities of dictatorships, almost no attention has been given to their *weaknesses*. Indeed, we have constantly given dictatorial regimes credit for being far more efficient, effective, powerful, and durable than in fact they are. All dictatorships, including totalitarian ones, contain inherent weaknesses which, over time, even without deliberate efforts to aggravate them, tend to make the system less effective and less dictatorial. In some cases these weaknesses could cause the dictatorship to disintegrate.

Dictatorships, even totalitarian systems, are not fully monolithic, and certainly not omnipotent or eternal. It is really nothing completely new to say that dictatorships do not always accomplish their objectives. David Riesman and Karl W. Deutsch both pointed to this fact in the 1950s.

In 1952 David Riesman wrote that we often overestimate the capacity of totalitarians "to restructure human personality."[1] While people under pressures may play certain roles and often conform outwardly, they also may be apathetic and even indifferent to ideological appeals and indoctrination. They may reject the dictator's "ethics" which all are supposed to accept. People may retreat from politics — the process of "privatization." Instead of being determined by the doctrines and programs of the system, people's behavior may be motivated by their greed. Corruption and even crime may become widespread. People may deliberately behave with excessive enthusiasm to support edicts of the system in order to disrupt it, as by accusing everyone in the Party of deviationism. Power conflicts may emerge within the regime or Party.[2] Such responses involve, Riesman wrote, "sheer unheroic cussed resistance to totalitarian efforts" to remake human beings into the new image.[3] Not even the terror can completely "destroy all bonds of organization among its victims."[4] These limitations on the effectiveness of controls affect those systems detrimentally, he wrote. However, our own absence of realism in understanding those limitations affects us also, for it leads us to "be unduly cowed or unduly aggressive...."[5] Instead, we ought to "seek ways to bring those regimes down without war...."[6]

We have assumed in the past that dictatorships, especially in their extreme forms, differ from other systems of government more than they actually do. Contrary to popular opinion, a totalitarian ruler is, in common with all rulers, dependent on his subjects. All rulers depend upon the cooperation, submission, and obedience of the subjects for their positions and power. Their power is drawn from sources in society, such as economic resources, military capacity, knowledge, skills, administration, and authority. These in turn are each closely related to, or directly dependent upon, the degree of cooperation, submission, obedience, and assistance which the would-be ruler is able to obtain from his subjects — both from the general corps of full-time agents and aides and from the population as a whole. This submission may be induced by the use of terror, but the underlying dependence of the ruler on the subjects is nevertheless present. If the help and submission of either or both of these groups is withdrawn, the ruler's power is seriously weakened. If the withdrawal can be maintained in face of various sanctions, an end to the regime is in sight.[7] This principle applies even to totalitarian rulers. This dependency may have considerable significance in the eventual solution of our problem.

Most people assume that this view is nonsense. They believe that with sufficient threats, intimidation, punishment, brutality, killings, and terror, the dictator can enforce his will upon any population without their having any choice or chance to change the situation. That view of enforced obedience and cooperation induced by repressive measures is very incomplete. It implies that this is always a one-way relationship. While on the surface that appears at times to be the case, the reality is fundamentally different. In special situations the regime in fact becomes incapable of enforcing its will. This may occur because too many people are defying it simultaneously, because its administrators are refusing to help, or because its agents of repression are not obeying orders to inflict the punishments. In some cases, these may all happen simultaneously.

In 1953 Karl W. Deutsch applied this view of the interdependence of enforcement and obedience to totalitarian systems. The passage is highly important:

> The...enforcement of decisions [by totalitarian government] depends to a large extent on the compliance habits of the population. Compliance and enforcement are interdependent; they reinforce each other, and the varying proportions in which they do so, form as it were a continuous spectrum. At one end of this spectrum, we could imagine a situation where everybody obeys habitually all commands or decisions of the totalitarian regime, and no enforcement is necessary; at the other end of this spectrum, we could imagine a situation where nobody obeys voluntarily any decision of the totalitarian system, and everybody has to be compelled to obey at pistol point, or under conditions of literally ever-present threat and ever-present supervision.
>
> In the first of these cases, enforcement would be extremely cheap and, in fact, unnecessary; in the second, it would be prohibitively expensive, and in fact no government could be carried on, on such a basis....Somewhere in the middle between these extremes of universal compliance and ubiquitous enforcement is the range of effective government. There a majority of individuals in a majority of situations obeys the decisions of the government more or less from habit without any need for immediate supervision.[8]
>
> These considerations apply to totalitarianism as they apply to all types of government, but in their application to totalitarianism they again suggest a paradox. Totalitarian power is strong only if it does not have to be used too often. If totalitarian power must be used at all times against the entire population, it is unlikely to remain powerful for long. Since totalitarian regimes require more power for dealing with their subjects than do other types of government, such regimes stand in greater need of widespread and dependable compliance habits among their people; more than that they need to be able to count on the active support of at least significant parts of the population in case of need.[9]

Severe problems exist in transforming this general insight into deliberate concrete resistance actions to undermine and destroy the totalitarian system. It is not easy, for example, to maintain the withdrawal of support in the face of severe repression from still faithful police and troops. As present policies for dealing with dictatorships also have their own problems, the existence of difficulties in possible options is no reason to halt exploration of their potential for dealing with modern dictatorships.

WEAKNESSES IN EXTREME DICTATORSHIPS

On the basis of what we know of the Nazi and Communist systems, and certain lesser dictatorships, it is possible to indicate various specific weaknesses in them. These are factors which will in time, even without deliberate efforts to aggravate them, produce changes which in differing degrees will modify the capacities and characteristics of the dictatorship. For example, these weaknesses may produce the following results:

- restrict the freedom of action of the regime;
- induce the regime to be more considerate of the needs and wishes of the population;
- reduce the brutality and repression;
- contribute to the regime's becoming less doctrinal in its own actions;
- reduce the degree to which the regime is in effective control of the society;
- destroy the myth of the regime's omniscience;
- at the mildest, cause the system to become somewhat "liberalized" or even democratized; and
- at the extremity, cause the system to disintegrate.

The following are some of the weaknesses of extreme dictatorships, including totalitarian systems:

1. The cooperation of a multitude of different people and groups which is needed to operate the system may be restricted or withdrawn.

2. The regime's freedom of action may be limited by past policies, the requirements and effects of which still continue.

3. The system may become routine in its operation, therefore more moderate and less able to shift its activities drastically at the service of doctrinal imperatives and sudden policy shifts.

4. The allocation of personnel and resources for existing tasks will limit their availability for new ones.

5. The central command may receive from the lower echelons inaccurate or incomplete information on which to make decisions, for subordinates may be fearful of inducing displeasure from higher echelons.

6. The ideology may erode, and the myths and symbols of the system become unstable.

7. Firm adherence to the ideology may lead to decisions injurious to the system because insufficient attention is given to actual conditions and needs.

8. The system may be inefficient due to deteriorating competency and effectiveness of the bureaucracy, or to excessive controls and red tape; consequently, the system's policies and normal operations may become ineffective.

9. The system's internal conflicts of various types may detrimentally affect and even disrupt its operation.

10. Intellectuals and students may become restless in response to conditions, restrictions, doctrinalism, and repression.

11. The general public may over time become apathetic or skeptical.

12. Regional, class, cultural, or national differences may become acute.

13. The power hierarchy will always be to some degree unstable, at times highly so.

14. Sections of the political police or the military forces may possess sufficient power to exert pressures to achieve their own ends, or even to act against the established rulers.

15. In the case of a new dictatorship, time is required for it to become firmly established, which allows an especially vulnerable period.

16. The extreme concentration of decision-making and command means that too many decisions will be made by too few people to avoid errors.

17. If the regime, in order to avoid some of these problems, decides to diffuse decision-making and administration, this will lead to further erosion of central controls, and often to the creation of dispersed new power centers which may seek to expand their power at the cost of the center.

Such weaknesses of extreme dictatorships do not, of course, mean that disintegration occurs quickly, or even at all, regardless of other factors at play in the situation. Dictatorial systems are often aware of at least some of their weaknesses, and take measures to counteract them. Also, under appropriate circumstances even very inefficient and incompetent regimes often manage to survive for remarkably long periods of time, and people may, as Riesman said, "mistake blundering compulsions or even accidents of 'the system' for conspiratorial genius."[10]

It should be possible, however, to learn much more than we now know about dictatorships and about alternative forms of opposition and resistance to them. With this knowledge, people living under dictatorships might be able to aggravate deliberately such inherent weaknesses in order to alter the system drastically or to disintegrate it. In such efforts, the interdependence of enforcement and patterns of obedience is especially important. Nonviolent forms of struggle are premised on the capacity of the populace to withhold its obedience and cooperation. This withholding makes it possible for the required sources of power of the dictatorship to be restricted or severed.

UNPREPARED RESISTANCE TO TYRANNY

Severe problems would be involved in such disobedience and noncooperation struggles against extreme dictatorships. We must remember that we do not have available an option without difficulties and dangers. The problems of this type of struggle need to be viewed in the perspective of the present limitations of the various types of political violence for resisting and destroying dictatorships. Serious exploration of the future potential of disobedience and noncooperation for aggravating weaknesses of dictatorships in order to control and destroy them needs to begin on the basis of an understanding of dictatorships, of the nature of nonviolent struggle, and of the history of the previous nonviolent struggles against dictatorships. Though still insufficient, all of these are necessary for a beginning. Instances of nonviolent action against lesser oppression are therefore relevant: one cannot understand how a major nonviolent struggle operating against a totalitarian system could be conducted, or what would be all of its problems, weaknesses, and strengths, without first studying its application against lesser obstacles. The general history of this technique is therefore relevant. Considerable understanding of the range of particular methods, strategic principles, basic requirements for effectiveness, and the dynamics and mechanisms of nonviolent action is necessary background for this exploration.* Without this, it is

*See the introductory discussions of some of these aspects in Chapter Nine, " 'The Political Equivalent of War' — Civilian-based Defense," subchapter: Control of Political Power and Conduct of Open Struggle, and Chapter Ten, "Seeking a Solution to the Problem of War." However, more in depth understanding is required. For this, see Gene Sharp, *The Politics of Nonviolent Action* (Boston: Porter Sargent Publisher, 1973).

impossible to appreciate adequately the general characteristics and capacities of this technique. These include:

- how nonviolent action wields power and counteracts the power of the opponent;
- how use of this technique breaks the spell of conformity and fear;
- the roles of symbolic and psychological resistance;
- the many ways in which economic and political noncooperation wield and affect power;
- the necessity of maintaining nonviolent discipline in order to apply political *jiu-jitsu* to counter violent repression and to use it to aid the resisters;
- the constantly changing strengths of the contending parties during a nonviolent struggle;
- the ways in which the struggle can continue after any recognizable leadership has been seized;
- the processes by which additional support can be aroused during the conflict from members of the general populace, the opponent's own camp, and third parties; and
- the mechanisms of change which may bring success (the operative mechanism is rarely conversion, more often accommodation, sometimes nonviolent coercion, and even disintegration of the opponent's regime).

In a number of important cases, nonviolent struggle has been applied against totalitarian systems, either alone or in combination with political violence. While no totalitarian system has been permanently overthrown by nonviolent struggle, more such resistance has occurred than is generally recognized. These cases establish that nonviolent struggle against extreme dictatorships including totalitarian systems is possible. The degree of success and failure of these cases has varied, depending in part on one's criteria. In several instances this type of struggle presented formidable problems for the regime. Sometimes it forced concessions and won at least partial victories.

The following cases are among the more significant ones:

- the civil disobedience, political noncooperation, and rescue of Jews by the Norwegian Resistance during the Nazi occupation 1940-45;
- the political noncooperation, labor strikes, psychological resistance, rescue of Jews, and the Copenhagen general strike, 1944, by the Danish Resistance, 1940-45;

- the political noncooperation, mass circulation of underground newspapers, massive adoption of new identities, religious opposition, and major strikes of 1941, 1943, and 1944 by the Dutch Resistance, 1940-45;
- the protest marches, strikes, and sit-downs before tanks during the East German Revolt, June 1953;
- the strikes in the political prisoners' camps (especially at Vorkuta) in the Soviet Union in 1953;
- the street demonstrations, general strikes, political defiance, formation of workers' councils, and establishment of a federated council substitute national government during the Hungarian Revolution of 1956-57;[11]
- the popular pressure and street demonstrations for political liberalization and on economic grievances in Poland in 1956 and 1970-71;
- the leafleting, public demonstrations, and sit-ins by Soviet civil rights activists and by Soviet Jews seeking permission to emigrate in the Soviet Union during the 1960s and 1970s;
- the refusal of collaboration, street demonstrations, resistance radio and television broadcasts, Government and Party defiance, student protests, and efforts to undermine the morale of Soviet troops in Czechoslovakia in 1968-69 against the Soviet invasion and measures to reimpose a rigid Communist dictatorship.*

All of these cases occurred without advance preparations. They were waged by people who had little or no real understanding of the nonviolent technique, its dynamics and requirements, except perhaps that gained by extremely limited experience or hearsay. It is, therefore, reasonable to explore whether by using increased knowledge of this technique with (where possible) advance training and other preparations based upon deep knowledge of extreme dictatorships and their weaknesses, we might be able to aggravate those weaknesses seriously and increase the effectiveness of nonviolent struggle against totalitarian systems.

---

*For a brief survey, with references, of the Czech and Slovak resistance, see Chapter Nine, " 'The Political Equivalent of War' — Civilian-based Defense."

PROBLEMS OF RESISTANCE UNDER TOTALITARIANISM

A host of difficult problems arises as soon as one begins to think seriously about waging nonviolent struggle in a liberation movement against a totalitarian system. Since variations in circumstances will influence to a high degree the course of a struggle against the system, we will need to know the particular situation as well as possible in order to deal with those problems. These variations will be revealed by the answers to such questions as the following:

Is the totalitarian system newly formed or long established? Have the subjects ever had any type of experience or previous practice which would constitute advance training, or preparation for nonviolent struggle? Has informative, analytical, and instructional literature on nonviolent struggle been circulated and read, as by *zamizdat*?* To what degree have any independent groups and institutions not under State or Party control (*loci* of power) survived the system or been newly created? Is the totalitarian system of domestic or foreign origin, or in what combination? Was the regime originally established with foreign assistance, or is it now foreign supported? How did the system originally develop: was it initiated by a coup d'état, guerrilla war, foreign invasion, gradual evolution, or in another way? To what degree are the present administrators, bureaucrats, civil servants, police, and troops loyal to the system and satisfied in their present positions? Do any significant groups or institutions exist, such as labor, religious, cultural, and the like, which are presently or potentially opposed to the system? What are the attitudes of the general public to the system as a whole, to any specific grievances or positive points of support, and how do they see the future?

PROBLEMS OF STRUGGLE REQUIRING RESEARCH

In addition to the background understanding of the particular situation revealed by the above questions, we also need greater knowledge about the problems of nonviolent struggle against

*The Russian term for illegally reproduced and circulated manuscripts and publications.

extreme dictatorships and the options available to the resisters. Here, advance research, analysis, and strategic planning can provide helpful insights for later use in actual struggles. These are the kinds of questions we can research to aid advance planning:

1. In face of the system's control over communications and publication and dissemination of literature, how can one spread information and understanding about nonviolent struggle? What role may exist for illegal literature, foreign-based radio broadcasts, and "teaching by example" through small planned actions or by spontaneous ones?

2. In face of effective political police, how can one solve the problem of leadership for nonviolent struggle? What role is there for an underground movement, for individuals and small groups setting examples, for spontaneous "leaderless" actions, or for "anonymous" or radioed instructions?

3. In face of the political police, censorship, and other controls, how can one plan action and resistance, and spread knowledge of such plans and instructions among the people who are expected to carry them out? What role is there for "underground" communications, spontaneous actions, and consensus on the types of issues to be resisted?

4. How are the particular problems related to the dynamics of nonviolent action operating under extreme dictatorships to be solved? These problems may be associated, for example, with the absence of civil liberties, and lack of access to public means of communication. Other problems may be linked to the strong ideological basis for the systems; this suggests a lesser role for attempts to "convert" the leaders and believers, and a greater role for actions which mobilize increased support for resistance, or which restrict or sever the ruler's sources of power.

5. How can one destroy confidence in the Leader and the Party, and achieve widespread and deep dissatisfaction? How can one at appropriate stages turn such dissatisfaction into withdrawal of cooperation and defiance of the regime?

6. How can one best approach the problem of the totalitarian ideology? Is it most effective to question it, reinterpret it, criticize it, or repudiate it? To what extent does the official ideology give meaning and direction to the lives of individuals? Is it better to offer a clear rival ideology with a different outlook on life, or to refuse to do that, encouraging people to develop a variety of outlooks and philosophies as they find most desirable?

7. How, under those political circumstances, can opposition and resistance be most effectively organized and conducted: with considerable openness, as in Russian Jewish and civil rights cases in the 1960s and 1970s, or with secrecy, as in many cases of resistance to the Nazis? What are the real implications and consequences of both positions? This is more complex than it might first appear.

8. How can one determine the optimal strategy for resistance during a crisis and in advance of one? Are there advantages to a prior determination of the points and conditions at which resistance will be offered without specific instructions? Under what conditions should a strategy of total noncooperation be practiced? When should selective noncooperation at particularly important points and issues be applied instead?

9. In the early stages of extreme dictatorships moving toward totalitarianism, how can one prevent the "atomization" of the population and the destruction of the society's *loci* of power?* In advanced stages of a totalitarian system when the destruction of independent institutions has gone very far, how can new groups and institutions outside of the system's control be created and strengthened?

10. How can one resolve the problems imposed on a resistance movement by the atmosphere of fear in a totalitarian society? Based on past experience and on analysis, under what conditions can subjects cast off such fear or act defiantly despite it? In a political atmosphere of extreme fear, what impact do acts of brazen defiance conducted apparently fearlessly have? How and why?

11. How can resisters withstand severe repression while continuing their defiance? Repression may include imprisonment, internment in concentration camps, execution, reprisals on nonparticipants, treatment with drugs, detention as mental cases, control of food, water, and fuel supplies, *agents provocateurs,* and selective and massive deportations. What different problems for the resisters may be produced by other responses by the system to the nonviolent challenges? These may include: (a) milder control measures applied to avoid creating martyrs or attributing exaggerated strength to the opposition, or (b) extremely severe repression and terror applied to

*See the discussion on *loci* of power in Chapter Two, "Social Power and Political Freedom."

force restoration of cooperation, obedience, and submission, their withdrawal being perceived as the most severe threat possible to the system. How can these problems be solved? Can some kind of balance be achieved between the need for action to win immediate objectives and the capacity of the subjects to defy and to withstand the resulting sanctions?

12. Ought external assistance to the struggle movement — such as radio broadcasts, smuggled literature, headquarters for exiled leaders, and international economic and political noncooperation with the dictatorial regime — be accepted? Can it benefit the struggle movement? Or, would external aid discredit the movement by allowing the resisters to be labeled "foreign agents"? Could such aid contribute either to dependence on, or to control by, foreign political groups or regimes? How could a resistance movement against an extreme dictatorship be completely independent of all foreign help in the internal struggle itself, while accepting external aid by embargoes and diplomatic sanctions, for example? What problems would this position present and how might they be resolved?

13. Does the extreme conformity and interdependence within a totalitarian system increase disproportionately the impact of acts of defiance and resistance, making very limited acts become very significant? Or, does the extreme conformity instead make it possible to dismiss the resisters as mentally ill, antisocial persons, or foreign agents, and easily to quarantine the acts themselves?

14. What are the implications for opposition strategy and tactics, and for the general course of the movement, of the fact that the nonviolent defiance may produce differing reactions among various sections of the population and types of personnel and officials in the system? For example, responses may vary among fully committed Party members, "soft" Party members, idealistic followers of the Party who lack real understanding, differing social classes, various religious, national, or cultural sections of the population, members of different branches and levels of the military forces, members of the political police, and the top hierarchy.

15. How can one maintain the necessities of life, such as food, water, fuel, against State restriction of them, and of employment and money, as repression to control resisters?

16. How can resistance strategy be deliberately aimed at aggravating identified inherent weaknesses in the system, thereby damaging the system fundamentally in ways which will be difficult to counteract?

17. Can resistance be designed to create conflicts, or aggravate existing ones, within the ruling echelons of the system? Could such internal conflicts help the resistance movement even though the resisters would rarely if ever know about them at the time unless they produced major changes in personnel, policies, or structures?

18. How can one encourage deliberate inefficiency, laxity in carrying out duties, and perhaps eventual mutiny among the system's officials, bureaucrats, administrators, police, and soldiers? What different effects on these possibilities tend to be produced by passivity, violent action, and nonviolent action? How might such failures and refusals to supply information to the center, to relay orders to lower personnel, to carry out policies and instructions, and even to carry out repression, be developed on a sufficient scale to be catastrophic to the dictatorship?

These eighteen questions illustrate the many practical problems which require investigation if we wish to learn how to destroy extreme dictatorships, including totalitarian systems. This effort to find solutions to extreme dictatorships and to explore the potential of nonviolent struggle against them must be based upon full appreciation of the diverse and serious problems involved. If the required research and analysis are carried out on a sufficient scale and are of the needed quality, however, we can obtain the knowledge required to enable people to formulate effective nonviolent struggle strategies to resist and destroy extreme dictatorships.

USING KNOWLEDGE FOR FREEDOM

The continuation and revitalization of political democracy require that we take deliberate measures to enrich it and to counter those developments and forces which restrict and endanger it. These measures include both the conscious cultivation of necessary underlying social and political conditions, and the improvement of democratic institutions, constitutional processes, and laws. Examination is urgently needed of democratic means of correcting social and economic injustices. This is because justice ought to be closely associated with freedom and democracy, and because many of the attacks on democratic government are launched in the name of justice. The development of new measures for emergency action against internal and external dictatorial threats to practicing democracies is also required.

The development of such means requires major research on the nature of dictatorships. This research should include both their means of control and *their weaknesses,* so that opposition might be concentrated on vulnerable points. The research should also focus on political violence in its various forms and its impacts on political systems, on possible alternatives to violence in serious domestic and international struggles against dictatorships, and on genocide. We need to know much more about the conditions under which genocide can occur and about past efforts to undermine and to defeat it. More knowledge is required on the viability of political freedom and optional forms of vitalized democratic structures and processes, and on underlying conditions which may be requirements for a practicing political democracy. Capacity to resist dictatorial attacks may be enhanced by greater knowledge of the modes of attack and requirements for success of the various forms of usurpation.

We also need to give attention to the ways to structure and prepare our society so that in the future we will be more able to avoid the development of dictatorships and more able to deal with them when we encounter them. These are some of the important long-term policy questions which we should examine:

1. How we should structure our social, economic, and political institutions to facilitate a free and democratic system, and to make most difficult or impossible any internal or external imposition of a dictatorship.

2. How we should organize people's resistance capacities to enable them to defeat attempts at internal usurpation and foreign rule which might occur.

3. How we should — without dangerous internal political violence or international war — assist people in other parts of the world to defend their independence and their abilities to maintain or to achieve democratic political systems and social justice without our doing it for them, and without dominating or manipulating them.

4. How people should act internally to undermine effectively a dictatorship which is already established — as by concentrating resistance on its inherent weaknesses, aggravating its internal problems, or creating dissension within the regime, rather than by using means which unify the regime and arouse the population to support it.

5. How we can develop alternatives to modern military struggle to provide effective self-reliant defense, even for smaller countries.

6. How we can develop ways to improve societies, increase justice, and distribute power more equitably among the population without dictatorial means.

Such research and policy studies may reveal some blind alleys which could be by-passed in the future. However, this work is very likely to provide fundamentally significant new political options which can contribute to the revitalization of political democracy, the development of programs of dictatorship prevention, and the introduction of new, more effective policies for constitutional and national defense.

We need not only to rededicate ourselves to basic political principles of freedom and justice; we need also to discover and develop policies and means of action which in the face of the dangers of modern dictatorships will enable those principles to survive, to be implemented, and to become revitalized both in theory and in practice. This will enable us to face both the internal and foreign threats of dictatorships with the confidence that we can withstand their assaults and triumph over them.

NOTES

1. David Riesman, "Some Observations on the Limits of Totalitarian Power," in David Riesman, **Abundance for What? And Other Essays** (Garden City, N.Y.: Doubleday, 1964), pp. 81 and 89.
2. Ibid., pp. 81-82.
3. Ibid., p. 92.
4. Ibid., p. 81.
5. Ibid., p. 92.
6. Ibid.
7. For a fuller presentation of this power theory, see Gene Sharp, **The Politics of Nonviolent Action** (Boston: Porter Sargent Publisher, 1973), Chapter One, "The Nature and Control of Political Power."
8. Karl W. Deutsch, "Cracks in the Monolith," in Carl J. Friedrich, ed., **Totalitarianism** (Cambridge, Mass.: Harvard University Press, 1954), pp. 313-314.

9. Ibid., pp. 314-315.
10. Riesman, "Some Observations on the Limits of Totalitarian Power," p. 81.
11. For references to various of the above cases, see Sharp, **The Politics of Nonviolent Action.**

5

Civil Disobedience in a Democracy

INTRODUCTION

A significant popular movement against nuclear weapons developed in Britain in 1958. This movement was largely expressed through the Campaign for Nuclear Disarmament which favored unilateral renunciation of British nuclear weapons and also opposed those of the Soviet Union and the United States. That Campaign applied a variety of means of protest, lobbying, pressure, and demonstrations. The latter included marches, public meetings, and picketing, but stopped short of deliberately illegal, though nonviolent, actions.

In early 1961 a new organization, the Committee of 100 was

established following a plea from Earl (Bertrand) Russell and the Reverend Michael Scott, well known for his work in Africa, to organize public acts of group civil disobedience against nuclear weapons. They argued that such illegal nonviolent action would advance the cause of unilateral nuclear disarmament more rapidly than the more conventional means used by the Campaign for Nuclear Disarmanent. The Committee of 100 included in its membership a diverse group of concerned citizens, actors, writers, social radicals, and intellectuals, including Vanessa Redgrave and Sir Herbert Read. The first deliberate act of public disobedience was a sit-down demonstration outside the Ministry of Defence, close to the Houses of Parliament, in February 1961.

Later, as part of its continuing activities, the Committee of 100 organized a different type of civil disobedience demonstration at the Wethersfield Air Base. That base was at the time used by the United States Air Force squadrons assigned to the Supreme Allied Command, Europe, whose planes regularly carried nuclear weapons. The Committee openly planned to attempt under strict nonviolent discipline to enter the base in order to immobilize it, or, if that effort failed, to block the entrance with their bodies.

Six members of the Committee, Terry Chandler, Michael Randle, Helen Allegranza, Pat Pottle, Ian Dixon, and Trevor Hatton, were later arrested and charged with violations of the Official Secrets Act (which had been enacted in 1911). However, it was not even charged that the accused had either attempted to obtain secret information of any kind or to pass secrets to an enemy.

The trial was held in London at the Central Criminal Court — the famous Old Bailey — 12–20 February 1961. After a little more than four hours of deliberation, the jury found the six guilty on both counts of conspiracy and incitement, but made a unanimous plea for leniency. The five men were sentenced to eighteen months imprisonment, and Helen Allegranza to twelve months.

The convictions were appealed to the House of Lords, where the case was heard by Lord Reid, Lord Radcliffe, Lord Hodson, and Lord Devlin. The appeal was dismissed on 12 July 1962.*

---

*In addition to newspaper accounts of the trial, the weekly *Peace News* (London) issued a special supplement, "On Trial," following the initial conviction. The dismissal of the appeal with the Lords' arguments was reported, for example, in the "Law Report" of *The Guardian* (London and Manchester) on 13 July 1962, and

The trial of General Raoul Salan, referred to in this chapter, was a consequence of a coup d'état in Algiers by French military officers and units which wanted to keep Algeria as French territory, and opposed the steps being taken by the French Government under President Charles de Gaulle and Prime Minister Michel Debré toward independence for Algeria. To be successful, the Algiers coup would need to have been followed by the ouster of the de Gaulle-Debré Government by a parallel coup within France, or by an invasion of France by the Algiers rebels. The coup was organized by four colonels but the declaration of a state of siege in Algeria by the rebel "Military Command" was issued under the names of four recently retired generals: Maurice Challe, Edmond Jouhard, André Zeller, and Raoul Salan. The coup collapsed four days later as a result of civilian defiance in France and widespread noncooperation and disobedience by the conscript soldiers in Algeria against their rebel officers.

The trial of Adolph Eichmann, also discussed in this chapter, was held at the District Court of Jerusalem, following his capture by Israeli agents in Argentina and his secret transport to Israel. Eichmann was tried for his role as organizer of the transportation of Jews to the death camps from all over Europe.

The views in this chapter were not offered in the original trial of the six members of the Committee of 100, although the general points had been made available to the defense. I was permitted to take the stand, but the judge refused to allow me to be questioned substantively about civil disobedience. Mr. Justice Havers declared: "I am afraid we can't turn this court into a college for non-violence." Evidence was also disallowed from Professor Linus Pauling, Archbishop T. O. Roberts, S.J., and John B. Witchell (a Canadian with expertise on electromechanical early warning systems). In addition to

---

initially in a nineteen page duplicated verbatim report on the case "Chandler and ors. v. Director of Public Prosecutions" from the shorthand notes of W. B. Gurney & Sons. For the full text of the Lords' decision, see either House of Lords and Judicial Committee of the Privy Council and Peerage Cases, *The Law Reports, 1964,* "Chandler v. Director of Public Prosecutions" (London: Incorporated Council of Law Reporting for England and Wales), pp. 787-814, or Cyril King and J. T. Edgerly, eds., *The All England Law Reports: Incorporating the Law Times Reports, Law Journal Reports,* 1962, vol. 3, "Chandler and Others v. Director of Public Prosecution" (London: Butterworths, 1962), pp. 144-160.

the six accused, defense witnesses included Vanessa Redgrave, Earl (Bertrand) Russell, and Sir Robert Watson-Watt, the inventor of radar.

This chapter is an analysis of the constitutional issues posed by the Committee of 100 trial.

*   *   *   *

Is organized civil disobedience democratic? Is it justified in a liberal democracy in which citizens possess the right of free speech, assembly, and a representative system of government with periodic elections? Should dissident groups in such a system be permitted to organize to express their dissent in open disobedience and to encourage others to join them? Or does such behavior strike hard against such a system itself? The constitutional questions raised by the application of organized civil disobedience in political conflicts are highly important and may influence not only later legal cases but the whole future development of democratic society.

In this chapter I have attempted to analyze the issues at stake, and to demonstrate, not only that individual civil disobedience is justified in a constitutional representative democracy, but also that organized civil disobedience may play an important role in the preservation and development of that system.

Questions about the role of organized civil disobedience in a constitutional representative democracy have so far been posed most frequently in India, where the independent government often found itself opposed by the very means which its own members once used to achieve independence, and in Britain where the activities of the Committee of 100 have raised in embryo the possibility in the West of mass civil disobedience against the chosen policy of an elected Government. They have also been raised in the United States where organizers of civil disobedience against war preparations have been prosecuted for "conspiracy." But unless the whole trend of the past half century in this field is reversed, the use of nonviolent action in general and civil disobedience in particular will continue to spread into an increasing number of countries and situations.

The question whether organized, as distinct from individual, civil disobedience is justified in a constitutional representative democracy was, in my opinion, the most important constitutional issue involved in the Committee of 100 "Official Secrets" trial.

THE PROBLEM OF EXTREME DISSENT

In the spring of 1962, within a period of two weeks, three significant events took place. On 23 May ex-General Raoul Salan, chief of the OAS (Organization of the Secret Army) was found guilty of five capital charges and sentenced to criminal detention for life. On 31 May Adolph Eichmann was hanged near Tel Aviv as the director of transportation for the murder machine which destroyed six million Jews during the Second World War. On 5 June the House of Lords dismissed the appeal of the six members of the Committee of 100 prosecuted under the Official Secrets Act. Each of these quite different events is important in finding answers to the questions I have posed.

The ancient moral problem of the limits of individual obedience to the established ruler has not been eliminated by majority rule. As far as the individual is concerned, when it is demanded that one submit to what one believes to be a violation of one's basic beliefs, it makes little difference to that individual whether the evil is one approved by a single ruler or by all the rest of one's fellow citizens. Nor has the system of constitutional represenative government solved the problem of how extreme dissent should be expressed.

One of the sobering aspects of politics is the number of occasions in history when a government's laws and policies have, in the perspective of later years, been condemned as wrong. The simple extension of the franchise is no guarantee against similar errors in the present or future. Yet in the past such laws and policies have generally been passively or actively supported at the time by the majority of the citizens. In such cases it was the minority dissenters (who opposed and often disobeyed those laws at the cost of persecution) who were thanked by later generations for their part in bringing about changes in those policies. There have also been other dissenters who were not right, but who sincerely believed that they were, and were therefore willing to take strong actions in support of that belief — yet were supporting a cause that was, in retrospect, wrong. Both of these groups dissented on moral or political questions on which they — rightly or wrongly — believed submission or compromise was not possible without a betrayal of their basic principles. They therefore pose the same problem for all political societies, including constitutional representative democracies: how should one express extreme dissent, and can this be done in a way which is effective but at the same time respects the opinions, persons, and rights of their opponents and the majority?

Elections and representative institutions, however imperfect, mark a distinct advance over the use of open political violence to achieve political ends. But if democracy is to survive, their usefulness must not be undervalued nor their limitations ignored. It is often forgotten that representative institutions are able to function effectively only so long as the issues with which they must deal are those on which there exists a fundamental agreement within the society. The disagreements must be limited to secondary matters on which compromise — which is essential to the present system — is possible, or on which the dissenting minority is willing and able to acquiesce.

There do exist, however, moral and political issues involving conscience or fundamental questions concerning the nature or future of the society on which compromise or acquiescence are — rightly or wrongly — regarded as morally and politically unacceptable.[1] Some of these are issues on which most of us would agree. For example, the election by majority vote of a party pledged to destroy liberty and democracy could not bind the democrat to submit passively to the ensuing dictatorship. Racial segregation, untouchability, or slavery do not become acceptable because of majority approval. Majority support can never justify the extermination of a minority. Abolition of religious liberty by the majority cannot bind the democrat. There may be other issues on which agreement is not so widespread but on which members of the dissenting minority nevertheless believe that they can neither compromise nor submit to the majority. The possibility of error — seen by others — does not alter the intensity of the minority's convictions.

These "no compromise" issues arise even when constitutional representative democracies operate as they ideally ought, with full civil liberties, full dissemination of information, and genuine debate. Almost by definition, the normal procedures of a representative democracy are inadequate in these cases of fundamental conflicts.

Much popular discussion about civil disobedience and democracy proceeds on the assumption that all differences of opinion and conviction are of equal intensity and that compromise or acquiescence is always possible. This is a false and dangerous view that may weaken the democracy in the name of which the argument is offered.

In addition to these "no compromise" issues, the problem of how to express extreme dissent is important for another reason. Increasing concentration of social, political, and economic power often reduces the degree of effective decision-making left to the legislature, the degree to which minorities even on lesser issues may effectively influence others not sharing their views, and the degree to which legislatures and governments may be controlled even by the majority of the subjects. Where the normal representative processes are thus imperfect, the need for examining ways to express dissent is extended beyond the "no compromise" issues into ones of lesser importance on which the subjects feel they have no effective conventional means to express their grievances.

In a world in which liberty is widely threatened, and resort is frequently had to violence in political conflicts, democratic society will be strengthened by finding creative ways of expressing strong dissent.

It is no answer to a dissenter on fundamental issues of the types cited to say that one has a right to maintain one's personal opinion, to exercise freedom of speech, and to work through established constitutional channels. When the dissenter regards an issue as crucial, the dissenter cannot be expected to compromise or acquiesce passively during a transition period while working for the cause in question. The dissenter feels driven to express disapproval by some form of action in order not to be involved in moral complicity in the policy which is opposed. And any such action, to have a chance to influence opinions and policy, necessarily leads to organization and the cooperation of others. To argue that while *individual* dissent is permissible, *organized* dissent by nonviolent means is not, is to postulate the atomizing of the population, isolating the individual in face of vast organized forces determining one's fate, and rendering the dissent impotent. It can then be ignored. This is hardly a democratic conception.

A firmly established regime need not take serious note of a minority opposition which is restricted to verbal dissent, while continuing passive submission and cooperation with the regime. If even a majority dissents only in words, while refraining from any action which the regime would have to take seriously, there is nothing that *requires* the regime even to consider the advisability of a change. As John Strachey stated: "It is true that governments always tell us they will never yield to force. All history tells us, however, that they never yield to anything else."[2]

The problem, therefore, is to find a mode of dissent which is both capable of wielding power proportionate to the number of dissenters and which simultaneously does not violate the rights of others or seek to impose minority rule. This mode of dissent must, however, be one which can be applied in *group action.* The dissenters face an organized opponent possessing vast resources; to deny their right to act together is to destroy the content of democracy.

INADEQUATE "ANSWERS" TO THE PROBLEM

Just as other constitutional channels are inadequate to resolve these issues, so also is the judicial system. It is unreasonable to assume that simply because a court of justice is involved, the basic "no compromise" issues somehow disappear or become secondary matters where compromise or submission is possible. Judicial decisions may usefully settle a variety of social and political issues; but there will be certain issues on which judicial ruling will not be accepted by both parties as a final settlement.

In the Committee of 100 Official Secrets case, for example, the House of Lords' decision explicitly stated that a current Government policy regarding the armed forces could not be challenged in the courts. The defense had in effect attempted to use this judicial system as a means of challenging and ruling on the validity and wisdom of the Government's defense policy. It is obvious that although relatively minor questions could be ruled on by the courts, no Government could permit decisions to be passed on such a fundamental policy as its whole defense program by a variety of judges and juries in the absence of any clear consensus in the society. The resolution of the problem of extreme dissent must therefore lie elsewhere.

There is a limited number of possible ways of acting when "no compromise" issues arise (that is, conflicts concerning morality, religion, or the whole nature and direction of the society), or when people believe the conventional channels to be effectively blocked.

One common response to such crises has been political violence — rioting, assassinations, terrorism, violent revolution, or civil war. These have occurred both in the presence and in the absence of a constitutional representative system.

The OAS in France and French Algeria was an important example of this. This "Organization of the Secret Army" applied violence and attempted a coup d'état in efforts to prevent the French Government from giving independence to Algeria. General Raoul Salan was one of the French Army officers who participated. The capital charges on which Salan was sentenced to criminal detention for life on 23 May 1962 are instructive. They were: taking part in the insurrection movement (the generals' abortive *Putsch* in Algiers); having been an accomplice in attempts aimed at changing the constitutional regime by force; encouraging citizens to take up arms against the State; having been an accomplice in attacks with the use of arms; having ordered attacks against members of the security forces and organized armed gangs to resist the security forces. The OAS, in both France and Algeria, was in fact facing a political conflict in which compromise on fundamentals was not possible. Passive submission was then rejected in favor of political violence. This took place under a system which included an elected legislature chosen by voters from a variety of parties.

Similarly, certain minority extremist sections of the Doukhobor religious group in Canada have resorted to bombings in their struggle for religious and cultural autonomy. John Brown's raid in slaveowning United States was a further instance. These are merely examples to show that political violence as a means of expressing dissent occurs in constitutional democracies as well as nonrepresentative systems. This is a response to our problem which we must reject. Political violence in our time has taken such forms as to convince most serious democrats that it is destructive of both moral principles and democracy itself.

Another response to such conflicts of principles has been passive submission. But although the dissenter may thereby avoid the undesirable consequences of political violence, there are good reasons why passive submission is unacceptable. First, the dissenter may be right. The Nuremberg and the Eichmann trials are particularly relevant here. The only legal basis upon which both those trials of Nazi leaders and officials for the deeds of their regime could be held was that the men charged had had a *legal* responsibility to *disobey* the orders of their political or military superiors. The British and other Allied Governments accepted this legal position at Nuremberg.

Throughout his trial Eichmann insisted that whatever his moral guilt, he was not legally guilty because he had acted under orders. "Obedience has always been a virtue." When he was executed on 31 May 1962, he said on the scaffold: "I had to obey the laws of war and the flag." The Nuremberg defendants made similar pleas, and the rebuttal was that they ought *not* to have obeyed orders.

The ruling in the Committee of 100 "Secrets" trial was the precise opposite of the verdict in the Nuremberg and the Eichmann trials. The judge in the "Secrets" trial, without attempting to justify himself, repeatedly forbade *mention* of both the above trials. While this doubtless simplified the case for the prosecution, it is difficult for an outsider to see the legal justification for the ruling. All three trials involved the question of the legal limits of obedience and of passive submission.

It is true that the Eichmann and Nuremberg trials involved crimes committed under a dictatorial regime. But this, though important, does not alter the fundamental problem. Whatever Adolph Hitler did afterwards, he came to power constitutionally. The nature of a government does not necessarily alter the nature of the moral problem posed by its actions. People not agreeing with the aim of the Committee of 100 and of the broader Campaign for Nuclear Disarmament to induce the Government to abandon nuclear weapons unilaterally, ought to have been able at least to understand (even though not agreeing) how their unilateralist fellow-citizens could find a similar moral problem involved in the extermination of six million Jews and in preparations for nuclear war which, if it occurs, may exterminate many more millions of people.

When people have a deeply-felt moral conviction, it is dangerous to them personally and to their society if they suppress and do nothing about that conviction. Their ability ever to act responsibly and true to their best convictions is reduced when knowingly they passively submit to what they believe to be a grave wrong. The history of the consequences of political passivity, authoritarianism, and dictatorship ought to be a warning that passivity on deeply-felt issues may weaken democracy.

There has always been a third, less common, response to fundamental conflicts: an attempt to withdraw from the "world" and to live as true as possible to one's convictions without attempting to influence the course of political events. This is, however, unsatisfactory for those who feel that their convictions require them to attempt to respond to wider responsibility to influence the course of society as a whole, and is, therefore, not an answer to our problem.

If, therefore, neither passivity nor political violence is acceptable, an alternative means of democratic peaceful action is needed to express extreme dissent — means which, while being effective, also recognize the democratic rights of the majority.

CIVIL DISOBEDIENCE

Civil disobedience — one of the methods of nonviolent action — has been suggested and practiced as a substitute nonviolent way of responding to these conflicts and of expressing extreme dissent. Civil disobedience is a deliberate and peaceful violation of particular laws, decrees, regulations, ordinances, military or police orders, and the like. These are usually laws, etc., which are regarded as inherently immoral, unjust, or tyrannical. Sometimes, however, laws of a largely regulative or "neutral" character may be disobeyed as a symbol of opposition to wider policies of the Government. This may take place where it is difficult to find a point of direct contact between the individual and the wider Government policy. Civil disobedience may be practiced by individuals, by small groups, and by masses of people. It may be reluctantly practiced by those who have no desire to disturb the status quo per se, but wish only to remain true to their convictions. Or it may be undertaken with the limited aim of changing a particular policy, law, or the like. It may also be used along with other methods of nonviolent action in times of major social or political upheaval as a substitute for violent revolution. Civil disobedience is not likely to be lightly undertaken for it involves the strong risk, and in some situations the virtual certainty, of incurring the penalties provided in the law for violations.

Civil disobedience has already been substituted for political violence in several cases, as in India, South Africa, and the American Deep South. The activities of the Committee of 100 in Britain have been an attempt, however imperfect, to make a similar substitution on the issue of nuclear weapons.

THE CONSTITUTIONAL ISSUE IN THE "SECRETS" TRIAL

The prosecution made it quite clear in the "Secrets" trial that the defendants were being prosecuted because they expressed their extreme dissent by *organized* civil disobedience. *They were charged not with committing civil disobedience, nor with approaching the Wethersfield base, etc., but with conspiring, that is, organizing to do so.* Though related, the committing of civil disobedience and the organizing of it are different questions, with different constitutional implications. The prosecution clearly recognized the important difference between them; the defense never gave evidence of having done so.

On 10 January 1962, when the six were sent for trial, Mr. M. Griffiths-Jones, for the prosecution, said:

> The reason why this prosecution has been brought is that these defendants were not content with the use of legitimate methods for putting forward their views and seeking support for them...as a matter of deliberate policy...they decided to break the law, to use their own expression: to engage in civil disobedience....[3]

At the Central Criminal Court on 12 February the six were charged on two counts:

> (1) Conspiring together to incite diverse persons to commit a breach of Section 1 of the Official Secrets Act, 1911, namely, for a purpose prejudicial to the safety or interests of the state, to enter the RAF station at Wethersfield.

> (2) Conspiring together and with other persons to commit a breach of Section 1 of the Official Secrets Act, 1911, namely, for a purpose prejudicial to the safety or interests of the state, to enter an RAF station at Wethersfield.[4]

On that same day the Attorney-General referred to minutes of various meetings of the Committee at which civil disobedience projects were discussed, saying:

> These minutes showed beyond any shadow of doubt that what was under contemplation was civil disobedience, which you may think is another way of saying breaking the law.[5]

In his summing up speech on 19 February 1962, at the end of the trial, the Attorney-General returned to this theme:

This is the point I want to emphasize once again: this prosecution is brought solely and simply because they have deliberately broken the criminal law of the land.

I ask you to consider for one moment what would happen if other bodies adopted the same course. If that happened it would be an end, would it not, to the rule of law. It would lead to the end of democracy, to anarchy, and possibly dictatorship. The rule of law protects our rights and privileges such as freedom of speech.[6]

The question posed was the role of organized civil disobedience in a constitutional representative democracy. This is fundamentally a constitutional question, despite the fact that the Attorney-General denied that the offenses were of "a political character." "This is not a political prosecution."[7] It is true that the defendants were not prosecuted because of their views. But it is also true that they were prosecuted for their role in applying organized civil disobedience in a political conflict. The prosecution therefore assumed undeniable political characteristics because the grounds of the prosecution and the views of the Committee combined to raise wider constitutional issues.

The judge, Mr. Justice Havers, in summing up, saw the question of organized civil disobedience as essential in the case.

One of the bulwarks of our constitution is that everybody, whatever his rank, position, status, whatever his views or creed, however strongly he hold those views, is subject to the law. If on moral or humanitarian grounds he is convinced a particular law is a bad law and contrary to the best interests of this country he is not entitled to break that law in order to protest against the Government. It is the bounden duty of every citizen of this country to obey the law.[8]

Mr. Justice Havers also said that his sentencing would be influenced if the six would assure him that they would give up the campaign of civil disobedience and would commit no more "criminal offences." Immediately before sentencing he said: "I have to pass a sentence which is adequate to the offences that you have committed and which will deter others from committing similar offences."[9]

In the Lords' decision, Lord Devlin returned to this constitutional question, saying that those who dissented from Government policy on nuclear weapons had "...every right to use all lawful means at their disposal to make them [their views] known. But so long as the contrary view was held by the majority and the policy of the country thus determined, I cannot see how it can be otherwise than prejudicial to the state to obstruct the execution of that policy."[10]

The defense apparently either did not fully grasp the constitutional issue involved in the question of organized civil disobedience in a representative constitutional democracy, or else regarded it as a minor issue. Much of the defense argument — when it was permitted to be developed — was more suitable for a prosecution brought for *violation* of Section 1, that is, with actually approaching or entering the place — than for *"conspiring" to commit* a breach of Section 1: *organizing and promoting* the civil disobedience.

The defense instead argued that the Official Secrets Act was being inappropriately applied to such a case, that it was the Government "defense" policy which was detrimental to the interest and safety of the State, and that the action and objectives of the Committee of 100 were, in fact, beneficial. It was also argued that civil disobedience was justified on such issues on moral grounds.

Questioned extensively by the Attorney-General, Michael Randle explained and justified civil disobedience against the existing nuclear weapons policy.[11] In his personal statement, Ian Dixon sought to justify civil disobedience, saying that "even though in this country we have certain democratic liberties which do not exist in other countries, it is necessary to step outside the law and to resort to unconstitutional actions."[12] Pat Pottle argued that civil disobedience was necessary if he were to avoid feelings of moral complicity in the present policy.[13] The judge refused to allow Pottle to question Archbishop Roberts, S.J., on the morality of civil disobedience. My own testimony was cut short before Pottle reached constitutional questions, after several questions on nonviolent action were ruled out of order.

This all meant that there was *no* defense argument or evidence offered to the central point presented by the prosecution concerning whether or not people ought to be prosecuted for organizing, as well as actually *committing,* civil disobedience in a parliamentary democracy. Although it is true that the judge ruled a considerable amount of the defense argument out of order, the fact is that the defense itself made no attempt to argue on this point, central though it was to the prosecution case and to the constitutional issues involved.

PROBLEMS OF CIVIL DISOBEDIENCE IN A DEMOCRACY

Where ordinary civil liberties exist, organized civil disobedience is not a substitute for verbal persuasion and the use of the existing constitutional means of influencing and changing governments. It is, rather, an alternative to political violence. This is basic for under-standing its role in a democracy.

Organized large-scale civil disobedience inevitably presents certain problems to the Government and the majority. They cannot ignore it because of the dissenters' challenge in openly disobeying a law, with willingness to accept the legal penalties, in order to bring wider public attention to their case and in order to withdraw their consent and support from the policy they oppose. Established governments will rarely feel they can tolerate open deliberate disobedience without their imposing the sanctions provided in the law for disobedience. This means that governments, operating from their established premises, must arrest the civil resisters and impose fines and sentences of imprisonment upon them. *This is to be expected, and when this is done the civil resisters normally cannot complain.* They must instead regard the sentences as a means of furthering their cause and strengthening their movement. Where civil disobedience is widespread, the government is compelled to provide the necessary enforcement personnel, administrative machinery, and penal facilities to cope with the large number of disobedient subjects.

The enforcement problems for governments facing large-scale organized civil disobedience are peculiar, partly because deliberate, open, peaceful disobedience is not usual, but mainly because the dissenters not only are not afraid of the penalties but virtually ask to be arrested. Governments have therefore often reacted with some uncertainty. The example of people willing to undergo penalties and hardships for their conscientious dissent may lead increasing numbers of people to think about the issues for the first time. This thus encourages policies to be chosen consciously, rather than accepted passively. It may even result in the minority becoming the majority. In that case, of course, the change of policy may be made by the usual constitutional methods. Where the Government does not bow to the changed views, or does not allow the usual constitutional means for changing Governments to be used, then the new majority of dissenters to Government policy have peaceful means of civil disobedience and other forms of nonviolent action by which they can act peacefully to alter the policy or the Government and restore majority rule.

But it may not happen that the dissenters are successful in convincing the majority. In that case, the minority cannot force the majority to accept the change of policy. There is no such thing as a "nonviolent coup d'état." Those who envisage that they could become some kind of incongruous "Gandhian Jacobins" and, while a clear minority, impose their will on the majority, are obviously ignorant of the nature of nonviolent action and are harboring ideas which are irresponsible and dangerous.

If a policy is to be permanently secured by nonviolent means it can only be done by building up conviction in its rightness among the population to the point where it has majority support. This is required to provide the strength needed to carry through its policy and to defend it nonviolently against minority attempts by violence to impose the old policy. It is possible that a minority could by purely obstructionist nonviolent tactics bring about the fall of a Government in a constitutional representative system. But to think that this would amount to victory is naive. This would not necessarily, nor even probably, bring about the desired new policy. With the majority still supporting the old policy, and alienated from considering the minority's case by their obstructionism, a new and more repressive regime supporting the old policy could come to power — either constitutionally or by coup d'état. Obstructionism could thus lead to the minority becoming a still smaller minority with reduced chances of achieving its objectives.

It is unlikely that a minority Government would come to power favoring the new policy against the wishes of the majority. If it did, it could only maintain itself in the face of strong opposition on such a crucial issue by itself becoming repressive of the majority. This would require it to depend for its existence, in the last resort, upon the very military means it allegedly opposed.

Understood in terms of the nature of civil disobedience, and of nonviolent action in general, a minority cannot impose its will upon a majority which believes in its own policy. There is no substitute for quality and genuine strength in a nonviolent movement, and there is no alternative to building up majority support for the views of the dissenters. If, therefore, nonviolent action in general, and civil disobedience in particular, are to advance the minority dissenters' cause, they must conform to certain standards which not only make the action effective in the long run, but also simultaneously make it compatible with democracy.

DEMOCRATIC QUALITIES OF CIVIL DISOBEDIENCE

Civil disobedience withdraws support and obedience from a policy or regime in proportion to the numbers of citizens who disapprove of it and are willing to pay the price (usually imprisonment) for that withdrawal. If the quality of the action, including nonviolent discipline, can be maintained, the seriousness of the challenge of the civil disobedience to the Government is thus roughly in proportion to the numbers among the citizens who feel strongly enough about the issue to take part in it.

Organized civil disobedience combines certain qualities which were formerly believed to be incompatible. It allows for direct, immediate militant action by those strongly dissenting from the established policy and who feel that they "must" act against it at once. This quality was formerly believed to be found only in political violence. With civil disobedience, however, there is no injury or death caused by the dissenters, and no destruction of property. There is respect for the opponents, and for the majority. The dissent is expressed in an orderly and peaceful manner — important qualities of democracy. It has even been argued that civil disobedience involves a profound respect for the law itself, the disobedients acting openly and being willing to accept the legal penalty for disobedience as the price in a democracy for expressing extreme dissent in direct action. All these are qualities which were formerly believed to be possessed only by adherence to the normal constitutional procedures of a representative democracy.

Civil disobedience, it is thus argued, combines the strengths of both direct action and gradualism in political conflicts, while avoiding the undesirable moral and political consequences of both political violence and inaction in face of fundamental conflicts.

THE CHOICE: VIOLENT OR NONVIOLENT ACTION?

The distinction between nonviolent action in general and civil disobedience in particular on the one hand, and political violence on the other, cannot be overemphasized. The moral implications and immediate human consequences, as well as the long-run social and political effects, are radically different. Civil disobedience is an attempt to act peacefully and democratically in cases of basic conflicts about issues on which the minority finds itself unable to compromise or passively to acquiesce. Civil disobedience is used only in cases of extreme dissent in which — in the absence of a nonviolent alternative — the dissenters would very possibly have resorted to political violence. *Civil disobedience as organized group dissent is thus not a substitute for conventional constitutional means, but instead is a substitute for political violence.*

It is, therefore, disturbing that the attempt is often made to equate civil disobedience with violence. For instance, the judge, in his summary of the proceedings at the "Secrets" trial, said:

> Great emphasis has been laid upon the fact that in this campaign strict directions were given that the campaign was to be conducted in a non-violent manner. Members of the jury, if a man deliberately commits a crime it is wholly immaterial whether he does so by non-violent or violent methods, unless the use of violence is an essential ingredient of the crime. . . . It is quite immaterial if in fact they all agreed to enter upon this air station whether they did so by violent or non-violent methods.[14]

In a legal sense, admittedly, the judge's statement is correct; the breaking of the law is the breaking of the law, and preparations to break one law may be technically as illegal as preparations to break another law. However, the six were not being tried for actually committing civil disobedience, but rather for organizing it. Such a prosecution is based upon a view of the social and political consequences of that act, and here the question of whether the means are violent or nonviolent *is* relevant to whether they should be tried on that charge because the social and political consequences of violent and nonviolent means differ radically.

In considering the constitutional question of whether or not people should be prosecuted for *organizing* civil disobedience, the question of whether the dissent is violent or not is therefore a highly important one. The social and political consequences for a democracy of acts to express extreme dissent by minority political violence and by minority nonviolent action including group civil disobedience, respectively, are vastly different. Such consequences differ so much that a legal distinction ought to be made between organization for violent disobedience and organization for civil disobedience. This difference is crucial in answering the question whether there should be prosecutions for *organizing,* as distinct from *committing,* civil disobedience. The attempt to equate the violent and nonviolent techniques, by ignoring their different consequences and implications, can only be based upon ignorance of these differences or a desire to crush the expression of dissent by civil disobedience at all costs.

Another example of this equating nonviolent with violent action was seen in the appeal to the Lords, where civil disobedience was likened to sabotage. Yet there was — to my knowledge — no reference to "sabotage" in the original trial of the six where it would have been easy to refute it. It is quite clear that the Lords, in pronouncing judgement, found it possible to stretch the Official Secrets Act, 1911 — an Act which was never intended to deal with prosecuting organizers of such things as nonviolent civil disobedience — to make it usable against the six by equating their intended action with "sabotage."

Lord Reid, for example, said that the side note to Section 1 (1), "Penalties for spying," could not be used as an aid to construction so as to limit the scope of the action (that is, to spying only). "Moreover, it is impossible to suppose that the section does not apply to sabotage, and what was intended to be done in this case was a kind of temporary sabotage."[15] Lord Radcliffe, concurring, said:

> The saboteur just as much as the spy in the ordinary sense is contemplated as an offender under the Act. But, if so [*sic*], the Appellants were saboteurs in this case, for...it was their avowed purpose to interfere with and obstruct the operation of this airfield....The question upon which this appeal turns is whether they were any the less saboteurs within the range of the Act because they wished to use their obstruction and interference as a demonstration in the hope that through some long process of agitation and persuasion the policies they canvassed would be adopted.[16]

Lord Devlin, similarly, referred to "sabotage" in his concurring judgement.[17] It would appear then that this was the basis upon which a law designed for dealing with spying and sabotage was interpreted to allow it to be used for prosecuting organizers of nonviolent civil disobedience — a method of protest for which existing legislation did not apparently otherwise allow. But this equation of "sabotage" with "nonviolent civil disobedience" is a blatant distortion of the facts. If this was, as it appears, the basis on which prosecution under the Official Secrets Act was justified, it is quite possible that in a future case a better informed judge or jury could dismiss such a prosecution.

"Sabotage," according to the *Shorter Oxford English Dictionary,* is defined as, "The malicious damaging or destruction of an employer's property by workmen during a strike or the like; hence *gen.* any malicious or wanton damage." Civil disobedience is a very different thing. There are many reasons why sabotage is inconsistent with nonviolent action, and why its introduction into such a movement would seriously weaken it. The equation of the two, unless backed by unquestionable evidence, must be assumed to be due to blatant ignorance or else a deliberate attempt to create a false impression to divert attention from the real issues.

Another misunderstanding of civil disobedience was shown by Lord Radcliffe's concurring judgement. Speaking of the appellants' intentions, he said: "Nothing short of an obstruction would have suited their purpose."[18] In civil disobedience, however, it is not the actual successful committing of the intended specific act which is the most important. It is the *attempt* to do so. For example, in India, in 1930, when there were massive attempts to manufacture salt illegally, if the person was arrested before the making of the salt was completed, this did not defeat his object, for the salt tax law had been violated by his attempt, and the State had demonstrated that in order to maintain its policies it was necessary to arrest thousands of peaceful subjects. This revealed the normally hidden violence of the system, trained the population in resistance, and further alienated the people from the Government. Similarly, if demonstrators against racial segregation in the Deep South were arrested *as they entered* a segregated waiting room instead of *after* they had been in it for a while, their action had not been defeated but had achieved its essential purpose.

If the number of disobedient subjects grows so large, owing to decreasing support for the Government's policy, or if there is a "change of heart" in the supporters of Government policy, so that the dissenters are ultimately permitted to continue the specific act without interference, so much the better from their standpoint. But — and this point is important in considering the role of civil disobedience in a constitutional representative democracy — *it is the attempt to commit the act which constitutes civil disobedience. If all the demonstrators are arrested as soon as this attempt is made, and outward formal "order" is quickly restored — thus satisfying the government — the act has still achieved its purpose in being an act of defiance and of withdrawal of consent which the Government has been forced to recognize.*

A DEMOCRATIC EXPRESSION OF EXTREME DISSENT

Thus, the answer to our original question of whether organized civil disobedience is democratic, gradually becomes clearer. Basic to that answer is our view of democracy. It involves, of course, civil liberties and respect for both the minority and the majority. But democracy means essentially that the citizens have a *genuine* voice in determining the course of their own lives and of the policies of their government and country. With the present increasing centralization of all kinds of power, the active participation of the citizenry is more important than ever. Equally important, democracy means that social and political changes are to be made without resort to political violence. Representative institutions in parliamentary and other forms have served as a means toward this end. It was always clear, however, that these were not the *sole* means of making peaceful changes.

No one questions the democratic qualities of a public protest meeting, distribution of leaflets, publication of political articles and books, a picket line or a strike, a petition to the government, or a campaign to educate the public on a particular issue. All these actions may be aimed at influencing the majority, the legislature, and the Government. But they are all clearly outside the electoral and legislative procedures. This does not make them less democratic. Similarly, organized civil disobedience is not intrinsically undemocratic because it too is outside those procedures.

Civil disobedience is often dismissed as coercive, but, as we have noted, though it may cause difficulties to the government and the majority, *minority* civil disobedience cannot *force* a government to reverse its policies if it and the majority really believe in them and are determined to carry them out.

In his summing up in the Official Secrets trial of the six members of the Committee of 100 in February 1962, the Attorney-General, expressing concern at what might happen were civil disobedience to become more widespread, said:

> I ask you to consider what would happen if other bodies adopted the same course. If that happened, it would be an end, would it not, to the rule of law. It would lead to the end of democracy, to anarchy and possibly dictatorship.[19]

It is my contention that this is simply not true. Rather than destroying democracy, the introduction of the right to organize civil disobedience would strengthen it by meeting one of its major existing weaknesses — the absence of a democratic means of expressing extreme dissent. Civil disobedience would also reduce the more serious dangers to democracy posed by passivity and political violence. Rather than being horrified at the prospect of other groups adopting civil disobedience, one might be gratified that they had thereby rejected political violence with its antisocial and antidemocratic effects.

Organized civil disobedience is somewhat comparable on the political level with strikes in the industrial field, except that in the former only a portion of the persons involved withdraw their cooperation from the system. Strikes are designed to take place when established procedures for dealing with disputes have failed to produce agreements. They, too, are a substitute for violent action, such as murdering the employer or bombing the factory. Instead, the workers nonviolently withdraw their cooperation. However misused strikes have been at times, it is generally agreed that the right to strike is an essentially democratic right. Even so, there are, of course, sanctions against strikes. While refusing to work laborers receive no wages. This, though not a legal sanction, operates to discourage strikes except where the issue is deeply felt.

Similarly, in organized civil disobedience, sanctions exist which would to a much greater degree discourage people from practicing it except in extreme cases. The number of groups, therefore, likely to adopt civil disobedience is not large, being limited to those who feel deeply enough about the issue to be willing to accept imprisonment and other suffering for their refusal passively to submit.[20] If the dissent is that deeply felt, it is desirable that the group should have some strong, but peaceful, means of expressing its objections.

Our present democratic system could be improved by making provision for the expression of extreme dissent through recognition of the right to organize civil disobedience with no prosecutions being made for such organizing and promoting. The *committing* of civil disobedience would of course by definition continue to be illegal. As long as arrests and prosecutions were made under the law chosen for disobedience they would be regarded as fair and reasonable within the framework of existing constitutional democracy. This would provide the society with a democratic outlet for extreme dissent and with a kind of barometer by which the extent and intensity of extreme dissent would be measured. *Organized civil disobedience would thus provide an orderly, peaceful substitute for political violence.*

On the other hand, the attempt itself to *prevent* the peaceful expression of radical dissent by organized civil disobedience poses grave threats to democracy. By interfering with such organization, the government forces the society to restrict the normal civil liberties which a dissenting group may wish to use to discuss their views or to promote a demonstration by civil disobedience.

Exactly this situation occurred in attempts by officials to control the preparations for civil disobedience and promotion of it by the Committee of 100. Permission for meetings to be held in Trafalgar Square, a traditional site for free speech, was refused when assurances were not granted that civil disobedience would not be discussed and literature advocating civil disobedience would not be distributed. The distribution of leaflets and the holding of poster parades were stopped when they referred to civil disobedience. The first political police raids for some time on people's homes and offices took place in searches for incriminating evidence.

If, on the other hand, the approach I have advocated here were adopted, while prosecutions for committing civil disobedience would be quite in order, such restrictions as those cited above on normal civil liberties for publicizing grievances or future civil disobedience would be quite unnecessary and inappropriate. Lifting these restrictions could, at certain stages of a movement, considerably ease and simplify the task of the police. At times in the past when restrictions were placed on civil liberties, one result was an increase in the numbers committing civil disobedience, for people then saw a connection between the act and the preservation of freedom. At such times, those restrictions have simply enlarged the scope of civil disobedience, by making it possible to commit it by holding prohibited meetings, distributing prohibited literature, and engaging in similar acts.

What if a government, faced with a significant movement of extreme dissent, persists in making organized, orderly civil disobedience not only illegal but also seriously attempts to make it impossible? Unless knowledge of the principles, theory, and application of nonviolent action are widely permeated throughout the movement and population, there is a strong likelihood of the movement organizing itself on an "underground," or secret, basis. This would have serious consequences for the movement as well as for the society. It would probably lead to a numerically smaller and more desperate movement, tending to use whatever means it could, very possibly including acts of political violence. As Gandhi asked when the British were so furious at his 1930 civil disobedience movement: would they prefer violence? That is in fact the alternative in such cases of radical conflict, and unfortunately it is often the case that rulers *do* prefer their protesting subjects to revolt with violence, for they are more easily crushed and discredited when they do so. This development would, however, be disastrous both for the cause of the dissenting group and for the society, as well as destructive of democracy. The chances of that development occurring will be greatly reduced if it is recognized that a democratic society requires some means of expressing extreme dissent and that this need can best be met by a legal recognition of the right to organize civil disobedience. Whether or not this is accepted may depend upon whether the citizens and government are more interested in suppressing dissent or in maintaining and improving a democratic society.

STANDARDS FOR CIVIL DISOBEDIENCE
IN A DEMOCRACY

When organized civil disobedience is to be practiced in a constitutional representative democracy, there must then be certain standards of behavior to which *both* sides must conform if fair play is to be observed and if the democratic qualities of that society are to be maintained and enriched. The failure of either side to conform to these may severely threaten the democratic qualities of that society. I tentatively suggest the following standards:

For the nonviolent actionist:

1. The action must be absolutely nonviolent in all circumstances, in face of all provocation, retaliation, and repressive measures. The actionists ought even to seek to avoid engendering permanent animosity and hostility and to maintain friendly relations with all involved (while recognizing that temporary hostility may sometimes, despite all efforts, be aroused by the mere existence of dissent).

2. The group responsible for laying the plans for the action must operate openly and above board. All plans for action must be revealed publicly in advance of the action, including to the police and other relevant governmental agencies.

3. As long as prosecution is brought under the law or regulation chosen for disobedience, the actionists must be willing to accept the penalties provided in the law for disobedience, such as fines or imprisonment.

4. Except where brutality, attempts at humiliation, or other unjust treatment have occurred, or in very special cases, the prisoner should cooperate with the police and prison authorities from the time of his or her arrest. Imprisonment is seen as the penalty the democrat must accept for practicing civil disobedience as a means of furthering his or her convictions.

5. The nonviolent actionists must behave in a disciplined, dignified manner in all circumstances.

6. The demonstrators will not seek to be simply obstructionists nor to bring down a Government supported by the majority.

For the government:

1. Where a law is not being violated, the nonviolent action must be allowed to proceed peacefully without interference. Basic civil liberties, including the right to picket, distribute leaflets, hold parades, public meetings, and similar acts, must not be interfered with, even when these advertise plans to commit civil disobedience and urge others to participate in it.

2. The penalties imposed on the disobedient demonstrators must be limited to the maximum — and this must be reasonable — contained in the law chosen for disobedience, and laws not intended to deal with such behavior must not be invoked.

3. Extralegal measures, such as beatings, shootings, brutalities, and the like, either before or after arrest must in no circumstances be permitted.

4. Disproportionate punishment of only a few of the demonstrators or organizers must be regarded as selective justice and hence unfair.

5. The right to organize and practice collective civil disobedience, subject to the above standards, must be recognized as a peaceful democratic substitute for political violence.

6. While conforming to the above standards, a government is justified in arresting and sentencing demonstrators practicing civil disobedience under the normal provisions of the law chosen for disobedience.

With both sides conforming to such standards as these, regardless of the rights and wrongs of the disagreements, the contest, while admittedly causing inconveniences to the government and the majority, will enrich the ability of the democracy to deal with extreme dissent in a democratic manner.

This set of "standards" presents nothing radically new, but amounts essentially to a return to the actual practice in London during the first two demonstrations by the Committee of 100. In both cases there was no restriction placed on advance publicity. Trafalgar Square was available for an advance meeting and assembly point, and demonstrators marched down Whitehall accompanied by police to the point where the demonstrators sat down and in an act of civil disobedience refused to move. In the first case no arrests were made and in the second, over eight hundred people were arrested. From the standpoint of democracy, these were far more creative ways of dealing with extreme dissent than by the later prosecutions under the Official Secrets Act.

CONCLUSIONS

My general proposal, that the organizing of civil disobedience be permitted in a constitutional representative system, admittedly involves a modification of some existing policies and perhaps even legal concepts. But this would enrich and strengthen the democratic system by providing a solution to the problem of how to express extreme dissent in ways compatible with democratic principles — a problem which existing democratic theory and practice have never really faced.

The development of nonviolent action, including civil disobedience, in facing conflicts within the society may, in turn, help the country to resolve other problems. Civil disobedience is not only a means of achieving the just consideration of minority views. It could also assist in providing a means — along with other forms of nonviolent action — by which the majority itself could act to defend the society and constitutional government when liberty is threatened, for example, by coup d'état, for which there is also at present no constitutional answer. At present, military action which may lead to civil war is the only means of dealing with it. But if the army, along with a minority of the citizens, supports the coup, the majority is virtually helpless against it.

The use of civil disobedience and other forms of nonviolent action within the society could thus help to prepare people as a whole for meeting such crises as this, and even invasion, by producing experience in the application of an alternative technique of struggle. The country as a whole would thus be more capable of effective action against internal or external threats to its liberty.

NOTES

1. See Joan V. Bondurant, **Conquest of Violence: The Gandhian Philosophy of Conflict** (Princeton: Princeton University Press, 1958; London: Oxford University Press, 1958; and Berkeley: University of California Press, 1965), pp. 216-219 and 223-235.
2. Quoted in E.H. Carr, **The Twenty Years' Crisis, 1918-1939** (London: Macmillan, 1942), p. 226.
3. **The Times,** 11 Jan. 1962.
4. **The Times,** 13 Feb. 1962.
5. Ibid.
6. "On Trial," **Peace News** Supplement, p. 11.
7. "On Trial," p. 2.
8. Ibid., p. 12.

9. Ibid.
10. **The Guardian,** 13 July 1962.
11. Ibid., p. 8.
12. Ibid., p. 9.
13. Ibid.
14. "On Trial," p. 12.
15. **The Times,** 13 July 1962.
16. Ibid.
17. **The Guardian,** 13 July 1962.
18. **The Times,** 13 July 1962.
19. "On Trial," p. 11.
20. Whether, and if so how, nonviolent sanctions might be developed in government to replace legal sanctions dependent upon violence is a separate question; we are not here attempting to describe an ideal nonviolent society but to make certain modifications in the present system which will improve it in the right direction and on which some general agreement might conceivably be possible at an early date. For discussions of more fundamental change involving replacing violent sanctions with nonviolent sanctions see Chapter Eleven, "The Societal Imperative" and Chapter Twelve, "Popular Empowerment."

6

Freedom and Revolution

*A Review of Hannah Arendt's On Revolution**

Was a basic error made in selecting the political institutions of Western democracy? Did the establishment of the United States federal constitution and the post-independence state constitutions contribute to *dis*empowering people rather than increasing popular control in politics? Do political parties help people to control governments, or are they used to control people?

Why is it that so many revolutions against tyrannies result in the establishment, not of freedom, but of new tyrannies, often worse than the old ones? Do revolutions contribute at all to freedom? Is there

*Hannah Arendt, *On Revolution* (New York: Viking Press, 1963, and London: Faber & Faber, 1963).

something basically different between throwing off a tyranny —
"liberation" — and establishing freedom?

What exactly is freedom in politics? Is the idea of people running
their own political system naive and romantic? Or, is there actual
experience which if utilized could make such participatory politics
realistic, even in this dangerous world?

These are the provocative questions with which Hannah Arendt
dealt in her 1963 book *On Revolution*. They merit continued examination and thought.

Oppressed people and democrats have long asserted the right of
revolution against tyranny. People have often assumed that freedom
is produced by the destruction of a tyrannical regime or by the
ousting or killing of the tyrant. Instead of freedom, however, a new
tyranny has often emerged. When this has happened, people who
wanted freedom have often been dismayed, confused, and at times
disillusioned.

In response, some people have turned against all popular revolution to end tyranny, and even all major structural change; they have
concluded that such means can only make the society more oppressive. Other people have denied that anything serious is really wrong
with revolutions, and instead blamed secondary factors, such as
"enemies of the revolution," external forces, individual personalities,
and usurpations by power-hungry persons and groups. Still other
people have assumed that every case of a revolution gone sour has
had a different cause. Some people have even denied that a tyranny
existed, or have excused its "excesses," and pointed instead to the
evils of the old regime, or the dirty hands of others. Some even
glorified the new tyranny as long as they themselves or their friends
controlled it. Tyrannical controls (called by kinder names) were
believed to be useful in the "right hands" in order to institute drastic
changes in the whole society, and even to change the nature of human
beings.

A deeper understanding of the societal conditions which make
tyranny possible or probable would have prevented surprised dismay
when the termination of one tyranny was followed by the establishment of a new one. If people had understood that a suitable societal
and political foundation is required for freedom to be vital and
durable, they would not have expected the ending of one tyranny to

be followed by the full blossoming of political freedom.* Very few people understood, too, that very different structural consequences are likely to follow from major use of violent sanctions and of nonviolent sanctions.† A revolution which both ends a particular tyranny and brings in substantive political freedom, is a rare phenomenon. Why is this?

These important questions rarely receive the serious attention they merit from political thinkers capable of dealing with them. Hannah Arendt was an important exception. In her 1963 book *On Revolution,* Dr. Arendt was primarily concerned with the problem of how political freedom can become a reality in the modern world — a world in which people are manipulated and controlled under constitutional regimes, as well as tyrannical ones, a world in which revolution has failed to bring freedom, and a world in which people are constantly threatened with annihilation.

Clearly, the status and condition of freedom in the modern world are in deep trouble, and something is seriously wrong when revolutions produce new tyrannies instead of establishing popular control. The problem of making freedom real despite the tendencies toward dictatorial control and the problem of preventing war despite the growth and dangers of modern military weaponry are, Arendt insisted, interrelated.

This chapter is primarily devoted to a presentation of Arendt's views (for they are not always easy to follow the first reading), to a discussion of structures and sanctions, and to a plea that we examine seriously whether and how participatory politics might contribute to reshaping modern politics to help implement the ideals which most people espouse. In her book Dr. Arendt dealt with problems and concepts which require very careful attention and thought in order to understand and to evaluate them, even in this more succinct and less complex presentation.

In the Introduction Arendt emphatically placed the problem of tyranny also in the context of the problem of modern war. War and

---

*On the societal and political conditions contributing to tyranny and freedom, see Chapter Two, "Social Power and Political Freedom."

†See the concluding section of Chapter Two, "Social Power and Political Freedom," Chapter Eleven, "The Societal Imperative," and Chapter Twelve, "Popular Empowerment."

revolution, she wrote, are still the "two central issues" of our world (p. 1). The confidence which people formerly placed in these to deal with serious human problems is no longer deserved. War can no longer defend civilians, and the military has changed into "a belated and essentially futile avenger" (p. 5). As for revolution, the word "freedom" has even disappeared from the revolutionary vocabulary (p. 2). Although war is often waged by tyrannical regimes, it should not be necessary to accept the destruction of freedom in order to prevent physical destruction by war; she rejected both the "better dead than red" and the "better red than dead" outlooks (p. 4). In an important note she argued that we ought to dare "face both the horrors of nuclear weapons and the threat of totalitarianism" simultaneously (p. 287 n. 1). Indeed, the two are intimately related, for violence is, Arendt argued, a "common denominator" for both revolutions and wars (p. 9), and violence is responsible for much of the tragedy which has accompanied and followed them. Later in the book, she continued this discussion only in terms of revolution.

LIBERATION OR FREEDOM?

The central focus of the book is the relationship between political freedom and revolution. Arendt distinguished sharply — and this is crucial — between "liberation" and "political freedom." "Liberation" is a negative notion of liberty, she argued; it is becoming "free *from* oppression" (p. 25, italics added). That condition does not necessarily require a democratic or republican form of government. "Freedom" has wrongly been confused with the ending of a particular tyranny and has lost its political meaning. Even in political theory the term "freedom" has come to be understood not as a political phenomenon but, wrongly, as "the more or less free range of non-political activities which a given body politic will permit and guarantee to those who constitute it" (p. 22).

Political freedom, argued Arendt, is a positive concept. It is not a condition of being ruled by those in charge of the political institutions and allowed certain personal, nonpolitical liberties. Instead freedom is, she insisted, the opportunity to participate directly in the operation of one's political society. "[T]he actual content of freedom . . . is participation in public affairs . . . ." (p. 25). Freedom is not simply a system of civil liberties, political parties, constitutionally-prescribed elections, and a parliament. Instead, freedom is a system of government in which the citizens become "the rulers themselves" (p. 34). Freedom is "a form of political organization in which the citizens [live] together under conditions of no-rule, without a division between rulers and ruled" (p. 22). This is *not* anarchism, she argued, as this freedom is dependent upon a system of government.

Freedom does not, however, occur under just any system of government, nor even under all governments which can be labeled democracies or republics. Arendt's concept of political freedom occurs only in "a body politic which guarantees the space where freedom can appear" (p. 121). That means that political freedom occurs when the citizen becomes, in Jefferson's words, "a participator in the government of affairs" (p. 123). This opportunity for direct participation constitutes "public freedom," and makes possible a unique feeling of satisfaction.

The colonial "Americans knew that public freedom consisted in having a share in public business, and that the activities connected with this business by no means constituted a burden but gave those who discharged them in public a feeling of happiness they could acquire nowhere else" (p. 115).

Popular revolutions in which people have themselves cast off a tyrannical regime which has oppressed them have also produced "this experience of being free" and "this experience of man's faculty to begin something new" (p. 26). The revolutionary spirit has included both the desire to liberate and the desire "to build a new house where freedom can dwell" (p. 28). This attempt both to end tyranny and to build freedom was, Arendt wrote, unprecedented and unequalled. Its promise, however, has not been fulfilled. Often the very process of "liberation," that is, the casting off of the old tyranny, has defeated the revolution, that is, the foundation of political freedom. In such cases, Arendt wrote in effect, the effort is not worth the result; rebellion and liberation are "futile" unless followed by "the constitution of the newly won freedom" (p. 141).

So disastrous has the process of liberation been for the establishment of a system of freedom that, she continued, freedom has been better preserved in those countries in which no revolution ever occurred, or even those in which one was defeated, than in those in which revolutions were supposedly successful. Whatever the various results of revolutions, freedom is not one of them, and it certainly does not follow automatically from the act of liberation. The revolutions of the nineteenth and twentieth centuries resulted in those in which the revolution became "permanent" (Russia and China) and those which ended in limited "constitutional" governments which ensured a moderate amount of civil liberties. The political systems of the countries with "permanent revolutions" do not even approximate freedom. The systems of the limited constitutional governments are often confused with freedom, and hence require more detailed consideration. Therefore, she turned her attention primarily to the American revolution and system of government as an example of that type of result.

Popular participation in self-government had been an important feature of colonial America. It brought the citizens a satisfaction they called "public happiness" (p. 123). However, following the War of Independence (which she called the American Revolution), a shift occurred from "public freedom" to "civil liberty." Representation replaced participation. The system of people's *share in* government was replaced by safeguards *against* government, illustrated by the bills of rights. Thomas Jefferson saw the danger which this shift contained. Civil rights are not, Arendt emphasized, the same as political freedom. That means instead "the right 'to be participator in government,' or it means nothing" (p. 220). At that time, Benjamin Rush clearly stated "the new and dangerous doctrine" which argued that although "all power is derived from the people, they possess it only on the days of their elections. After this it is the property of their rulers" (p. 239).

Important gains have been achieved under the two-party system of government, as distinct from tyrannical systems. These gains include a certain control over the rulers, constitutional liberties, and "private happiness," Arendt conceded. Contrary to the popular view, she argued that the political parties are not instruments of popular control but instead "the very efficient instruments through which the power of the people is curtailed and controlled." Under this system public freedom and public happiness "have again become the privilege of the few" (p. 273). Indeed, a basic premise of representative democrarcy is false: only "interest" and "welfare" can be represented, not "actions" and "opinions" (p. 272).

The contradiction between public freedom and the political

order arising from the revolution was much sharper in France. The aim of constitutional government, said Maximilien Robespierre, was the preservation of a new republic founded to establish political freedom. But then he added, "it is almost enough to protect individuls against the abuses of public power" (p. 134). In the latter situation, Arendt pointed out, power is still public and in the hands of government, but the individual has become powerless and must be protected against it. Freedom no longer resides in the public realm but is relegated to the private lives of the citizens. That private freedom must, therefore, be defended against the public and its power. "Freedom and power have parted company, and the fateful equating of power with violence, of the political with government, and of government with a necessary evil has begun" (p. 134).

In contrast to Europe, Arendt argued, "the revolutionary notions of *public* happiness and *political* freedom have never altogether vanished from the American scene" (p. 134). It is uncertain, however, how much of what is left of those notions will survive under the impact of economic affluence.

The establishment of representative government as distinct from participatory public freedom spelled danger. It meant, argued Arendt (quoting Jefferson), "that the people must either sink into 'lethargy, the forerunner of death to the public liberty' or 'preserve the spirit of resistance' to whatever government they have elected, since the only power they retain is 'the reserve power of revolution' " (p. 240). America then became predominantly the promised land of plenty for Europe's poor. The "taste for public freedom" (p. 136) — while not completely lost — was no longer prominent as the individual withdrew from politics into his or her private domain.

WHY REVOLUTIONS HAVE FAILED

Why did the revolutions which were intended to achieve freedom not lead to freedom? Seven interrelated problems hold the explanation, in Arendt's opinion. Presented systematically, they are:

1. Violence. Violence has occurred widely and has been assumed to be necessary in liberation and revolutionary movements. However, Arendt was convinced, such violence has been a major reason why they have failed to achieve political freedom. There have been, in her opinion, four main reasons for this violence:

a. It has been assumed that the beginning of something new "must be intimately connected with violence..." (p. 10). However, violence cannot create. It can only sweep away. A new free political order can come only by deliberate creative efforts, "by men in common deliberation and on the strength of mutual pledges..." (p. 215).

b. Revolutionaries have failed to distinguish between "violence" and "power" (p. 134). It has been wrongly assumed that violence produces power. Power, however, Arendt argued, instead comes from the mutual assistance and loyalty of people binding themselves together for some purpose.

c. Violence and terror in revolutions followed, she maintained, the introduction of the "social question" (especially poverty) into the attempt to establish political freedom. Rage and compassion led to the demand "for swift and direct action, that is, for action with the means of violence" (p. 82). (This is not, of course, necessarily true.)*

d. Revolutionaries have often lost their capacity to see people as human beings and have become cruel, not hesitating to sacrifice people "to their 'principles,' or to the course of history, or to the cause of revolution as such" (p. 85).

2. Rigidity. Rigidity in the thought of the "professional revolutionaries"† has also helped to prevent the achievement of freedom as a consequence of revolution.

---

*This part of Dr. Arendt's analysis is, in my opinion, the least adequate in the book. She did not mention the relevant and frequently close relationship between economic and political control. Struggles of the poor do not inevitably produce terror. Compassion and rage do not always lead to violence. And swift direct action can be nonviolent. This does not, however, invalidate the overall analysis of the book, as her point is not that the social question *directly* leads to disaster in the revolution, but that it leads to violence and terror, and "it is terror which sends revolutions to their doom..." (p. 108).

By saying that violence is one reason why revolutions have not led to the establishment of political freedom, Arendt was in effect saying that the means used in a political struggle are instrumental, and that they help to determine the type of political order which results from the conflict. Furthermore, if the assumption that violence is necessary for all foundations and new beginnings is false, so too must be the assumption that violence is "supposedly unavoidable in all revolutions" (p. 215).

†"Professional revolutionaries" are persons who have accepted a doctrine or ideology of revolution, and are usually organized into a disciplined, hierarchically structured Party which is believed by its members to be the necessary vehicle for instituting the revolution, to the service of which they have committed their lives.

Revolutions, mass popular uprisings against oppressive systems, are of course not the work of professional revolutionaries. Revolutions, instead, result from the collapse of the ruler's authority — belief in the ruler's right to rule — and the consequent withdrawal of support and obedience by the citizens, especially members of the military forces. In the period of instability which occurs during this revolution, the professional revolutionaries become influential and rise to power. Their influence, Arendt continued, is invariably exerted in accordance with the past pattern of revolution, especially the French Revolution, directly or indirectly. This was scarcely an ideal model, for it disintegrated into a chaos of internal and international violence, and led not to freedom but to a new dictatorship and war throughout Europe. Yet, from *this* revolution the professional revolutionaries "learned" how to make a revolution, trying to imitate its course of events which were believed to be "necessary." Other experience which differed from that model was ignored. Specifically, the professional revolutionaries have persistently ignored or belittled a quite different revolutionary tradition which did not fit their preconceptions, as we shall explore shortly.

3. Authority. In order to last, a new body politic must have "authority" — that is, the people's belief in its legitimacy. Every revolution therefore faces the problem of how to make the new order legitimate.

People have often believed that such authority must come from some source which is believed to be absolute, which is comprehensive and unchallengeable. Before the revolution, such an absolute source of authority was provided by religion or an absolute sovereign ("the divine right of kings" to rule as they wished without challenge or interference from others). When the old ruler was deposed and these sources of absolute authority were repudiated, however, the quest for an absolute source of authority was continued; this was supplied by the abstract concepts of "the Nation" or "the Revolution" or a combination of both. This enabled the new rulers who claimed to speak and act for the Nation or the Revolution also to claim the right to rule without challenge or interference from others, and hence contributed to despotism, not to freedom.

For a political system to last, for it to possess the needed authority to provide legitimacy, there is no need for an absolute source of authority, Arendt argued. Authority need not come from some high source capable of pronouncing on the way the political institutions of mere people must operate. Authority can instead come "from below," from the people coming together and themselves founding their new political order by deliberation, joint decision, and action (p. 165). *That* source of authority is compatible with freedom.

4. Sovereignty. Revolutionaries have failed to think afresh about the problem of sovereignty: the idea that there exists what Burlamaqui called "an ultimate right of command in society" deriving from a transcendent principle, with absolute authority. Such sovereignty is believed to bestow on the rulers who claim to possess it the right to control and coerce the citizens without their having the right of resistance. In the French Revolution the doctrine of sovereignty was never really attacked, Arendt continued. Instead, the abstraction *le peuple* ("the people" as a unity and with one will) simply replaced the king (p. 89).

The Americans dealt with the problem very differently. For them, "the people" was *not* an abstraction nor a unity, nor a single will. Instead, the people were conceived as a plurality, as a "manyness," as a large number of individuals possessing different opinions. In prerevolutionary colonial America the settlers had constituted themselves into "civil bodies politic" which were not really governments as much as political societies (p. 167). These formed a political system which possessed power and claimed rights, but which neither possessed nor claimed sovereignty. ". . . [P]erhaps the greatest American innovation in politics as such was the consistent abolition of sovereignty within the body politic of the republic, the insight that in the realm of human affairs sovereignty and tyranny are the same" (p. 152).

5. Creativity. Revolutionaries, in Arendt's opinion, have also failed to establish a new order which is both lasting and creatively adaptable. Instead they have destroyed freedom, either in the effort to preserve the new order against change, or by the effort to impose on the nonparticipating citizens continuous change directed by the political minority which claimed alone to "know" what was required and was good for the revolutionary society.

The American system perhaps approached the solution to this problem of how to establish a lasting but creatively adaptable new order more closely than did other postrevolutionary regimes. But even the American system did not solve it, Arendt insisted. Thomas

Jefferson was acutely aware of this failure, and feared lest " the abstract political system of democracy lacked concrete organs" (p. 238). He sought ways to meet this danger. First, he advocated periodic new rebellions. Then, after seeing more clearly the dangers of such rebellions, Jefferson proposed frequent revisions of the constitution. When he later saw this, too, to be inadequate, he developed a third proposal. This was closely related to Arendt's own recommendation, which we shall shortly explore.

6. Government. Despite the aim of establishing political freedom, all the regimes which have followed revolutions have continued the division between the rulers and the ruled — a division highly dangerous for freedom, Arendt argued. Such regimes were not all equal, of course. The degree to which the ruler's power has been limited or tyrannical in such regimes has varied considerably, and that difference is important. By Arendt's definition of freedom, however, that very separation means that political freedom has not been established; that division makes it possible for even mild rule to open the way to more blatantly antidemocratic rulers.

Although some people would argue that this division between the rulers and the ruled is inevitable and in the very nature of government, she insisted that this is not true. This division need not exist. A modern political system could be developed in which people could in political matters become their own rulers. She based that view on certain participatory political systems which have emerged in various countries and circumstances, but which have been largely ignored by both the professional revolutionaries and those who have studied revolutions.

7. Theory. A last reason why revolutions have not achieved political freedom has been the failure of people to develop the theory appropriate to that system of freedom. Concepts and theories have important practical consequences, Arendt insisted. Without the development of theory and the preservation of the memory of past experience in political freedom, there are no guideposts for the future. Instead, we get the "automatic thought-reactions" and the automatic pursuit of the sterile tradition of the French Revolution (p. 225). Political freedom in the future may, therefore, in large degree depend on the development of political thought on how to achieve, operate, and preserve a society characterized by political freedom.

ORGANS OF DIRECT SELF-GOVERNMENT

Past revolutions have failed to establish political freedom, therefore, for reasons which reach down into the very nature of politics itself. Obviously, no ready-made system exists which can be adopted overnight in place of the various present systems of government. There exist, however, Arendt argued, very important contributions to a solution to this problem. Certain experiences — and a very little theory — give us some direction. The experiences she listed are European and American, although examples could also have come from non-Western sources.

Important modern experience exists with direct participating democracy in the course of various revolutionary situations, Arendt pointed out. This constitutes the beginnings of a new system of government which could potentially avoid the dangers of violent revolution, solve successfully the above seven problems, prevent tyranny, and also transcend the limitations of party-parliamentary democracy. This experience which provides the germ of an alternative political system is drawn from America, France, Russia, Germany, and Hungary.

Colonial Americans had, as we noted, considerable experience with direct participating self-government without a division between the ruler and the ruled. After the War of Independence, when the state and federal constitutions were established, however, the local units of direct self-government were not incorporated into the new political system. Because of this, Jefferson "feared an 'elective despotism' as bad as, or worse than, the tyranny they had risen against..." (p. 241). Under the new American machinery of government, Arendt argued, only the representatives of the people, not the people themselves could exercise political freedom. The failure to incorporate the town meetings and the townships was equivalent to their "death sentence" (p. 242), while the people were condemned to "lethargy and inattention to public business" by their exclusion from direct participation (p. 241). Periodic elections were an insufficient substitute for direct involvement in deliberations and decisions.

After Jefferson retired from active political life, he argued that the "elementary republics" of direct participation must be incorporated into the new political system (p. 252). He saw them as a peaceful alternative to his earlier notion of the need for recurring revolutions.

These small units would enable people to *be* republicans and to *act* as citizens, to *participate* in public business, even though the county, state, and federal governments were too large to permit immediate participation of all citizens. Thus, Jefferson argued, "these little republics would be the main strength of the great one" and would be part of the wider political system (p. 257).

> The elementary republics of the wards, the county republics, the State republics, and the republic of the Union would form a gradation of authorities, standing each on the basis of law, holding every one its delegated share of powers, and constituting truly a system of fundamental balances and checks for the government [p. 258].

This system would prevent tyranny, because with every citizen feeling himself to be a "participator in the government of affairs" and "a member of some one of its councils, great or small, he will let the heart be torn out of his body sooner than his power wrested from him by a Caesar or a Bonaparte" (pp. 257-258). Jefferson, writing in 1816, thus clearly connected this system of government to the society's will and capacity to maintain and defend its freedom against usurpation by would-be tyrants.

While the bodies of popular participation in the governance of the political society had developed in colonial America before the War of Independence ("the Revolution"), in France comparable bodies emerged during the revolution. They were, Arendt wrote, "the unexpected and largely spontaneous outcome of the Revolution itself" (p. 242). These bodies were the Paris Commune (with its 48 sections) and the independent spontaneous clubs and societies called *sociétés populaires,* which spread all over France. Collot d'Hervois wrote that these societies "openly aimed at the establishment of a new federalism" (p. 248).

Each of these organs of direct self-government possessed an internal power structure of its own. Together such bodies diffused effective power throughout the political society, removing the distinction between the ruler and the ruled. This popular movement constituted the first beginnings "of a true republic" and was, Arendt continued, a clear danger to centralized State power (p. 248). A conflict existed, therefore, between the communal movement of popular self-government and the revolutionary parties committed to centralism which sought control of politics and the State for themselves. This was *not,* Arendt insisted, a fight between the street and the body politic as it has sometimes been represented, but instead "the conflict between the people and a mercilessly centralized power apparatus" (p. 247). It was a conflict between the concept of the Nation-State and the federal principle with its separation and division of power which derived only from the spontaneous efforts of the people to organize themselves.

Both Robespierre and Saint Just* once supported these popular bodies, but when they came to power they assisted in their destruction. The Jacobin Government and the parties infiltrated these popular bodies and destroyed them from within. The Jacobins and the parties then converted what was left of the popular bodies into organs of the parties and of the central Government, and into instruments of terror. Freedom then ceased to be public and political, and became restricted to the individual's private life.

The American colonial experience, Jefferson's plan, and the French experience were followed by the emergence elsewhere of similar bodies of direct participating democracy, Arendt pointed out, the workers' councils, *soviets,* and the *Räte,* "which were to make their appearance in every genuine revolution throughout the nineteenth and twentieth centuries" (p. 252). Such bodies appeared in Paris under the Prussian siege in 1870. More importantly, they were present in the Paris Commune of 1871, the Russian Revolutions of 1905 and Februrary 1917 (continuing on until the Bolshevik coup), in Germany in 1918-1919, and in the 1956 Hungarian Revolution. Contrary to the expectations of the professional revolutionaries, these new instruments of popular self-government did not regard themselves as mere temporary instruments but "clearly intended to survive the revolution" (p. 260).

This development contradicted the theories of the professional revolutionaries and — what is more important — the assumptions about the nature of power which they shared with their former rulers. The professional revolutionaries had thought of revolution as a seizure of power; this, they had imagined, meant a monopoly of the means of violence. But both had disintegrated, and a new power structure had been formed which owed its existence only to the organizational impulses of the people themselves.

---

*Antoine Louis Léon de Richebourg de Saint Just.

With "no power left to seize," the professional revolutionaries could only seek to impose their party organization in the place of the defunct Government, or simply join "the new revolutionary power centers which had sprung up without their help" (p. 259). Even sympathetic historians generally did not understand that out of the revolution had emerged "an entirely new form of government, with a new public space for freedom..." (p. 253).

Occasionally a single professional revolutionary was temporarily caught off guard by the new development of the council system, and momentarily faltered on the path of centralization. Karl Marx, for example, pondering on the Paris Commune of 1871, temporarily allowed himself to suggest that it might well contain "the political form, finally discovered, for the economic liberation of labor" (p. 260). With only such temporary diversions, Arendt argued, both professional revolutionaries and anarchists alike failed to grasp the importance of these developments. Parties of both the "Left" and the "Right" opposed this development. (The *soviets* as vital bodies were undermined and effectively destroyed by the Bolsheviks, surviving only in name.) Statesmen, historians, and political theorists have ignored these organs of direct democracy.

FOUNDATIONS OF A NEW REPUBLIC

Political "realists" have usually rejected direct democracy under modern conditions. They have assumed, Arendt wrote, that there must be a separation between "the party experts" who "know" and the mass of people who are to "do." In assuming the need for this cleavage, however, the "realists" have ignored "the average citizen's capacity to act and to form his own opinion.... Wherever knowing and doing have parted company, the space of freedom is lost" (p. 268). These "realists" have ignored the reality of the councils, she continued, and have assumed "that there is not, and never has been, any alternative to the present system" (pp. 274-275).

The council system is, however, as old as the party system. Ignored, without a conscious tradition, an organized influence, or a developed theory, this system of direct popular political participation has repeatedly emerged spontaneously. This provides the basis for a hope that "a new form of government" is possible which "would permit every member of the modern egalitarian society to become a 'participator' in public affairs..." (p. 268). That hope was, however, "buried in the disasters of the twentieth-century revolutions," Arendt continued (p. 268). Buried? Perhaps. But the author's whole discussion was based upon the conviction that this hope is not dead. Instead, she argued that it may yet revivify politics, and establish a new system of government, one which will go beyond limited constitutional government to a system of genuine political freedom.

The councils have combined stability with capacity for creative change. While being organs of action they have also been organs of order. They have sought, not to bring in utopia, but to lay the foundations of a new republic which would establish freedom and end forever the era of invasions and civil wars. People who have witnessed these developments have sensed the development of a force which might transform the State, as Oskar Anweiler wrote in his study of the Russian *soviets* (p. 268). Both the *soviets* of the 1917 Russian Revolution, and the workers' councils of the 1956 Hungarian Revolution showed, Arendt continued, the bare outlines of the emergence of a government based on the council system. In these cases, the local councils quickly began "a process of co-ordination and integration through the formation of higher councils of a regional or provincial character, from which the delegates to an assembly representing the whole country could be chosen" (p. 291).

Hannah Arendt acknowledged limitations to the council system of government. These include past failure to distinguish between participation and administration. She also — I think too quickly — brushed aside workers' control in industry, arguing that management of factories is not an appropriate area for direct participation of the people involved. She acknowledged, also, that many people would not wish to take part in political deliberations; they would not be forced to do so, although they should always have that opportunity.

The author did not imply that there would be no serious problems under the proposed new system. She pointed insistently, however, to the importance of giving major attention to the discovery and examination of means by which public freedom can be achieved in our world — if, indeed, it is to be achieved at all. Wisely she recognized that the council system cannot be imposed on people from without, but must, if it is to be genuine and lasting, grow from them. She therefore concluded that it is best to say with Jefferson: "Begin them only for a single purpose; they will soon show for what others they are the best instruments" (p. 283). In a participating and creative political order people will have the opportunity, Arendt wrote, to achieve a genuine satisfaction and happiness which can be gained in no other way.

POLITICAL ORGANIZATION AND SANCTIONS

It is easy in reviewing any book to argue about details rather than coming to grips with the essence of the author's thinking. *On Revolution* is too important for that; I have devoted this much space to the simple presentation of Dr. Arendt's thought because our basic responsibility is to think about *what* she has said. Our comments and criticisms should largely be devoted to examinations of the validity of the analysis and proposal, and to related questions not adequately considered by Arendt.

Perhaps the most serious substantive criticism of the book is that Dr. Arendt — at least in 1960-61 when this book was written — did not distinguish sufficiently between the structure of political organization on the one hand and techniques of struggle and sanctions on the other. She clearly gave the impression that the council system constitutes the alternative to political violence, which can be only partly true. The provision *only* of an alternative form of government is an incomplete solution to the problems Arendt posed. The council system of government is a possible substitute for other types of government. Although violence for political ends may be especially intimately connected with certain types of government, it is not a form of political organization. Violence in politics is a technique of action, a means of struggle, and the usual ultimate sanction used to preserve a political system under attack or to impose its will upon dissident members of the society. The council system is not, therefore, the exact counterpart and substitute for political violence.

The problem is illustrated if we ask *how* a widespread council system of government is to defend itself against the political police and troops of the professional revolutionaries who are trying to impose a one-party dictatorship — as happened in Russia following the 1917 revolution. Or, we may ask how an established council system of government is to defend itself from attack by foreign troops of a neighboring dictatorship — as happened in Hungary in 1956-57. Against such internal or international violent attack, the council system is *by itself* an inadequate answer. A technique of struggle, a system of sanctions, is also required which is both effective and compatible with that system of government, that is, sanctions which are harmonious with freedom, popular participation, and the diffusion of power.

The basic choice is between violent and nonviolent techniques of struggle, violent and nonviolent sanctions. The council system of government is unsuited to wielding effectively the modern forms of military warfare against formidable opponents. If it were to do so, the strong centralizing tendencies of such violence would weaken or destroy the council system itself. Guerrilla warfare is a possible answer, but it presents other difficulties, such as ensuing social destruction, the tendency to immense casualties, and even in case of success strong long-term centralizing effects. Another possibility is nonviolent action; that technique would require further refinement and development, with attention to the difficult problems it would pose in the effort to be made effective against extreme opponents.

Violence in politics is *not* — as Arendt sometimes gave the impression — simply the result of irrational rage. Violence (as she would probably have agreed) is often in politics intended to be instrumental in achieving some desired goal. Ultimate sanctions of some type, reserved as threats or used in struggles, are necessary for all political societies, no matter how limited or widespread territorially, and no matter how tyrannical or how free. Arendt blamed violence for much of the disasters accompanying revolutions. Yet, if the sanctions used in conflicts are not to be violent ones, they must take nonviolent forms.

The technique of nonviolent action is, in fact, based upon the very theory of power which Dr. Arendt presented: ". . . power comes into being only if and when men join themselves together for the purpose of action, and will disappear when. . . they disperse and desert one another" (p. 174). She wrote of "a sudden refusal to obey [which] initiates what then turns into a revolution" (p. 230). ". . . [H]uman power. . . is simply non-existent unless it can rely on others; the most powerful king and the least scrupulous of all tyrants are helpless if no one obeys them, that is, supports them through obedience; for, in politics, obedience and support are the same" (p. 230).

A nonviolent technique of struggle based upon this theory of power exists and is being developed.[1] Therefore, contrary to the view expressed in *On Revolution,* "war" and "revolution" without violence *are* possible. (In fact, one of the classics on this technique is titled *War without Violence.*[2]) This has fundamental implications for the discussion of means for dealing with tyranny under present conditions.

We need to give serious attention both to the question of the structure of a society which is compatible with political freedom, and also to the question of the sanctions relied upon by the society to defend itself and to enforce its standards and policies. Usually both of these questions have been largely ignored because so few people have been able to think very much outside the political assumptions of our own society. Hannah Arendt has opened the way for a discussion of political organization, just as Joan V. Bondurant in *Conquest of Violence*[3] opened the discussion of sanctions. Neither book was intended by its author to be the last word, but only to initiate a rethinking of politics in light of the inadequacies of traditional thought and practice. These are especially serious in light of the dual problems of modern war and totalitarianism. In their respective books Arendt and Bondurant have issued challenges to others to join in this effort to rethink politics. Those challenges still stand, awaiting those who are prepared to accept them.

NOTES

1. On the technique of nonviolent action, see Gene Sharp, **The Politics of Nonviolent Action** (Boston: Porter Sargent Publisher, 1973).
2. Krishnalal Shridharani, **War without Violence: A Study of Gandhi's Method and Its Accomplishments** (New York: Harcourt, Brace, & Co., 1939, and London: Victor Gollancz, 1939. Reprinted: New York and London: Garland Publishing, 1972. Revised updated edition: Bombay: Bharatiya Vidya Bhavan, 1972). See Gene Sharp, **Gandhi as a Political Strategist** (Boston: Porter Sargent Publishers, 1979), Appendix A, "Shridharani's Contribution to the Study of Gandhi's Technique."
3. Joan V. Bondurant, **Conquest of Violence: The Gandhian Philosophy of Conflict** (Princeton: Princeton University Press, 1958; London: Oxford University Press, 1958; and Berkeley: University of California Press, 1965). See also Gene Sharp, **Gandhi as a Political Strategist,** Chapter Four, "*Satyagraha* and Political Conflict."

7

What Is Required to Uproot Oppression?

Strategic Problems of the South African Resistance

The problem of how to uproot oppression effectively with minimal casualties and maximum long-range benefits to the liberated people still remains without an adequate solution. The people of South Africa have long awaited its resolution. Although this chapter is an edited synopsis of four articles published in 1963, with only a few changes and additions, its major points are, in 1980 — seventeen years later — still as relevant as when they were written, despite certain very limited new signs of Government flexibility.

In whatever way the South African conflict may be finally resolved, many people throughout the world will continue for many years to face the general problem of how to uproot oppression. It is hoped that this chapter will raise questions and suggest possible directions for consideration by people who are still seeking more adequate answers to the question of what is required to end oppression.

*   *   *   *

The situation in South Africa is now a desperate one. The Government, backed by the "opposition" United Party,* has for years increased its dictatorship over the predominantly non-European population. Every means of change has been dammed up. The flood waters are rapidly rising. For South Africa there is no way out which does not involve severe suffering and bloodshed. If nothing is done the situation will grow worse, and the constant suffering of the people and violence of the Government will increase, contributing finally to a terrifying explosion. Whether nonviolent or violent means of resistance are used, great suffering will be incurred by the non-European people. Anyone who opposes action on the grounds that it will lead to suffering is profoundly ignorant of the situation. The problem is how to act effectively to change that situation, and whether the suffering will help to achieve a free, humane society.

This chapter is an attempt to contribute to an understanding of that problem, and thereby shed some light on its solution. My aim, therefore, is not to "judge" or "condemn" or "instruct" but to contribute a few thoughts to the general quest for a solution. The problem of South Africa is one for all humanity. We all have much to learn from the South African experience.

In seeking a course of action we must accept the fact that no matter what is done, there will be a hard core of Afrikaners who will never agree voluntarily to the abolition of apartheid. One must also accept that many European South Africans are so committed to their position of power and wealth that they will continue to react to every challenge, by whatever means, with increased rigidity. One must, therefore, expect that they will respond by vigorous repression, and that the abolition of apartheid and European domination will come only after a protracted struggle.

*The United Party collapsed in 1977 as the result of internal dissension. Two new parties were created: the New Republic Party and the South African Party. Other former United Party members joined the Progressive Reform Party, which was renamed the Progressive Federal Party, now the second largest party in the country.

Simple moralizing about how to deal with this problem will not suffice. A course of action is required. In addition to specific methods of action in particular situations, attention must be given to the tactics to operate in particular phases of the struggle, and to the overall strategy to guide the course of the struggle.

A consideration of some of the problems of an overall strategy should include three areas:

1. How to achieve the maximum strength and involvement in the struggle by the non-Europeans, mainly the Africans.*

2. How to split some of the Europeans from support for the Afrikaner Nationalists and European domination, and move them toward action in support of the non-Europeans.

3. How to bring the maximum international pressures to bear on the South African Government toward change compatible with the self-determination of the South African people as a whole and their future development.

There are two main techniques of struggle which could be applied by the non-Europeans of South Africa: some form of revolutionary violence, or large-scale noncooperation and defiance without violence — that is, nonviolent action. The violence would probably follow the general model of the Algerian struggle, a type of terrorist guerrilla warfare. An exact model for the nonviolent alternative does not exist, although there are experiences and thought both within and without South Africa on which to draw.

RECONSIDERING THE EFFICACY OF VIOLENCE

The pendulum has swung heavily in favor of violence. "On all sides now there is a fatalistic acceptance of the inevitability of vio-

---

*Despite the time-honored practice of referring to persons of European descent as "white" and of African descent as "black," I have resisted this. These terms are themselves a product of a racist society, and make it inevitable that we see not the actual color variations with infinite gradations — which make dichotomous racism extremely difficult — but instead two clear separate groups. That makes racism, and its practices of prejudice, discrimination, slavery, segregation, and apartheid thinkable, and therefore possible. The *view* of reality behind our words often has grave consequences when it results from false preconceptions, distorts reality, and is a precursor of disastrous practices.

The term "non-Europeans" was used by the Unity Movement to refer to Africans, Cape Colored people, Indians, and other Asians.

lence," wrote Colin Legum in *The Observer*. "The long period of support for [African National] Congress's methods of nonviolent struggle (as embodied in Chief Luthuli) is past. All talk now is about the tactics of violence, no longer about its relevance."[1] Bitterness, frustration, and helplessness build up to the point where a violent explosion becomes almost inevitable. The past failure of nonviolent action to achieve major victories leads to its rejection. The Government attempt to prevent all forms of protest leads to the understandable feeling that one must strike back.

Despite widespread lip service, the world's response to the non-Europeans' pleas for economic boycott and political, diplomatic, and cultural ostracism of the Afrikaner Government has been pitifully small, so that non-Europeans naturally become disillusioned with the potential of such means. Despite some gestures, the world's nonviolence movement has been unable to offer any major assistance, whether in the form of spearheading the international boycott or by providing helpful information and analyses of problems of resistance, or consultants (where wanted) to contribute to the consideration of serious strategic and tactical problems in an effective nonviolent struggle.

Although they have obviously been inadequate, significant and sacrificial efforts to apply nonviolent struggle have been made by the non-Europeans. No one would deny that if a peaceful way out of the situation were believed possible, they would choose it.

Nevertheless, the doctrinal approach of salvation by violence has gained such a following that fair consideration of alternative courses of action may not be given unless the adequacy of violence is challenged on strategic grounds, and unless certain qualities of nonviolent action are examined. This consideration of the advantages and disadvantages of violent and nonviolent action is often difficult because of impatience with intellectual analysis of revolutionary problems and because of justified distaste for the vague generalizing and moralizing which has often been poured out by exponents of nonviolent means.

There are important reasons for *not* accepting the inevitability of the resistance movement's relying upon violence to achieve victory. It is not sufficient to have an emotional release of hatred in acts of violence, any more than it is enough to have a growth of self-respect in the person defying the government in nonviolent action. Consideration must also be given to the way in which the proposed course of action will contribute to the success of the movement.

Recognition of the difficulties and dangers of a future struggle by nonviolent resistance, and of the inadequacy of the past nonviolent movement, is not in itself an argument in favor of adopting violence. It is also necessary to consider the difficulties and dangers of a future struggle both by guerrilla warfare and terrorism and also by possible new types of nonviolent struggle. If a responsible consideration of the alternatives is to be made it must include a comparison of the advantages and disadvantages of each technique of struggle, and a consideration of whether the disadvantages of each can be overcome or are counterbalanced by other factors. There is little evidence that this is taking place. Colin Legum wrote that "the loss of faith in the efficacy of the old methods does not always go with a realistic assessment of the chances that violence might prove to be equally unsuccessful."[2]

So many difficulties and dangers are involved in the choice of struggle by violence in South Africa that a reconsideration of *its* efficacy is now merited alongside an exploration of whether a struggle by nonviolent means can be developed which is more effective than that of the past. While military superiority does not guarantee victory — especially in guerrilla warfare — it is important to note that the South African Government possesses vast military superiority over anything that the non-European South Africans could hope to muster, barring extensive and highly dangerous international intervention.

Indeed, it is in many ways an *advantage* to the South African Government for the non-Europeans to resort to violence. This provides the excuse for extremely harsh repression which could produce still further demoralization among the Africans, Cape Colored people, Indians, and other Asians. It has been suggested that in at least one instance the government may already have deliberately provoked violence by the use of *agents provocateurs* at the end of the 1952 Defiance Campaign of civil disobedience. The riots between 18 October and 9 November 1952 — while the campaign was at its peak — resulted in the deaths of six Europeans and thirty-three Africans. This greatly helped the Europeans to identify the nonviolent campaign with the violent African Mau Mau movement in Kenya — and thus counter the tendency of some Europeans to sympathize with it.

The riots also helped crush the spirit of resistance among the non-Europeans. In October 1952, for example, 2,354 volunteers defied apartheid laws, while in November and December combined, only 280 did so. This violence was not the only factor involved in the collapse of the movement. (Fear of increased severity of sentences was important, as were, it is suggested by some, internal activities of Communists within the movement.) Yet, said Leo Kuper in his study of this campaign, "Clearly the riots played a decisive role." They also "provided the opportunity for the government to take over the initiative and to assume far-reaching powers with some measure of justification."[3]

The killing of African demonstrators at Sharpeville on 21 March 1960 is often cited as a justification for abandoning nonviolent action. This view is, however, based upon a lack of understanding of the dynamics of nonviolent action. (It is not widely remembered that the shootings at Sharpeville began after some Africans broke nonviolent discipline, throwing stones at the police, and that this was preceded by a riot at Cato Manor not long before, which may have made the police more jumpy, and may have increased their brutality at Sharpeville.) It was, however, precisely because the killings were perceived as committed against peaceful unarmed demonstrators that there was aroused in South Africa and throughout the world such deep feeling and vigorous protests. Had the same number of Africans been killed in police firings against an undisciplined mob invading a European residential area to commit arson and murder there would have been no such reaction. Compare, for example, the attention and protests aroused over the deaths of less than a hundred Africans at Sharpeville with the indifference to the deaths of any particular hundred Algerians in the Algerian struggle.

The murders at Sharpeville revealed, to those who had not yet realized it, the real nature of the South African Government and its policies. Immediately following this there was very considerable international support for the boycott programs. In Norway, flags all over the country were flown at half-mast after Sharpeville. This was symbolic of its impact — an impact that would have been sharply reduced if the South African Government could have shown that those shot were terrorists rather than courageous nonviolent demonstrators. Witness, for example, the comparatively small reaction to the executions of the Poqo terrorists.

COSTS AND EFFECTS OF NONVIOLENT STRUGGLE

There are some very naive conceptions about the nature of nonviolent resistance prevalent among both its advocates and opponents. It is not true that if opponents of a regime struggle nonviolently the oppressive regime will be nonviolent too, and quietly acquiesce. It is not true that by being nonviolent one avoids suffering and sacrifices. It is not true that if the opponent reacts with brutal, violent repression, the struggle has been lost and the movement defeated. It is not true that the nonviolent way is an easy way.

Quite the contrary. One must expect that if the non-Europeans resist by nonviolent but militant means, there will be suffering and deaths. This is in part a consequence of the very violence of the social and political system which is being attacked. And violent repression is in part a tribute to the power of nonviolent action and a recognition of the threat it poses to the continued existence of that system.

At the time when the opponent intensifies his repression, the resisters must demonstrate great courage and not only continue but also *increase* their resistance. This has not always taken place in South Africa. This willingness to persist despite repression produces political *jiu-jitsu*. That is, the government's supposed greater power is made ineffective and turned to its own disadvantage. The repression of nonviolent people tends to alienate sympathy and support for the government — among those who might join the resistance, the government's usual supporters, and throughout the world — as the regime is seen as dependent upon, and willing to use, naked, brutal violence against nonviolent human beings. This may lead to increased numbers of people becoming determined to resist such a system. It may also lead to divisions within the government's own camp. Given a sufficient growth of numbers, the massiveness of the defiance by courageous resisters may, in an advanced stage, be so vast as to immobilize even the agencies of repression.

The cost of change may thus be a terrible one, but no worse than that incurred by violence. The indications are that although in a nonviolent resistance movement there is severe suffering, this is far less than in a violent resistance movement. In proportion to the numbers involved there were far fewer deaths in the nonviolent struggle in India than there were in the Mau Mau campaign in Kenya — both struggles waged against British rule. The information we have about the series of strikes in Russian prison camps, occurring primarily in 1953, indicates that where the strikes were conducted largely nonviolently, the number of casualties was much lower than where a great deal of violence occurred. Similarly, among the Indian campaigns themselves, those in which there was little or no violence were accompanied by fewer injuries or deaths than those campaigns in which there was substantial violence. In the Indian struggle for independence as a whole, probably not more than eight thousand died directly or indirectly as a result of shootings and other injuries inflicted in the course of the struggle over a long period. The immense number of casualties in Algeria — estimated as high as one million — in a population not exceeding ten million — a fraction that of India — is quite alarming. This is *not* explained by accusing the French of being by nature more savage than the English.

The cost of a violent revolt is likely to be much higher than that of a nonviolent revolt. Impatience with the *expected* slowness of change by nonviolent action (based only on South African experience) ought not to blind one to the length of time that a violent struggle would take. Defeats and stalemates also occur when violent means are used, and sometimes nonviolent means work rapidly. Both violent and nonviolent techniques of struggle require sacrifice and time in which to operate. In certain circumstances one technique may appear to be somewhat quicker than the other. But, even then, other important factors must be considered, such as the likely number of casualties and the kind of a society which will result from the struggle.

The South African struggle is a movement to cast off tyranny and achieve freedom. It is, therefore, very important whether the technique of struggle used is likely to do this, or whether, at best, it is likely to remove one dominating minority and replace it by another. Violent struggles tend to be followed by the concentration of power in the hands of those who control the effective means of violence — usually the army and the police. The population, then disarmed and knowing no other means of struggle, is relatively helpless in the face of rulers with such means of violent repression.

The simple destruction of one form of tyranny does not in itself bring freedom. That would require the diffusion — not the further concentration — of power. The simple destruction of European domination in South Africa without diffusing power among the people and their organizations and institutions will mean that at least as much power will be concentrated in the hands of the new government as is now the case. Probably it would be more, as there are constant pressures for centralization in newly liberated countries. This is serious, for we know from experience that the leaders of a resistance movement often do not remain rulers after victory, and that a single party or even a single man often becomes dominant. Even if this does not develop immediately in its extreme forms, the very concentration of power even in the hands of the most restrained and benevolent ruler makes it possible, if a coup d'état takes place, for a usurping despot to impose an especially thorough and complete form of tyranny.

In contrast, nonviolent struggle tends to diffuse power through the population as a whole. The course of the struggle itself depends on voluntary widespread popular support and participation. After a successful conclusion to the struggle, the concentration of military power in the hands of the commanders (which could be used to bolster a new dictatorship) does not occur, and the population is trained in effective means of struggle by which it can maintain and extend its freedom against new usurpers. These considerations are highly important if one is really concerned with achieving freedom, and not simply with replacing one tyrannical system with another. The disastrous consequences of violence for political ends should prod us to seek other, nonviolent, solutions to even the most difficult problems.

INADEQUATE NONVIOLENT STRUGGLE

These criticisms of violence by no means imply that the nonviolent movement in South Africa has been adequate. First, there has not been enough of it. *That is, inaction, nonresistance, and an absence of violence are by no means to be equated with nonviolent action.*

The Indian minority in South Africa, using nonviolent action under Mohandas K. Gandhi's leadership between 1906 and 1914, achieved great improvements in their situation. However, nonviolent action was not again used in South Africa on a comparable scale against segregation and discrimination until 1946, again by the Indians to gain relief from the "Ghetta Act." Since then there have been several African bus boycotts (some successful), the 1952 Defiance Campaign (in which over 8,500 non-Europeans were imprisoned for civil disobedience of apartheid laws), the Pan-Africanists' defiance of the pass laws in 1960 which culminated in Sharpeville, and attempts to organize widespread strikes (which were apparently more success-ful than the Government admitted at the time — for example, the three day general strike in 1961). There have been other similar actions. But it is clear that nonviolent action has been sporadic, and there have been long periods of inaction. This has often been for very understandable and necessary reasons. But where these periods of inaction have been necessary, that necessity has been produced by the weakness of the resistance movement and the non-European popula-tion. (Imagine an army which only fought scattered skirmishes after intervals of weeks or months in a war, or major campaigns only after intervals of months or years!)

Inaction, however, even in such situations as South Africa, sometimes tends not to strengthen but to weaken the subordinates still further. *The belief that advances will be made as long as there is simple abstention from violence is false.* If a resistance movement in situations such as South Africa only undertakes nonviolent action sporadically, it will not achieve significant results unless the subordi-nates are considerably strengthened and their organization grows in the "silent" periods.

Nor can a nonviolent struggle be successful if the participants and the population are unwilling to pay the price of resistance. This is something which is very similar in the case of a violent struggle. If in a war of the old type the infantry collapses under heavy enemy fire, that side cannot win. The fault in such a situation is not with war itself, but with the ability of the troops to *wage* war. Similarly, in nonviolent struggle, when the opponent applies repression and increases that repression, to have a chance of victory the nonviolent actionists must have the strength to persist and court the greater penalties for their defiance. If they lack sufficient strength to do so, the fault is not in the technique but in the actionists themselves.

Thus in 1952, when the Government instituted severe punish-ments for civil disobedience, it was a grave tactical error not to *increase* the defiance. Nor should the Pan-Africanists have been taken by surprise in 1960 when in response to their defiance the Government declared an emergency. Withdrawal at such a point allows the Government to regain the upper hand and for an atmosphere of fear and conformity to become predominant among the non-Europeans once again. Yet another weakness existed in past nonviolent movements. One of the clever means which the Government has frequently adopted for dealing with nonviolent action has been to remove the non-European leaders from the political struggle without making them martyrs and sources of inspiration by imprisonment. For example, a person may be "named" and "liquidated" under the Suppression of Communism Act and thereby be prohibited from maintaining or taking out membership in specific political organizations, exercising leadership of them, or attending political gatherings. National leaders were sometimes tried under that Act, found guilty, sentenced to several years' imprisonment, to be suspended *provided they did not again commit an offense under that Act.* Under the Riotous Assemblies and Criminal Law Amendment Act a person can be exiled to an area far from his or her home, work, and activities. The alternative for the non-European leaders has been years of imprisonment. This alternative is personally severe, but so also can be the political consequences of accepting withdrawal from political activities and even exile.

One of the objective results of the leaders' choice of accepting these limitations, instead of refusing to comply and going to prison, has been to set an example harmful to future resistance. The ordinary opponent of apartheid is not likely to risk a greater punishment than the leaders are seen to be suffering. Yet willingness to undergo imprisonment and other suffering is a primary requirement of change. It is significant that Robert Sobukwe, who founded the Pan-Africanist Congress, chose to be among the first to go to prison for civil disobedience.[4] Albert Luthuli, on the other hand, implied in his autobiography that he intended to conform to the ban until it expired in May 1964 (though it was doubtful under the circumstances that he would then be allowed to resume political activity).[5] The Government thus achieved the advantages which come from imprisoning the non-European leaders without incurring any disadvantages.

All of these and other influences have tended to reduce the militancy and activity of the nonviolent resistance movement. Yet in such a situation if there is no vigorous nonviolent resistance and defiance, no sufficiently strong movement to be a source of real hope (if not of major immediate victories), then it is virtually certain that in desperation a shift to violence will take place.

THE MAIN TASK: STRENGTHEN THE OPPRESSED

The South African Government — like every government no matter how democratic or how tyrannical — is dependent for its continued existence upon the willingness of its subjects to continue to cooperate with it and submit to it. This cooperation and submission may take various forms, such as helping to run the economic system, serving as government employees, and simple obedience of the laws and orders of the regime.

This consent may at times be "free" — based upon support for the regime or passive submission to it. At other times, it may be "forced" — that is, acquiescence may be procured because the people are afraid of the imprisonment or other sanctions which may be imposed upon them if they refuse to cooperate. But even "forced consent" reflects the choice that it is better to submit and avoid the penalties than to defy and incur the suffering. In either case the continued existence of any regime is the result, not simply of the wishes and determination of those persons and groups directly controlling the State machinery, but primarily of the submission and cooperation of the people as a whole. The cost of defiance may vary. In some situations, as South Africa, it may be terrifyingly high. The people's ability to withdraw their consent may also vary, depending upon their determination, strength, and willingness to pay the price for change.

The problem of altering the existing Government or of achieving a revolution is, therefore, not simply one of attacking the existing rulers and their immediate agents. The primary responsibility, both for continuing the present system and for producing change, thus falls on the majority of the population, without whose submission and cooperation the system — after a bloody attempt to force a resumption of cooperation — would collapse. The achievement of change in South Africa thus depends upon increasing the strength of the non-Europeans, predominantly the Africans.

Change can thus be achieved even if the present rulers are never convinced that it is desirable. *The main task is to strengthen the people. Their determination to abolish the system must be increased. Their organizational strength and ability to act corporately and spontaneously must be improved. Their willingness to persist in defiance despite repression must be strengthened.*

The condition of real liberty or tyranny in any political society is thus largely a reflection of the past and present strength or weakness of the people as a whole. If the people are now weak and fearful, unable or unwilling to pay the price of suffering for the withdrawal of their consent, then no real and lasting freedom can be achieved. Real freedom is not something which is given, but rather something which is earned and taken, and which can therefore be defended and extended even in the face of new attacks.

Therefore, those — including important non-European leaders — who now look to liberation of South Africa by *solely* external intervention are attempting to by-pass the most important single revolutionary problem and to achieve a short cut to freedom when there is none. Even if the present Afrikaner Nationalist Government is abolished by external intervention, and European domination is thereby ended, that will not necessarily bring an end to oppression in South Africa. If in the process the people as a whole are not strengthened and their own ability to win and defend their freedom is not increased, if no effective diffusion of power among them occurs, if no increase takes place in their ability to control their rulers themselves, then the succeeding Government — no matter what its color — will be at least as tyrannical as that which it replaced. Having depended on external aid to end one system, the people would then still lack the ability to achieve real freedom.

Terrorist and guerrilla movements often recognize to a considerable degree the importance of the withdrawal of cooperation and consent from the government. This helps to explain why so often the terror is directed not against the "enemy" as one might expect, but primarily against one's own people, to force them into resistance. (There are signs that this is already beginning in South Africa.) It is thus an attempt to force people to be free, an attempt to achieve the impossible. Even if politically successful in destroying the existing Government, the kind of society and the kind of liberation which is thereby produced is of highly questionable worth.

Evidence exists that nonviolent action can significantly assist in increasing the strength of oppressed people. Mohandas K. Gandhi always argued that the *primary* aim of the nonviolent struggles he led in India was not to attack the British, who were an important but secondary factor in the situation, but to strengthen the determination, independence, and ability to resist of the Indians. *They* were the most important factor.

This was demonstrated in South Africa in 1952 in the Defiance Campaign, during which membership of the African National Congress jumped from 7,000 to 100,000. The number of members is not the only criterion for increased strength, but this is one indication of the contribution of nonviolent action to increased capacity to resist, and increased organizational strength. Similarly, in India the Indian National Congress was transformed under Gandhi's program from a tiny group passing yearly resolutions into a mass fighting organization capable of shaking the mighty British Empire.

Among the factors which could help strengthen the capacity of people to resist are:
- increased self-respect;
- strengthening of their institutions and capacity to act in solidarity;
- dissemination of knowledge on the use of nonviolent struggle, and how to organize for group action;
- awareness of what others have done elsewhere in difficult situations;
- the example of some people among themselves resisting the tyranny — which may inspire others and be contagious;
- an imaginative accepted leadership to spark the situation;
- a new idea (or a new insight into an old idea) which may suddenly give people a new confidence, especially if it relates something they can do to help solve the problem;
- unplanned actions, breaking the spell of conformity and moving others to action also; and
- participation in nonviolent action on a small scale: this may itself contribute to increased confidence in one's capacity to change the situation, especially if limited objectives can be won.

Often — though not always — as people begin to act, the qualities of courage, willingness to serve others, and concern about the social and political evils around them grow within themselves. Further, their example often helps others to gain these qualities. This, along with other results of nonviolent action, helps to improve that society's capacity for freedom.

It has been argued, for example by Patrick Duncan, that because the South African Government has made all conventional political efforts by non-Europeans to produce change illegal and has forbidden the use of nonviolent action to alter apartheid, violence is now justified. It is, however, very superficial reasoning to conclude that because nonviolent action has been made illegal, violence should now be used. Violent resistance is equally unlawful, and this argument does not address in practical terms the need for effectiveness.

Increasing government repression now makes it much more difficult to organize nonviolent resistance — especially openly — than it was in 1952. But it is no easier to organize violent resistance. It is true that nonviolent resistance is usually most effectively organized openly. However, in a violent movement, agents and informers make secrecy less than totally effective. Also, while we should keep in mind the dangers involved, nonviolent resistance has been effectively organized secretly while practiced openly — as with much of the Norwegian resistance under the Nazi occupation. Furthermore, not all nonviolent resistance need be organized in advance to be effective. At times, highly effective resistance has been quite spontaneous. At other times, actions planned and initiated by a very small number of people may strike a responsive chord, and their example may be followed by large numbers of people.

FACTORS IN A STRATEGY FOR CHANGE

It is extremely difficult now to work out wise strategy and tactics for the struggle in South Africa, yet very important that serious efforts be made to do this. Only thus can a serious alternative to terrorism and guerrilla warfare and to military invasion gain a serious hearing. Unfortunately, we do not have all the knowledge we should have for developing wise strategy, one reason being the lack of interest in, and resources for, the kind of research and analysis which could have expanded our knowledge.

At least five major tasks need to receive careful consideration in working out that strategy:

1. Examine the present condition of South Africa, signs of rigidity and flexibility, strengths and weaknesses, and in particular the condition and potentialities of various groups which may hinder or aid resistance, especially:

(a) the Government;

(b) the European opposition and potential opposition to the Government;

(c) the non-European activists and organizations;

(d) the potential non-European resistance; and

(e) the remainder of the population.

2. Study the technique of nonviolent action, its power theory, methods, dynamics, requirements for success, and possible relevant experience elsewhere.

3. Reduce present weaknesses among the non-Europeans which would increase their ability to cast off oppression. In particular, this includes such questions as:

(a) how to increase self-esteem;

(b) how to cast off fear and increase willingness to persist in resistance despite repression;

(c) how to increase knowledge and ability to resist most effectively;

(d) how to gain confidence in their ability to change the situation (as by winning small local victories, as has already been done in the earlier bus boycotts); and

(e) how to select the specific issues (especially limited economic ones) for immediate changes.

4. Separate sections of the European South African population from support for the Government, including especially liberals, religious groups, the English minority, and the industrialists. It is significant that the 1952 Defiance Campaign was effective in this direction, leading to the establishment of both the Liberal Party and the Congress of Democrats, and leading also to limited religious opposition.

5. Stimulate the maximum international assistance and make the most effective possible use of it. There are several concrete ways in which international assistance could be given to an internal nonviolent resistance movement. These suggestions are simply illustrative:

(a) communicate news, encouragement, resistance plans, etc. to the people of South Africa by, for example, a radio station based outside South Africa, newspapers and other literature printed outside South Africa for distribution within the country;

(b) improve effectiveness of publicity and educational campaigns directed toward the rest of the world about conditions in South Africa and the resistance movement there;

(c) provide selected literature on the characteristics, requirements, and options in nonviolent struggle and additional means of training people in the use of that technique;

(d) apply more effective economic pressures against South Africa, such as a much more serious boycott and embargo movement than has been practiced hitherto (recommended by the United Nations General Assembly as long ago as November 1962);

(e) exert more effective diplomatic and cultural pressures, such as the breaking of diplomatic relations (also recommended by the UN General Assembly) and refusal of cultural cooperation, except where this involves the breakdown of apartheid practices;

(f) cut off all supplies of military weapons, replacement parts, and ammunition to South Africa (also recommended by the UN General Assembly) and of supplies which could be used for their manufacture within South Africa;

(g) withdraw all foreign investments except where the industries are willing to pay reasonable wages to non-Europeans and to abandon apartheid practices; and

(h) apply throughout the world various types of nonviolent action, as well as conventional means, to achieve these objectives.

Naturally, the major role of people outside South Africa must be in advocating and participating in such international action. International action and internal action are, however, *interdependent,* and certain types of action within South Africa are more likely to stimulate international assistance than are other types of action or inaction.

These measures could be of great assistance in (1) strengthening the morale, determination, and capacity of the non-Europeans to resist; (2) weakening the morale, determination, and capacity of the Government to continue the present course; and (3) weakening the willingness of the European population in general to support the present Government and apartheid.

The alternative to this general course of action is doubtless some form of war, probably involving either a long terrorist campaign and guerrilla struggle on the Algerian model or major international military intervention by a United Nations army, an all-African military alliance, or more direct Russian or Chinese military assistance. All of these are highly dangerous, especially where the East-West power struggle could become involved and where the conflict could degenerate into nuclear war.

At this late stage the odds are not great that the struggle will shift to a more effective application of nonviolent resistance internally, with powerful external aid. If it does not happen, however, it will be because of insufficient daring, understanding, strength, and initiative — not because, if intelligently and courageously applied, nonviolent action could not have been effective. If that does not happen, the tragedy of South Africa in the future may make the tragedy of South Africa in the past and present appear insignificant. There is still hope, however, and the opportunity. If these are seized, the world may be given a lesson in how to deal with tyranny and simultaneously to establish genuine and lasting freedom.

NOTES

1. **The Observer** (London), 5 May 1963.
2. Ibid.
3. Leo Kuper, **Passive Resistance in South Africa** (New Haven, Conn.: Yale University Press, 1957, and London: Jonathan Cape, 1956), p. 145.
4. **Robert Sobukwe (1924-1978)** became Secretary-General of the African National Congress youth league while attending Fort Hare University. He broke with the ANC in 1958 and formed the Pan-Africanist Congress, intended to conduct more militant nonviolent struggle against apartheid without the Communist influence he felt in the ANC. Under his leadership, the PAC organized mass nonviolent demonstrations and civil disobedience in 1959 and 1960 against the pass laws. He was convinced that violent resistance was suicidal and militant nonviolent struggle was the effective alternative.

   Sobukwe was arrested on 21 March 1960 on charges of incitement. He was sentenced to three years' imprisonment, detained a further six years, then released in mid-1969 and sent to Kimberly. He died there on 27 February 1978 after a long illness.

   He was regarded as a gentle, humble, intellectually brilliant man, one of the great African nationalists. Sobukwe was wrongly accused of being a racist. He urged Africans to stand on their own feet, and look forward to a South Africa in which people of different colors could live in equality.

5. **Albert Luthuli (1898?-1967)** was elected Chief of the Unvoti Mission Reserve in 1936, after serving as Secretary and President of the African Teachers' Association. In 1952, at the time of the Defiance Campaign against segregation laws, he was

President-General of the African National Congress. When he refused that year to resign from the ANC the Government stripped him of his chieftainship.

Luthuli was among the 155 arrested in 1956 for opposition to apartheid, but after the long Treason Trial was released. Under the Suppression of Communism Act he was restricted to an area around his home near Stanger, about thirty miles north of Durban. In March 1960, after the Pan-Africanists had initiated defiance of the pass laws, Luthuli burned his pass in Praetoria and urged all Africans to do so also. The South African Government allowed him to travel to Oslo, Norway in 1961 to receive the Nobel Peace Prize, but Luthuli was prohibited from leaving the country after that. Under his banishment, he was prohibited from making speeches and attending public meetings. His statements were banned from publication in South Africa. His autobiography, **Let My People Go,** was banned in that country.

8

The Problem of
Political Technique in
Radical Politics

The basic problem of all radical politics is *how* to act with political relevance to improve the social, economic, and political life of the people. This is the problem of political technique — the fundamental problem of all politics. Even conservatism is not excepted. The problem there is the choice of means to use in the face of forces of change in order to preserve that which is deemed to be of value in the existing institutions and traditions.

The problem appears more acutely in radical politics — primarily because "radicals" have aimed at fundamental or basic change. The problem has not been solved, the intended goals have not been reached, and people have widely become disillusioned with the results produced by yesteryear's radical political movements.

The present adequacy of the usual answers offered by radicals to this problem of how to act to achieve the society of their dreams therefore requires careful examination. This may be both disturbing and difficult, but it is by far preferable to repeating existing answers which may be either incomplete or wrong. Such an examination is also better than seeking to absolve one's social and political responsibility by escaping into an extreme individualistic personal philosophy, or an atomistic brand of pacifism or of anarchism. Nor should the inadequacies of one political doctrine or program lead us simply to adopt another. Instead, we need to rethink politics fundamentally.

The overall problem of political technique in radical politics may be divided into at least three subproblems: (1) how to convince others of the need for change; (2) how to counteract the political, social, economic, and military power of those groups opposing the changes; and (3) how to implement the desired changes. This chapter is largely devoted to the second question because it has been the least satisfactorily solved, and because the answer to the third is to a large degree dependent upon the solution provided to the second.

These three problems must be faced for all political or quasi-political movements seeking to achieve change — whether liberal, socialist, social reform, anarchist, pacifist, Communist, or fascist. This chapter focuses on the problem of political technique in relation to the "socialist" movements. We shall briefly examine three types of such movements which have dealt with the problem of how to achieve the desired future society in distinct ways: the utopian socialists, the Social Democrats, and the Communists. Very important variations exist within each of these which are not discussed here. However, those variations do not affect the basic points of their approaches which have been selected for this critical analysis.

The reexamination which has begun in some quarters of socialist thought and programs makes this focus especially topical. The analysis here, however, is only illustrative of the kind of analysis of political technique which could be made of any political doctrine and movement. Similar critical analyses are needed for other approaches which have aimed to produce more humane societies, including both liberal and anarchist ones.

The following analysis of these "socialist" movements is critical — despite the writer's fullest sympathy with the ultimate socialist objective of a just, free, classless, warless, and Stateless society, and despite having been for a few years, as a student, an active member of the Socialist Party, U.S.A. My conclusion that socialist thought on political technique is inadequate came gradually, and even regrettably; it is never easy to conclude that the movement and means in which one has placed confidence are inadequate. This is especially so when there are severe difficulties in developing an adequate alternative conception and capacity for change and an alternative political technique.

SOCIALIST GOALS AND TECHNIQUE

The common goal of the utopian socialists, Social Democrats, and Communists has been to replace capitalist society with a more just system in which need, exploitation, oppression, and war will not exist, and in which people will be able to develop their potentialities to the fullest. These movements have differed in their analyses of the nature of capitalism. But their most significant differences have been over what means should be used to achieve "socialism," or, finally, "communism" (with a small "c" to indicate the ultimately desired goal of a free, just, peaceful society in which even the State* would have ceased to exist).

In order to achieve a new society the utopian socialists concentrated primarily on education and persuasion to convince others of their aims, and on the power of example in building the new social order by establishing pilot social and economic experiments. However, they largely ignored the problem of how to counteract the power of those groups opposed to the changes they aimed to achieve. In large degree, this was their fatal weakness. Because they did not really confront and deal with questions of power, including how to meet determined opposition, their relevance was minimal in the field of

---

*"State" is used here to indicate the particular form of government which includes a permanent bureaucracy to administer the policies of the ruling group in control of the whole governmental apparatus, a permanent police and prison system to punish violators of the laws and policies of the regime, and a permanent military system, the use of which may be threatened or applied against external enemies and even the home population in times of unrest.

practical politics. They were able to make little lasting contribution to the actual reorganization of social, economic, and political life. The choice, therefore, presented to those desiring to build "socialism" has been largely between the Social Democrats and the Communists.

TWO ANSWERS

The problem of how to meet determined opposition to a program of change and to institute the desired policies and system is a question of political technique. The socialists who faced up to the fact of power were forced to answer this question: What means are to be used to ensure that the desired changes can be made even in the face of powerful opposition?* Fundamentally, both the Social Democrats and the Communists answered this question in the same way: gain control of the State apparatus and use the power of the State to meet such opposition.

However, the two movements answered very differently the question of how to gain control of the State and the question of how to use it once it was gained. The Social Democrats favored peaceful, electoral, and parliamentary means, while the Communists were willing to use whatever means they viewed as "necessary." If, despite electoral victory for the Social Democrats, the capitalists and their supporters refused to turn over the State apparatus to them, or where political democracy did not exist, the means proposed by the Social Democrats varied, but included violent revolution and the general strike. The Communists have been prepared to use coup d'état, violent seizure of power, and guerrilla war, with or without electoral participation and victory. In fact they have seemed often to prefer the

---

*Another question must also be faced: What is to be done if control of the State is gained by antisocial and dictatorial groups? Here the usual procedures of a liberal democracy are demonstrably inadequate. But violent revolt suffers also from severe disadvantages and weaknesses — arising in large degree because such dictatorial groups would then have at their disposal the full police and military resources of the State. Without a major mutiny of the military forces, the chances of a successful revolt by violence would therefore be virtually nil. The failure of socialists, other radicals, and democrats in general to develop a political technique for dealing with such eventualities was undoubtedly a significant reason for the Nazi era.

violent means, apparently because they would facilitate their continued use of political violence and centralization *after* seizure of the State in order to remake the society. Once in control of the State, the Social Democrats were willing to relinquish control if defeated in an election, while the Communists allowed for no such eventuality.

Generally speaking, the Social Democrats' reliance upon liberal democratic processes meant building a new party, or converting an existing one to their objectives, and then campaigning in elections until by an electoral victory they were able to gain control of the State apparatus. Once the Social Democrats had taken over the State, all the State's bureaucracy and means of repression — police, jails, militia, army, navy, etc. — were at their disposal (within the accepted limits of political democracy) to implement and enforce their policies in the face of opposition. Widespread acceptance of constitutional democratic procedures, the pressure of popular endorsement of the elected government, and the ability and willingness, if necessary, of the Social Democrats to use these means of repression, were usually sufficient to guarantee that their conservative opposition would acquiesce without a struggle.

In contrast to the Social Democrats' peaceful, constitutional methods, the Communists refused to allow "bourgeois values" to prevent them from sweeping aside all obstacles to their goal. They were, therefore, willing to use whatever means were deemed "necessary," especially the coup d'état. Once they had obtained control of the State they were more sweeping than the Social Democrats in the changes they instituted, and willing to use all means of the State for repression to enforce their policies far more totally and ruthlessly than the Social Democrats. This willingness facilitated popular acquiescence. However, the radical changes, the speed with which they were carried out, and the methods used could arouse intense opposition. To meet this eventuality, the Communists were willing to use greater severity in repression and to concentrate effective power in the hands of the Communist-controlled State.

In addition to the answers of the Social Democrats and the Communists to the problem, other radicals such as syndicalists advocated different means — especially strikes and other "direct action" — to deal with opposition to the introduction of socialism. Their views did not prevail in the socialist movements, however.

The Social Democrats could with some degree of fairness regard themselves as being true to democratic principles, and hence to a socialism which was based on "human values." The Communists, however, could charge them with being content with minor reforms, compromising with capitalism, and betraying the objective of a full socialist — and ultimately the desired classless, Stateless, warless — society. The Social Democrats, however, could reasonably charge the Communist with forgetting in their ruthlessness the basic attitude to human beings which had originally inspired the socialist pioneers, with betraying the revolution by the establishment of dictatorship, and by willingness to inflict mass human suffering in the name of the Revolution — thereby determining that the ultimate goal would never be reached.

The arguments were about political technique.

NO OTHER WAY?

Within the range of means from which both groups deemed they could choose while being politically relevant, there lay no solution to this problem. The peaceful, constitutional methods of the Social Democrats also involved reformism, compromise of principle, and acceptance of the restrictions imposed by the inadequacies of parliamentarianism.[1] The all-out means of the Communists also involved inhumanity, executions, dictatorship, concentration camps, and other means of oppression. In the eyes of both Social Democrats and Communists there existed no technique of political action capable of being simultaneously revolutionary, peaceful, effective, democratic, and humane. If such a technique had been seen to exist, the course of history might have been changed.*

The perceived absence of a peaceful yet militant and effective technique of combatting oppression had yet another major effect upon the Social Democratic and Communist movements: their reaction to war. It had once been the clear socialist doctrine that wars

---

*The problem was also in part how to organize and structure the industrial and political institutions. The contribution of guild socialism was potentially significant at this point. The whole field of thinking on "industrial democracy" and "workers' control" is relevant here, but because this chapter is limited largely to the question of political technique and because others are far more qualified to write on industrial democracy, this important area will be left for others to discuss.

arose from capitalism, and that workers had no interest or stake in them. There was no reason why the workers of one country should go to war to kill the workers of another country in a quarrel between their respective capitalist masters when their common real enemy was capitalism.

Two important factors, however, altered the application of this principle: (1) because of genuine or perceived foreign threats involving expansion and conquest by a neighboring State, workers in several countries became convinced of the need to defend their homeland from such threats; (2) after the Russian Revolution, the defense of the homeland came to be identified with the defense of the Revolution and of the first "Workers' State." In both cases the choice was understood as being among: (1) passive submission out of cowardice or because of sympathies with the "enemy," (2) military resistance, and (3) individualistic pacifism, which politically meant acquiescence in face of the threat.

In the absence of a perceived alternative technique of defensive resistance instead of war, there remained in the eyes of most Social Democrats and Communists only one possible course for all who believed in the defense of their homes, chosen social system, or country against the external threat. That was support for war.

The existence, however, of an alternative technique of resistance against oppression, which was both nonmilitary and effective, might have drastically altered the willingness of socialists and workers to support both World Wars. This, too, might have changed the course of history.

CONCENTRATED POWER

The decision of the Social Democrats and the Communists to depend upon the State to establish socialism, and to support war made a decisive change in "socialist" thought, programs, and achievements. The socialist movements had once opposed concentrated capitalist economic and political power. They had emphasized the right of the workers to be free from domination and insisted that the workers should own and control the means of production. Now these movements came to pursue themselves the further concentration of economic and political power in the State which they had once wished to abolish. They came to rely upon the State with its bureaucracy, police, and military forces to achieve, defend, and consummate the "Revolution." Thus the focus of decisive power in society was *not* in fact shifted to the working people themselves, but extended and stabilized in the hands of a governing "class" and its professional bureaucrats and agents of repression.

The fact that this ruling class was largely political and included the top hierarchy of the Party, the bureaucracy, the police, and the military officials, rather than the capitalists and their representatives does not refute that this was a far cry from the ultimate society envisaged by early socialist pioneers. The one-time aim of socialists to create a classless, warless, and *Stateless* society has been radically altered in favor of the Welfare State, a Workers' State, a Socialist State. Even in an age in which these can often be honestly translated as a "Warfare State" it is regarded as almost heresy to recall the original aim. The earlier plea that this was a necessary transitional phase toward the goal is now rarely heard.

The early dreams of a cooperative democracy, guild socialism, and workers' control of industry are largely forgotten in the organization of nationalized industry by both the Social Democrats and the Communists. The establishment of State-owned centralized industry, combined with technological developments, changes in mass communications, and the requirements for "efficient" military preparations — all of which have had socialist support — has meant that the working people in "socialist" countries are now more subject to controls by the State, more manipulated by mass media, more threatened by war, than they were before the parties espousing socialist aims came to power.

Simultaneously, under "socialist" rule, the concentration of economic, social, political, and military power in the hands of the State has meant the workers and others have often faced increased difficulty in controlling their own lives, in counteracting undemocratic tendencies, in maintaining significant democratic liberties and resisting war, or have been given no opportunity to develop these qualities which were formerly believed to be inherent in a socialist society.

This is not to deny the important progress that has taken place in the Western world toward the removal of extreme poverty, hunger, and sickness, nor to deny that the socialist movements have contributed significantly to these changes. It is, however, to say that in achieving these important gains, sight has often been lost of other — perhaps even more important — socialist objectives.

An important reason for the loss of early socialist objectives, I suggest, is that the "socialist" movements had not satisfactorily solved the problem of political technique. They lacked the knowledge of how to struggle for humane socialist objectives by humane socialist methods. In default, they relied heavily upon the methods and institutions of the system they abhorred, and these were at sharp variance with their socialist goals. Thereby, they helped to create — not their new equalitarian, democratic, peaceful, "brotherly" world, but — a world in which some of the unwanted tendencies of the system they had hated were nurtured and matured.

People themselves have not been trained in a technique of political action which they can effectively apply independently of the State or against the State if it itself violates justice, peace, and freedom. To carry over uncritically the superficial thought of the "socialist" movements on political technique into the present, with its threats to human freedom and life itself, is to do something less than to think seriously about one's responsibility for the future of humankind.

NEW POLITICS

A quest has begun [1960] in several countries for the development of a "new politics" more able to serve humanity than the politics we have hitherto known. In my view this new politics must include a vigilant maintenance and achievement of civil liberties, a shift of effective political and economic power to the hands of people themselves, opposition to all colonialism and exploitation, replacement of military with civilian means of defense, and a restoration of humanity and warmth in social, economic, and political life.

If the "new politics" is not to crash on the same rock as did the old politics — that of political technique — it is imperative that it must develop new means of action. Such a technique must be able to:

1. Supplement parliamentarianism, especially by correcting in theory and practice two erroneous assumptions often associated with it: (a) that the only acceptable and effective political power is that which is channelled through the governmental and electoral machinery, and (b) that nothing really significant politically can be done without gaining control of the State;

2. Reduce drastically or eliminate reliance on the State's means of repression to cope with opposition to change; and

3. Replace violent revolution and war with nonviolent struggle as means of conducting acute conflicts in which important issues are at stake.

Such a technique must therefore basically be a peaceful means of struggle and of counteracting the power of opposition. This requires more than words and good intentions. Words only become applied in this world when the ideas and principles which underlie them become actualized in terms of some combination of moral, psychological, social, economic, or political power.

There is no escape in this world from power. It is present in interpersonal situations — such as the influence of a mother on her baby and of lovers on each other — and also in social situations such as workers producing or not producing certain goods; people making decisions together, establishing and operating an institution to educate youth, produce and distribute food, or achieve any other objective; traders buying, selling, or not doing either; conscripts entering or refusing to enter the army; workers striking or employers resisting strikes; a country waging war or in other ways refusing to acquiesce to threats. All these and many other examples involve various types of power.

Nor is power itself inherently immoral. The most serious single factor which can render power immoral is the willingness to inflict physical injury and death upon others — the threat or use of physical violence.[2] Unless one abdicates all responsibility for one's fellow humans, all responsibility for opposing injustice, tyranny, and war, and all participation in or support for any social relationships beyond onself, one cannot avoid exercising, supporting, or advocating *some kind* of power.

The problem then is to find a kind of power which is peaceful and noninjurious while enabling one to fulfill one's responsibilities toward others. Putting it another way, the problem is what kind of power can be moral, is nonmilitary, can be applied by people themselves, and can contribute significantly to the solution of the problem of political technique.

A more direct peaceful technique of socio-political action is thus needed which: (1) can supplement the procedures of liberal democracy where these have proved inadequate or where they have retained their outward forms while the democratic content has been weakened or destroyed; and (2) can be substituted for violent direct action, including violent revolution and war. Within the context of socialist objectives, once the problem of how to counteract and overcome the opposition without violent direct action, or sole reliance on State power, is solved, the question of how to organize the institutions of the society on democratic lines and with more direct control by the populace becomes greatly simplified. There are already indications of the general form this technique of action must take, and some experience in its application. Within the socialist and labor tradition itself there are clues to this answer — clues which most modern "socialists" often would prefer to forget.

CLUES TO THE ANSWER

The way war should be prevented in capitalist systems, socialists once believed, was for the workers to conduct general strikes in their own country and for the troops to mutiny and fraternize with those of the other side. The syndicalists placed confidence in the use of the general strike to achieve the transfer of the ownership and control of industry into the hands of the workers, rather than in the gaining of control of the State and using it to take over ownership. Boycotts and many forms of strikes have had their important role in the labor and socialist struggles of the past, although they are now used almost entirely to achieve higher wages, better working conditions, and the like, rather than a socialist organization of society. Very often in the West, strikes have been accompanied by bitterness, hatred, and sometimes by physical violence on both sides. Such emotions and behavior are not, however, inherent in those methods.

The significant point here is that these methods are inherently nonmilitary and extraparliamentary. They are direct and can be applied by the workers when other means have failed. In these qualities, they meet the qualifications we have indicated are needed now for a new socio-political technique. That is not to say, of course, that they are completely adequate in their present forms.

Another important clue in the solution to this problem of political technique comes from India: the Gandhian struggles against injustice and to achieve political independence.[3] These struggles — nonmilitary and extraconstitutional — were waged with considerable effectiveness. In contrast to the Indian experience, the uses of strikes and boycotts in the Western labor struggles appear relatively crude. To a remarkable degree in India the bitterness, hostility, and hatreds usually accompanying such major struggles were greatly reduced and a spirit of nonhatred, and personal consideration of the opponent accompanied these struggles.

There are other clues: from Africa, especially various nonviolent struggles of the non-Europeans against apartheid in South Africa, including the 1952 Defiance Campaign; from the United States, especially the 1955-56 Montgomery, Alabama, Afro-American bus boycott and later struggles; from Hungary, especially the general strike and nonviolent defiance of the 1956-57 Revolution; from East Germany, particularly the predominantly nonviolent Revolt of June 1953; from Spain, especially the bus boycotts in Madrid and Barcelona under Franco's rule; and from many other places throughout the world.[4]

The past half-century has seen a remarkable development of these means of resistance and struggle, in the extent of their application, in the degree to which moral qualitites have become fused with the forms of action themselves, and in the degree to which they seem to have met the political needs of the day.

It becomes, therefore, important to examine closely the possible relevance of this newly refined but very old technique of nonviolent struggle for correcting the serious gap in political philosophy and practice concerning political technique. Within the limits of this chapter it is possible only to indicate in general outline how nonviolent action may contribute to the solution of the contemporary problem of political technique in socialist politics, assuming the original aims of socialism. That contribution largely consists of the technique of nonviolent struggle providing a suitable supplement to, or substitute for, present constitutional and extraconstitutional political methods and techniques at several important points.

Nonviolent action can supplement or replace existing means in such cases as the following:

1. Instead of military preparations and war, nonviolent struggle can be used to resist an occupation and deter an invasion. The potential invader would be faced with the prospect of having to govern a defiant population already trained in means of action by which they could most effectively undermine his power.

2. Instead of violent revolution, in an age in which the existing regime has overwhelming military superiority, nonviolent struggle can be used to undermine and ultimately to disintegrate the regime by noncooperation, disobedience, and defiance.

3. Instead of using the State apparatus and means of repression to achieve changes in ownership of industry, nonviolent struggle can be used on a plant-by-plant or industry-by-industry basis to supplement persuasion to convince the management and owners of the desirability and necessity to broaden ownership and accept increased workers' and consumers' participation in the control of the industries in which they work and whose products they use.

4. Instead of reliance on the usual means of State repression, nonviolent sanctions can provide substitute means of enforcing social policies set by legislative means. For example, for violations of child labor laws, instead of imprisoning owners or managers, offical government backing might be given to boycotts of the company's supplies and products by suppliers, handlers, workers, and consumers until the policy was changed and perhaps some type of restitution made.

5. Instead of relying exclusively upon court decisions and hoped-for changes in the law to achieve and preserve civil liberties, nonviolent action can be used to obtain and modify policies and to halt intrusions of government into the spheres of private liberties.

6. Where the normal democratic processes have been blocked, destroyed, or made inoperative by institutional incrustations, regulations, coups d'état, or other extraconstitutional operations of the power structure, instead of acquiescence, nonviolent struggle can be used to break through the impediments and blockages to establish popular control.

7. Instead of passivity or acquiescence on matters of extreme importance or involving basic moral principles — such as genocide — in the face of majority opinion in support of the undesirable policy, nonviolent resistance can be used as a peaceful yet militant means of action against the unacceptable policy.

Each of these suggested points at which nonviolent action can supplement or replace existing political methods requires extensive further study and analysis. In the development of a "new politics" this will include exploration of theory, a further examination of the requirements, implications, limitations, and probable consequences of nonviolent action in each circumstance, and planning of the most suitable means of achieving its adoption.

Refinements and improvements in the technique are still needed. More experiments in its application are still required and the transition in each of the above suggested seven areas where nonviolent action may be applied will require some time.

It has not been my intention in this chapter to do more than to point the direction in which the solution of a major part of the problem of political technique may be found. It is not suggested that nonviolent action is a panacea, or the answer to all political problems. It is claimed, however, that it constitutes the core of the answer to the present problem of political technique, and that the seven above areas may be regarded as points of departure for achieving the resolution of that problem in the framework of socialist aims. Different initial programs could be developed for conservatives, liberals, libertarians, and others.

In the shadow of the results of yesteryear's radical movements, and in view of the human and political needs of our day, it is not too much to ask present-day radicals to look in a new direction. Nonviolent struggle may have a unique contribution to make in the building of a "new politics" which is realistic, moral, and effective.

NOTES

1. See Joan V. Bondurant, **Conquest of Violence: The Gandhian Philosophy of Conflict** (Princeton: Princeton University Press, 1958; London: Oxford University Press, 1958; and Berkeley: University of California Press, 1965), pp. 214-225.

2. For discussions on violence and problems of political ethics, see Gene Sharp, **Gandhi as a Political Strategist, with Essays on Ethics and Politics** (Boston: Porter Sargent Publishers, 1979), Chapter Eleven, "Ethics and Responsibility in Politics," and Chapter Twelve, "Morality, Politics, and Political Technique."

3. On Gandhi and the Indian struggles, see Sharp, **Gandhi as a Political Strategist,** the chapters of Part One, and Appendix D for an extensive classified annotated bibliography.

4. On nonviolent struggle, its history, methods, and dynamics, see Gene Sharp, **The Politics of Nonviolent Action** (Boston: Porter Sargent Publisher, 1973).

9

"The Political Equivalent of War" — Civilian-based Defense

THE PROBLEM OF WAR

Decades have now passed since Hiroshima and Nagasaki. In the days and years since 6 August 1945, awareness of the need to abolish war has steadily increased, both among ordinary people and among the world's rulers. Although progress has been made during these decades in some important areas related to international peace, the overall danger remains, and our continued existence is still highly uncertain. The problem of war remains unsolved, and the proliferation of nuclear weapons is well under way.

It is possible that the failure to abolish war may have its roots in a

195

failure to appreciate adequately the nature of the problem itself and, therefore, the requirements for its solution. "To find an answer to a problem it is necessary to know what it is," Jawaharlal Nehru reminded us. "Indeed it is as important to know the problem as to seek a solution for it."[1] This essay is primarily an attempt to define the problem. We shall try to determine what conceivably useful function war has played that might help to explain why it has not been abandoned, and to outline an alternative policy — a political equivalent of war — which might serve the same function.

William James' essay "The Moral Equivalent of War," which the title of the present essay may call to mind, is frequently believed to propose an equivalent of war that is also moral.[2] There is, however, only a very slight suggestion of this in his 1910 essay. He sought instead a "substitute for war's disciplinary function" as a contribution to peace, and for the preservation of such "martial virtues" as the "ideals of honor and standards of efficiency." It was Walter

Author's note: The term "civilian-based defense" is used in the title and text of this essay to indicate a defense policy against foreign invasions and internal take-overs relying on prepared noncooperation and defiance by the trained civilian population and their institutions to deny the attacker's objectives and make lasting control impossible.

The original 1965 edition of this essay used instead simply "civilian defense." That term was adopted in 1964 specifically to provide a name for this policy which indicated something of its nature and distinguished it from ideological associations and pacifism.

The term "civilian defense" was never perfect although it had clear advantages over the various alternatives which either tied the skeletal policy to moral nonviolence or only indicated what the policy was *not,* such as nonviolent defense, nonmilitary defense, unarmed defense, and the like. I think we were essentially right in picking the term, although it was possible to improve on it by a minor modification.

In 1975 in efforts to clarify the nature of the policy and remove some confusion about it in conversations with officers at the U.S. Army War College I found that the term "civilian-based defense" had distinct advantages. It did all the things we had wished "civilian defense" to do; it was nonideological, it indicated more effectively that the policy was based upon the civilians, it avoided the lingering confusion with the similar term "civil defense," and it stood in contrast to its counterpart "military-based defense." For those who like to use initials — as my Army friends do — it quickly became "CBD." In this edition, along with certain other changes, I have thought it best to use this newer term, with a recommendation that it be more widely adopted.

Lippmann eighteen years later who pointed to the inadequacy of James' analysis:

> It is not sufficient to propose an equivalent for the military virtues. It is even more important to work out an equivalent for the military methods and objectives. For the institution of war is not merely an expression of the military spirit. It is not a mere release of certain subjective impulses clamoring for expression. It is also — and, I think, primarily — one of the ways by which great human decisions are made. If that is true, then the abolition of war depends primarily upon inventing and organizing other ways of deciding those issues which have hitherto been decided by war....
>
> Any real program of peace must rest on the premise that there will be causes of dispute as long as we can foresee, that these disputes have to be decided, and that a way of deciding them must be found which is not war.[3]

This thesis of Lippmann rather than that of William James is the antecedent of this chapter which hence borrows the title of Lippmann's 1928 essay — "The Political Equivalent of War."[4]

The following analysis is based upon the assumption that the proposed solutions to the problem of war that have been presented so far are inadequate and give rise to some difficult questions which need to be faced candidly. Although a detailed analysis and critical examination of these solutions cannot be attempted within the scope of this essay, it is possible to suggest several reasons for the inadequacy of each particular proposal. Since we are here concerned with possible solutions to the problem of war and not with measures designed merely to allay the danger of war, methods such as arms control, partial disarmament, or ways to improve the international climate will not be considered. We shall take a brief look, instead, at four general approaches often presented as adequate and permanent solutions to the problem of war: removal of the "causes" of war; pacifism and its political corollary, unilateral disarmament; world government; and negotiated total disarmament. The purpose of this survey is not to deny the virtues that may inhere in them, but to indicate their shortcomings as real solutions and thus clear the air for fresh thought about the problem of war itself and the characteristics of its resolution.

REMOVAL OF THE "CAUSES" OF WAR

While efforts to remove conditions conducive to war are of course very necessary and desirable, they are not likely by themselves to lead to the abolition of war for three reasons. (1) At best, there would still remain the problem of how to deal with present and future conflicts, the causes of which have not been removed. (2) It may never be possible, or even desirable, to remove conflict from human society. Max Weber insisted, for example, that "conflict cannot be excluded from social life. . . . 'Peace' is nothing more than a change in the form [of the conflict] or in the antagonists or in the objects of the conflict, or finally in the chances of selection."[5] Conflict may help to keep human society creative[6] and free and to remove oppression and injustice, which are constant potential sources of open struggle. The important issues often at stake in international conflicts — as, for example, Mussolini's attack on Ethiopia or Hitler's ambitions with regard to Czechoslovakia — are not resolved by long-term attempts to remove future grievances. (3) The view that wars are caused by misunderstandings which can be corrected ignores the fact that understanding and even friendship do not dissolve conflicts or make unimportant the genuine issues at stake in international conflicts. Further, a fuller understanding of an opponent's intentions (as in the case of the Nazis) may even heighten the conflict and increase the chances of open struggle.

PACIFISM AND UNILATERAL DISARMAMENT

Pacifism refers to various belief systems of persons and groups which refuse participation in all international or civil wars or violent revolutions, and base this refusal on a moral, ethical, or religious principle.[7] These groups call for a national application of pacifism in the form of unilateral total disarmament.[8] While this approach may serve to solve an individual's moral dilemma, it contains serious inadequacies as a proposed solution to the problem of war. Many pacifists have a strong tendency to ignore or play down the importance of genuine issues in international conflicts, especially if they involve the problem of tyranny, and to give the intentions of aggressive dictators the most optimistic interpretation.

There are, however, other motives for military aggression than provocation by the victim's military preparations. In fact, history records cases of military conquest without provocation. Nor is it true that all international conflicts can be satisfactorily resolved by negotiation and compromise. This view ignores the role of power[9] in international relations, especially of sanctions,[10] whether held in reserve or applied in crises. For example, if an acceptable agreement is not reached, negotiations are often influenced by the reserve capacity to take what is demanded or to resist forcibly such an attempt.[11] Moreover, while compromise can be useful and desirable, there are issues on which it is morally and politically dangerous.[12] The mere abandonment of military capacity would leave a country defenseless in the event of international dangers and, therefore, would be rejected even as a means to peace. Although military defense may itself be highly ineffective and destructive, a merely negative caution about what *not* to do in conflict situations leaves most people with no choice but to continue to support the familiar governmental military responses in which they still have some confidence.

WORLD GOVERNMENT

While international organizations are undoubtedly necessary and desirable, the belief that the solution to the problem of war lies in the establishment of a world government needs careful reexamination. Two broad criticisms of this approach merit special consideration. First, world government is likely to be a *consequence* of world peace and world community (and then a means to preserve and extend them) rather than a means of *achieving* world peace. Hans J. Morgenthau, who accepted the thesis that permanent international peace requires a world State, cogently pointed out that "a world community must antedate a world state." However, because the conditions for the community do not now exist, "a world state cannot be established under the present moral, social, and political conditions of the world."[13] Despite the urgency of the problem of war, such a process is likely to take "generations,"[14] as Amitai Etzioni pointed out. The second criticism relates to the fact that world government would involve not the abolition of military capacity, but rather the concentration of overwhelming military power in the hands of a world State.[15] This would be necessary to take that capacity away from national governments and to ensure world-wide enforcement against rebellious units.

The establishment of a world State could no more preserve peace than has the existence of much smaller States automatically prevented violent revolutions, civil wars, coups d'état, and guerrilla wars within their boundaries. Several decades after the establishment of its federal government, even the United States, with its exceptionally high degree of cultural, political, and historical unity, experienced an extremely bloody civil war. An incomparably greater degree of conflict exists in the world today than was the case among the thirteen American colonies, and there is no sign that present world conflicts will be significantly reduced for many decades. But, as Morgenthau has noted, where serious conflicts exist within a society and are not muted by overriding loyalties, "the peace of such a society cannot be saved by the state, however strong."[16] The policies of a world government might face the opposition not merely of a few individuals but of whole constituent States and geographic areas bound together by regional, political, and national solidarity. The government would require the capacity to repress widespread rebellion and guerrilla warfare. Moreover, the seizure or manufacture of conventional and even nuclear weapons by dissident groups would be possible. Thus, the attempt to bring diverse political and ideological groups under a single government might increase, rather than reduce, the chances of war.

The potential danger of both insurgency and conventional war might lead to pressures to make world government all-powerful and, combined with other pressures, could enhance the possibility of a world dictatorship. The difficulties in establishing and maintaining popular control over any government would be vastly increased on a world scale. Written constitutions would be inadequate. The tendency in federations for power to gravitate to the central government would add to the difficulties of citizen participation. Any attempt to prevent the reestablishment of autonomous military capacity would probably require extensive and very close control over individuals, raw materials, industrial capacity, constituent governments, divisional police forces, and so forth.[17] These controls could also be used for less noble purposes, particularly if one considers twentieth century developments in totalitarianism and the fact that a world State would be a prize plum for seizure by would-be dictators or totalitarian parties.

Whether in fact a world government can be the primary means for achieving peace, or whether it would genuinely serve the cause of internationalism in a conflict-filled world merits study in the light of the problems listed above. Perhaps it is *not* national sovereignty itself that threatens world peace, but the ability and willingness to use military power as an ultimate sanction in international relations. Moreover, independence and military capacity may after all prove to be separable.

NEGOTIATED UNIVERSAL DISARMAMENT

The proposal that war be eliminated by negotiating an agreement, or a series of agreements, among all countries to abandon their capacity to wage international war has great appeal. If such were possible, tensions and fears would diminish, and the capacity for aggression and the need for defense would be drastically reduced. There are, however, five major difficulties to the realization of this solution.

1. The international situation is in a state of constant flux, with some countries wishing to maintain the status quo and others desiring to change it. As long as States continue to regard military capacity as the most effective ultimate sanction for preserving and changing existing relationships, it is almost impossible to obtain agreement to abandon this capacity.

2. In negotiations for the reduction or limitation of military armaments, opposing sides almost inevitably attempt to ensure that their relative security position will not be endangered but will, preferably, be improved. The history of negotiations on arms reduction and arms limitation has demonstrated this fact.[18]

> No power is prepared to contemplate a treaty unless the situation that results from it is one in which its own military interest is firmly secured [Hedley Bull has observed]. Two facts stand persistently in the way of agreement: the inherent uncertainty as to what constitutes an equal balance between opponents, and the determination inherent in all military policy to err on the safe side.[19]

3. Inspection has been proposed as a means of overcoming the possibility that the agreement will be violated. Although technological developments facilitate inspection, violation is still possible. It is doubtful whether world-wide inspection or even inspection limited to the superpowers could have the degree of certainty that would remove distrust and the possibility of a major violation. Even the retention of a small number of powerful weapons would create a substantial military advantage in an otherwise largely disarmed world. For example, while rocket delivery systems might be eliminated, less dramatic means of delivery (even in a suitcase) could be devised. Hiding some existing nuclear weapons or manufacturing new ones would also be possible with limited likelihood of detection. It is infinitely more difficult and "not remotely feasible in present circumstances" to inspect chemical and biological weapons, which can be produced in small but lethal quantities.[20]

4. Lowering the level of military preparations may cause some reduction of international tensions, but it does not remove war. "Men do not fight because they have arms. They have arms because they deem it necessary to fight,"[21] as Hans Morgenthau has reminded us. As long as confidence rests on military means as the most powerful technique of resolving international conflict, there will be strong pressures to resume preparations for war even after agreed disarmament, if acute conflicts erupt or ambitious leaders seek aggrandizement.

5. The problem of dealing with countries that violate the disarmament agreement must also be faced. The purpose of the agreement is frustrated if the violation is ignored or countries simply rearm in self-defense. Economic sanctions would have little value if the violating country is relatively selfsufficient. Moreover, war against the violator would not bring about the intention of the treaty, namely, international peace. Therefore, although partial arms reduction measures may be useful in lessening tensions, there are no foolproof formulas or feasible sanctions that would make war permanently impossible.[22] Moreover, it is difficult to get governments to go beyond the point at which their military capacity for resistance, in case of attack, is seriously damaged or destroyed.

> We cannot expect [Morgenthau wrote] that...the complete and voluntary elimination of national armaments will be put into effect by governments for all of whom there are issues over which they will resort to violence rather than accept defeat.[23]

The failure over the decades to abolish war by negotiation and the increased difficulties since the development of nuclear weapons should induce caution in accepting disarmament as the panacea for the problem of war.

BEYOND ESTABLISHED AXIOMS

This does not mean that continued examination of these proposals should be abandoned, but rather that the questions raised here suggest the need for skepticism in considering them as possible solutions. The idea that a permanent solution exists and needs only to be discovered is ill-founded.

> We...do not believe the problems of war and peace and international conflict are susceptible of any once-for-all solution [wrote Thomas C. Schelling and Morton Halperin]. Something like eternal vigilance and determination would be required to keep peace in the world at any stage of disarmament, even total disarmament.[24]

International conflict is inevitable, and political groups or countries will continue to be tempted to impose their wishes by military means.

The future, however, is not completely hopeless. Other possible views of the nature of the problem and alternative proposals in addition to the familiar ones must be explored. A reexamination of long-established axioms about defense and peace may help in looking at the problem from a different direction. This may lead not to a "once-for-all" solution, but to a new policy susceptible of making a fundamental contribution and of serving at the same time as a means of exercising the necessary "eternal vigilance" to ensure peace and freedom.

THE NEED FOR A SUBSTITUTE

In seeking a solution to the problem of war, we must start with the world as it actually is and not assume that it is now the way we would like it to be. As has been indicated, military action is still believed to be the only effective ultimate sanction for dealing with extreme tyranny and especially with expansionist designs. Furthermore, modern totalitarianism is a far more formidable opponent and a more serious problem than past forms of tyranny. Developments in technology and the use of psychological manipulation have steadily increased the potential capacity of a tyrant to implement his will, thus magnifying the difficulties of exercising any form of restraint over such regimes. Nor can one safely assume that totalitarian phenomena are occurring more rarely merely because the Nazi system has been destroyed and the Stalinist system modified. Totalitarian regimes are likely to reappear in one guise or another for many decades.

Almost simultaneously we have seen the emergence of total war and of totalitarianism equipped with unprecedented powers. If we are to survive and maintain our humanity, we must deal with both these extreme developments in political violence. However, the search for a peaceful solution to international conflicts does not mean the passive acceptance of political slavery. Conflict exists — and ought to exist — between antidemocratic forces in many countries and in all parts of the world and those people everywhere who believe in freedom, the dignity of the individual, political democracy, and the ways intrinsic to those principles. This conflict ultimately requires that people believing in those principles and ways possess the capacity (in reserve or in action) to struggle and apply sanctions in order to further democratic principles and institutions. At a time when an effective technique of struggle is most needed, however, the concentration of military power and the nature of modern weapons have, for reasonable persons, removed the traditional, ultimate sanction of war. We are faced with a political dilemma and an apparent paradox. There is grave danger in failing to meet such conflicts head-on, but even greater danger in handling them by the accepted means. Thus, not only is the question of war at stake today, but also the whole direction of political society. It may be that the solutions to both war and oppression are interdependent.

FUNCTIONAL SUBSTITUTES

Major social institutions (of which war is one) do not continue to exist without reason. They persist because they fulfill a social need that must be taken into consideration if they are to be altered or abolished. Consequently, if an institution is to be eliminated, it must be replaced with a substitute that fulfills the same function, as Robert

K. Merton has insisted.* *"Any attempt to eliminate an existing social structure without providing adequate alternative structures for fulfilling the functions previously fulfilled by the abolished organization is doomed to failure."*[25]

The term "function" has been subject to a variety of definitions both in popular usage and in social science. For the purposes of this discussion, the definition given by A. R. Radcliffe-Brown will be used: "The *function* of any recurrent activity...is the part it plays in the social life as a whole and therefore the contribution it makes to the maintenance of the structural continuity."[26] If one asks what is the function of a social or behavioral pattern, one really asks, wrote John Bennett and Melvin Tumin, "what does it 'do for' people and their groups?"[27] Merton pointed out that the existing social structures — patterns of action, institutions, or "means" toward a social goal — are not the only possible ones. There also exist other ways of fulfilling the function served by the present structure. In contrast to the "concept of indispensable cultural forms (institutions, standardized practices, belief-systems, etc.), there is, then, the concept of *functional alternatives, or functional equivalents, or functional substitutes."* Furthermore, *"just as the same item may have multiple functions, so may the same function be diversely fulfilled by alternative items."* Functional needs in these terms are considered as "permissive, rather than determinant, of specific social structures."[28] In other words, a given function can be fulfilled by a variety of structures. Lewis Coser made the same point: "In realistic conflicts there are also possibilities of choice between various forms of contention, such choice depending similarly on an assessment of their instrumental adequacy."[29]

These eminent social theorists, especially Merton, apparently believe that these theoretical principles are applicable to all major social institutions and, therefore, may be applied to the problem of war. What follows is an attempt to do this, based upon the assumption that theoretical insights are often relevant to the solution of practical problems and may at times point the way toward more fundamental solutions than would otherwise have been possible. The conclusions of such a theoretical analysis, however, need to be carefully examined and tested in terms of their practical applicability.

---

*This functional substitute analysis is presented more fully in Chapter Ten, "Seeking a Solution to the Problem of War."

A FUNCTION OF WAR

As a complex and varied phenomenon, war has served a number of functions. Some are no longer as important as they once were; others continue to play a major role. One function is widely believed to be more necessary and justifiable than all the others and may, therefore, help significantly to perpetuate war. Whatever else it may have done and with whatever results, war has provided an ultimate sanction which can be held in reserve to give weight to arguments advanced in negotiations, and which can be used when other means have failed to defend a country's freedom, beliefs, and way of life. War has relieved people and governments of a sense of impotence in times of danger and given them a technique of struggle to defend and to further their objectives. Helplessness, cowardice, and submission to a felt evil have been considered the alternatives to war. Nuclear weapons as well as conventional war are viewed as providing both relief from impotence and a source of power. Although their use may be rejected as socially undesirable, their existence, it is believed, will deter an enemy from carrying out his threats, thus preventing the conflict from turning into a major war and endangering the nation's way of life.

None of the traditional proposals to control, replace, or abolish war has served this same function, although both collective security and an international police force have been intended to provide effective means for warding off the danger of aggression and for dealing with it should it occur. As Morgenthau has pointed out, however, it is most doubtful that in a particular situation the necessary conditions for the effective operation of collective security will in fact be present. In the absence of the prior development of a world community, an international police force capable of defending itself by its own means is not practicable.[30]

If war has been a final technique of struggle to discourage and resist international aggression, if a given social structure cannot be removed unless it is replaced with a substitute that fulfills the same function, and if the proposals for eliminating war have not provided such a substitute, then only one conclusion is possible. Such proposals for abolishing war could not possibly be successful, even under the shadow of nuclear weapons.

What is needed is a substitute means of struggle, which could be used at least as effectively as war has been used to defend freedom and a way of life against tyranny and aggression. The application of these aspects of sociological theory has thus produced a view of the nature of the problem of war that differs sharply from the assumptions about the nature of the problem underlying both the "once-for-all" solutions and most of the more limited measures that have been proposed. Is there a significant degree of validity to this analysis of the nature of the problem? Can there be developed a functional equivalent of military defense, or a political equivalent of war, that will be effective and also meet the broader political conditions and problems discussed earlier?

Although this precise formulation is not usual, there has already been significant acceptance of its important elements. The arms control approach, for example, seems to be based on the assumption that the elimination of defense capacity is either impossible or undesirable under present international conditions. Morgenthau's analysis of the issues involved in disarmament is fully compatible with the above analysis, although he came to somewhat different conclusions.

> The more thoughtful observers have realized that the solution for the problem of disarmament does not lie within disarmament itself. They have found it in security. Armaments are the result of certain psychological factors. So long as these factors persist, the resolution of nations to arm themselves will also persist, and that resolution will make disarmament impossible. The generally professed and most frequent actual motive for armaments is fear of attack; that is, a feeling of insecurity. Hence, it has been argued that what is needed is to make nations actually secure from attack by some new device and thus to give them a feeling of security. The motive force and the actual need for armaments would then disappear; for nations would find in that new device the security they had formerly sought in armaments.[31]

Consideration of the problem of war from these various perspectives has thus brought us back to Lippmann's 1928 diagnosis: there is need for a political equivalent of war.

A POLITICAL APPROACH?

Two factors should be kept in mind when determining whether a political equivalent of war is possible. The first is that there can be no simple, safe solution. Any course of action incurs risks and involves

potentially severe difficulties because of the complexity and seriousness of the problems of war and tyranny. It is, therefore, important to
make a fair comparison of alternative courses of action. The second
factor is that careful use of the term "defense" is required. National
defense has traditionally been identified with military defense, and,
conversely, rulers of States and ordinary people have usually
assumed that military means were effective for defense purposes. Are
these assumptions necessarily correct?

It has been stated that there are psychological, sociological, and,
above all, political needs for effective means of defense against
aggression, and, at the same time, that war must be removed from
human society. "Every generation," Amitai Etzioni stressed,
"believed its war to be just, defending values that could not otherwise
be protected...."[32] But, what would happen if our generation and
the next could develop a political equivalent of war capable of
providing the necessary protection without military armaments?
Could there be a nonmilitary policy for deterring attack and, in case
of attempted usurpation or occupation, for struggling actively to
defend one's principles and social system? If there did exist an effective defense policy that avoided both passive submission to tyranny
and the dangers of modern war, the whole international situation
might be fundamentally changed. "Nothing is worth the destruction
of mankind, nor would anything be worth risking it, if it were clear
that there were a third alternative,"[33] as Hedley Bull has written. The
question thus arises whether the answer may lie in a peaceful counterpart of war — "war without violence" — by which people can defend
liberty, their way of life, and humanitarian principles when all other
hopes have failed. The way to peace may not be through complete or
partial disarmament but through "transarmament" — the change
from one "weapons" system for defense to a very different "weapons"
system.[34]

This possible approach to the dual problem of war and tyranny
is little known and as yet relatively undeveloped. Some of the early
pleas for such a third approach have been formulated in doctrinal and
ideological terms and have not always given sufficient weight to the
complexity of the problem and to the multitude of serious difficulties
that would have to be faced. However, these are not adequate reasons
for dismissing such a policy without further consideration. In light of
the gravity of the threat of modern war, all reasonable proposals

merit careful examination and investigation. Initially crude ideas, theories, and measures are susceptible to testing, refinement, and development into infinitely more adequate measures for dealing with the particular problem in question. This is evident in much of the history of modern social, political, scientific, and military developments. There is no reason to assume that such a development would not be possible here as well.

CONTROL OF POLITICAL POWER AND CONDUCT OF OPEN STRUGGLE

The assumption that only military action can be effective in resisting an opponent using military action is belied by evidence of nonmilitary types of resistance. These have proved so powerful and effective that the will of the military-supported opponent has been thwarted, and significant concessions or major objectives have been won. Too little study has been devoted to these cases and to the means of struggle employed. Not only is our knowledge unduly limited, but, in addition, there exists serious misunderstanding about these nonmilitary means of struggle.

INDIRECT STRATEGY

A frequent reaction to the idea that resistance without military arms could be effective against an enemy able to use military power is to dismiss the idea. It is generally assumed that resistance to a military attack must be made frontally by the same means, at the same time, and at the same place. Since nonmilitary resistance cannot do this, the whole idea is deemed unworthy of consideration. A closer look at strategic problems of resistance, within the narrow context of military struggle, shows that it is not necessarily true that the wisest course is to resist an enemy's attack head-on, precisely because that is where he expects resistance and where he has concentrated his strength. Napoleon, for example, laid down as a basic principle that one should never "attack a position in front which you can gain by turning."[35] Similarly, B. H. Liddell Hart argued that "throughout the ages, effective results in war have rarely been attained unless the approach has had such indirectness as to ensure the opponent's unreadiness to meet it."[36]

If even in military conflict it is not always the wisest strategy to resist and attack where the enemy has concentrated his combat strength, there is no reason to dismiss lightly another kind of indirection that would attack the enemy's power, including his military capacity, by means other than a direct matching of forces of the same type. It is very possible that the basic principle in that indirect strategy, never to resist or attack frontally where the enemy is strongest but instead to fight by such indirect ways that the enemy is unable to counteract, could be further developed and extended. The principle might be taken even to a point where a nation might decide to fight not with the weapons chosen by the opponent, but by different means entirely; the result of such action might be a significant increase in combat effectiveness over that possible by reliance on military weapons.

There is a need, therefore, to explore the possibility of a defense policy in which the opponent's means of military action are always confronted indirectly by quite different means of resistance and intervention; in which his power of repression is used against his own power position in a kind of political *jiu-jitsu;* and in which the very sources of his power are reduced or removed, with the inevitable result that his political and military position is significantly weakened or destroyed.

SOURCES OF POWER

The opponent's power is often assumed to be a relatively fixed entity, a kind of monolith, a "given" factor in the situation which, by and large, can only be controlled or destroyed by the threat or use of overwhelming physical might. Faced with the potential destruction of people, weapons, cities, industries, communications, and so forth, the enemy is forced to agree to an acceptable settlement. But this view of a ruler's power as a kind of stone block that can only be reduced or destroyed by blasts of explosives is extremely crude and ignores the nature of the power at the disposal of any ruler or regime.

For an intelligent study of the possible ways to control political

power, it is necessary to examine the nature and roots of the phenomenon to determine whether it can be attacked at the source instead of
trying merely to deal with its manifestations. The enemy's capacity to
wage war must be viewed, therefore, within the context of his overall
political power, and that political power must be seen in the context
of the society as a whole, with regard to the sources of that power.[37]
"The notion that force is the creator of government is one of those
part-truths that beget total errors,"[38] Robert MacIver wrote. It is a
simple truth of fundamental political significance that power wielded
by any ruler comes from sources external to the power-holder. The
wielding of political power by a ruler involves the ability to direct the
behavior of other people, to draw on large resources (human and
material), to wield an apparatus of coercion, and to direct a bureaucracy to administer his policies. These capacities have their origin in
the society itself.[39]

Political power appears to emerge from the interaction of all or
several of the following sources.[40]

1. *Authority:* the extent of the ruler's authority among the
subjects, that is, the quality which leads some people's judgements,
decisions, and recommendations to be accepted voluntarily as right
and to be implemented by others through obedience or assistance in
achieving certain objectives.

2. *Human resources:* the number of persons who accept the
ruler's authority, obey and cooperate with him, or offer special
assistance, and the proportion of these persons to the rest of the
general population.

3. *Skills and knowledge:* the types of skills, knowledge, abilities,
and similar qualities possessed by the persons accepting the ruler's
authority, and the relation of these to the ruler's needs.

4. *Intangible factors:* the psychological and ideological factors,
such as habits and attitudes toward obedience and submission, presence or absence of a common faith and ideology, a sense of mission,
and similar factors.

5. *Material resources:* the degree to which property, natural
resources, financial resources, the economic and industrial system,
and the means of communication and transportation are under the
control and at the disposal of the ruler.

6. *Sanctions:* the type and extent of sanctions — punishments
— at the ruler's disposal, both for use against his own subjects and in
conflicts with other rulers.

TO OBEY OR TO DISOBEY?

The degree to which these factors are present varies, but they are seldom, if ever, completely present or completely absent. Variations induce an increase or a decrease in the ruler's power.[41] A closer examination of the mainsprings of a ruler's power indicates how intimately they depend upon the obedience and cooperation of the subjects. This is true even in the case of sanctions. The very ability to inflict sanctions depends upon the obedience and cooperation of the subjects. In turn, the effectiveness of sanctions depends upon the subjects' particular pattern of submission, and whether or not their fear of sanctions is greater than their determination to resist. Even the threat and infliction of sanctions does not necessarily produce the necessary degree of obedience, cooperation, and support.[42] The ruler's power is thus not a "given" static factor but varies with the availability of its sources, and this is in turn dependent upon the degree of cooperation received from the governed.[43] "If the state is to exist," Max Weber insisted, "the dominated must obey the authority claimed by the powers that be."[44] In this "two-sided relationship," as Franz Neumann called it, it can never be assumed that the necessary degree of obedience and cooperation will occur automatically.[45] Any government's power, both domestic and international, therefore, "is in proportion to its ability to make itself obeyed and win from that obedience the means of action. It all turns on that obedience,"[46] Bertrand de Jouvenel declared. Prominent cases of mass disobedience, defiance, and noncooperation are simply the more dramatic evidences of this general truth. Since the reasons for obedience are not constant and the degree of obedience varies, there is a possibility of controlling or destroying the ruler's power by deliberately withholding the necessary obedience, cooperation, and submission.

In order to achieve this, noncooperation and disobedience must be made sufficiently widespread to achieve and maintain an effective impact, despite repression inflicted by the ruler in an effort to force resumption of the previous submission and cooperation. Once people are willing to accept the sanctions as the cost of disobedience for righting political wrongs, it is possible for them to practice disobedience and noncooperation on a large scale and to continue such defiance despite repression. Such action then becomes politically relevant, and the ruler's will is thwarted in proportion to the number of disobedient subjects and the degree of his dependence on them.

POLITICAL POTENTIALITIES

One of the most vivid expositions of the theory that tyrants can be controlled and freedom restored if only the citizens refuse to give them the necessary sources of power was written in the sixteenth century by the French writer Etienne de la Boëtie. If tyrants

> are given nothing, if they are not obeyed, without fighting, without striking a blow, they remain naked and undone, and do nothing further, just as the root, having no soil or food, the branch withers and dies. . . . Only be resolute not to be servile and there you are free. I don't want you to push him or shake him, but just don't support him, and you will see him like a great colossus whose base has been stolen, of his own weight sink to the ground and shatter.[47]

Niccolo Machiavelli, similarly, noted the dangers for a prince of disobedience by both his agents and his ordinary subjects, especially in times of transition from a civil to an absolutist system of government. The prince must then depend on the uncertain goodwill of his agents (magistrates), who may refuse to assist him, or of his subjects, who may not be "of a mind to obey him amid these confusions."[48]

In the face of noncooperation and disobedience from anything less than the total population, the ruler would inflict severe sanctions through those agents remaining faithful. The repression *may* force a resumption of submission, but not necessarily, as John Austin pointed out:

> If the bulk of the community were fully determined to destroy it [the government], and to brave and endure the evils through which they must pass to their object, the might of the government itself, with the might of the minority attached to it, would scarcely suffice to preserve it, or even to retard its subversion. And though it were aided by foreign governments, and therefore were more than a match for the disaffected and rebellious people, it hardly could reduce them to subjection, or constrain them to permanent obedience, in case they hated it mortally, and were prepared to resist it to the death.[49]

Machiavelli even argued that the prince "who has the public as a whole for his enemy can never make himself secure; and the greater his cruelty, the weaker does his regime become."[50] As Jean Jacques Rousseau observed, "It is easier to conquer than to rule."[51]

There is historical evidence that these theoretical insights are valid and that massive noncooperation can be effective, at least in certain circumstances, in controlling rulers' political power. Jawaharlal Nehru's experiences in the Indian struggle for independence led him to the opinion that "nothing is more irritating and, in the final analysis, harmful to a Government than to have to deal with people who will not bend to its will, whatever the consequences."[52]

It is perhaps more instructive, however, to consider the conclusions of occupation officials themselves on the need to obtain and maintain the support of the populace, and on the dangers to their regimes posed by the withholding of that cooperation with or without violent resistance. In the midst of the 1930–31 civil disobedience movement in India, the British Viceroy, Lord Irwin (later known as Lord Halifax), warned of the political power of such means of resistance.

> In my judgment and that of my Government it is a deliberate attempt to coerce established authority by mass action, and for this reason, as also because of its nature and inevitable developments, it must be regarded as unconstitutional and dangerously subversive. Mass action, even if it is intended by its promoters to be nonviolent, is nothing but the application of force under another form, and, when it has as its avowed objective the making of Government impossible, a Government is bound either to resist or abdicate....So long as the Civil Disobedience Movement persists, we must fight it with all our strength.[53]

THE NAZIS' NEED

The German occupation of major sections of the Soviet Union during World War II, which was vastly different from the circumstances prevailing in India, also led certain officials and officers with the Nazi army and agencies to an appreciation of the necessity of cooperation and obedience for the maintenance of the occupation regime. Reviewing the history of the occupation, Alexander Dallin wrote:

> While the whip continued to be the rather universal attribute of German rule, there slowly matured an elementary realization that the active co-operation of the people was needed for maximum security and optimum performance. A pragmatic imperative, perceived primarily in the field, dictated a departure from the practice, if not the theory of Nazi-style colonialism.[54]

In 1942, for example, Kube, the Reich Kommissar in Byelorussia, became persuaded that "German forces could not exercise effective control without enlisting the population."[55] A memorandum of the Propaganda Ministry in Berlin, on the basis of dispatches from Minsk, stated:

> Once one gets to the point where our awkward policy uproots the huge and heavy mass of neutrals who want to risk nothing, then one gets a popular movement that cannot be suppressed unless one has an overpowering police machine, and such a machine Germany does not possess.[56]

Lecturing in a General Staff training course, Captain Wilfried Strik-Strikfeldt concluded that "Germany . . . faced the choice of proceeding with or without the people: it could not succeed without them if only because such a course required a measure of force which it was incapable of marshalling."[57] In May 1943, General Harteneck wrote: "We can master the wide Russian expanse which we have conquered only with the Russians and Ukrainians who live in it, never against their will."[58] This change of view is all the more significant because it was diametrically opposite to the Nazi ideological position concerning the East Europeans, regarded as *Untermenschen,* and to the earlier plans for annihilating the population in major areas of the occupied territory. Adolph Hitler's staunch supporter in Nazi-occupied Norway, Vidkun Quisling, who by this time had considerable experience in the difficulties of dealing with a defiant noncooperating population, submitted a long report to Hitler in early 1944 which also contained the thesis that Russia could not be held without the support of the population.[59]

Remarkably, Hitler himself admitted that "force" alone was inadequate in ruling conquered peoples. In July 1943, he noted that German policy had to be so tough in the occupied East that it would numb the population's political consciousness. However, he continued:

> Ruling the people in the conquered regions is, I might say, of course a psychological problem. One cannot rule by force alone. True, force is decisive, but it is equally important to have this psychological something which the animal trainer also needs to be master of his beast. They must be convinced that we are the victors . . . .[60]

What happens if the subjects, despite occupation, refuse to be convinced that they are beaten? Hitler might possibly have been better prepared for this difficulty if he had paid even a little attention to a rather different political leader, M. K. Gandhi, who stated nearly four and a half years earlier that:

> ...at the back of the policy of terrorism is the assumption that terrorism if applied in a sufficient measure will produce the desired result, namely, bend the adversary to the tyrant's will. But supposing a people make up their mind that they will never do the tyrant's will....[61]

WEAKNESSES OF TYRANTS

Thus, even totalitarian regimes cannot free themselves from dependency upon their subjects. Karl W. Deutsch has explained why this is the case:

> Compliance and enforcement are interdependent; they reinforce each other, and the varying proportions in which they do so, form as it were a continuous spectrum....Totalitarian power is strong only if it does not have to be used too often. If totalitarian power must be used at all times against the entire population, it is unlikely to remain powerful for long. Since totalitarian regimes require more power for dealing with their subjects than do other types of government, such regimes stand in greater need of widespread and dependable compliance habits among their people; more than that, they need to be able to count on the active support of at least significant parts of the population in case of need.[62]

This interdependence of enforcement and obedience in totalitarian systems is but one possible illustration that they are not necessarily as monolithic and omnipotent as the totalitarians themselves would like potential opponents to believe. There exist in these systems various weaknesses which reduce their efficiency, totality of control, and permanence.* While further investigation is necessary before a comprehensive list can be drawn up, some of these weaknesses can be suggested.

The totalitarian ideology, if maintained in a relatively "pure" form, may interfere with political judgement and adaptability. If it

---

*For a fuller discussion of weaknesses of dictatorial systems, with a more extensive selection of the quotation by Karl W. Deutsch, see Chapter Four, "Facing Dictatorships With Confidence."

adapts to new knowledge and new political events, it is likely with the passage of time to become eroded or modified. Pressures for regular allocation of resources may limit the regime's maneuverability and contribute to tendencies toward a more regular and traditional system. Subjects may cease to be enthusiastic and become apathetic or resentful, thereby altering the psychological situation within which the regime operates. The concentration of decision-making power in fewer hands, combined with the multiplication of decisions because of greater control over the society, may lead either to a greater risk of errors or to the devolution of decision-making from the center. Intermediate layers of command may gain increasingly independent power and the capacity for collusion against the top ruling group. Inaccurate or incomplete information passed up the hierarchy to the center may lead to decisions harmful to the regime. Inefficiency or inaccuracy in the relay and interpretation of central decisions and orders to subordinate agents and to the general population may hamper their implementation. Economic problems may lead to or aggravate political difficulties. Despite outward appearances of unity, deep conflicts may exist within the regime, party, and even the top hierarchy, which may reduce efficiency and capacity for concerted action and facilitate the modification or disintegration of the system. Subordinate officials, agencies, soldiers, and the police may carry out instructions with less than complete accuracy and efficiency.

Many of these possible weaknesses are related to the general requirement of obtaining the cooperation, obedience, and assistance of the subjects. If these or similar weaknesses exist in a totalitarian system and tend in the long run to a liberalization or disintegration of the system,[63] is it possible deliberately to produce conditions in which this tendency is accentuated? Might certain types of resistance aggravate the weaknesses? Putting it a different way, can there be a means of defense against an aggressive tyrannical system, which, instead of reinforcing the system and attacking at its strongest points, strikes at the weak points and stimulates or facilitates the operation of forces, thus helping to alter the system itself? Obviously, even if such means of defense were developed, severe problems of implementation in any given crisis situation would still remain. This would not provide an easy way — without dangers and suffering — to solve the problem of war. But that is not a reason for not considering such a policy.

TECHNIQUE OF NONVIOLENT ACTION

The technique of nonviolent action, while still relatively undeveloped in comparison with other political techniques, such as parliamentary democracy, guerrilla war, and conventional war, is rooted in
both current theory and practice. Based on the theory that rulers are
dependent on those they rule, and that persistent withholding of the
necessary cooperation, obedience, and submission means an inevitable weakening and possible collapse of the regime, this technique
offers the possibility of implementing (in T. H. Green's words) the
"withdrawal by the sovereign people of power from. . .legislative or
executive representatives."[64] Moreover, it applies, perhaps most
importantly, not only to potential domestic tyrants but also to foreign aggressors.

In his classic study of the strike, E. T. Hiller stated that "cooperation produces dependence, and withholding co-operation provides each party with a means of coercion and of opposition against
the other." The strike "is conflict in the form of a corporate refusal to
participate." He goes on to discuss the wider characteristics of political noncooperation, which most frequently takes the form of a "refusal to share in the prescribed institutional activities or to participate
in political affairs."[65]

This is the broad technique of nonviolent action, which includes
types of behavior known as nonviolent resistance, passive resistance,
satyagraha, nonviolent direct action, and a large variety of specific
methods. Because serious misunderstandings about the nature of this
technique are widespread, a detailed definition may be useful.[66]

Nonviolent action refers to those methods of protest, resistance,
and intervention without physical violence in which the members of
the nonviolent group do, or refuse to do, certain things. They may
commit acts of *omission* — refuse to perform acts which they usually
perform, are expected by custom to perform, or are required by law
or regulation to perform; or acts of *commission* — perform acts
which they usually do not perform, are not expected by custom to
perform, or are forbidden by law or regulation from performing; or a
combination of both.

The technique has three main categories of methods. Where the
group acts largely by symbolic acts of disapproval, its behavior may
be called "nonviolent protest." Included in this category are demonstrations of protest and moral condemnation, such as marches,

parades, and vigils. Where the group acts largely by noncooperation, its behavior may be described as "nonviolent resistance," for it is in a sense reacting to the policy and initiative of the opponent group. The many types of strikes and economic boycotts, the social boycott, and a considerable number of forms of political noncooperation, including, for example, boycotts of political institutions, civil disobedience of "immoral" laws, and mutiny, may be grouped under this heading. Where the group acts largely by directly intervening in the situation, its action may be referred to as "nonviolent intervention." Examples of this category are sit-ins, nonviolent obstruction, nonviolent invasion, and parallel government.

Nonviolent action includes struggle in which violence is rejected because of considerations of expediency or practicality, mixed motivations of various types, and at times religious, ethical, or moral reasons. The technique is *not* synonymous with pacifism.[67] The rather exaggerated claim sometimes pressed by pacifists that only they can practice nonviolent action is simply not true; in an overwhelming number of cases of nonviolent action, neither the participants nor the leadership have been pacifists, although those groups have often cooperated. This technique has nothing to do with passivity, submissiveness, and cowardice. By no means is it to be equated with verbal or purely psychological persuasion; it is a group of sanctions and a technique of struggle that wields power; it is not dependent on the assumption that people are inherently "good." As repeatedly stated, the major justification here for nonviolent action is pragmatic.

Although the opponent is usually well equipped to apply violent means of struggle, the actionists, by using nonviolent methods, fight with quite different weapons. They use weapons with which the enemy is least equipped to cope, and which tend to maximize the actionists' own strength while disrupting and weakening the opponent's power position. Nonviolent action has been successfully practiced by "ordinary" people. Its success does not require — though it is, of course, helped by — shared standards and principles, a high degree of community of interest, or a high degree of psychological closeness between the contending groups. Nonviolent action has been used with effectiveness against opponents with radically different outlooks and objectives from the actionists. It is at least as much a Western phenomenon as an Eastern one.

Nonviolent action may be used to change, modify, or abolish; to defend against efforts to change, modify, or abolish established outlooks, attitudes, social patterns, customs, laws, policies, programs, or social and political structures; or for a combination of these purposes. Attitudes toward the opponent and the conflict may vary widely, ranging from a desire to change the opponent's attitudes and beliefs and a determination not to allow time to change the resisters' outlook, to a determination to thwart attempts to change policies and other factors whether or not the opponent changes his views. Moreover, "conversion" and "nonviolent coercion" may be attempted simultaneously.

There is no assumption that the opponent will not resort to violence as an irrational reaction to the challenge or as a deliberately chosen means of repression against the nonviolent actionists. Whereas it is possible for both sides to rely on nonviolent action, the technique has primarily developed as one that can be practiced against an opponent willing and able to use his police and military power to maintain or extend his position and to carry out his objectives.

LEARNING FROM PAST CASES

There is a multitude of socially and politically significant instances of nonviolent action, some successes, some failures, and some with mixed results, all of which could, if carefully studied and analyzed, shed important light on the political potentialities of nonviolent action. In many cases the nonviolent technique has been accompanied by varying amounts of violence; in others violence has been largely excluded. But they are all relevant.

In studies of war, one can learn from lost battles and unsuccessful campaigns how to avoid similar mistakes and how to increase combat effectiveness in the future. Similar studies should also be useful in this type of struggle. An overwhelming number of past instances of nonviolent action have occurred without advance preparations. Until recently, there has been almost no serious thought or study about the operation of the technique, and relatively little in the way of experience and insight has been passed on from past struggles to present and future practitioners. Even under such unfavorable circumstances, and even in a world based on the assumption of the necessity of violent struggle, nonviolent action has won significant victories and forced concessions from harsh occupation regimes and tyrants. It is reasonable, therefore, to explore whether its political applicability might be expanded.

The following list of only a few examples illustrates the wide variation in political, cultural, and geographic conditions under which nonviolent action has occurred:

- American colonial economic boycotts, tax refusal, and political noncooperation, 1765-75;
- Hungarian passive resistance to Austria, 1850-67;
- Belgian general strikes for broader suffrage, 1893, 1902, and 1913;
- Finnish resistance to Russian rule, major aspects, 1898-1905;
- Russian revolutions, major aspects, 1905-06, and February and later, 1917;
- Chinese anti-Japanese boycotts, 1906, 1908, 1915, and 1919;
- South Africa, Indian campaigns, 1906-14 and 1946;
- Samoan resistance to New Zealand rule, 1919-36;
- Germany, general strike and noncooperation to Kapp *Putsch,* 1920;
- Ruhr, government-sponsored passive resistance to French and Belgian occupation, 1923-25;
- Indian independence movement, various campaigns;
- Danish resistance, major aspects, including 1944 Copenhagen general strike, 1940-45;
- Norwegian resistance, major aspects, 1940-45;
- Dutch resistance, major aspects, including various large strikes, 1940-45;
- South Africa, non-Europeans' struggles, 1952, 1959, and 1979-80.
- Soviet Union, political prisoners' camps, various strikes, especially in 1953 (particularly at Vorkuta);
- East German uprising, major aspects, June 1953;
- United States civil rights movement, various campaigns and demonstrations, especially during the 1950s and 1960s;
- Hungarian Revolution, major aspects, 1956-57;
- Johannesburg, Pretoria, Port Elizabeth, and Bloemfontein, African bus boycotts, 1957;
- Kerala State, India, nonviolent resistance to elected Com-

munist government's education policy, 1959;
- Belgian general strike, 1960-61;
- South Vietnam, Buddhist campaign against the Ngo Diem regime, 1963; and
- Czechoslovak resistance to the Soviet invasion and occupation, 1968-69.

NONCOOPERATION

Because of the variety of methods, issues, attitudes, objectives, types of action groups, and so forth, it is impossible to say that nonviolent action always "works" in one precise way. Within the technique various influences and forces may produce change by one of three broad mechanisms: conversion, accommodation, and nonviolent coercion. The relative strength and power of the contending groups in such a struggle are always subject to continuous and wide variation, depending on the course of the conflict.

The methods of nonviolent protest described above, such as marches and vigils, operate largely as extensions of verbal persuasion and protest into the field of social action. Unless the opponent is so authoritarian that he prohibits demonstrations of dissent (and the use of such methods then becomes a direct challenge to his position), the impact is likely to be limited to the level of changes in attitudes and ideas. However, when the methods of noncooperation are utilized, the picture changes. They may contribute to changes in attitudes and ideas, but they are primarily methods of exerting pressure and wielding power. Directed toward the attainment of certain objectives, they effect the deliberate withholding of various types of cooperation which the opponent expects or demands. Whether the noncooperation takes the form of a bus boycott, an industrial strike, a general strike, a civil disobedience campaign, or the open mutiny of soldiers, the action has the potential of seriously disrupting the social or political system, depending, of course, on the numbers involved, the importance of the withheld cooperation, and the duration of the resistance.

BOYCOTT IN MONTGOMERY

Two examples of the withdrawal of cooperation may serve as

illustrations. The first is the Afro-American bus boycott in Montgomery, Alabama, in 1955-56. The struggle began on 1 December 1955 when Mrs. Rosa Parks refused to give up her seat to a newly boarded (so-called) "white" man and was arrested. This unleashed a general protest boycott that was nearly 100 percent effective. Afro-Americans of that city walked, took taxis, and shared rides, but stayed off the buses. Negotiations failed to produce a satisfactory settlement. The use of taxis at reduced fares was prohibited. A car pool of three hundred vehicles was organized. Money began to pour in, and a fleet of over fifteen new station wagons was added. Drivers were arrested for minor, often imaginary, traffic violations. Police intimidation became common. Houses were bombed. As the result of a suit filed by civil right leaders, the Federal District Court declared the city bus segregation laws unconstitutional. The city appealed to the U.S. Supreme Court.

Meanwhile, the bus boycott continued, with the new objective of ending bus segregation. Insurance policies on the station wagons were cancelled; the policies were transferred to a London firm. City officials declared the car pool illegal. The same day the U.S. Supreme Court affirmed the unconstitutionality of the bus segregation laws. The Court's bus integration order finally reached Montgomery on 20 December 1956. On the first day of integration there were no major incidents.

Then the "white" extremists began a reign of terror. Shots were fired at buses. A teenage girl was beaten. A pregnant Afro-American woman was shot in the leg. The Klan paraded again. But the fear of them had gone. A small boy warmed his hands at one of the burning crosses. Then the homes of more leaders and several Afro-American churches were bombed. This turned the tide against the "white" supremacists. The local newspaper, several "white" ministers, and the businessmen's association denounced the bombings.

The boycotters adhered to nonviolence. More bombs exploded. Arrested "whites" were quickly found "not guilty," but the disturbances abruptly ceased. The desegregation proceeded smoothly, and in a few weeks transport was back to normal with Afro-Americans and "whites" sitting where they pleased on integrated buses — a compliance with the court order that would have been virtually inconceivable without the forces set in operation by the nonviolent struggle.[68]

STRIKE AT VORKUTA

The second example occurred in the Soviet Union in 1953 after political prisoners in the coal mining camps at Vorkuta established strike committees. The central leadership was arrested and removed to Moscow; a new committee was elected. Many prisoners remained in their barracks, refusing to work. They insisted on presenting their demands only to the commandant of all the Vorkuta camps, which they did two days later when 30,000 had joined the strike. Then the commandant, a general, made a long speech containing vague promises and specific threats.

A week passed without decisive action against the strikers; no clear orders came from Moscow. Food would continue only while existing provisions lasted, it was announced. A strike leaflet appeared in the thousands of copies urging self-reliance to gain freedom, and calling the strike the only possible means of action. Sympathetic soldiers helped to spread these and to maintain contacts between the camps. Twenty big pits were shut down.

Russian-speaking troops were then withdrawn and replaced by soldiers from the Far East tribes. With the strike at its peak in early August 1953, the State Prosecutor arrived with several generals from Moscow, offering minor concessions: two letters home a month (instead of a year), one visit a year, removal of identification numbers from clothes and of iron bars from barracks windows. In an open letter, the strike leadership rejected these. The Prosecutor spoke at the camps, promising better food, higher pay, shorter shifts. Only a few wavered. The Strike Committee leaders went to an interview with the General, but never returned. Some strikers were shot.

After holding out for over three months the strike finally ended in face of food and fuel shortages. Considerable material improvements were made, and a spokesman of the International Commission on Concentration Camp Practices considered the strike action in this and other camps to have been one of the most important factors in the improvement in the lot of the political prisoners.[69]

Methods of nonviolent intervention, such as sit-ins, nonviolent raids to demand possession of certain objects or places, nonviolent occupation of specific places by multitudes of people, or parallel government operating in rivalry to the opponent's regime, are all methods that go beyond the withholding of desired or expected cooperation. They challenge the opponent's authority and capacity to rule. Although undoubtedly of more limited applicability than the methods of noncooperation, in particular circumstances they may be used advantageously to the detriment of the opponent's authority and capacity to maintain his system. The choice of methods determines to a considerable degree how the technique will work in a given situation. This, however, is not the only factor.

CHALLENGE IN BERLIN

It is assumed in the following discussion that while methods of nonviolent protest may be used, the bulk of the action is conducted by noncooperation with a limited use of nonviolent intervention. If the nonviolent action is then applied at vulnerable points with appropriate numbers and maintained over an adequate period of time (these will vary with the case), the result is likely to be a challenge to the opponent's position, policy, or power, which he may not be able to ignore as was evident, for example, in Berlin in 1943.

The Gestapo carried out a massive raid, arresting every remaining Jew in Germany. Those with "Aryan kin" from Berlin were placed in a separate prison. The following day wives of the Aryan-related prisoners turned up en masse at the prison where they were held. Heinz Ullstein includes this account in his memoirs:

> In vain the security police tried to turn away the demonstrators, some 6,000 of them, and to disperse them. Again and again they massed together, advanced, called for their husbands, who despite strict instructions to the contrary, showed themselves at the windows, and demanded their release. For a few hours the routine of a working day interrupted the demonstration, but in the afternoon the square was again crammed with people, and the demanding, accusing cries of the women rose above the noise of the traffic like passionate avowals of a love strengthened by the bitterness of life.

> Gestapo headquarters was situated in the Burgstrasse, not far from the square where the demonstration was taking place. A few salvoes from a machine gun could have wiped the women off the square, but the SS did not fire, not this time. Scared by an incident which had no equal in the history of the Third Reich, headquarters consented to negotiate. They spoke soothingly, gave assurances, and finally released the prisoners.[70]

The opponent may find that, if he is not to give in readily to the demands of the nonviolent actionists, he must apply sanctions against them in an effort to halt their action and restore cooperation and submission. Exactly how severe his sanctions may be will vary with the seriousness of the nonviolent challenge, the importance of the issue at stake, the political situation, and the nature of the opponent.

REPRESSION IN NORWAY

Repression or other countermeasures are to be expected in most situations. This repression would probably involve the threat or use of physical violence, including imprisonment, beatings, shootings, and perhaps executions. But these means do not necessarily produce submission; nonviolent action is a technique designed to operate against opponents with the capacity for violence and the willingness to apply it to attain their objectives. For sanctions to be effective, they must operate on the minds of the subjects and produce fear and the consequent willingness to obey. In nonviolent action, danger of injury or death does not necessarily cause the combatants to withdraw any more than it does on the battlefield. If the nonviolent actionists are willing to pay the price of resistance, the repression may not produce the desired submission. Arrests and selected reprisals may increase the spirit of resistance as they did in Nazi-occupied Norway. This, for example, was evident in the attempt to put all the teachers into a "corporation" under the head of the Norwegian SS. This was part of the effort to create a fascist system and to use the schools to indoctrinate the children.

The underground called on the teachers to resist by writing to Quisling's Education Department, stating they could not assist in promoting fascist education of the children nor regard themselves members of the new teachers' organization. Between 8,000 and 10,000 of the country's 12,000 teachers wrote such letters, each signing their names and addresses to the prescribed wording. After threatening dismissal, the Quisling Government closed all schools for a month. The teachers then held classes in private homes. Despite censorship, news of the resistance spread. Tens of thousands of letters of protest poured into the Government office from parents.

After the deadline for compliance had passed, about 1,000 teachers were arrested and sent to concentration camps. In the camps, the Gestapo imposed an atmosphere of terror. On starvation rations, the teachers were put through "torture gymnastics" in deep snow. Only a very few gave in. When the spirit of resistance remained unaffected, the "treatment" continued.

When the schools were reopened, the remaining teachers told their pupils they repudiated membership in the new organization and spoke of a duty to conscience. Rumors were spread that if the teachers at their jobs did not give in, some or all of those arrested would meet death in one way or another. The teachers stood firm.

Then, by cattle car train, the arrested teachers were shipped to Trondheim. On the way, as the train passed through the mountains, children sang at the railway stations. Then, by an overcrowded steamer, the teachers were sent to a camp near Kirkenes, in the Far North.

Their suffering strengthened the home front morale, while it posed several problems to Quisling and his followers. On one occasion, Quisling raged at the teachers of a school near Oslo, ending: "You teachers have destroyed everything for me!"

Fearful of alienating the Norwegians still further from his regime, Quisling finally ordered the teachers' release. Eight months after the arrests, the last of the teachers returned home to triumphal receptions. The new teachers' organization never came into being, and the schools were never used for indoctrination. Finally, even the plan to establish the Fascist Corporate State was abandoned.[71]

POLITICAL *JIU-JITSU*

It is fairly commonly assumed that victory inevitably comes to the one who wields the greatest military power. It seems incredible that citizens without military weapons can thwart an enemy willing and able to use violence to achieve his goals. The military or paramilitary, it can be argued, are a highly professional group, responding not to their own self-imposed drives but to commands and trained reflexes. How can any citizenry turn itself, of its own volition, into a "sitting duck"? The answer is that this has happened in the past — the 1963 struggle of the Buddhist priests in South Vietnam is one of the

most dramatic of such examples. There is no reason that it cannot
and will not happen again. In fact, the opponent may find that
nonviolent action is more intangible and difficult to overcome than
overt violence. Not only is it difficult to justify repressive violence
against nonviolent people, but such violence, instead of strengthening the opponent's position and weakening the nonviolent actionists,
may achieve the reverse. In short, the nonviolent technique applied
against a violent opponent uses the opponent's "strength," as in
jiu-jitsu, to upset his balance and contribute to his own defeat. This is
not simply because of the novelty of nonviolent action, which with
the spread of the technique is already wearing off, but because of the
inherent nature of the technique itself.

Violence applied against nonviolent citizens may also alienate
the general populace from the opponent's regime. Repression may
rally public opinion to the support of the nonviolent actionists
(though its effectiveness varies), which may lead to supporting action.
Repression may even alienate the opponent's own subjects, usual
supporters, and agents; initial uneasiness may lead to internal opposition and, at times, to noncooperation and disobedience. If the repression does lead to a significant increase in the number of nonviolent
actionists, and conceivably also to action such as strikes, disobedience, and troop mutiny among the opponent's own supporters, the
repression clearly will have rebounded against the regime.

Furthermore, apart from this *jiu-jitsu* effect, the repression may
be highly ineffective in bending the actionists to the opponent's will.
The arrest of the leadership may simply lead to the movement developing in such a way as to enable it to carry on, first, with secondary
lines of leaders (either preselected or who have emerged from the
ranks) and, possibly later, even without a recognizable leadership.
The opponent may make new acts illegal only to find that he has
opened up new opportunities for defiance. While he attempts to
repress defiance at certain points, the nonviolent actionists may
develop sufficient strength to broaden their attack on other fronts
and challenge his very ability to rule. Instead of mass repression
forcing cooperation and obedience, the opponent may discover that
the repression is constantly being met with refusal to submit or flee.
In extreme cases, the very agencies of repression may be immobilized
by the massive defiance. Physically incapable of enforcing the opponent's will, the police may abandon the struggle, officials resign, and

troops mutiny. This situation, it is emphasized, cannot be produced except when the aims of the nonviolent actionists have the overwhelming support of the populace and when the activists and the population are willing to pay the price.

RECLAIMING THE POWER

There have been situations in the past when mass defiance by the populace has made a government powerless. One vivid illustration of this is the defeat of the 1920 military coup which attempted to overthrow Germany's young Weimar Republic. On 10 March, a year after the Republic had been established, the Government was presented with a virtual ultimatum by General von Lüttwitz on behalf of a right-wing promonarchist group led by Lüttwitz and a German politician, Wolfgang Kapp. The group's demands included new elections, a cabinet of "experts," and a halt to the disbandment of the military forces (in accordance with provisions of the Versailles Treaty). The ultimatum was rejected, and the same day the Kappists began their march on Berlin. Police officers sided with the conspirators, and the Government army officers and their troops could not be trusted to oppose them.

President Friedrich Ebert and his Government abandoned Berlin without a fight, retreating first to Dresden and then to Stuttgart. Berlin was occupied on 13 March and Kapp proclaimed himself Chancellor of the Reich. The Ebert Cabinet and the Executive Committee of the Social Democratic Party retaliated by calling for a general strike:

> There is but one means to prevent the return of Wilhem II; the paralysis of all economic life. Not a hand must stir, not a worker give aid to the military dictatorship.

Thousands had already initiated a spontaneous strike in Berlin, so that by 14 March the general strike, supported by workers of all political and religious groups, was in full swing. No "essential services" were exempted. Seizure of two pro-Ebert newspapers in Berlin led to a printers' strike. The Kappist regime lacked money, and civil servants struck and refused to head ministries under Kapp.

On 15 March, the Ebert government rejected proposals for a

compromise. Leaflets entitled "The Collapse of the Military Dictatorship" were showered by plane on Berlin. Some *Reichswehr* commanders defected from the Kappist regime. The strike continued to spread despite severe threats and the shooting of some strikers. On the morning of 17 March, the Berlin Security Police changed its attitude and demanded Kapp's resignation. Later that day Kapp resigned and fled to Sweden. Bloody clashes took place in many towns, but by evening most of the conspirators had left Berlin and Lüttwitz had resigned. The attempted coup had been defeated, and the Weimar Republic was preserved.[72]

Most nonviolent struggles have been directed toward other objectives than national defense. Some cases, such as Dutch, Norwegian, and Danish resistance during World War II, were improvised efforts to oppose occupation rule. In two Europeans cases, however, nonviolent resistance without advance preparations was consciously substituted for military resistance to oppose invasions and occupations. Probably the first case in history of nonviolent resistance being applied as official government policy to oppose a foreign take-over was the German struggle in the Ruhr against the French and Belgian occupation in 1923.[73] The result of this struggle was a mixture of failure and success.

CZECHOSLOVAKIA'S DEFIANCE

The next comparable case after World War II was Czechoslovak opposition to the August 1968 Warsaw Pact invasion and the ensuing occupation, which continued until April 1969, and in certain ways even later. This is the most significant attempt thus far to apply improvised civilian struggle for national defense. In the end, the result was defeat. However, for eight months the Czechs and Slovaks denied the Russians their political objective: a conservative regime which would do their bidding.

Reportedly, the Russians originally expected military resistance and had estimated they could crush it with their half-million troops, install a puppet regime in place of the reform Dubček Government, and withdraw within a few days. Czechoslovak troops were ordered to stay in their barracks. Instead, nonviolent noncooperation and defiance were waged against the occupation. Important Czechoslovak Government and Party leaders were kidnapped by the K.G.B. as soon as possible, and the President, Ludvik Svoboda, was placed under house arrest.

Almost immediately employees of the Government news agency refused to issue a press release claiming that Czechoslovak leaders had requested the invasion. President Svoboda refused to sign a document legitimizing the invasion. A clandestine radio network called for peaceful resistance, reported on such activities, and convened several official bodies which then denounced the invasion. These included the Extraordinary Fourteenth Party Congress. Government and Communist Party officials and bodies condemned the invasion. The National Assembly demanded the release of the arrested leadership and the immediate withdrawal of the foreign troops. Students and the general public demonstrated in the streets, workers held symbolic brief general strikes, police refused collaboration and aided the resistance. Owing to resistance at several key political points, and strong social pressures, a collaborationist Government was prevented.

As a result of such resistance, the Russians found they could not control the country. In face of unified civilian resistance and the increasing demoralization of their troops, the Soviet leaders flew President Svoboda to Moscow for negotiations. There he insisted on the presence of the kidnapped leadership.

A compromise — probably a major strategic mistake — legitimized the presence of Soviet troops and sacrificed some of the reforms, while keeping many of them; it also removed the troops from the cities, and returned the reform group to their official Party and Government positions. The general population saw this as a defeat and for a week refused to accept it. The reform regime and many of the reforms were maintained until April 1969 when anti-Russian rioting — which may have been staged — provided the pretext for intensified Russian pressure. This time the Party and Government capitulated and replaced the Dubček group with the Husak regime. The Russians had been delayed eight months in gaining their basic objective, and had shifted from military means, which had not worked, to gradual political pressures and manipulations. Of all the types of resistance applied, none had been prepared in advance except the hidden radio transmitter which had been set up in case of an invasion from the West.[74]

ENHANCING EFFECTIVENESS

Such cases of nonviolent struggle in the past have always been improvised by people who had little or no knowledge of other practice of the technique, and of its requirements for effectiveness. Large-scale preparations and training have always been absent or minimal.

Almost certainly the effectiveness of this technique and its capacity to struggle successfully against repressive dictatorial systems could be very significantly increased by research, analysis, preparations, and training of participants. It should also be possible deliberately to adapt it to serve specific purposes, or functions, much more adequately than have the past improvised attempts. It should be possible deliberately to create the political equivalent of war to provide effective defense against invasions and internal take-overs and by that same defense capacity to deter such attacks.

Limited efforts have been made in several countries to think about such a possible policy, to conceptualize how it might work in face of various types of attack, and to explore what might be required to develop the proposed policy to the point at which it could be viable. This policy is called "civilian defense" in various countries, "social defense" in the Netherlands and Germany, and increasingly in the United States since 1975 "civilian-based defense."

CIVILIAN-BASED DEFENSE POLICY

In civilian-based defense,[75] the civilian population wields diverse social, political, psychological, and economic "weapons," rather than military ones, for national defense purposes. Civilian-based defense can be defined as a defense policy utilizing prepared civilian struggle to preserve the society's freedom, sovereignty, and constitutional systems against internal coups d'état and external invasions and occupations. The aim is to deter and to defeat such attacks. This is to be done not simply by efforts to alter the will of the attacker, but by the capacity to make effective domination and control impossible by both massive and selective noncooperation and defiance of the population and their institutions.

Civilian-based defense is a projected refinement of the general technique of nonviolent action, or civilian struggle, as it has occurred widely in improvised forms in the past. This policy is an attempt deliberately to adapt and develop that technique to meet defense needs, and thereby potentially to provide, by the same capacity, deterrence to those particular forms of attack.

WHAT IS IT?

A civilian-based defense policy has three main characteristics. First, it is designed to be a defense policy capable of practical operation under existing political and international conditions, although it may also contribute to significant changes in international relations. Second, it is a civilian as contrasted to a military defense policy. Military attack would be met with the quite different nonmilitary sanctions of defiance and nonviolent noncooperation. Present military personnel would not by definition be excluded from the implementation of the policy, but military means of defense would be replaced with civilian means. Third, it is a policy to be carried out by the civilians as a whole and not conducted for them by a small group of professionals or by an organization set apart from the rest of the society (although specialists and organizations would be needed). In crises, the effectiveness of this policy would ultimately depend to a much greater degree on the active participation of the citizens themselves in the defense of their political freedom and political society than in the case of military defense.

There is almost no doubt that a civilian-based defense policy would have to be considered and adopted through the normal democratic process and governmental decision. The governmental apparatus and resources would then be available for the preparation of the new policy, which would have to be considerable, and for assistance during the changeover. It may, however, be worth exploring other possible models for adoption.

There are two important differences between civilian-based and military-based defense. Civilian-based defense is designed not only to deal with external threats to freedom by invasion, but also to defeat attempts to destroy democratic government by means of a coup d'état, with or without external encouragement and assistance. Many parliamentary regimes have been ousted by such coups. Barring civil war, however, there has been virtually no defense capacity for such contingencies if the army leads or backs the coup as has often happened. This extension of defense capacity in the new policy would help to deter both the usual types of coups d'état and possible coups by very small political extremist groups once the military establishment has been abolished. Civilian-based defense cannot defend geographical borders or territorial integrity as such, but as a rule neither can military means. Even the superpowers cannot ensure their territories against nuclear devastation.

The purpose of civilian-based defense would be to make the establishment and maintenance of control over the country impossible and, at the same time, set in motion influences in the invader's own country that would be internationally harmful to his regime and to the military venture. The primary attempt to defend free social and political institutions, and the principles underlying them, would thus finally lead to a geographic withdrawal or collapse of the invader. The advantage of this approach is the probability that it would considerably reduce physical destruction and loss of life, while making it possible to refuse to surrender despite occupation.

CIVILIAN-BASED DEFENSE AS A DETERRENT

If an aggressive regime is deciding whether or not to attempt an invasion to take possession of another country, it will usually take into consideration a number of factors. These include estimates of the relative ease or difficulty of the invasion and subsequent control of the country, and estimates of anticipated gains as compared to costs of the whole operation, including economic, political, ideological, military, and other aspects. If the prospective invasion is not based on a huge gamble or pure irrationality, the likelihood of considerably greater losses and disadvantages than gains will probably discourage or deter the invader.

It is commonly claimed that strong military defense capacity can serve as an effective deterrent by making an invasion extremely costly, reducing possibilities for success, running a very low chance of defeating it, or promising massive retaliatory destruction. There is no reason to assume, however, that military power is the only available deterrent. Invasion is not an objective in and of itself. It is seen as a way to achieve a wider purpose, which almost inevitably will involve occupation of the country. If, however, a successful invasion is to be followed by immense difficulties in occupying and controlling the society and population of the invaded territory, this may be at least as effective a deterrent as military capacity to combat the invasion. Such control on a large scale is a problem even in the absence of well-prepared capacity for resistance. George F. Kennan has argued the difficulties of achieving and maintaining control over large conquered areas.

> There is no magic by which great nations are brought to obey for any length of time the will of people very far away who understand their problems poorly and with whom they feel no intimacy of origin or understanding. This has to be done by bayonets, or it is not done at all.[76]

Although he is not an advocate of civilian-based defense and has urged continuation of the nuclear deterrent, his 1957 Reith Lectures stressed the importance of the nonmilitary component of Western resistance to Communism. "The Soviet threat," he declared, "is a combined military-political threat, with the accent on the political." He propounded a "strategic doctrine addressed to this reality." This doctrine, which included military or preferably paramilitary forces, emphasized the need to strengthen the "internal health and discipline of the respective national societies, and of the manner in which they were organized to prevent the conquest and subjugation of their national life by unscrupulous and foreign-inspired minorities in their midst." Such a strategy would not be designed primarily to defend the frontiers;

> but rather its defense at every village crossroads. The purpose would be to place the country in a position where it could face the Kremlin and say to it: "Look here, you may be able to overrun us, if you are unwise enough to attempt it, but you will have a small profit from it; we are in a position to assure that not a single Communist or other person likely to perform your political business will be available to you for this purpose; you will find here no adequate nucleus of a puppet regime; on the contrary, you will be faced with the united and organized hostility of an entire nation; your stay among us will not be a happy one; we will make you pay bitterly for every day of it; and it will be without favorable long-term political prospects."

A country in a position to demonstrate its ability to do this would, he maintained, "have little need of foreign garrisons to assure its immunity from Soviet attack." Moreover, defense based largely on organized civil resistance "could be maintained at a fraction of the cost per unit of the present conventional establishments."[77]

DEFENSE OF FREEDOM

A reconsideration of policies and preparations for civilian-based defense would necessitate a careful examination of the principles, qualities, and institutions of the society that were deemed worthy of defense. Widespread understanding of, clarification of, and commitment to democratic principles and institutions would be an important early stage in transarmament to civilian defense.[78] But, while defense motivations and aims ought to be under regular development and consideration, there are certain minimum principles in which general agreement should be possible. The formulation that Arne Næss has offered in regard to Norwegian defense might serve, in a modified form, as the basis for a description of the defense motivations and aims of other countries.

> To defend Norway today means to defend our independence, our freedom to shape our lives within the framework of Norwegian social traditions and cultures and to change them as we wish. It is to defend a way of life against all external forces that would alter it without our consent.[79]

One of these basic principles in combatting attempted occupations and seizures of power is, as has been emphasized, that defense is the responsibility of the citizens themselves. Civilian-based defense extends the principle that the price of liberty is eternal vigilance to the strategy and specific implementation of the country's defense policy. This principle, of course, is not new. Its earlier applications are symbolized by the guns above the fireplaces in Swiss houses, the early American Minutemen, and the constitutional guarantee of the "right to bear arms." But, as Carl J. Friedrich has reiterated, technological developments, primarily in modern weaponry, have virtually destroyed this as a practical principle (except perhaps in a very indirect and abstract sense).[80] Civilian-based defense, by relying on a technique of struggle not dependent upon military technology, restores the role and importance of individuals in the defense of their freedom and political society. "Eternal vigilance" ceases to be a romantic slogan of an earlier age and becomes a fundamental principle on which the defense policy is built.

PREPARATIONS FOR CIVILIAN-BASED DEFENSE

There is general agreement that, although it is never easy, it is less difficult to resist a tyrannical regime while it is seeking to establish itself rather than after it has succeeded. Kennan, in reference to the seizure of power by a totalitarian regime, points to the necessity for certain states of mind and behavior among the subjects. "For the seizure of power, a certain degree of mass bewilderment and passivity are required."[81] The advanced preparations and training for a civilian-based defense policy are designed precisely to prevent that condition; the usurper will encounter a population prepared to fight for its freedom. Thus, subject to the adequacy of such preparations and the effectiveness with which the struggle is conducted, the invader or internal usurper is likely to face an extraordinarily difficult task in establishing and consolidating his regime.

Adoption of a civilian-based defense policy would require both general and specific preparations. Since no country is likely to abandon military defense until it has confidence in and is prepared to apply an alternative defense policy, for a significant period these preparations would be carried out simultaneously with continued military measures. Because of their different natures, the two policies would probably require separate institutional arrangements; during the transitional period, personnel and money would be needed for both. Detailed consideration of the various aspects of preparations for civilian defense necessarily lies outside the scope of this chapter. The broad types of preparations listed here, therefore, are only suggestive of the extensive program that would have to be developed.[82]

A major educational program to introduce the nature and purpose of the new defense policy would be needed for the country as a whole. This probably could best be implemented by central, state, and local governmental bodies, assisted by various independent institutions, such as schools, churches, trade unions, and business groups. People would be given the broad outlines of the new policy, the method of operation, and the results expected. This basic education would be designed to encourage justifiable confidence in the new policy and to instill in the general population the broad principles on which resistance in times of crisis would be based.

More specialized training would be required for particular occupational groups and for those wishing to participate in more advanced aspects of the defense policy. The specific forms of training would vary, and the levels would range from that required by local defense workers to specialist education, which could be offered by civilian-based defense counterparts of West Point. Careful consideration would be needed to determine the most desirable and effective means of such educational preparations and organizational structures for those actively involved in preparation and training programs.

Specialists in civilian-based defense could play an important role in initiating resistance, especially at the beginning of an occupation or a coup, and could in specific situations serve as special cadres for particularly dangerous tasks. They could not and should not be depended upon to carry out the resistance on behalf of the general population. Responsibility for the bulk of defense measures should be assumed by the citizenry. The specialists' role should be primarily that of assisting in training and in launching the initial resistance. It may be highly desirable to keep some specialists in reserve to guide the later stages of the resistance. In general, the leaders will be among the first imprisoned or otherwise dealt with by the usurper; thus, the population will need to have the capability to continue civilian-based defense measures on its own initiative.

None of this should be interpreted as an implication that preparations for civilian-based defense should consist only of central instructions carried out at the base of the pyramid. An effective strategy of civilian-based defense would require an analysis of the potentialities of particular factors — means of transportation, government departments, schools, and so forth — to identify the specific points at which selective noncooperation might have a maximum impact in disrupting the operation of the whole institution or system. This is simply illustrative of the interplay that would be needed between the group largely responsible for formulating various general strategies of defense and those carrying out measures on the local level. The specific organization of a contact system or an underground would probably have to wait until after the launching of the invasion or coup; otherwise it might be much easier for the opponent to know the exact personnel and structure of the resistance system.

Civilian-based defense "war games" and defense maneuvers, as part of the preparations, have been proposed by Theodor Ebert.[83] Such war games would offer the specialists a chance to examine the viability of proposed alternative strategies and tactics for dealing with various types of threats. Maneuvers, ranging from ones to be held in local residential areas or factories to ones in cities, regions, and even the whole country, could be useful means by which the population would learn in a small way something of the practical application of the civilian-based defense principles. Such exercises might help to avoid the uncertainty and bewilderment often experienced by the population in times of invasion or coups d'état, and thereby facilitate the launching of the resistance with the maximum of resolution and unity.

Preparations for civilian-based defense should also include continued efforts to improve the society and system. In the last analysis, the more worthy the society is of defense, the better that defense will be. Alienated or unjustly treated sections of the population can be a serious threat to success. Since diffusion of power and responsibility is important in the conduct of civilian-based defense, reforms designed to give such groups a sense of participation in the community and to eradicate injustices could be a contribution by increasing both the degree of democracy and the defense potential.

Technical preparations are also necessary for civilian-based defense. It would be most desirable, for example, to provide, in advance, provisions and equipment that would lessen difficulties of communication with the population after the enemy has occupied key centers and seized established newspapers, radio stations, and other mass media. Printing and duplicating equipment for underground newspapers and resistance leaflets and broadcasting equipment could be distributed in advance. Thus, if large stocks were discovered and seized, considerable supplies would still be available to counter the enemy's propaganda and to disseminate instructions for resistance. Advance arrangements might often be possible for locating such broadcasting stations or printing plants in the territory of a friendly neighboring country as part of a civilian-based defense mutual aid agreement. Since an enemy might seek to force submission by starving the population, and since certain resistance methods (such as a general strike) would disrupt the distribution of food, emergency supplies of food should be stored locally. Alternative means of providing fuel and water during emergencies could also be explored. In particular types of crises, plans might be considered for the dispersal of major sections of the population from large cities to rural areas where control would be more difficult to exercise.

It is difficult at this point to determine what would be the best governmental arrangements for the preparation and organization of a civilian defense policy. A Department of Civilian-based Defense might be set up to provide leadership and coordination. Various types of legislation concerning the adoption and implementation of civilian-based defense, the responsibility of the citizens, and so forth, would probably be necessary.

UNDERMINING THE OPPONENT

The strategists and other experts in or associated with this Department of Civilian-based Defense would have prime responsibility for considering a variety of possible strategies and tactics for dealing with all conceivable forms that usurpation might take. The strategy most appropriate to a given situation would be determined in a large degree by the nature of the enemy and his objectives. All possible present and future threats and aims, therefore, would require careful advanced study, carried out together with a consideration of various strategies for dealing with each threat. In the United States this should include possible usurpations by an elected President and pseudo-constitutional seizures of power. While anticipation of and preparation for all eventualities should be made, the exact course of events is extremely difficult to predict. Provisions would also have to be made to ensure the flexibility and capacity for innovation to meet unexpected situations.

The initial stages of an attempted usurpation will be crucial in setting the mood and pattern of behavior to be developed in later periods. The attitude of the population to the invasion or coup is crucial. Traditionally, occupation following the defeat of military forces has been accompanied by feelings of dismay, confusion, and hopelessness. The defense capacity has been exhausted to no avail, and the population is left to fend for itself. This situation contributes significantly to the psychological condition that Hitler prescribed as necessary for successful occupation rule: the people of the occupied territories must admit defeat and recognize the occupation regime as their conqueror and master. Under a civilian-based defense policy, a radically different situation would exist. The country and the defense capacity would not have been defeated. The combat strength would not yet have been tested in struggle. The citizenry would have been so trained and prepared that it would not feel dismayed or confused. It would be understood that the physical distribution of soldiers and functionaries throughout the country did not constitute defeat but instead was the initial stage of a longer struggle at close range. This admittedly would be difficult, but the civilian defenders would hold advantages. Setbacks and defeats might occur; they would lead, however, not to acceptance of the usurpation but to a period of building strength and regrouping of forces under a different strategy in preparation for greater success in future campaigns. There are no white flags of surrender in civilian-based defense.

Although civilian-based defense cannot defend the geographic borders, this does not mean that nothing can be done at this initial stage. The deployment of troops can be delayed by obstructionist activities at the docks if major troop shipments come by sea, by refusing to operate the railroads, or by blocking highways with thousands of abandoned automobiles. Such acts will also make clear to the individual soldiers that any propaganda concerning the population's desire for protection against a threatening third power is not true. Other more symbolic actions with primarily a psychological intent can be undertaken to establish an attitude of resistance and defiance as early as possible. This will serve a dual purpose: *(a)* to give notice to the usurping regime, its functionaries, and its troops that the attempt to seize control and occupy the country will be firmly resisted; and *(b)* to influence the morale and behavior of the general population so that no inactive period will exist during which submission and collaboration could spread because of the absence of articulate opposition.

It will be important, as has been previously indicated, to make special efforts to communicate with the usurper's ordinary troops. They should be informed that there will be resistance. But, to minimize future suffering and increase the chances of victory, they must be helped to understand that, despite what they may have been told, the resistance will be a special type, directed against the attempt to seize control but without threatening harm to the individual soldiers. If this can be communicated, the soldiers may be more likely to help the resisting population in small ways, less likely to carry out brutalities or to conduct repression efficiently, and more likely to mutiny at a crisis point than if they expected at any moment to become targets for snipers or plastic bombs. Radio, leaflets, and personal conversations (preferably in the soldiers' own language) may be used for this purpose. Certain types of demonstrations may conceivably be held at the border or at other points where troops may enter, but their limited role will have to be recognized. Other initial actions may include the wearing of black by the whole population as a symbol of disapproval, a stay-at-home for one or more days, a general strike for a limited predetermined period, and the defiance of curfews with multitudes of the people flooding the streets and behaving in a friendly fashion to the individual soldiers, asking them to visit their homes, and urging them not to believe the propaganda they may have heard.

STRATEGIES OF CIVILIAN STRUGGLE

Depending on the assessment of the opponent and the situation, a well-prepared population might possibly undertake a hard campaign of comprehensive noncooperation intended to force quick defeat of the attempt to seize power. The general strike would be a key method for this kind of campaign, which has been called a "nonviolent *Blitzkrieg*."[84]

A program of total noncooperation with the enemy would doubtless be the most effective strategy, if the population could maintain such noncooperation with something approaching unanimity even in the face of severe repression, and if it were able to organize and continue life itself during the struggle. The difficulties of fulfilling these conditions may mean that sometimes such extensive noncooperation will not be attempted. In any case, it could be effectively practiced only for limited time periods. This strategy, therefore, might be reserved for initial attempts at quick defeat of usurpation, applied as short, extra severe resistance at particular points in the course of a long struggle, or used toward the end of a prolonged struggle to bring it to a swift, successful close.

It should already be obvious, even from this very sketchy discussion, that a variety of possible strategies may be applied in civilian-based defense.[85] If one strategy is inappropriate in a given circumstance or after use has not proved effective, other possible strategies exist, and within each one there is considerable room for variation. Transitions from one strategy to another and from one phase of the conflict to the next are very important; flexibility without a sense of failure and realistic assessments of the state of the struggle without an abandonment of confidence and loss of initiative are crucial though difficult to achieve. If a "nonviolent *Blitzkrieg*," or total resistance, has been attempted and has not produced victory after a reasonable time, a transition to more selective resistance over a longer time schedule would be necessary.

Directly after the stage of initial symbolic resistance or after a period of general strike or total resistance, the strategy of selective resistance could be applied. Such a strategy provides for the concentration of resistance at specific points crucial to the usurper's control, or at those particularly important for the maintenance of the principles and way of life of the country.

There are several potential advantages of this strategy. First, it may involve an economic use of combat strength. For a certain period of time the main brunt of the struggle may be borne by a particular section of the population, such as an occupational group, and the rest of the population, though involved in various ways, does not constantly have to be the primary target of attack. Other sections of the population may take the lead later and assume the brunt of the struggle. Second, as tyrannical, and particularly totalitarian, regimes seek to achieve and maintain control by the stage-by-stage destruction of independent groups and institutions and the atomization of the population, selective resistance can be focused on defense of the independence of particular groups and institutions, such as trade unions, schools, and churches, that may be subject to attack at any given point. Successful resistance at these points helps both to retain and to develop the society's capacity for future resistance and its qualities of freedom. Third, selective resistance in either defensive or offensive forms may be directed at those points which symbolize important issues, for example, the freedoms of speech, religion, and assembly, in the battle of ideas between the two systems. In addition to being simply the battlegrounds over which the contest of forces takes place, they are, by the very selection and formulation of the specific issues, important factors in the ideological and psychological aspects of the struggle. "Resistance at the right point can help to communicate to an enemy, to the civilian population, and to third parties, exactly what is being fought for, and what is being opposed."[86] Last, selective resistance applied to transportation, industry, and other aspects of the economic system can be very effective in thwarting the enemy's general control and specific economic objectives. Careful selection of the issues and points of resistance may go a long way to maximize the power of the civilian defenders and to achieve successes against the usurping regime.

As selective resistance is likely to be more frequently applied than total resistance, it would be crucial to decide well ahead of time on the types of issues to which resistance must be offered and on the points at which ground must never be given even for tactical reasons, whatever the price. These would generally be points of overwhelming ideological significance or points that, if granted, would ensure the enemy control of the society. Citizens as a whole and each occupational group should be familiar with these preselected points, thereby facilitating response to particular resistance instructions or ensuring resistance at such points even if the resistance organization were destroyed. Within selective resistance, the strategy may be developed in various specific ways to counter most adequately the opponent's objectives and to accord with particular social and political conditions.

It is impossible here to suggest detailed courses of resistance in particular conflict situations or to explore all the kinds of strategic considerations and alternatives that lie within the field of strategy in civilian-based defense. No two situations are ever exactly alike. Careful investigation and planning are required to determine for a particular conflict what are the more promising strategies and tactics. The consideration of general principles of civilian-based defense strategy is a vast task, which for several reasons may be more comprehensive and difficult than military strategy. The whole population and all the institutions of the society potentially are directly involved in the struggle itself. In a nonviolent war, the battleground is not limited to geographic front lines or foreign targets. It includes the whole country, the international theater of operations in which nonmilitary support is sought against the invader, and the invader's own homeland where domestic opposition to the invader's regime and its aggression should be encouraged.[87]

As long as the citizens remain firm and refuse to cooperate and obey, they hold the real power. The usurper can only impose that which the population is too weak to resist.[88] A dictator is no less dependent upon the sources of power granted to him by the subjects than any other ruler. If these sources of his power can be withheld by the noncooperation and disobedience of the population, he, too, will be unable to maintain himself as a ruler.

DIFFICULT QUESTIONS

The problem of defense, therefore, is the problem of how to act by means that undermine and finally dissolve the usurper's power to maintain his usurpation. There are admittedly a multitude of difficult questions involved in such an attempt. In addition to those already suggested, four merit special mention. (1) What is the most desirable and effective approach to the opponent's troops and functionaries in order to encourage disaffection, obtain cooperation, and perhaps finally induce a mutiny? Two diametrically opposite approaches have been suggested: social boycott, and individual fraternization combined with political noncooperation. (2) With varying degrees of individual commitment and involvement, how can the maximum level of citizenry participation be obtained? (Total participation is not necessary for success.) Since certain occupational groups may be especially vulnerable and simultaneously hold extremely important positions, their behavior requires special attention. (3) In the face of repression and brutalities, how can the defenders' capacity to persist be strengthened to the utmost? Military might has been demonstrated to be incapable of imposing a regime on a population firmly determined not to accept it.[89] It is necessary, however, to study the conditions under which this is possible and the influence on these of various types of repression, including psychological warfare, drugs, *agents provocateurs,* seizure of hostages, selective acts of terror, and vast physical destruction. (4) Can civilian-based defense be combined with military defense or at least with sabotage? Although this requires careful investigation and research, there is one important argument against the attempt to do so. The mechanisms of change in the two techniques of struggle are quite different from those in nonviolent action; the latter is seriously weakened by violence from the resisters. A combination of these may destroy the effectiveness of the civilian-based defense actions and the operation of the political *jiu-jitsu* process in which the opponent's violence, in the face of the defenders' nonviolence, rebounds against his power position. This suggests that in the absence of greater knowledge it is unwise to make a hasty decision to combine them.

POSSIBILITY OF DEFEAT

A defense of political freedom such as that proposed here would never be easy. There would be suffering, tragedies, and setbacks as well as dignity, heroism, and successes. There would be no certainty of easy or short-term victories; there would be no way of guaranteeing that such a struggle would inevitably lead to success even in the space of a few years. No technique of struggle can guarantee clear victory in every instance in which it is applied. There is a multitude of factors involved in a civilian defense struggle. If the qualities and conditions necessary for the successful operation of the mechanisms of nonviolent action are not present to a sufficient degree, victory cannot follow. Many of these factors, however, are directly and indirectly controllable by the nonviolent actionists. This is one reason why research, planning, preparations, and training are so important for civilian-based defense and significantly increase the chances of victory.

In considering the possibility of failure or of only very limited success, two factors need to be kept in mind. First, even failure after an heroic struggle by civilian-based defense is preferable to any outcome of a major nuclear war. At worst, it would mean a long, difficult, and painful existence under severe tyranny, but life would still remain, and with life the hope for eventual freedom. Emphatically, this is not a brief for the "better red than dead" type of slogan. It is not the abandonment of strength but the reverse. Nonviolent action is not a course for cowards. It requires the ability to sustain the battle whatever the price in suffering, yet would, in any case, allow a future for humanity. Second, in this type of struggle, the failure to achieve total victory does not mean total defeat. Even if the population of the occupied country should lack the capacity to drive out the invader, it could have the strength to maintain a considerable degree of autonomy for the country and a large degree of independence for the social and political institutions upon which the country's capacity for freedom largely depends. The defense struggle could also exert pressures to lessen the brutality and rigidity of sections of the invader's own government and population.

There are many reasons for believing that an adequately prepared civilian-based defense policy would make it possible to overthrow an occupation or a coup and restore political freedom. If a country makes the maximum possible effort to fulfill the requirements of a civilian-based defense policy, there are grounds for thinking that, under present international and technological conditions, civilian-based defense offers a much greater chance of success than does military defense.

THE TYRANT FACES IMPOTENCE

A number of the responses that may be used to create a political ambush and to deny the invader his political and economic objectives has been indicated. It may be worthwhile, however, to briefly recapitulate these possible activities.

At the initial stage, he may find that the railways, airlines, buses, and even private vehicles are not available to transport his soldiers and officials because of the refusal of transport workers and transportation experts to cooperate. He may discover the removal of key parts from the equipment or the absence of necessary fuel. He may meet a blanket refusal on the part of the existing government bureaucracy and civil servants to take any action, or they may continue to carry out the old policies, ignore his orders, and disrupt the implementation of new policies. The existing police, instead of helping to make arrests, carry over some resemblance of order, and encourage obedience to the new regime, may blatantly go on strike, disappear under new identities, or at least warn the resistance movement and population of impending arrests. Furthermore, the police may also selectively refuse to carry out orders or carry them out with such inefficiency that they are of little use.

The invader's parades of troops throughout the cities may be met with empty streets and shuttered windows, and his public receptions boycotted. Efforts may be made to undermine the loyalty of his individual soldiers and functionaries. They may be invited to dinners and parties with individuals and families and tactfully explained the aims and nonviolent means of the resistance. Attempts to utilize the economic system may be met with limited general strikes, slow-downs, refusals of assistance, or disappearance of indispensable experts, and the selective use of various types of strikes at key points in industries, transportation, and the supply of raw materials. The resistance may be publicized through prearranged channels throughout the world, including the invader's homeland.

At the intermediary stage, the enemy may gradually try to gain control of the various social institutions, either because their independence contributes significantly to the population's capacity to resist or because control is required by the tyrant's ideology or political program. By its very nature, totalitarianism must seek to bring all major social institutions under the control of the State, as a part of the atomization of the population and the regimentation of the society. If this is achieved, the future capacity for resistance will be largely destroyed for a long period. Thus, because of democratic principles and future combat capacity, civilian-based defense will firmly resist any efforts to control the society's institutions.

The attempt to use the legal court system to bolster the authority of the new regime or to enforce its orders would be met by refusals to recognize the usurping regime as legal and constitutional, and often by refusal of judges to continue to operate the courts under existing political conditions. The attempt to bring the school system under State control by dissolving independent teachers' organizations and school boards, by setting up substitute politically controlled bodies, and by introducing propaganda into the curriculum would be confronted with a refusal to recognize the dissolution of the former organizations, a refusal to include antidemocratic propaganda in the curriculum, explanations to the pupils of the issues at stake in the defense struggle, and perhaps the closing of school buildings and the holding of free private classes in the children's homes. Efforts to destroy the independence of trade unions and to establish politically controlled puppet organizations would be met by refusal to attend meetings of or pay dues to the new bodies, by persistence in recognizing only the earlier organizations, and by engaging in a series of disruptive strikes and boycotts that would cause grave difficulties for the usurping regime. Innumerable ways can be envisaged by which attempts to take over other institutions and occupational groups (the churches, management, newspapers, radio, farmers, electricians) could be opposed by similar noncooperation and defiance. There are historical precedents for all of these types of resistance. Even without advance preparations they have been highly effective in important cases. With careful advance instruction, training, and other types of preparations, there is every reason to believe that the effectiveness of such noncooperation could be greatly increased.

The failure to bring the occupied country to heel and to destroy social institutions would indicate that the society's capacity to resist had been sustained; its skill in doing so may have increased with combat experience. Moreover, the psychological climate created would tend to produce or increase a miasma of uncertainty and dissent within the usurper's regime, in his country, and among his soldiers and functionaries. International pressures may also have been encouraged by the course of events and the defender's evident will to resist. The usurper may find that he faces not only the opposition of world public opinion but serious diplomatic pressures and economic embargoes on important fuels, raw materials, and manufactured products. In such a situation, repression feeds resistance — the greater the repression, the stronger the resistance. The simple numerical multiplication of noncooperating and disobedient subjects may thus defeat the would-be tyrant and bring about a restoration of liberty, enhanced with new meaning, vitality, and durability. The initial apparent success of the invasion or early stages of the coup is revealed as a mirage without lasting political reality. The real conquest is effected by the determined civilian defenders of freedom.

THE POLICY AND THE WORLD COMMUNITY

If it is at least conceivable that a well-developed and well-prepared civilian-based defense policy can serve as a deterrent to international aggression and internal coups d'état, and can defeat attempted occupations and seizures of power, what bearing does this have on the abolition of war? What contributions, both indirect and direct, can civilian-based defense make to this goal? Where will the adoption of such a policy meet the greatest resistance? Can civilian-based defense be initiated in one or only a few countries and with what effect? How can civilian-based defense, which is designed to be a viable alternative defense policy in a world in which most countries still maintain military capacity and where international aggression is still possible, play a major role in the abolition of war on a global scale?

No defense policy — military or civilian — operates in a vacuum. It influences and is influenced by the country's foreign policy. It has been effectively argued that the nature and requirements of military defense today impose limitations on the country's other international policies in ways that reduce the country's contributions to world peace. Transarmament to civilian-based defense is likely to remove these limitations and facilitate the choice and implementation of policies in closer harmony with the country's political principles and with conditions conducive to world peace. Civilian-based defense is not a panacea that would eliminate the need for other peace policies but, on the contrary, would serve as a stimulus. The foreign policy of a country with a civilian-based defense policy would thus be far from isolationist. It would continue to participate in a variety of international activities and organizations and deal with the causes of conflict as well as actual outbreaks of violence.

INTERNATIONAL RESPONSES

Civilian-based defense has a potentially significant contribution to make to the reduction of international tensions. It virtually eliminates the fear and distrust that a country's military defense preparations often arouse because they can also be used for aggression. Since civilian-based defense has no such capacity, many of the fears created by the build-up of military defense capacity are removed. Confirmation of the peaceful intentions of a country is in itself a contribution to international peace.

Civilian-based defense is also intended to contribute directly to the elimination of war from international society. It provides a political equivalent to military defense that is currently available and not dependent, as universal disarmament or world government is, upon a prior transformation of human society. Both the deterrent effects of civilian-based defense and its appeal to countries that still rely on a traditional military establishment would depend, in part, on the ability to make clear that the policy is neither a smokescreen to hide secret weapons nor an admission of helplessness. The policy would, therefore, need to be accompanied by a thorough international information program concerning the nature and potential of the policy.

There would inevitably be strongholds of resistance. Democratic powers with large military establishments are unlikely, and probably unable, to eliminate these in a short span of time. They might, however, add a civilian-based defense component, if its effectiveness could be convincingly demonstrated. They might increasingly rely on this component until the substitution is completed. Dictatorial regimes and unstable governments probably would cling hardest to military capacity for both domestic and international purposes. Civilian-based defense cannot be used to "liberate" another country or to provide the foundations of national solidarity and stability where these are lacking. In the case of a dictatorship, however, two possibilities of exerting influence exist. First, where the dictatorship has been motivated partly by fear of foreign attack, the adoption of civilian-based defense by its erstwhile potential aggressors could lessen this fear and permit some relaxation. Second, the absence of military threats from countries with civilian-based defense policies removes, as far as these countries are concerned, the opportunity to use such threats to keep the population submissive. Moreover, the example set by countries employing civilian-based defense policies might inspire the population to press for greater freedom. If the reduction of tyranny is encouraged as a byproduct of civilian-based defense in a number of countries, this is potentially an important contribution to international peace as well as to political freedom. Similarly, unstable governments might find aspects of civilian-based defense that would help them establish a sense of national loyalty among the people.

COULD COMMUNISTS ADOPT THE POLICY?

The adoption by Communist countries of civilian-based defense would be a radical development, but this is not inconceivable, as the improvised nonviolent noncooperation by Czechoslovakia in 1968-69 shows. Adoption of prepared civilian-based defense by such countries would depend, to a great extent, on the seriousness with which early socialist ideals and ultimate socialist goals are taken by their present and future leadership. Early socialist doctrine was strongly antimilitarist. The political intention was to abolish capitalism, war, and tyranny as well as the State itself.

After the Bolshevik seizure of power in Russia, there was some consideration of the type of defense appropriate for a socialist country. Military defense of the traditional type was settled upon to deal with actual or potential foreign intervention and invasion. This not only led to a defense policy in the Soviet Union virtually indistinguishable from capitalist countries, but, according to Josef Stalin himself, also influenced the whole development of Party and government. Stalin used arguments of national security against pleas for freedom of discussion within the Communist Party: Russia was "surrounded by the wolves of imperialism; and to discuss all important matters in 20,000 party cells would mean to lay all one's cards before the enemy."[90] He also maintained that the needs of military security were among other reasons why a workers' democracy was "impossible." At one point, Stalin explained the divergence of the Soviet regime from the original ideal — "the attainment of which [is] still far off" — by this prescription:

> ...what is needed to free the state from bureaucratic elements...is a high degree of civilization in the people, a completely secure, peaceful condition all round, so that we should not need large military cadres...which put their imprint on the other governmental institutions....[91]

It would be possible to interpret a change to civilian-based defense as justified by socialist ideology. Past military defense could be explained as an unfortunate historical necessity beyond which it is now possible to move. It could also be attributed partially to the distortions of socialism encouraged by Leon Trotsky, who organized the Red Army, and by Stalin. Civilian-based defense could be interpreted as more in harmony with earlier socialist doctrine that placed confidence in the power of the workers. In one of V.I. Lenin's last speeches, for example, while complaining of the noncooperation of the bureaucrats, he reminded his followers of times in history when the civilization of the conquerors was inferior to that of the conquered. In these situations, according to Lenin, the latter was able to impose its civilization on the former.[92]

A change to civilian defense in Communist countries is thus not inconceivable at some future time. Such a change would hinge on the best possible view of those societies and intentions of their current officials. It would require genuine popular support for the system, absence of aggressive military intentions, and a willingness to de-Stalinize to the extent of devolving and diffusing power throughout the society to a hitherto unachieved degree. It would be a serious error to be optimistic about the likelihood of such changes, however.

TRANSARMAMENT: THE FIRST CASES

The most likely candidates for adoption of civilian-based defense are instead several small West European countries for which instrumentally effective military defense cannot exist because of their size and the destructive capacity of present military weaponry.

Although one can assume that initially only a few countries would adopt a civilian-based defense policy, it is still impossible to outline with any precision or certainty the effect this would have on the course of international relations. The decision and transarmament would have to depend on the state of knowledge and understanding, the adequacy of the strategic planning, the quality and extent of preparations, the type of citizen training, and the determination, skill, and heroism with which the policy was implemented. All of these factors will be highly influential in determining whether or not the particular application of civilian-based defense utilizes and demonstrates the maximum potential of the policy. A visual demonstration of a carefully prepared civilian-based defense successfully defeating a seizure of power or occupation might make a significant contribution toward the adoption of the policy by other countries. If, however, early applications of this policy were poorly prepared and conducted, the result could be to discredit the whole idea.

If the initial developments and applications in civilian-based defense were to show sufficient promise and effectiveness, it is quite possible that more and more countries interested in both adequate defense and international peace would investigate, consider, and finally transarm to the new policy. This type of development could be directly encouraged by the countries that had already investigated and adopted civilian-based defense. Countries with civilian-based defense policies could help each other in various ways: by such measures as civilian-based defense mutual assistance pacts under which they could cooperate in a detailed sharing of knowledge and experience in various aspects of civilian-based defense; by providing certain types of aid (food and other supplies, financial help, diplomatic and economic pressures against the aggressor, a haven for escapees, safe printing and broadcasting facilities) at times of attempted usurpation; by cooperative efforts to provide interested countries with information on civilian-based defense; and by various combined activities designed to reduce the pressures and temptations for aggression and coups.

As contrasted with military data, a sharing of results of research, investigation, planning, preparations, and training programs would not normally endanger future combat effectiveness. The expansion and accumulation of such knowledge added to increased experience could lead, first, to greater general confidence in the viability of civilian-based defense and, eventually, to a significant acceleration in the rate at which countries transarmed to civilian-based defense. This development would be of major importance in a step-by-step removal of war from the international arena.

It is quite conceivable that some countries might never abandon military capacity. That would not, however, be a reason for abandoning civilian-based defense, but rather for expanding it and improving its effectiveness. The need for defense capacity against internal and external would-be dictators will long be present.

THE NEED FOR RESEARCH

The state of knowledge of this technique and policy, however, is still extremely primitive. It will be necessary, as has been stated, to analyze the nature of totalitarian regimes, with particular reference to their sources of power, means of repression, and their inherent weaknesses.* How can these weaknesses be accentuated by nonviolent means to induce the regimes either to liberalize themselves or to disintegrate? Under what conditions can the disaffection and mutiny of their troops be successfully fomented?

A study of past occupations by totalitarian and nontotalitarian regimes and of violent and nonviolent resistance movements will have to be made. What are the theories, mechanisms, and dynamics of nonviolent action, including the variant strategies and requirements for success? What is the relationship of nonviolent action and civilian-based defense to various social and political systems; which are most compatible with the policy and which most alien to it? What problems are encountered in preparing and training for civilian-based defense, in operating a resistance movement, and in maintaining an underground organization under conditions of severe repression and totalitarian controls? What is the effect of combining civilian-based defense with sabotage and military defense? What are the foreign policy requirements for an optimal civilian-based defense policy?

MEETING REALITIES

Civilian-based defense is designed to operate in a world of conflict, aggression, and broken promises; a world of distrust and suspicion; a world in which not only tyrants but political mad-men sometimes occupy positions of power and honor; and a world in which, even if all military weapons systems are destroyed, they can be built again. Civilian-based defense, therefore, has not been developed as a policy for a future Utopia. It is based on the premise that defense today, if it is to be real and not simply destructive, must be self-defense. Lasting and genuine freedom depends upon internal strength and the capacity of the citizens to defend it against all usurpers. Civilian-based defense may ultimately prove to be a major contribution to the solution of the problem of war. Upon investigation it may also prove to be a dead end. However, considering the

*See Chapter Four, "Facing Dictatorships With Confidence," for a discussion of these weaknesses and their significance.

seriousness of our need, no possible solution for which a reasonable case can be made ought to go uninvestigated.

An answer to so grave a problem as war should be based on an accurate perception of the real and tragic world in which we must live. Such an answer has to be formulated in concrete and practical terms to meet the realities of that world. It will also have to be a solution susceptible of application by ordinary men and women, who are capable, it must be remembered, of extraordinary qualities. The answer cannot be a doctrine or a system that is simply accepted in order to solve the problem once and for all. Measures for abolishing war will have to operate stage-by-stage and be applied, tested, improved, and reapplied as one seeks to move from one situation to the creation of another, which in turn makes possible a new move and a new situation, and on and on until war is removed from human society.

NOTES

1. Jawaharlal Nehru, **Toward Freedom** (Rev. ed.; New York: John Day, 1942), p. 346.
2. William James, **The Moral Equivalent of War** (Cabot, Vt.: International Voluntary Service, 1960), pp. 1-12.
3. Walter Lippmann, "The Political Equivalent of War," **Atlantic Monthly,** vol. 142 (Aug. 1928), pp. 181-182. Copyright © 1928, by The Atlantic Monthly Co., Boston, Mass.
4. This does not imply that in other respects Lippmann's essay followed the same line of thought. He went on to advocate the development of world governmental institutions. In this chapter, however, such institutions are not regarded as a full functional equivalent of war.
5. Max Weber, **The Methodology of the Social Sciences** (Trans. and ed. by Edward A. Shils and Henry A. Finch; Glencoe, Ill.: The Free Press, 1949), pp. 26-27.
6. See Lewis Coser, **The Functions of Social Conflict** (Glencoe, Ill.: The Free Press, 1956), pp. 31, 80, and 124-125.
7. See Gene Sharp, "The Types of Principled Nonviolence," in **Gandhi as a Political Strategist, with Essays on Ethics and Politics** (Boston: Porter Sargent Publishers, 1979), Chapter Ten. Note especially the discussion of nonresistance, active reconciliation, moral resistance, and nonviolent revolution.
8. Proposals for "unilateral initiatives" or for unilateral nuclear disarmament are considered to fall within the group of preventive or ameliorative measures. Discussion of these measures lies outside the scope of this chapter.
9. Political power is here briefly defined as the total authority, influence, pressure, and sanctions which may be applied to achieve the implementation of the wishes of the power holder. Sanctions are usually a key element in power.

10. A sanction is here defined as a punishment applied as a reprisal for failure to behave in the expected or desired manner and/or which is intended to produce the originally desired behavior by the person or group on which the sanction is inflicted.

11. For a further discussion of the difficulties of negotiations, see pp. 201-202.

12. See Joan V. Bondurant, **Conquest of Violence: The Gandhian Philosophy of Conflict** (Princeton, N.J.: Princeton University Press, 1958, London: Oxford University Press, 1958, and Berkeley: University of California Press, 1965), pp. 218-222, and Daniel Katz, "Consistent Reactive Participation of Group Members and Reduction of Intergroup Conflict," **Journal of Conflict Resolution,** vol. III, no. 1 (Mar. 1959), p. 35.

13. Hans J. Morgenthau, **Politics Among Nations: The Struggle for Power and Peace** (Third ed.; New York: Alfred A. Knopf, 1960), pp. 519 and 513.

14. See Amitai Etzioni, **The Hard Way to Peace: A New Strategy** (New York: Collier Books, 1962), pp. 112 and 173-202.

15. See Hedley Bull, **The Control of the Arms Race: Disarmament and Arms Control in the Missile Age** (London: Weidenfeld & Nicolson for the Institute of Strategic Studies, 1961), p. 5.

16. Morgenthau, **Politics Among Nations,** p. 509. See also Bell, **The Control of the Arms Race,** p. 36.

17. See Arthur Waskow, **Unintended War** (Philadelphia: American Friends Service Committee, 1962), pp. 53-54.

18. See Morgenthau, **Politics Among Nations,** pp. 389-411.

19. Bull, **The Control of the Arms Race,** pp. 67-68. See also pp. 66-69.

20. Ibid., p. 135. See also pp. 97-101 and 136.

21. Morgenthau, **Politics Among Nations,** p. 408. See also Bull, **The Control of the Arms Race,** p. 8.

22. Ibid., pp. 101-102.

23. Ibid., p. 203; see also p. 77.

24. Thomas C. Schelling and Morton H. Halperin, **Strategy and Arms Control** (New York: Twentieth Century Fund, 1961), p. 5.

25. Robert K. Merton, **Social Theory and Social Structure** (Rev. ed.; Glencoe, Ill.: The Free Press, 1949), p. 79. Italics are Merton's. See also Chapter Ten in this volume.

26. A. R. Radcliffe-Brown, **Structure and Function in Primitive Society** (New York: The Free Press of Glencoe, 1963), p. 180.

27. John W. Bennett and Melvin M. Tumin, **Social Life: Structure and Function** (New York: Alfred A. Knopf, 1949), p. 245.

28. Merton, **Social Theory and Social Structure,** p. 35.

29. Coser, **The Functions of Social Conflict,** p. 50.

30. See Morgenthau, **Politics Among Nations,** pp. 412-424.

31. Ibid., p. 412.

32. Etzioni, **The Hard Way to Peace,** pp. 11-12.

33. Bull, **The Control of the Arms Race,** p. 81.

34. The term "transarmament" was introduced by Kenneth Boulding in the 1930s and reintroduced by Theodor Ebert in the early 1960s.

35. Napoleon Bonaparte, **Maxims of War,** Maxim XVI (New York: James G. Gregory, 1861).

36. B.H. Liddell Hart, **Strategy: The Indirect Approach** (New York: Frederick A. Praeger, 1955), p. 25.
37. See Auguste Comte, **The Positive Philosophy of Auguste Comte**, 2 vols. (Trans. by Harriet Martineau; London: George Bell & Sons, 1896), vol. II, pp. 223-225. See also Thomas H. Green, **Lectures on the Principles of Political Obligation** (London: Longmans, Green and Co., 1948 [1895]), pp. 121-141.
38. Robert M. MacIver, **The Web of Government** (New York: Macmillan Co., 1947), p. 15.
39. See Comte, **The Positive Philosophy of Auguste Comte,** pp. 222-223; MacIver, **The Web of Government,** pp. 107-108; and Harold D. Lasswell, **Power and Personality** (New York: W.W. Norton and Co., 1948), p. 10.
40. This power analysis is presented at considerably greater length in Gene Sharp, **The Politics of Nonviolent Action** (Boston: Porter Sargent Publisher, 1973), Chapter One, "The Nature and Control of Political Power."
41. See Introduction by Arthur Livingstone in Gaetano Mosca, **The Ruling Class (Elementi de Scienza Politica)** (Trans. by Hannah D. Kahn; ed., rev., and with an Introduction by Arthur Livingstone; New York and London: McGraw-Hill, 1939), p. xix.
42. See John Austin, **Lectures on Jurisprudence or the Philosophy of Positive Law** (Fifth ed.; London: John Murray, 1911 [1861]), pp. 295-297 and 453; Kurt H. Wolff, trans. and ed., **The Sociology of Georg Simmel** (Glencoe, Ill.: The Free Press, 1950), pp. 183 and 250; and Bertrand de Jouvenel, **Sovereignty: An Inquiry into the Public Good** (Chicago: University of Chicago Press, 1957), pp. 32-33.
43. See Jeremy Bentham, **A Fragment of Government** (London: Oxford University Press, Humphrey Milford, 1931 [1891]), pp. 168 and 223; and Bertrand de Jouvenel, **On Power: Its Nature and the History of Its Growth** (New York: Viking Press, 1949), pp. 27-28.
44. Max Weber, "Politics as a Vocation," in H. H. Gerth and C. Wright Mills, trans. and eds., **From Max Weber: Essays in Sociology** (New York: Oxford University Press, 1946), p. 78.
45. See Franz Neumann, "Approaches to the Study of Political Power," **Political Science Quarterly,** vol. LXV, no. 2 (June 1950), p. 162. "No conceivable motive will certainly determine to compliance, and no conceivable motive will render obedience inevitable." (John Austin, **Lectures on Jurisprudence,** vol. I, p. 90).
46. Jouvenel, **On Power,** p. 27. See also Lasswell, **Power and Personality,** pp. 10-12; and Wolff, ed., **The Sociology of Georg Simmel,** pp. 183-186 and 250.
47. Etienne de la Boëtie, *Discours de la Servitude Volontaire Suivi du Mémoire* (Paris: Editions Bossard, 1922), pp. 57 and 60. Trans. by Madeline Chevalier Emerick. See also Etienne de la Boëtie, **The Politics of Obedience: The Discourse of Voluntary Servitude** (New York: Free Life Editions, 1975).
48. Niccolo Machiavelli, **The Prince** (London: J. M. Dent & Sons, 1944), p. 77.
49. Austin, **Lectures on Jurisprudence,** p. 296.
50. Niccolo Machiavelli, "The Discourses on the First Ten Books of Livy," in **The Discourses of Niccolo Machiavelli** (New Haven: Yale University Press, 1950, and London: Routledge and Kegan Paul, 1950), vol. I, p. 254.
51. Jean Jacques Rousseau, "The Social Contract," in **The Social Contract and Discourses** (New York: E. P. Dutton & Co., 1920, and London: J. M. Dent & Sons, Ltd., 1920), p. 64.

52. Nehru, **Toward Freedom,** p. 249.
53. Government of India, **India in 1930-31** (Calcutta: Government of India, Central Publication Branch, 1932), pp. 80-81.
54. Alexander Dallin, **German Rule in Russia, 1941-1945** (New York: St. Martins Press, 1957, Toronto: Macmillan Company of Canada, 1957, and London: Macmillan Co., 1957), p. 663.
55. Ibid., p. 218.
56. As quoted in ibid., p. 220.
57. As quoted in ibid., p. 516.
58. As quoted in ibid., p. 550.
59. Ibid., p. 585, n. 4.
60. As quoted in ibid., p. 498.
61. For text, see M. K. Gandhi, **Non-violence in Peace and War** (Ahmedabad: Navajivan Publishing House, 1948), vol. 1, p. 174. For a more comprehensive presentation of Gandhi's views on power and defense against aggressors, see Gene Sharp, **Gandhi as a Political Strategist** (Boston: Porter Sargent Publishers, 1979), Chapter Three, "Gandhi on the Theory of Voluntary Servitude," and Chapter Eight, "Gandhi's Defense Policy."
62. Karl W. Deutsch, "Cracks in the Monolith: Possibilities and Patterns of Disintegration in Totalitarian Systems," in Carl J. Friedrich, ed., **Totalitarianism** (Cambridge: Harvard University Press, 1954), pp. 313-315.
63. For a discussion of such weaknesses, see ibid., pp. 309-331. Some of the internal conflicts within the Nazi regime are documented by Dallin, **German Rule in Russia, 1941-1945.**
64. Green, **Lectures on the Principles of Political Obligation,** p. 77.
65. E. T. Hiller, **The Strike: A Study in Collective Action** (Chicago: University of Chicago Press, 1928), pp. 125, 12, and 234.
66. For a full presentation and analysis of the nature of nonviolent action, see Sharp, **The Politics of Nonviolent Action.**
67. Pacifists may support or oppose the use of nonviolent action. See Gene Sharp, **Gandhi as a Political Strategist,** Chapter Ten, "Types of Principled Nonviolence."
68. See, for example, Martin Luther King, Jr., **Stride Toward Freedom: The Montgomery Story** (New York: Ballantine Books, 1958, and London: Victor Gollancz, 1958).
69. This account is based on the articles by Brigitte Gerland, who was a prisoner at Vorkuta during the strike. See **The Militant** (New York), 28 Feb. and 7 Mar., 1955.
70. From Heinz Ullstein's memoirs, *Spielplatz meines Lebens* (Munich: Kindler Verlag, 1961), pp. 338-340. This passage (translated by Hilda Morris) is reprinted from Theodor Ebert, "Effects of Repression by the Invader," **Peace News** (London), 19 Mar. 1965.
71. See Sharp, "Tyranny Could Not Quell Them" (pamphlet) **Peace News,** (London,) 1958 and later editions. Norwegian sources include: Magnus Jensen, "Kampen om Skolen," in Sverre Steen, gen. ed., *Norges Krig* (Oslo: Gyldendal Norsk Forlag, 1947-50), vol. III, pp. 73-105; and Sverre S. Amundsen, gen. ed., *Kirkenes Ferda, 1942* (Oslo: J. W. Cappelens Forlag, 1946).
72. For more details, see Wilfrid Harris Crook, **The General Strike: A Study of Labor's Tragic Weapon in Theory and Practice** (Chapel Hill: University of North Carolina Press, 1931), pp. 496-527; and D.J. Goodspeed, **The Conspirators: A**

Study of the Coup d'Etat (New York: Viking Press, 1962), pp. 108-143 and 211-213.

73. See Wolfgang Sternstein, "The *Ruhrkampf* of 1923," in Adam Roberts, ed., **Civilian Resistance as a National Defense: Nonviolent Action Against Aggression** (Harrisburg, Pa.: Stackpole Books, 1968), pp. 106-135.

74. On Czechoslovak resistance, see Robert Littell, ed., **The Czech Black Book** (New York: Praeger, 1969); Robin A. Remington, ed., **Winter in Prague** (Cambridge, Mass.: M.I.T. Press, 1969); Philip Winsor and Adam Roberts, **Czechoslovakia 1968** (New York: Columbia University Press, 1969); and Vladimir Horsky, *Prag 1968: Systemveränderung und Systemverteidigung* (Stuttgart: Ernst Klett Verlag, and Munich: Kösel-Verlag, 1975).

75. On civilian-based defense, see Anders Boserup and Andrew Mack, **War Without Weapons** (New York: Schocken, 1975); Roberts, ed., **Civilian Resistance as a National Defense;** Gene Sharp, **Exploring Nonviolent Alternatives** (Boston: Porter Sargent Publisher, 1971), Chapters Three and Four; and Brigadier General Edward B. Atkenson, "The Relevance of Civilian-Based Defense to U.S. Security Interest," in **Military Review,** vol. LVI. no. 5 (May 1976), pp. 24-32, and no. 6 (June 1976), pp. 45-55.

76. George F. Kennan, **Russia and the West Under Lenin and Stalin** (Boston: Little, Brown and Co., 1961), p. 276. Copyright © 1960, 1961 by James K. Hotchkiss, Trustee, with permission of Atlantic-Little, Brown and Co.

77. George F. Kennan, **Russia, the Atom, and the West** (New York: Harper and Bros., 1958), pp. 62-65.

78. See Arne Næss, "Non-military Defence and Foreign Policy," in Roberts, **Civilian Resistance as a National Defense,** p. 36.

79. Ibid., p. 34.

80. Carl J. Friedrich, "The Unique Character of Totalitarian Society," in Carl J. Friedrich, ed., **Totalitarianism,** p. 56. "If men wish to defend themselves against a violent invader on the level of violence, it is the invader who dictates to the defender what methods of control he shall use." (Bart. de Ligt, **The Conquest of Violence: An Essay on War and Revolution** [New York: E.P. Dutton & Co., 1938], p. 198.)

81. George F. Kennan, "Totalitarianism in the Modern World," in Friedrich, ed., **Totalitarianism,** p. 23.

82. For brief discussions of preparations for civilian defense, see Theodor Ebert, "Preparations for Civilian Defence," in T. K. Mahadevan, Adam Roberts, and Gene Sharp, eds., **Civilian Defence: An Introduction** (Bombay: Bharatiya Vidya Bhavan, and New Delhi: Gandhi Peace Foundation, 1967), pp. 150-157; and Theodor Ebert, "Organization in Civilian Defense," in Adam Roberts, ed., **Civilian Resistance as a National Defense,** pp. 255-273.

83. See Ebert, "Organization in Civilian Defense," in ibid., pp. 271-273.

84. See Theodor Ebert, "Preparations for Civilian Defence," p. 155, and "Initiating Popular Resistance to Totalitarian Invasion," pp. 159-160, in Mahadevan, Roberts, and Sharp, eds., **Civilian Defence.**

85. See Ebert, "Initiating Popular Resistance to Invasion," and "The Crisis," in ibid.; Adam Roberts, "Civilian Defense Strategy," in Roberts, ed., **Civilian Resistance as a National Defense,** pp. 215-254; and Boserup and Mack, **War Without Weapons,** pp. 37-54.

86. Roberts, "Civilian Defense Strategy," in Roberts, ed., **Civilian Resistance as a National Defense,** p. 248.
87. Theodor Ebert, "The Strategy of Civilian Nonviolent War," an unpublished paper prepared for the 1964 Civilian Defense Study Conference held at Oxford.
88. Krishnalal Shridharani, **War Without Violence: A Study of Gandhi's Method and Its Accomplishments** (New York: Harcourt, Brace & Co., 1939, and London: Victor Gollancz, 1939. Reprinted: New York and London: Garland Publishing Co., 1972. Revised updated edition: Bombay: Bharatiya Vidya Bhavan, 1962), p. 305.
89. According to some military officers, the odds in favor of the use of nuclear weapons against a country using civilian-based defense are extremely low.
90. As quoted in Isaac Deutscher, **Stalin: A Political Biography** (London: Oxford University Press, 1949), p. 258.
91. As quoted in ibid., p. 263; see also pp. 226 and 285.
92. V. I. Lenin, "Political Report of the Central Committee of the R.C.P. (B.) March 27 [1922]," in V. I. Lenin, **Selected Works in Three Volumes** (New York: International Publishers, 1967), vol. III, pp. 692-693.

10

Seeking a Solution
to the Problem of War

A reexamination of the problem of war and the possible means for its solution must begin with a recognition of the failure of past movements and proposals for the abolition of war. These have failed despite the widespread understanding of the destructiveness of modern war. Hardly anyone believes that we are on the way to end war. Military technology stands at its highest stage of development ever. During this decade and the past, military institutions in many countries have been, for a period which is not one of world war, the most powerful ever in comparison to civil branches of government and to the rest of society. Except for world wars, a higher proportion of resources has been devoted in this period to military purposes than ever before. A larger number of lives can now be threatened and destroyed more quickly than earlier imagined.

Defenders of the status quo are not the only practitioners and supporters of war and other political violence. Political movements, parties, and governments which espouse change are often equally committed to military means — as was the case in the war in Vietnam. Nor are we on the verge of a popular rebellion against war as such. The time when the general public might have been capable of significant shock and revulsion at the nature of modern weaponry to rebel against it — as in its early atomic and thermonuclear forms in the late 1940s and the 1950s — has gone.

True, there are antiwar groups. For example, some people object to all war, perhaps even more now do so than previously: the perpetually small minority which witnesses against all war by a refusal to participate in it. Many other people may oppose a *particular* war, as that in Vietnam, when it is perceived as especially unjust or inhuman.* (Some of the opponents of the United States' actions in Vietnam were, however, silent about, or even supported, the war effort of the other side.) Still other people, and even governments, support more limited measures and seek to limit the development, manufacture, spread, and use of certain military weapons while accepting that serious disarmament is outside the realm of reality.

But, with very few exceptions, the dream in which many people only a few decades ago firmly believed — that war, along with certain other objectionable aspects of society, could and would be abolished — is for the most part no longer even dreamed. The few persons who still believe in and voice that dream are perceived as out of touch with political reality. If ever in world history awareness of the destructiveness and brutality of war and of the relative power of military systems might have been expected to increase efforts to abolish the military system and to enhance the prospects for doing so, it should have been by now. Instead, we have witnessed the demise of even major efforts to end war.

---

*On the varieties of pacifism and on selective nonviolence, see Gene Sharp, *Gandhi as a Political Strategist, with Essays on Ethics and Politics* (Boston: Porter Sargent Publishers, 1979), Chapter Ten, "The Types of Principled Nonviolence."

REEXAMINING THE PROBLEM

It is, of course, possible that one or several of the previously proposed solutions to the problem of war have been partially or largely valid. In any case, those more orthodox approaches will continue to receive attention, as they generally should. However, our further examination of the problem of war should not be limited to those past approaches. It is not reasonable to presume that the answer to it must lie in an existing proposal, or course, or system, which has not yet moved us perceptibly closer to the resolution of that problem. A careful and critical reexamination of those earlier proposals to ensure peace and to abolish war is impossible here, although it is important that it be done. Since the past proposals have not yet worked, we shall here instead concentrate on developing a different analysis of the nature of the problem of war which will point the direction toward a possible alternative policy and solution. We are unlikely to find a solution to the problem of war if we do not adequately understand the nature of that problem. We need to examine afresh whether war might be abolished for particular societies, or generally — and, if so, how this might be done.

DISTASTEFUL "GIVENS"

A new effort to abolish war requires a prior rejection of any romantic illusions we may have about such abolition; the effort also requires a willingness to recognize certain facts which are often distasteful to exponents of peace. It is assumed here:

- that there will always be intra-societal and inter-societal conflicts;
- that in any such conflict, some type of power will always be present and needed, on both sides;
- that what is crudely called "human nature" need not, and most likely will not, be changed;
- that people and governments will not, and should not be asked to, sacrifice either freedom or justice for the sake of peace;
- that peace is not identical with maintenance of the status quo, nor with revolution;
- that individual conversions to pacifism are not going to hap-

pen by the hundreds of millions, and world peace will have to come in a different way;

- that there is no break in the spiral of military technology within the context of military technology and military assumptions;
- that there have been, and are, brutal dictatorships and oppressive systems in the world, which may continue and recur, use new forms of control, and may expand against other countries in various ways;
- that the abolition of capitalism does not produce the abolition of war (the military system is more powerful now in noncapitalist States than before the change, and military action is threatened and used by noncapitalist States against each other);
- that negotiation is not a substitute for the capacity to wage conflict and wield sanctions (a capacity which itself is a crucial factor in negotiations);
- that unilateral "disarmament" (understood as the major reduction or abandonment of defense capacity) is not possible (for reasons which will be discussed);
- that major multilateral disarmament is nearly as unlikely because of the fear of every country to be at a relative disadvantage, and also because of the constantly changing nature of the international situation;
- that national independence is *not* the origin of war, but instead reliance on military means as the ultimate sanction of the independent State;
- that peace through world government is either a dangerous illusion because it is unrealizable, or, if achievable, would constitute a severe danger to world peace (likely to produce a world civil war), to freedom (if capable of preventing war it would be capable of tyranny), and to justice (who would control, to what ends, and how could shifts of control and ends be prevented?).

Other such factors may also need to be recognized. Our search for an understanding of the problem of war, and for a solution to it, must not rest on utopian illusions. Neither must our search be naive concerning the political intentions of protagonists to international conflicts.

Nor can we neglect the role of the basic nature of certain social and political systems. The recognition of this role does not require agreement that any particular system be identified as the "devil." Critical analyses of any and all such systems are desirable; but it is unnecessary and dangerous to gloss over their unsatisfactory characteristics in order to contribute to peace. However, this attention to social and political systems should not lead us to neglect the military system itself. It has its own major requirements and structural consequences; without elimination of reliance on military means, structural or systemic change is unlikely to be very significant, and the new system is likely to find itself distorted or controlled by the military system it has accepted.*

FUNCTIONAL ALTERNATIVES

One possible approach to the problem of war has rarely been applied: analysis of the military system's capacity to wage war in terms of its function of providing defense (either in reality, or belief that it does), and exploration of whether or not defense could be provided in some other way. Functional analysis is sometimes dismissed as a status quo approach, but it is utilized here as a tool precisely because it may provide insights making possible fundamental change which may otherwise not be possible. Here the sociological terminology of "function" and "structure" will be used, which might instead be called "need" or "task" and "instrument" or "institution" for the particular purposes of this discussion.†

A.R. Radcliffe-Brown defined function as "the part it plays in the social life as a whole and therefore the contribution it makes to the maintenance of the structural continuity."[1] John Bennett and Melvin

---

*See Chapter Eleven, "The Societal Imperative," and Chapter Twelve, "Popular Empowerment," subchapter Sanctions and Society.

†Here I will in part repeat and enlarge upon a portion of the discussion in Chapter Nine, " 'The Political Equivalent of War' — Civilian-based Defense." See also the discussion on functions and structures in Chapter Twelve, "Popular Empowerment."

Tumin wrote that to ask the function of something is to ask "What does it 'do for' people and groups."[2] The recognition that human institutions have functions and perform certain jobs for society in no way blocks the way to change, even fundamental change. Instead, examination of the existence and possibilities of "functional substitutes," or "functional equivalents," or "functional alternatives" opens the way for basic change. Functional substitutes have been referred to by various analysts and theorists, including Theodor Newcomb,[3] Talcott Parsons,[4] Parsons and Edward A. Shils,[5] Lewis Coser,[6] and especially Robert K. Merton.[7]

Merton pointed out in 1949 that the existing social structures — that is, patterns of action, institutions, instruments, or "means" to a social goal — are not the only possible ones. There also exist other ways of fulfilling the function served by the present structure. The specific existing social structures, he insisted, are *not* functionally indispensable. Merton offered "as a major theorem of analysis": "*...the same function* [*may*] *be diversely fulfilled by alternative items.* Functional needs are here taken to be permissive, rather than determinant, of specific social structures."[8] In fact, alternative social structures have served the functions necessary for groups to continue to exist.[9] This, he wrote, "unfreezes the identity of the existent and the inevitable."[10] Since there may be a range of ways in which a particular functional need may be fulfilled, we should look for functional alternatives. He insisted that this was relevant to conscious efforts to produce social change, and offered also as "a basic theorem":

> *...any attempt to eliminate an existing social structure without providing adequate alternative structures for fulfilling the functions previously fulfilled by the abolished organization is doomed to failure.*[11]

Parsons similarly wrote: "There must be a development of 'functional alternatives' to the structures which have been eliminated."[12] And Coser, too, argued:

> In realistic conflict, there exist functional alternatives as to means ....[T]here are always possibilities of choice between various forms of contention, such choice depending...on an assessment of their instrumental adequacy.[13]

FUNCTIONS OF WAR

War is such a prominent institution of modern society that if these theoretical views are valid they must apply to the military system which wages war. Let us therefore explore the application of this functional substitute theory to war.

Such a complex and diverse structure as the military system has doubtless served many purposes or functions. A careful analysis of *all* of them is needed (a task which is not attempted here), including examinations of alternative ways of fulfilling those functions which seem lasting, and exploration of whether some of the functions of the military — especially those deemed undesirable — may be required only under specific conditions and not universally, and may hence be removed, reduced, or dealt with in some other way.

We shall here identify four functions of a military capacity which are primarily political and are associated with national policy of the governments:

Attack: especially international aggression, motivated or justified variously, including the desire for: economic benefit, power expansion, egocentric aggrandizement of rulers, "liberation," extending "civilization," seizure of territory, and extermination of "inferiors." Sometimes the attack is internal, against the governmental system of that very country, or against another part of the society, as in a coup d'état or civil war.

Domination: control and oppression of the home population, or foreign populations and countries, or both, also with diverse motivations remarkably similar to those just listed.

Deterrent: that is, prevention of attack by possession of sufficient capacity to cause the potential attacker to anticipate greater losses than gains, or that the attack will fail, and hence to decide against initiating the venture.

Defense: that is, "defense" in the literal sense of the term, as warding off, protection, resistance against attack, denial of the objective of the attacker, and upholding or maintaining one's own objectives against the attacker. This includes both defense against genuine attack and preparations to defend in case of attack. Also at times the excuse of "defense" is used to assist in internal domination or is used to disguise for the home population what is in fact an attack on another country. (This last point is very important, and the following analysis is by implication relevant to it, although that specific kind of situation requires separate analysis.)

The relative importance of each of the several functions of war may vary from case to case, culture to culture, and time to time, although certain ones may be both far more persistent and perceived to be more generally justifiable than others. Let us now look at these four functions more closely, in two groups.

FUNCTIONS OF ATTACK AND DOMINATION

It appears that the functions of attack and domination may be dealt with in other ways than by providing substitute nonmilitary means of attacking and dominating, functions which are in any case undesirable. These functions might be removed, or attempts to carry them out might be frustrated, and thus the functions in practice are finally drastically reduced in two ways:

1. Changes may be carried out in the society which is, or potentially is, the origin of an attack, to reduce or eliminate both motives and ability to attack, by changes in its social institutions, distribution of power, economic system, beliefs and attitudes as to legitimacy, acceptable policies, and the like. Those social changes require separate attention, which unfortunately is not possible here.* If attacks can be reduced or eliminated by social changes which remove the "need," functional alternatives are not required here.

---

*However, the view that institutional or systemic changes (with or without accompanying attitude changes) will lead to the abandonment of the military system without specific attention to that abandonment is rejected here. In fact, social changes and social revolution may *increase* the military system, and popular support for it, because of a perceived greater need to defend the changes against counterrevolutionary threats (domestic or foreign), or because the society is perceived to be more worthy of defense, and the like. If violent struggle has produced the social revolution, the relative role of the military system in comparison to civil branches of the government and other institutions is likely to increase. If the struggle was largely nonviolent but with confidence remaining in military means for defense, an increase in the military system is also likely, only to a lesser degree. Almost without exceptions, countries which have undergone avowed social revolutions possess stronger military systems after the revolution than they did under the old order. Attention is therefore needed to

2. The capacity of the attacked society to defend itself by some means might be increased, so as effectively to deter attacks, to defeat attacks if they occur, or to liberate itself from the oppression caused by past attacks. Successful and repeated defense (and liberation) to such internal or external attacks, denying the objectives to the attackers is likely to reduce the frequency with which military systems are used to attack, *provided that* the defense is by means which do not confirm the attacker's belief in the omnipotence of the military system to gain ends. In other words, in the case of this function, it may not be a functional substitute means of *attack* which may be required, but a functional substitute means of *defeating* the attack. There are very important reasons (which are developed elsewhere) why such deterrence and struggle against internal or external attacks may be more advantageously and effectively achieved by means *other than* the military forms of conflict.*

FUNCTIONS OF DETERRENCE AND DEFENSE

Military systems also are widely used to deter and to defend. The reasons offered by most people, policymakers, and government spokesmen for keeping and relying upon the military system even today are that a strong military capacity can, better than anything else, deter an attack, and defend against an attack. In the face of these perceived functions of military systems, pleas to abandon military capacity on moral, religious, humanitarian, or political grounds have historically been accepted by only a small minority, while the general population has, with few exceptions, rejected the antimilitary pleadings. War may be brutal, immoral, and even suicidal, but people have perceived that it provided an ultimate sanction and means of struggle for which they have perceived no alternative. Even where deterrence

---

other means of abolishing war than changes in the social system unaccompanied by abandonment of the military system. See the fuller discussion of these points in Chapter Twelve, "Popular Empowerment," subchapter Sanctions and Society.

*See Chapter Nine, " 'The Political Equivalent of War' — Civilian-based Defense."

and defense are *not* the real motives for military systems, popular support for those systems and war efforts will be forthcoming even for aggressive purposes, as long as people believe they have no alternative means of defense.

Whether to be held in reserve to back up one's position in international negotiations, to deter attack by adequate preparations, or to defend in case of attack, military systems have been believed necessary since no other way to fulfill those functions of deterrence and defense has been believed to exist. It has been commonly assumed that the alternative to war is impotence, cowardice, and passive submission, and that perception of "ordinary" people has been shared by statesmen, policymakers, intellectuals, and academics. Even nuclear and similar weapons have not changed this, for people believe that, although nuclear weapons normally ought not to be launched, their existence will prevent attack, and thus provide safety and avoid helplessness.

All of this analysis is fully compatible with the application of Merton's "basic theorem" to the problem of war, for Merton postulated that efforts to remove a basic structure without providing an alternative structure for fulfilling its function would be doomed to failure.[14] The need for defense of a society, its populace, its institutions, way of life and the like, is such a basic societal need that in conditions of perceived and actual threats of attack, the military system will not be abandoned when it is understood that this will leave the society helpless and defenseless in meeting real or imagined dangers. This is, however, precisely what proposals for abandonment of war and the military system have almost always meant or been perceived to mean.

SEPARATING STRUCTURE AND FUNCTION

Peace movements and most peace proposals have in their assumptions and analyses often confused structure and function, or, putting it in other ways, confused institution and job, or instrument and task. Exponents of peace have largely accepted the identity of the structure (the military system and war) with its perceived most justified functions (deterrence and defense), just as have the exponents and practitioners of the war system itself. It has been assumed that effective defense and strong military capacity are synonymous. Whether judged by Merton's theorem, by statements of political officials, or by the views of "ordinary" people, it was predictable and inevitable that past efforts to abolish war would fail. This also explains why present and future efforts which are primarily antimilitary and antiwar cannot succeed.

The simple distinction between structure and function, or instrument and task, applied to war and defense may free us from the axiomatic presumption of the identity of defense with the military system. The distinction between defense and the military system enables us to ask whether there can be alternative means of defense which are not military — a question which to most people has been inconceivable.

This ought not to be as ludicrous a question as it might appear to others, since, even with present policies, defense and military capacity are not identical. First, the growth and development of military technology means that in its extreme forms the actual use of military means can in some cases provide only vast destruction and death, *not* actual defense. Second, in some cases, the advance perception of such possible destruction, or of overwhelming military capacity by the attacker, may lead to a realization that military resistance for defense is futile and hence to a decision not to attempt it. Third, and most important, in some international conflicts, nonmilitary means of resistance have already been improvised and used for national defense purposes. Also, such nonviolent means of struggle, in crude and undeveloped forms, have been widely used and often highly important in internal conflicts.

The analysis in this section of the chapter has pointed in this direction:

The path to the abolition of war may lie through the substitution of nonmilitary means of defense, if these exist, can be created or refined, and if they are, or can be made to be, at least as instrumentally effective as military means of defense have been and now are.

NONVIOLENT STRUGGLE

The world, much less politics, is not divided neatly into categories of "violence" and "nonviolence." There are many intermediary phenomena which are neither violent nor nonviolent. But in terms of ultimate sanctions and means of struggle, which are used when milder means are judged inadequate or have failed, there do appear to be two broad techniques, one violent action — which includes several types of violent conflict, among them conventional and nuclear war — the other, nonviolent action — which is also a broad and diverse technique. It is to the nature and potential of this nonviolent technique of struggle that our attention now turns.

Our awareness and understanding of the nonviolent counterpart of violent struggle is generally sharply limited and filled with many serious distortions and errors of fact. Therefore, an initial effort is usually required to free our minds from inaccurate perceptions of this type of struggle which we have accumulated from a culture in which belief in violence as the ultimate form of power and as the most significant single fact in history — both of which are now challenged — are fundamental axioms. This belief in the omnipotence of violence, and ignorance of the power of popular nonviolent struggle, may have also been compatible with the interests of past dominating elites who did not want people to realize their power potential.

Because of preconceptions, it is necessary to indicate some of the things that nonviolent action is *not*. This technique is the opposite of passivity, submissiveness, and cowardice. Nonviolent action uses social, economic, psychological, and political power in the matching of forces in conflict, and is not to be equated with verbal or purely psychological persuasion. This means of struggle does not assume that humans are inherently "good." This is not "pacifism"; in fact, this technique has been predominantly used by "ordinary" people who never became pacifists, and also some pacifists find it offensive. Nonviolent conflict may operate even in cases of extreme social distance between contending groups. The technique may be more "Western" than "Eastern," and certainly is not the reverse. It is designed to combat a violent opponent, and does not presume a nonviolent response to the nonviolent challenge. This technique may be used for both "good" and "bad" causes, though the social consequences of its use for "bad" causes differs sharply from those of violence.* While violence is believed to work fast, and nonviolent

_____

*See the discussion on this point in Chapter Twelve, "Popular Empowerment."

action slowly, often violence takes a great length of time and nonviolent struggle may operate extremely quickly. Finally, and most importantly for this chapter, nonviolent action is not limited to domestic conflicts within a democratic system; it has been used widely against dictatorial regimes, foreign occupations, and even totalitarian systems,* and it has already been applied without advance preparations internationally, even in improvised national defense struggles.

Our recent studies of this technique have revealed it to be infinitely richer, more variable and powerful than hitherto dreamed.[15] It has been widely thought that, for the most part, politically significant nonviolent struggle began with Gandhi. We now know that it has a rich and vast history which we are only beginning to piece together which goes back at least to several centuries B.C., and ranges over many cultures, continents, countries, historical periods, issues, types of groups, and opponents. Instead of the list of specific methods, or forms of action included within this technique being relatively few (a dozen or so as was once thought) we now know that even with a partial listing the number is at least 198, arranged in three main classes of nonviolent protest and persuasion (the milder forms), noncooperation (including boycotts of social relations, economic boycotts, strikes, and political noncooperation), and nonviolent intervention.

It was thought by some that conversion of the opponent by the sufferings of the nonviolent actionists was the only, or at least the best, way in which nonviolent action produced change. We now know that this is not true, and that nonviolent struggle can also be coercive, possibly even more so than violence against an obstinate opponent. This is because nonviolent struggle is capable of severing the various sources of the opponent's power, as by massive civil disobedience of the population as a whole paralyzing the political system, strikes by workers and noncooperation by management paralyzing the economic system, noncooperation by civil servants paralyzing the governmental structure, mutiny by soldiers destroying the repressive capacity, and in many other equally important but more subtle ways.

*See Chapter Four, "Facing Dictatorships With Confidence."

COMPARISON WITH VIOLENT STRUGGLE

A survey of the knowledge we now have of the history of nonviolent action would facilitate our consideration of this largely neglected socio-political technique, but that is not possible within the scope of this chapter. Suffice it to say that it is a remarkable history which when more fully revealed will require and produce major reexaminations of not only social but political history, and fundamental reinterpretations of very significant historical cases where violence is widely presumed to have been the only form of struggle, or the only possible successful one. In this, the American Revolution,* the Russian Revolution, and struggles against Nazism are only three of the more dramatic such cases.

This new understanding and information about the nature, history, dynamics, and existing capacities of nonviolent struggle is of a magnitude to require major reevaluation of the judgements which have been made or assumed about its effectiveness and potential in comparison with violence. That is but the beginning, however.

Nonviolent action has almost always been improvised without significant awareness of the history of this type of struggle. It has usually been waged without qualified leadership, or without compensating wide popular understanding of the technique, without thorough comprehension of its requirements for effectiveness, without preparations and training, without analyses of past conflicts, without studies of strategy and tactics, without conscious development of its "weaponry," and often without a consciousness among the actionists that they were waging a special type of struggle. In short, the most unfavorable circumstances possible have accompanied the use of this technique. It is amazing that the significant number of victories for nonviolent struggle exists at all, for these conditions of the lack of knowledge, skill, and preparations have been to the highest degree unfavorable. In contrast, for many centuries military struggle has benefited from conscious efforts to improve its effectiveness in all the ways which nonviolent action has lacked.

---

*See Walter Conser, Ronald McCarthy, Gene Sharp, David Toscano, and Kenneth Wadoski, eds., *To Bid Defiance To Tyranny: Nonviolent Action and the American Independence Movement 1765-1775* (Boston: Porter Sargent Publishers, 1981).

INTERNATIONAL RELEVANCE

Some people assume that means of conflict which have predominantly been used in domestic conflicts — as nonviolent action — are intrinsically limited to that range of conflict situations, while military struggle is the means obviously appropriate to the international level. On closer reflection it becomes obvious that this distinction is by no means as clear-cut as is often assumed. Violent action, of course, is also widely used internally — in repression, resistance, coups d'état, revolution, guerrilla war, civil war, and the like. Also, certain forms of nonviolent action are used internationally far more frequently than is usually recognized — such as embargoes, freezing the assets of another country, economic boycotts, cancellation of planned conferences and diplomatic visits, and refusal of diplomatic recognition. Other forms — which are far more relevant to our analysis — are the cases of widespread civilian resistance against invasion forces and occupation regimes.

The reality may be that whether a given technique is applicable to domestic or international conflicts is not determined by whether it does or does not use physical violence but by whether people have tried to adapt it as effectively as possible to that particular type of conflict situation. The presumption that nonviolent struggle is only appropriate to domestic conflicts is not valid.

Nonviolent struggle has already been applied in international politics *without planning or preparations and at times even without advice decision* (all of which are regarded as essential for maximum effectiveness). These international struggles do not refer to international economic boycotts and embargoes. Contrary to Thomas Jefferson, who saw those economic weapons as the basis for a substitute for war, they are probably not models, or even primitive prototypes, upon which to build a nonviolent functional substitute for war. Other cases exist which, although not models, might be early prototypes upon which to build more successful prepared and trained nonviolent defense capacities.

The resistance of Czechoslovakia in 1968–69 is the closest to what is envisaged. This was a nonviolent war of resistance to invasion and occupation, a war which in the end was lost. We learn from lost military wars, however, and we can learn from lost nonviolent wars. According to some reports, the Russians anticipated military resistance from the able Czechoslovak army, and expected they could overcome it and install a puppet government within four days. Despite very considerable Czechoslovak military capacity based on years of preparations and training, the obvious futility of military resistance in face of five invading armies, including that of the Soviet Union, produced a decision not to resist with military force.

Instead, an unprepared, improvised nonviolent resistance occurred. Despite serious problems, and apparent major strategic errors, and sometimes without adequate assistance from the official leadership, this resistance managed initially to frustrate completely the Russian efforts to install a puppet government in spite of the distribution of troops throughout the country. This resistance also forced the Soviet Union to negotiate with Czechoslovak leaders (some of whom, as Dubček, already had been arrested and kidnapped). All this was produced by people whose country was already totally occupied and whose army had never entered the field, conditions under which negotiations should not — by conventional views — have been required or expected!

Even after those negotiations, such resistance in less dramatic forms in fact maintained the Dubček regime, so hated by the Russians, in power (after their release from arrest and imprisonment) until April of 1969 — eight months! Even then, it can be argued, the demise resulted more from the collapse of resistance by the Government and Party at a time of anti-Russian riots (a break in the nonviolent discipline, possibly caused by *agents provocateurs*) than it did from any intrinsic weakness in the means of resistance.

That initial week of unified nonviolent resistance and complete denial of political victory to the Russians, and the eight-month life of the very regime which was the stimulus for the Russian invasion, are achievements of immense proportions. This is especially true considering that this nonviolent resistance capacity was *unprepared,* and hence probably less effectual and certainly less reliable than if it had been adequately prepared. Had unprepared military struggle against such odds held off the Russians for eight months it would have been hailed as victory even in defeat, with courage and historical significance comparable to Thermopylae.

There have been other cases, such as the struggle in the Ruhr against the French and Belgian occupation in 1923 in which nonviolent resistance was launched as offical German Government policy.

(The situation became mixed with sabotage later with detrimental effects for the German cause.) This case is widely regarded as a complete German defeat. Nevertheless, it led to an end of the occupation, and disastrous economic consequences for France (as well as Germany), and the French people's revulsion against the French Government's repression policies of their former enemies. This revulsion is said to have contributed to the unexpected electoral defeat of Prime Minister Poincaré's Government in the next election — achievements which Germany was militarily unable even to *attempt* at the time.

Significant other cases of nonviolent resistance can be classed as nonviolent struggle for national defense. These include the Hungarian struggle against Austria for home rule from 1850 to 1867, and Finland's struggles against Russification, especially from 1898 to 1905. Even the Gandhian struggles in India against British rule were those of an occupied country seeking restoration of independence — surely an international conflict. (Gandhi was far from the first Indian nationalist to advocate or organize nonviolent struggle for independence.) During the Second World War, Norwegian, Danish, and Dutch resistance against the Nazi occupations and certain other anti-Nazi struggles, including limited efforts to save Jews, produced some modest but significant victories. Some of these actions had the support of, or were even initiated by, the Government-in-exile.

A BASIS FOR A SUBSTITUTE FOR WAR?

Nonviolent action generally, and its use for national defense purposes specifically, has never even yet received systematic efforts to develop its capacity, to increase its effectiveness, and to expand the areas of its utility. The nonviolent technique is thus an underdeveloped political technique, probably at the stage comparable to violent group conflict several thousand years ago. Hence, nonviolent struggle as waged to date may only have revealed a small fraction of its potential fighting power and effectiveness.

The challenge now is to bring to nonviolent struggle research, analysis, experimentation, planning, preparations, and training, with the objective of attaining greater knowledge and understanding, facilitating our ability to evaluate it fairly, increasing the effectiveness of this technique, and, finally, exploring its progressive extension to serious conflict situations where most people have presumed that only military, or other violent, conflict was adequate.

Specifically, the question is this: can a national defense policy, for both small and large countries, be created by the capacity of the civilian population, trained, prepared, knowledgeable, to wield non-violent struggle? Can this policy make the consolidation and maintenance of control by an invading force or a coup d'état impossible? Even cursory examination of strategies for civilian-based defense lies outside this chapter. We note only that they are diverse, and flexible, and always need to be related to the specific situation and the objectives of the attacker in order to defeat his specific aims as effectively and efficiently as possible.

Also, the question arises as to whether such preparations can be perceived as sufficiently effective to deter invasions and coups. Finally, can this policy be relevant to the present nuclear powers? Would such a country which (1) had gradually built up its capacity to wage civilian-based defense, and then (2) had by unilateral action or negotiated agreements gradually phased down and dispensed with its military weaponry, including its nuclear capacity, as unneeded, be likely to be threatened or attacked with nuclear weapons? (This needs careful attention even though today it is generally the nuclear powers that fear attack, while the nonnuclear powers generally do not expect it.)

In comparing nonviolent struggle with military struggle for defense capacity the same criteria must be used in evaluating both, in terms of the degree of risk, what is risked, the costs if it comes to an open clash, the nature of failure and success in such a clash, and the possible gains in case of success.

IS IT POSSIBLE?

This type of policy is called "civilian defense," in some countries, "social defense" in Germany and the Netherlands, and increasingly "civilian-based defense" in the United States. It is direct defense of the society, its principles, people, way of life, chosen institutions, right to maintain or change itself, by action of the civilian population as a whole, and their institutions, using civilian (nonmilitary, nonviolent) means of struggle. It should go without saying that this is not a panacea and other diverse programs are needed to help meet many other needs.

This approach on a serious policy level began only in 1957. it has thus far received the most respectful attention from people regarded as hard-headed realists, strategists, defense analysts, planners, and military officers, as well as others interested in social change and world peace. The response is as yet small, but it includes limited governmental interest in several European countries. Books and other publications now exist on the subject in several European languages and Japanese. Thus in the relatively few years since 1957 this idea has been transformed from a vague conception into a strategic proposal receiving serious thought from the most unlikely people.

Some people still see this as a romantic conception unassociated with the real and the possible. Yet, there is profound truth contained in what Kenneth Boulding calls "Boulding's First Law"; "What exists, is possible."[16] Nonviolent action exists. It has occurred in human history on a scale, seriousness, and with a degree of success (nothing is ever always successful) which has hitherto been unrealized (despite the noted lack of understanding). Nonviolent struggle has even been applied against ruthless tyrants, and as we observed has already been used for national defense. Social science research, policy development, and strategic analysis also exist and can be applied to this phenomenon. We have more evidence today that a civilian-based defense policy is possible, and, if adequately prepared, could work more effectively than military means for real defense at this stage of history, than there was in August 1939 that atomic bombs were possible. That was the date when Dr. Einstein wrote the famous letter to President Roosevelt saying that *maybe* a new highly explosive bomb could be made from atoms.

It is popular today to pronounce that war is inevitable because of the aggressive nature of human beings, and hence some people conclude that this nonviolent "thing" is all nonsense. That is not the view of significant writers on human agressiveness. Konrad Lorenz has insisted that: "modern war has become an institution and . . . being an institution war can be abolished."[17] Robert Ardrey, no less, has asserted: "We must be nonviolent. Yes, we can do it — but are we going to have to work at it."[18]

Civilian-based defense is set forth for study and research as a possible functional substitute for war, as a means of abolishing war while providing real defense by nonviolent means against tyrants and aggressors. If it could be made to work at least as well as military means, it would be possible for individual countries, alone or in groups, without waiting on others, to "transarm," that is to change over to this defense system. This would be possible (in contrast to disarmament) because if it does work, civilian-based defense will maintain or increase defense capacity while making possible abandonment of military means as unneeded. It would thus by-pass the most serious blockage to disarmament proposals, fear of reduced fighting capacity, or an unfavorable relative fighting capacity for providing defense against attack.

FOUR TASKS

A vast amount of research, analysis, and problem-oriented investigation is required to examine whether this approach to provide a functional substitute for the military system and defensive military warfare is indeed a fruitful one, and whether, and if so how, the multitude of difficult problems associated with it can be solved. These problems include such questions as the means of training and preparations, how to handle the transarmament period, ways to meet the particular defense needs of individual countries, and the potential of this policy (compared with violence) in confronting successfully the most extreme and ruthless regimes.

Four tasks now urgently need to be tackled simultaneously to determine whether the approach to the problem of war presented in this chapter contains the basis for its solution.

First, a major program of research, analysis, and problem-oriented investigation, involving thousands of scholars of many disciplines, analysts, and other specialists. Outlines of some general research areas which might be tackled have been already proposed,[19] and others are needed. Dozens of research centers and programs are required.

Second, public and private discussion and evaluation of this substitute-for-war-policy, the problems with which it attempts to deal, existing knowledge relevant to whether it could work, and the difficulties which must be overcome if the policy is to be viable, and its potentialities and possible consequences.

Third, serious investigation and evaluation of this policy by civilian governmental bodies, defense departments, private institutions and groups, organizations, institutions, and individuals.

Fourth, high school, college, university, and general public education courses on the nature of nonviolent action, its potential as an alternative to domestic violence, and on the potential and problems of civilian-based defense as a substitute for war.

Each of these four tasks will require major resources and personnel. Considering the seriousness of our problems, this is a very modest proposal.

NOTES

1. A. R. Radcliffe-Brown, **Structure and Function in Primitive Society** (Glencoe, Ill.: The Free Press, 1952), p. 180.
2. John Bennett and Melvin Tumin, **Social Life: Structure and Function** (New York: Alfred A. Knopf, 1948), p. 245.
3. Theodor Newcomb, **Social Psychology** (New York: Dryden Press, 1950), p. 351.
4. Talcott Parsons, **Essays in Sociological Theory, Pure and Applied** (Glencoe, Ill.: The Free Press, 1949), p. 58. Also, Parsons, **The Social System** (Glencoe, Ill.: The Free Press, 1951), p. 210.
5. T. Parsons and Edward A. Shils, **Toward A General Theory of Action** (Cambridge, Mass.: Harvard University Press, 1951), p. 5.
6. Lewis Coser, **The Functions of Social Conflict** (London: Collier-Macmillan, and New York: The Free Press, 1956), p. 50.
7. Robert K. Merton, **Social Theory and Social Structure** (Glencoe, Ill.: The Free Press, 1949), pp. 35-36, 52 and 79.
8. Ibid., p. 35. Italics are Merton's.
9. Ibid.
10. Ibid., p. 52.
11. Ibid., p. 79. Italics are Merton's.
12. Parsons, **The Social System,** p. 167.
13. Coser, **The Functions of Social Conflict,** p. 50.
14. A longer discussion of some aspects of this exploration is contained in Gene Sharp, "The Need of a Functional Substitute for War," **International Relations** (London), vol. III, no. 3 (April 1967), pp. 187-207.
15. See esp. Gene Sharp, **The Politics of Nonviolent Action** (Boston: Porter Sargent Publisher, 1973). This is a comprehensive presentation and analysis of the nature of nonviolent struggle. Discussion in this chapter of that technique is documented in that book. It does not contain, however, discussion of the "civilian-based defense" policy, although it provides the necessary groundwork to that

policy. On Gandhi, see Gene Sharp, **Gandhi As A Political Strategist, with Essays on Ethics and Politics** (Boston: Porter Sargent Publishers, 1979), esp. Chapters One, Two, and Three.

16. Kenneth Boulding, quoted in Jerome D. Frank, **Sanity and Survival: Psychological Aspects of War and Peace** (New York: Vintage Books, Random House, 1968), p. 270.

17. Konrad Lorenz, **On Aggression** (New York: Harcourt, Brace and World, 1963), p. 284.

18. Louis S. B. Leakey and Robert Ardrey, in a dialogue, on "Man, the Killer," **Psychology Today,** vol. 6, no. 4 (September 1972), p. 85.

19. Gene Sharp, **Exploring Nonviolent Alternatives** (Boston: Porter Sargent Publisher, 1970), pp. 73-114, and Gene Sharp, "Research Areas on the Nature, Problems and Potentialities of Civilian Defense," in S. C. Biswas, ed., **Gandhi: Theory and Practice, Social Impact and Contemporary Relevance: Proceedings of a Conference,** (Simla: Indian Institute of Advanced Studies, 1969), pp. 393-414.

11

The Societal Imperative

We have not solved the grave problems of our time, nor are we even on the way toward their solution. Few of us are confident that we can solve them; few really expect that a more hopeful future lies ahead.

We face many serious problems today. In this chapter we will focus on four of these: dictatorship, genocide, war, and systems of social oppression.* If we can achieve adequate understanding of these problems, we may become able to chart strategies and develop programs to deal with them and to prevent them. We can do this long before we are able to create an ideal world. That should be our goal, rather than simply expressing dissent. While vigorous dissent is a

*See the initial discussion of these in Chapter One, "Rethinking Politics."

moral and political imperative for people whose convictions transcend the limitations of present policies and systems, too often dissent
is the last option of people who are unable to effect significant
change. Dissent is at best a less than adequate response. Our responsibility is to seek to achieve fundamental change in harmony with the
widely espoused ideals of freedom, human dignity, peace, and justice.

Before acting to achieve fundamental change we must think.
First, we must face the fact that we have so far failed to solve some of
our most severe problems. Then, we need to reexamine what makes
those problems possible and what is required to solve them. Let us
look again at the problems which were introduced at the beginning of
Chapter One.

The most extreme forms of dictatorship which the world has
ever seen — Nazism and Stalinism — have thrived in the twentieth
century along with lesser tyrannies waving different flags in many
other parts of the world. Despite this, we still do not have programs to
prevent the development of dictatorships, or preparations to enable
people to undermine and destroy those systems once they are
launched. Some people purporting to be committed to progress and
peace even object to using the terms "dictatorship" and "totalitarianism" to describe such systems, claiming that the terms are reactionary
or are conducive to war. Other persons positively justify certain
dictatorships as necessary and beneficial.

We have not faced, let alone solved, the problem of genocide.
Deliberate extermination has been glaringly demonstrated in the
Nazi slaughter of about six million Jews, perhaps one hundred
thousand Gypsies, many million Eastern Europeans, and others. We
know that these were not the first mass slaughters — witness the
killings of the Native Americans and Tasmanians by the European
settlers, and the massacres of Armenians, Africans, Bengalis, Cam-
bodians, and others. We know these have not been the last. We
express horror at these events. Yet we have no program to prevent
genocide and no credible policy to stop future attempts.

The destructive capacity of modern war has reached a pinnacle
which was in earlier centuries inconceivable. In significant ways the
situation is worsening. New weapon systems are being developed,
and the governments of both industrialized and nonindustrialized
countries, Western, Communist and Third World, supported by
most of their populations are seeking systemically to achieve maxi-

mum military capacities in both conventional and often nuclear weaponry. This occurs despite the awareness of the potential consequences of large scale use of weapons of mass destruction. Everywhere noble motives are avowed to justify this increased capacity to destroy; the weapons are needed, it is said, to protect, defend, combat evil, deter attack, and make peace possible. We must now presume that it is possible that none of the past proposals to abolish war is adequate or even valid.

Systems of social oppression, injustice, and exploitation rooted in the past continue, and often take new forms with enhanced capacities for the control of whole societies. Movements to create a new society instead of such systems have often fallen far short of their original objectives. Even where changed or new systems have achieved equitable economic distribution, the general populace has usually not gained increased capacities to determine their own present and future; economic classes have been replaced with political classes which also control the economic systems. In place of popular empowerment, the bureaucratic, police, and military structures of the new systems have grown. At times, instead of liberty, equality, and fraternity, the new order has resulted in political enslavement, terror, and indoctrination.

GROUNDS FOR URGENCY

None of these four problems — dictatorship, genocide, war, and systems of social oppression — should be ignored or sacrificed in an attempt to resolve another. This has often happened in the past, out of choice or a perceived necessity. In the interest of "peace," some people have been silent about dictatorship, injustice, and even genocide. In the interest of freedom, some have been willing to wipe out the lives of multitudes of people. In the interest of justice, some have imposed brutal dictatorships, killed off many people, and waged internal and foreign wars. Even then, the results achieved for the particular goal have often been meager, or even counterproductive.

We have not developed comprehensive programs capable of solving the four problems at the same time. Even when we have recognized a moral responsibility to do so, we have often assumed it to be an impossible task. It is not impossible, but it is not becoming easier. Unless major progress is soon made toward resolving these four problems, however, the developments in technology, political organization, the behavioral sciences, and genetics will increase their severity in the future, producing new types of dictatorship, genocide, war, and social oppression hitherto unequalled in human history. These will all be far more difficult to solve than the present problems. It is, therefore, our societal imperative to resolve these four problems and to develop a program for their prevention.

In addition to moral reasons for facing all four simultaneously, it may be politically impossible to solve any one of these problems unless we recognize their interrelationships and common features.

SEEING THE OBVIOUS

Our past failures to solve these four problems and to create the four corresponding positive conditions of freedom, respect for life, peace, and social justice may be due to an insufficient understanding of the problems. The analyses upon which the attempted remedies were based appear to have been inadequate or incomplete. Let us, therefore, look at these problems in a different way.

The significance of simple insights sometimes escapes us. We may not see the "obvious," and therefore fail to understand the problem. Let us look at the four phenomena, and ask whether there is a particular element without which they could not exist. Without what single factor would they be eliminated or be so radically transformed as not to be the same phenomena at all? Such a single element in fact does exist. *It is the application of organized violence as the ultimate sanction applied to achieve the objectives of the systems in which those four phenomena occur. Those systems all use institutionalized political violence to achieve their aims.** This is not, of course, violence of any and all types; it is not violence which is the result of

---

*Political violence** here means the application or threat of physical injury or death against persons for political objectives, and actions, such as imprisonment, which depend on that use or threat.

Political violence is here defined on the basis of the nature of the act itself and not on whether the act is deemed to be illegitimate or legitimate. The common practice of calling the same types of acts of violence "force" if they are deemed to be legitimate and are used on behalf of the system, and "political violence" if they are deemed to be

individual frustration or hostility, for example. Instead, it is violence as sanctions,* which is purposive and which is applied on behalf of some societal or political objective. The objectives of this institutionalized political violence in the four problems are to dominate, control, combat, or destroy the general population, hostile groups, disliked people, subjected groups or classes, political opponents, and enemy States.

Without such violence each of the four phenomena upon which we are focusing either could not exist, or would assume a radically different form. Dictatorship without violence would bear little resemblance to the political systems called by that name in the past. Unless psychological conditioning were fully effective as a substitute for violent repression, these new systems without political police, prisons, concentration camps, or military repression against the population would be the most fragile systems imaginable. Genocide

---

illegitimate and are used against the system, interferes with our perception of reality and our ability to analyze those political systems. The use of separate words for identical or similar acts of physical violence, or the threat of it, applied for political objectives on the basis of whether the use is judged to be legitimate or illegitimate can only blur our understanding of the political reality and cloud important issues. The distinction assumes that, for example, when the *imprimatur* of legitimacy is given to killing a person the act itself is totally different from the same act carried out without such legitimation. The distinction made between "violence" and "force" has contributed to our failure to perceive sharply that the ultimate sanction upon which even the most free, liberal, and democratic political systems of the West ultimately rely to enforce their will, to achieve their objectives, and to preserve their autonomy and existence is political violence. It is much more honest and accurate to refer to "illegitimate violence" and "legitimate violence." Even that, however, is not fully satisfactory, because it implies that objective and unchallenged criteria exist for determining legitimacy, and that major differences of judgment about that do not arise. That is demonstrably not the case. Sharp differences in criteria, judgements, and such determinations exist. Therefore, it is far better to indicate whether the given reference group has accepted the action as legitimate or has not done so by using instead the terms "legitimated violence" and "nonlegitimated violence."

*Sanctions here mean punishments, pressures, and means of action used to penalize, thwart, and alter the behavior of other persons, groups, institutions, or States. Sanctions are used not only by States to help enforce the obedience of the populace. Sanctions are also applied by the citizenry against the State, by certain nongovernmental groups against others, and by States against each other. Sanctions in domestic and international politics are usually a key element in political power. In many situations simply the capacity to wield, or the threat to apply, sanctions may induce the desired behavior.

without violence would be reduced to simple bigotry and discrimination. War without violence would be so different from military war that many pacifists would find it acceptable. Systems of social oppression without violence to threaten and to repress and to keep unjustly treated people "in place" would be fatally weakened and could not survive. These four grave problems may have other relationships also, but they clearly all share a common major dependency on institutionalized political violence as the ultimate sanction of the systems which carry out those activities. It is their common ingredient.

It is therefore possible that no resolution of any of those problems is possible without full consideration of that simple fact. The four may all be individual forms of the use of institutionalized violence for political purposes, four expressions of a single problem.

In contrast, the four opposites of those phenomena — broadly described as freedom, respect for life, peace, and systems of social justice — appear to be characterized by the significantly reduced use, or even the absence, of political violence. This reduction appears to allow other social influences and forces a freer reign, producing qualitatively different societal and political results than does the intensive and extensive application of political violence. For example, one of the several characteristics of political freedom is the absence of the use of police, troops, imprisonment, and executions against political opponents.

Of course, these four opposite positive conditions have only been imperfectly achieved, and the political systems within which they have developed have also ultimately relied on political violence as their ultimate sanction, perceiving no other one as realistic. However, sufficient restraints and restrictions have sometimes been placed on the use of that violence to make highly significant differences in the societal and political results.

Closely associated with the four positive conditions are two characteristics: (1) the existence of effective nonviolent means of conducting conflicts not resolvable by milder means, and (2) the possession by people and groups of effective power to influence and control their lives and shape their society.

VIOLENCE AS THE ULTIMATE SANCTION

"Rulers" in command of the State apparatus, their opponents and advocates of change, and the general population of a society all require sanctions of some type. These may be held in reserve to facilitate the successful operation of more routine procedures of the society's institutions, and may also be wielded directly when regular procedures are closed, are inappropriate, or have failed. In Western and many non-Western societies some type of political violence is viewed as the ultimate sanction in politics. Such violence may be threatened or applied, and used on behalf of, or in opposition to, the established system. History is perceived to a large extent as a past shaped by powerful governments and rulers, by the repressive violence of "law and order" of the established systems, by armies and battles, by violent revolutions, slaughters, assassinations, and riots. Most people assume that in the present violence is the only possible ultimate sanction in all political systems. People, theorists, and regimes have generally been confident that in extreme situations in domestic and international politics, political violence, threatened or applied, provides the most powerful available type of realistic sanctions for use as means of last resort offering reasonable chances of effectiveness in extreme situations. The view that "power comes out of the barrel of a gun" is simply a crude way of expressing the widely held view that violent sanctions are at times necessary to support, defend, or advance one's objectives amidst the dangers and conflicts of politics.

Violent sanctions applied for political purposes take a variety of forms. When used by individuals, private organizations, and mass movements, violent sanctions take the forms of physical assaults, murders, bombings, kidnappings, riots, terrorism, violent uprisings, and guerrilla warfare. When used by the State and paragovernmental bodies, violent sanctions take the forms of imprisonment, organized terrorization of the population, police action, executions, civil war, conventional military action, aerial bombings and rocket attacks, coups d'état, weaponry of mass destruction, and other forms. The specific means, the scale, and the extent and precise nature of the threatened or inflicted injury all vary widely.

The purposes for which political violence is applied differ greatly. It may be used with the intent of advancing the public good, supporting "law and order," maintaining an oppressive system, establishing a dictatorial regime, achieving social change, crushing opposition, righting ancient wrongs, intimidating hostile regimes, or destroying foreign enemies. The permanent institutionalized capacity to inflict violent sanctions internally and internationally, in the forms of the police and penal systems, and a standing military institution, is a major characteristic of the State as such.

We have not always been completely happy about violence as the ultimate sanction in politics. Various groups and systems have denounced political violence as a sanction for all causes of which they did not approve. Some have attempted to set criteria to determine when it might legitimately be applied. Some have objected to particular forms of political violence (as torture or certain weapons). Some have focused on the institutional procedures for determining when legitimate use could be made of such violence. Still others have asked in whose "interests" the violence was being applied. Liberal democratic systems have probably gone as far as any modern political system to minimize at least the internal reliance on violence as the ultimate sanction of the system.

Recognizing certain problems associated with violent sanctions, but also accepting them as needed, liberal democracies have attempted by various *procedures* to restrict the purposes and situations in which the violent sanctions can be used, and who may legitimately use them. In these liberal democracies, however, the ultimate dependence on such institutionalized political violence remains intact, even when disguised by the code word "force." When such systems face domestic or international crises, the reality of that ultimate sanction to maintain those systems is revealed.[1] In contrast, in blatant dictatorships there is usually little doubt that the ultimate political sanction lies in the capacity to imprison, to wound, and to kill. Whatever the other merits and benefits of the limiting procedures of liberal democracies, they do not solve the problem of institutionalized political violence. Violence, even when disliked by idealists, has been recognized as the foundation of realistic politics.

Violence is widely seen to be so natural and essential that serious consideration is rarely given to the possibly harmful structural consequences of such violence, nor to the possibility of alternative effective sanctions, including means of struggle. It has been almost impossible to conceive that institutionalized political violence could itself be the indispensable component of the four grave problems which we are considering.

INSTITUTIONALIZED POLITICAL VIOLENCE

As societies have grown in size and complexity, it has become necessary for violent sanctions to be organized in advance of each particular need, that is, they must be institutionalized. This particular type of violence has characteristics and capacities not possessed by other violence; not all violence, nor even all political violence is directly relevant to this analysis of the four problems. The violence with which we are dealing involves particular State institutions which have been established to apply certain violent sanctions to achieve objectives of the political system. We are dealing here with the *institutionalized* capacity for political violence. These institutions include regular military forces, reserves and national guard units, police, prison systems, internment and concentration camp systems, execution groups, assassination squads, and similar bodies. These institutions differ somewhat from country to country, and in particular States certain of these bodies may not exist, or may operate only rarely. In all cases, however, the capacity for violence is neither accidental nor incidental: these institutions have been established deliberately to serve given objectives — not necessarily bad ones, and indeed often noble ones.* The institutions to apply political violence are set up to act under the direction of officials of the political system to apply the ultimate sanction of political violence when it is deemed necessary.†

---

*However, whether those institutions for applying political violence in fact serve those objectives optimally may require attention.

†The general population may or may not have any voice in that decision. In extreme cases officials may order the use of widespread violence against the general population. The applications of political violence may be ordered in accordance with the constitution and laws of the society, or in violation of those rules.

TRANSFERABLE CAPACITY

This organized capacity for violence has an especially serious characteristic: once an institution is established to apply violence for one political purpose, that same institution can be shifted to apply that violence for *other* objectives. These may even be objectives prohibited by the constitution or laws. Such shifts can produce unanticipated and unwanted consequences. These shifts may be made under orders of officials of the legitimate government, or by autonomous action of officers and staff of the institution, deliberately defying contrary orders and laws. Such actions by these institutions or sectors within them may even overthrow the established government by an executive usurpation or a coup d'état. Additional shifts of the uses of the institutionalized capacity for political violence can then be made by the usurpers who have newly gained control of the State.

The same army that has fought foreign enemies may repress civilians at home during political unrest, a labor strike, or a revolt against an internal dictatorship. Regular police forces established to protect the public may shift to political repression, or even to the rounding up of persons for deportation or extermination. Political police in a revolutionary country can shift from detecting counter-revolutionaries to expurgating those deemed ideologically impure, or possible rivals or opponents of the new dictatorship. An organization for gathering domestic political intelligence about terrorist actions may instruct angry protestors in methods of arson and demolition in order to discredit and destroy them. An army which has fought against domestic or foreign forces to achieve a revolution may later be turned to invade neighboring countries, or to kill vast sections of the population. An agency for carrying out political assassinations and coups d'état in other countries may do the same at home.

Such shifts may not occur, of course. Conditions may not be suitable, or officials and staff may be deeply committed to the constitutional and legal system, and therefore abide by its rules. That does not remove the problem, however. The fact that these shifts *can* happen is sufficiently serious to require attention.

PREREQUISITES FOR DANGERS

We have seen that dictatorship, genocide, war, and systems of social oppression are four expressions of the use of institutionalized violence for political purposes, a capacity which can be shifted from one purpose to another. Reliance upon political violence as the ultimate sanction of political societies therefore intrinsically brings the *potential* to produce highly dangerous results.

Two important points follow from this. First, any significant *increase* for whatever purpose in the society's total institutionalized capacity for political violence, and in the relative and absolute power of the institutions for applying political violence, will increase the *capacity* to apply political violence for different and undesired objectives, including the capacities for the four phenomena upon which we are focusing to occur, for it is the *same* capacity. Those potentialities will not always be realized but the capacity is there. For example, the build-up of the military institutions to deal with foreign enemies has in many countries resulted in their becoming more powerful than both the civilian branches of the government and the nongovernmental civilian institutions of the society. This has, in many countries, led directly to military coups d'état and establishment of domestic dictatorships. Anti-regime violence appears also to contribute in different ways to the increase in the society's total quantum of political violence and hence to enhanced capacity for other unwanted purposes.

Conversely, the major *reducton* or removal of the institutionalized capacity for political violence will reduce the *capacity* for those phenomena to occur or to develop as fully as the State officials might wish. Such a reduction will lessen the likelihood and capacity of the present regime or a future one to establish and maintain a dictatorship, to carry out genocide, to wage war, and to impose and operate a system of social oppression. Without the institutionalized violence these cannot occur. It should, therefore, be of little surprise that the use of violence to combat any one of these four phenomena is so often followed by more of the same one, or by one or more of the other three. War may lead not only to increased capacity for further war, but also to diminution of freedom or even to dictatorship at home.

War may contribute to systems of social oppression, and create conditions facilitating genocide, especially when it was desired earlier, as it did in the Nazi case.* Repressive dictatorships may contribute to war, genocide, and social oppression. Systems of social oppression may increase the capacity of the society for both dictatorship and war, and at times genocide.

Institutionalized political violence as the ultimate sanction is a necessary cause of this and directly and indirectly makes these dangers possible. Therefore, it may only be possible to solve each of these four problems by facing them in the context of institutionalized political violence as the ultimate sanction of modern politics. The trend of modern politics has clearly been, however, to *increase* the institutionalized capacity for political violence.

This does *not* mean that none of the four grave problems can be effectively tackled until *all* are simultaneously solved. It *does* mean that efforts to solve one of these problems require a consideration of both the other expressions of political violence and also the role of this general reliance upon institutionalized political violence as the ultimate sanction in politics.

The expansion of the institutions for applying political violence, the growth of weapons technology and other means of control, and the capacity of such institutionalized political violence to be shifted to different purposes than originally intended, have combined to contribute significantly to our grave problems — even though the original expansion, growth, and controls derived, in part at least, from genuine social needs and innocent motives.

THE NEED FOR SANCTIONS

Difficulties with institutionalized political violence as the ultimate sanction of the society, and disapproval of its use for certain objectives, does not remove the need for a general sanction of some type, or the need for particular sanctions for approved objectives. All human societies seem to require and to possess some kind of final sanctions to apply in their internal and external relationships when milder influences and forms of power have not produced the desired

---

*See Chapter Three, "The Lesson of Eichmann," especially the later sections.

and often necessary objectives. A political society with no final sanctions would have difficulties maintaining internal compliance with certain basic norms against harming people, preventing an internal group from running roughshod over the remainder of the population, dealing with extreme internal disruption or usurpation, and finally, maintaining its own chosen way of life, institutions, beliefs, system of legitimate government, and independent existence in face of external aggression. This need for sanctions applies even to the most altruistic, benevolent, and egalitarian society, including nonviolent and anarchist ones.* All societies require some type of final sanctions for at least minimal purposes.† The need for sanctions cannot be removed from human societies, either at present or in the future.

Whatever certain individuals may do, there is no evidence that whole societies and political systems can renounce the only ultimate sanction they know in favor of an abstract principle or moral sentiment. Political violence may be ubiquitous because it derives from this fundamental social and political need for effective sanctions (including means of struggle) which can be applied for crucial issues when milder means have not succeeded. If so, utilization of political violence cannot be significantly reduced, much less removed, unless that need is recognized and some alternative way is found to fulfill it.

This need for sanctions is especially important in our society, in which widespread and often deep conflicts exist.†† Serious issues are often involved in acute domestic and international conflicts. Their outcomes are therefore frequently highly important. Failure in such cases to wage conflicts, or failure to do so successfully, often has lasting serious results, as much of the history of the twentieth century demonstrates.

---

*Even a deliberate withdrawal from contact with an alien group, as small nonliterate societies sometimes do, is a kind of sanction, albeit very different from the more usual types.

†For a more detailed development of this analysis as applied specifically to war, see Chapter Ten, "Seeking a Solution to the Problem of War," and as related to sanctions generally see Chapter Twelve, "Popular Empowerment."

††**Our society** here refers specifically to the United States, but the statement is also applicable to all Western societies and others undergoing major changes or which possess serious internal problems.

This discussion of the need for sanctions is not invalidated by the fact that sanctions may also be used for ignoble motives, as to dominate and oppress people and to attack other societies. Such cases in fact establish the need for sanctions, for countersanctions are then required.

With intuitive or reasoned recognition of the need for some ultimate sanction, and with political violence accepted as the only realistic way to provide that sanction, any suggestion to renounce or remove political violence is rejected by most people, and by political leaders, as naive and utopian.* They hold to that capacity for violence despite its problems and dangers, being both unwilling and unable to give it up.

As long as institutionalized political violence is seen to be the necessary type of utlimate sanction in political societies, whether for maintaining or changing those systems, there is almost no chance of reducing significantly this reliance on violence. Therefore, given that perception, it is impossible to diminish or remove the capacities and consequences of institutionalized political violence, including its crucial role in the four grave problems on which we are focusing.

SUBSTITUTE NONVIOLENT SANCTIONS

We need not despair, however. If an instrumentally effective substitute ultimate sanction indeed exists, can be developed, or can be refined from imperfect prototypes, then a basic change in the ultimate sanction of a system becomes possible. Finding, developing, and applying a substitute nonviolent sanction may therefore provide the key for resolving the problem of political violence. Such a substitute may also initiate broader fundamental societal change.

Grounds now exist to challenge the standard assumptions that violence is: (1) human nature; (2) the foundation of realistic politics; (3) the key factor in history; and (4) the only effective ultimate sanction. In different societies, and within the same society at various times in history, the deeds which are selected for punishment, the processes by which it is determined to inflict sanctions, and, very importantly, the forms of the sanctions used have differed widely.

---

*See Appendix A, "Doctrinal Responses to the Choice of Sanctions."

Some sanctions possess very different characteristics than others. Wide variations exist in the nature of the pressures applied. This diversity in the forms, characteristics, and pressures of different sanctions may be highly relevant to our situation, in which we continue to require sanctions but the commonly accepted institutionalized violent sanctions suffer from serious disadvantages.

Alternative sanctions to political violence are far from unknown. Fundamentally different sanctions have been used to achieve the same objective. For example, in one society the act of murder may be punished by the socially-approved killing of the murderer. In another society such an act may be punished by universal social boycott and temporary or permanent exile. In the early twentieth century in the Russian Empire exploited factory workers who wanted to take radical action were urged by some people to practice "economic terrorism" — the killing of managers and owners — and by others to exert economic pressure by withdrawing their labor by striking. Even today, a State with grievances may send bombers, naval ships, and troops against another country. Or, at other times a State may cancel loans, halt trade, or sever oil supplies.

These alternative nonviolent sanctions have been widely applied both domestically and internationally by individuals, groups, movements, and governments in diverse conflict situations. Domestically, they have included civilian insurrections, civil disobedience campaigns, labor strikes, economic boycotts, civil liberties struggles, minority rights movements, mutinies, and even nonviolent sanctions for law enforcement. Internationally, nonviolent sanctions have been applied in resistance to foreign occupation, economic embargoes, diplomatic boycotts, and nonviolent invasions. These nonviolent sanctions have been used in widely differing periods of history, cultures, and political conditions, and for a wide variety of purposes.* At diverse points in U.S. history, from the embargo and nonintercourse policies of Presidents Jefferson and Madison to the boycott, embargo, and diplomatic nonrecognition policies in recent decades against the Soviet Union, Communist China, Castro's Cuba, and Iran during the 1979–80 hostage crisis, nonviolent sanctions have been accepted as legitimate tools of U.S. foreign policy. Other States

---

*See the brief survey of this history in Chapter Nine, " 'The Political Equivalent of War' — Civilian-based Defense," and for more extensive accounts, Sharp, *The Politics of Nonviolent Action,* especially Chapter Two, "Nonviolent Action."

and bodies of the United Nations have similarly on occasion accepted these sanctions as appropriate instruments of policy.

Nonviolent sanctions share significant features with violent sanctions. Both are penalties or punishments intended to increase one's ability to accomplish or to resist some objective. Both are based on recognition of the reality of conflict, and of the frequent need to engage in it by active means of struggle. Both are used to wield power and to combat the power of opponents.

The focus is therefore clearly not on all peaceful responses to conflict, but specifically on nonviolent forms of action applied as sanctions instead of violent sanctions. These diverse social, psychological, economic, and political sanctions, or "weapons," are used by people and institutions to achieve or to oppose given objectives. These "weapons" include not only mild symbolic protest and popular demonstrations but also the potentially paralytic means of social, economic, and political noncooperation, and even diverse disruptive forms of nonviolent physical, psychological, social, economic, and political defiance and intervention. Nearly two hundred available nonviolent weapons or methods have already been catalogued.[2] The action is without violence but also without submission to violent repression.

Sometimes nonviolent sanctions have failed to achieve their objectives, but this is true also of violent sanctions. Even with preparations and training, one side normally loses in every war — even without considerating the original issues in the conflict. On the other hand, even without preparations and training, improvised or spontaneous nonviolent sanctions have often succeeded in varying degrees in actually reaching the intended objectives, even in highly unfavorable circumstances and when applied against highly repressive opponents with considerable institutionalized capacity for political violence. At the very minimum, this practice establishes that nonviolent sanctions can be substituted for violent sanctions when sanctions of some type are required.

POWER-WIELDING WEAPONS

Nonviolent sanctions are not defined by doctrine, but rather on the basis of their nature as revealed by practice. Nonviolent sanctions are not rooted in norms or commandments which begin, "Thou shall not. . . ." Instead, these alternative sanctions are rooted in the human capacity for stubbornness, in insights into the societal sources of political power, and in the utilization of people's roles in society and of institutional controls over the society's necessary functions as power leverages. These insights into the origin and nature of political power are far more sophisticated and accurate than the crude, naive, and antidemocratic statement that "power comes out of the barrel of a gun." Nonviolent sanctions are based upon the following perception of power: the ruler's power has sources; these can be located; they depend upon the cooperation of people and institutions; this cooperation can be restricted or cut off, with the result that the ruler's power is weakened. If the resisters' noncooperation can be maintained in face of repression, the ruler's power may be disintegrated. Hence any given institution, policy, or regime can be controlled, limited, or destroyed by the application of nonviolent sanctions. This is, in highly simplified terms, the theory of power upon which nonviolent struggle is based.[3] The alternative technique of nonviolent sanctions is therefore primarily societal and political, and not religious, in origin. Full discussion of how nonviolent struggle "works" is impossible here.* It is, however, necessary to point out a few key aspects of this. Repression will *not* always crush nonviolent struggle; nonviolent sanctions can operate successfully against a violent repressive regime *without* requiring a shift to violence.[4] In face of repression the noncooperation continues to restrict or sever the regime's sources of power. When confronted with nonviolent discipline, solidarity, and persistence by the nonviolent actionists, repression may rebound against the opponent to undermine further his power position by political *jiu-jitsu*. Nonviolent sanctions use three basic mechanisms of change: conversion, accommodation, and nonviolent coercion. Sometimes, also, nonviolent sanctions disintegrate the opponent's regime or system.

Nonviolent sanctions have been used by a great variety of people of diverse religious beliefs or none at all, and of many political viewpoints. These nonviolent ways of applying pressure and waging

---

*See the brief discussion of this in Chapter Nine, " 'The Political Equivalent of War' — Civilian-based Defense," and the full discussion in Sharp, *The Politics of Nonviolent Action,* Part Three, The Dynamics of of Nonviolent Action.

struggle have been overwhelmingly used by people who under other circumstances would have resorted to violent sanctions. Therefore, basic changes in people's beliefs, world-views, or personalities, are *not* required as a prerequisite to their use of nonviolent sanctions.

Nonviolent sanctions have also been used for objectives which many people would reject as undesirable or immoral.* Actually, that is encouraging, for it means that in a world of diverse beliefs and objectives conflicts about them can be fought out nonviolently rather than violently.

Nonviolent sanctions have been applied in a great variety of societies and political systems. These include highly imperfect societies where according to certain doctrinal interpretations of nonviolent means they should have been impossible, including class-ridden, oppressive, patriarchal, and dictatorial systems. This demonstrates that fundamental social change is *not* necessary — however desirable it may be — *before* nonviolent sanctions can replace violent ones. To the contrary, it is possible that lasting fundamental change which resolves the four problems on which we have focused and which shifts control to the population as a whole is not possible without the prior or simultaneous shift from violent to nonviolent sanctions, for reasons which are developed below and in the next chapter.

Nonviolent sanctions are already substituted for violent sanctions more widely than is usually recognized. Such substitutions are therefore in principle possible. The question then becomes whether nonviolent sanctions are or can be made to be at least as effective as violent sanctions, and to what extent, and how, nonviolent sanctions can be systematically substituted for violent ones to reduce drastically or eliminate institutionalized political violence in the society. These can be answered.

INCREASING EFFECTIVENESS

In the exploration of the potential of nonviolent alternatives to replace institutionalized violent sanctions for political purposes, we

*This does not mean, however, that nonviolent sanctions can serve all causes equally in the long run. See the discussion of the decentralizing and empowering effects of nonviolent sanctions in Chapter Twelve, "Popular Empowerment."

need to utilize past and present experience to gain knowledge, and to develop hypotheses and theories about how nonviolent sanctions operate and achieve their objectives. This phenomenon needs to be subjected to research, analysis, and rational evaluation. Our approach, therefore, must be exploratory, investigative, analytical, rigorous, and hard-headed.

Nonviolent sanctions in the past have always constituted a crude and improvised technique at the best of times, at a stage of refinement and sophistication comparable to the condition of military action several thousand years ago. People have not usually known what was required for effectiveness. Nor have they had the benefit of widespread, in-depth training, and preparations. People have lacked knowledge of previous uses of nonviolent sanctions and of what they must do, and not do, to maximize the chances for success. That situation is not good enough if people are to take seriously the possibility of replacing institutionalized political violence with nonviolent sanctions. Such substitutions will be rejected until and unless the nonviolent sanctions are, and are seen to be, at least as instrumentally effective as the standard violent sanctions. The "state of the art" of nonviolent sanctions at present is not adequate to make such substitutions acceptable to most people immediately on a comprehensive scale.

Nonviolent sanctions of the past ought not to be simply imitated or mildly modified for use in new settings. They should be studied and analyzed carefully. Using the tools of historians, social scientists, philosophers, psychologists, economists, lawyers, strategists, and others, conducting massive basic and problem-solving research, we could almost certainly multiply the effectiveness of these alternative sanctions. Because many nonviolent sanctions use a variety of society's necessary functions as power leverages, it is possible that refinement of these sanctions would produce a capacity for power not merely equal to institutionalized political violence but significantly greater. To the degree that nonviolent sanctions can be made more effective by deliberate efforts, the chances of their being substituted in particular cases for violent sanctions will be increased. Enhanced effectiveness leads to new possibilities for their substitutions, as in the fields of defense, internal conflicts, maintaining domestic order, revolution against tyranny, and others.

SPECIFIC SUBSTITUTIONS

Specific efforts to adapt nonviolent sanctions to serve particular needs would be required. These substitutions would vary widely, corresponding to many of the differing purposes for which institutionalized political violence supplies sanctions to meet present needs. The largest single substitution is the task of providing effective national defense — defense strictly defined as protection, preservation, or warding-off — against attack. Until and unless effective substitute nonviolent sanctions are developed, countries will continue to rely upon military means, with the consequence of maintaining and even expanding the quantum of institutionalized political violence in the society, with its capacity to be shifted to other purposes. Small scale but serious discussions are already underway about the potential of utilizing a researched, refined, and developed nonviolent sanction to provide deterrence against such attacks and defense against both types of attack if they occur. This is called civilian-based defense.* Focusing primarily on the problem of external invasion and occupation, the policy has reached the level of governmental discussion in several smaller West European countries,† and limited government-financed research has begun. This is now a legitimate topic among certain strategists and military officers in various European countries and the United States who are considering the range of options which may exist for meeting future security crises. It is possible that during the next decade several countries may initiate official preparations and training for civilian-based defense by nonviolent struggle, initially alongside their usual military capacity. Given a perception of effectiveness, that nonviolent component could gradually be built up during the period of "transarmament" and the military component, as an antiquated weapons system, might then be gradually phased down.

Substitutions for specific violent sanctions are possible in other areas. Some of these are cases in which the sanctions are, and would

---

*See Chapter Nine, " 'The Political Equivalent of War' — Civilian-based Defense."

†As of 1979 these were Sweden, Switzerland, the Netherlands, Norway, and Denmark.

be, institutionalized. Others involve noninstitutionalized replacements for violent sanctions (such as terrorism and guerrilla war) which are used in internal conflicts and against the established system. Even the latter type would also contribute to the progressive reduction of the quantum of institutionalized political violence in the society. Joan V. Bondurant has suggested that we could build nonviolent sanctions into our laws in place of the present violent sanctions.[5] Certain types of laws on social policy seem especially suited to the use of nonviolent sanctions. These include laws against child-labor, poor working conditions and inadequate pay, racial discrimination, environmental pollution, poor quality goods, and excessive size of economic institutions. If investigation and negotiations had failed to produce compliance, these might be enforced by officially approved economic boycotts by suppliers, transporters, and consumers, and by strikes by workers. Also, as a vehicle for meeting social needs more adequately and for controlling irresponsible and excessively powerful firms, new competing economic establishments owned and controlled by workers and consumers (rather than by the State) might be created. Both of these could serve as substitutes, not only for the old firms and new government bureaucracies, but also for institutionalized violent sanctions such as arrest, fines backed by threat of imprisonment, and imprisonment itself. The aim of the substitute nonviolent sanctions would not be punishment or retribution for its own sake but compliance with socially determined standards and policies. When that was achieved, the nonviolent sanctions could be lifted. Other types of laws would not be suitable for these particular nonviolent types of enforcement, but could potentially be suitable for other measures. Among these are "half-way" houses in place of imprisonment, and retribution by financial compensation to the victims and service to the community. Nonviolent sanctions could also operate in acute internal conflicts. Here the nonviolent "weapons" could be used as substitutes for rioting, terrorism, violent revolt against dictatorships, and guerrilla warfare aimed at social and economic transformation. All of these substitutions are highly likely to result in significantly less institutionalized political violence in the ensuing society.

We can, if we wish, examine whether these various substitutions might be viable, how they might be prepared, and how the transitions might be effected. The steps toward adoption of nonviolent sanctions and the changeovers to them will differ with each type of substitution and situation.

In this concept of change the substitute nonviolent sanctions for a particular task must be developed and the preparations made *before* the established violent sanctions can be given up. The shift to the new ones cannot be universal and sweeping initially, but must instead move from one particular substitution to another over a significant, but not infinite, period of time. Such changes would be slower than optimistic millenarian social prophets might wish, but far more rapid than is today realized. This is because the replacement of types of sanctions is a relatively simple process as compared to efforts to change all of the society's institutions as part of a single comprehensive plan. We have already seen a multitude of such shifts to nonviolent sanctions — in the labor movement, and in diverse resistance and revolutionary movements — not only made without preparations but frequently carried out by people who did not realize what they were doing. During a deliberate shift to nonviolent sanctions, more than one planned changeover could sometimes take place simultaneously, but each would require prior individual evaluation, policy development, planning, preparation, and training.

With this grand strategy, it could soon be possible to initiate responsibly important political changes in this highly imperfect and dangerous world. The task before us therefore becomes finding ways to make nonviolent sanctions at least as effective as violent sanctions, and adapting them for specific purposes. Otherwise, continued reliance on institutionalized political violence will ensure that the capacity for producing the four problems on which we have focused will be perpetuated.

STEPS TOWARD SYSTEMIC CHANGE

Such replacements of violent sanctions with nonviolent ones, both in the domestic and international spheres, are likely to have profound ramifications. *Minimally* one would not have increased the total quantum of institutionalized political violence. Since, as we saw, the institutionalized capacity for political violence can be shifted to other and unwanted purposes, the simple halt of its expansion would limit increases to the future capacities for dictatorship, genocide, war, and social oppression. On the other hand, the step-by-step specific replacements of institutionalized political violence with substitute nonviolent sanctions would gradually *reduce* the total quantum of institutionalized political violence. This would lay the basis for fundamental systemic and institutional change in the society. Step-by-step, reliance on such violence would be limited, reduced, and removed. This would progressively reduce the possibility of the four grave problems from occurring by removing the capacity for their operation. This removal would allow a freer reign to other social forces contributing to the positive improvement of the political society.

During the extended transitionary period significant institutionalized capacity for political violence would still exist as the population's knowledge and ability to apply nonviolent sanctions was growing. Already in the short run, however, the population's enhanced ability to resist effectively would likely have a major impeding effect on any elite which might wish to impose its will by use of the institutionalized capacity for violence. In the long run, this drastic reduction of institutionalized political violence and the empowerment of the population through learning the use of nonviolent sanctions would contribute both to ending the four problems and also to acceptable fundamental change harmonious with the ideals of our society.*

Every part of this analysis requires careful examination, testing, and research. If we wish to increase the effectiveness of nonviolent sanctions, including their use against new tyrannical systems and attempts to commit genocide, we clearly require greater knowledge of both nonviolent and violent sanctions. Therefore, we need to:

1. Conduct basic research into the nature of both violent and nonviolent sanctions, and the four problems on which we have focused attention;

2. Conduct problem-solving research on whether, and if so how, limits or problems in the utility, effectiveness, and application of nonviolent sanctions might be removed;

3. Carry out policy studies to discover, develop, and examine the potentials and limitations of the two types of sanctions in present

---

*See Chapter Twelve, "Popular Empowerment."

and refined forms for meeting social and political needs, especially for dealing with the four identified problems; and

4. Develop educational resources and methods to spread knowledge, stimulate thinking, and promote independent evaluation of the problems, both types of sanctions, and options within this whole field.

These are all achievable steps* which will contribute significantly to the progressive substitution of refined and developed nonviolent sanctions in place of institutionalized political violence.

The cumulative results of this change are likely to be profound. The positive conditions which would replace the four problems lie beyond our present conceptions of freedom, respect for life, peace, and social justice. That goal and this approach to achieve it are not utopian. Instead, this concept of change is based on a new, more complete, realism, rooted in history, which builds on human potential and enables us to chart a course for the reconstruction of human society. We can restore hope — one rooted in reality — depending on the choices we make, if only we will. This is our societal imperative.

*For an expansion and development of these points, see Appendix B, "Twenty Steps in Development and Evaluation of Nonviolent Sanctions."

NOTES

1. See Joan V. Bondurant, **Conquest of Violence: The Gandhian Philosophy of Conflict** (Princeton, N.J.: Princeton University Press, 1958; London: Oxford University Press, 1958; and Berkeley, Calif.: University of California Press, 1965), pp. 214-218.
2. For this classification, definitions, and examples, see Gene Sharp, **The Politics of Nonviolent Action** (Boston: Porter Sargent Publisher, 1973), Part Two, "The Methods of Nonviolent Action."
3. For a more complete presentation of this theory of power, see ibid., Chapter One, "The Nature and Control of Political Power."
4. See ibid., Chapter Ten, "Challenge Brings Repression," Chapter Eleven, "Solidarity and Discipline to Fight Repression," Chapter Twelve, "Political *Jiu-jitsu*," and Chapter Thirteen, "Three Ways Success May Be Achieved."
5. See Joan V. Bondurant, "The Case for Redefining the Legal Sanction of the Democratic State," in K.P. Misra and Rajendra Avasthi, eds., **Politics of Persuasion: Essays Written in Memory of Dr. G.N. Dhawan** (Bombay: Manaktalas, 1967), pp. 42-57.

12

Popular Empowerment

HUMAN NEEDS AND THE
DISTRIBUTION OF POWER

Most people in our society* do not participate to a significant degree
in the decisions and actions which shape their lives and institutions,
and which determine the direction of the society as a whole. This is a
major indication that we do not yet implement adequately the ideals
of our heritage.

Our society here specifically refers to American society, but the discussion
also applies to other Western societies, and also — sometimes to an even larger degree
— to other modern large-scale political systems.

"We" — most members of our society — say that we believe in the worth of human beings, freedom, justice, peace, economic well-being, and related principles. If so, we have a responsibility both to try to implement these principles in the world in which we now live, and also to do what we can to build a society which more closely approximates those ideals for succeeding generations. Sometimes the effort to implement our ideals means preserving the best parts of our present society which put these principles into practice. That is insufficient, however, for despite these positive achievements, our society has major shortcomings which need to be corrected. In these cases, implementing our ideals means seeking fundamental changes.

CONSIDERING HUMAN NEEDS

Our society fails to meet basic human needs, and these are even understood far too narrowly. Our extremely restricted view of these needs is a major cause of the failures of past efforts to build a better society.

It is of course true that without food, clothing, shelter from the elements, and fuel for warmth and cooking — and work to produce or obtain them — life could not exist. It is shocking that these needs are not being met for all people, and that control over them is not usually in the hands of the people who need them. *That* fact should shock us even more than the hunger and other results of deprivation, for with control in their own hands people could provide their own physical necessities.

Physical necessities are not the only basic human needs, however, and providing them alone does not produce an ideal society. Those necessities can be effectively supplied in prisons. In addition to our basic physical needs, human beings have other biological, psychological, social, and even "political" needs. Let us look briefly at these. They may appear very simple, or inappropriate to structural analysis. Yet, without this broader awareness we are likely to repeat past mistakes in our efforts to build a society which meets human needs more adequately — mistakes which derive from concerns to provide only food, housing, or jobs, for example, while neglecting other less tangible needs.

As human beings, we need to love and to be loved. We need sharing, tenderness, and to be needed by others. As a species, we need to reproduce and to rear our children. We need to learn the ways of our society, and hopefully others, and to learn and share the heritages of our past. We need to learn who we are, to develop self-respect and appreciation of our capacities and worth. We need joys, relaxation, creativity, opportunities to grow and to change, and to satisfy our curiosities as we seek new knowledge, insights, and truths. We need to develop our minds, our intellectual capacitites, our ability to think and to reason. Our capacities to relate to each other, to other forms of life, and to the world and universe of which we are a part, all need developing. We need to identify with others, to belong to groups, and to have group pride. We need protection from dangers and attacks and from threats to our lives. Our groups need to survive against both cultural and physical threats.

Very importantly, as individuals and groups we also need the capacity for power to determine how we shall live. We need power to control our lives, to withstand the forces that would mold us, harm us, or destroy us, a capacity to shape our lives and futures, even in the face of hostile forces. Most of the proposed remedies for our social ills have given too little attention to these wider human needs and particularly to this need for effective power.

Unless we are able to meet these various needs that go beyond our physical necessities, we lack the qualitites and capacities of human beings. Therefore, our efforts to meet human needs more adequately ought to be directed toward meeting *all* of them, not only our physical ones. Efforts to provide physical necessities must not negatively affect provision of our less tangible requirements or our need for power to control our lives. To the contrary, efforts to meet any human needs ought to be compatible with, and where possible actively to assist, the meeting of all of them. That will produce qualitatively different results from efforts based on a more restricted focus. Meeting these broader human needs more adequately will also help us to solve the problems of dictatorship, genocide, war, and systems of social oppression which have been discussed in previous chapters.

OUR PROBLEMS AND THE CONCENTRATION
OF POWER

All of our grave social, economic, and political problems involve at some point a serious maldistribution of power.* That is to say that effective power has become highly concentrated in certain parts of the population and institutions, and, most seriously, in the hands of the State apparatus. Other groups, or even the general population, are then in comparison weak, and therefore vulnerable to the will of the power group.

The power capacity of specific groups in a society at a certain time is by no means inevitable or unchangeable. It is the result of: (1) the degree to which the various groups have mobilized the sources of power at their disposal — that is, their *power potential;* (2) the relationships between the different degrees of *effective power* which the respective groups currently possess; and (3) the degree to which the social, economic, and political structures are flexible and responsive to the will of all sections of the population. The existing distribution of power is very real, but it is not permanent, and it will not be sustained under all conditions. Indeed, it can at times change dramatically. Such a change occurs when the sources of power at the disposition of relatively weak groups are mobilized to a far greater degree than previously, so that their effective power increases and comes closer to realizing their power potential. A major change in the distribution of power also happens when the sources of power at the disposal of the established powerful groups are weakened or withdrawn, thereby reducing drastically their effective power. Unless the sources of power of weaker groups are mobilized, or the sources of power of established powerful groups are reduced, or both, the subordinated and oppressed groups inevitably remain in essentially the same relative positions, despite any other particular changes in the society. (These other changes may even include the correction of specific grievances, provision of new services, and installation of a new person or group in the position of ruler.)

*"Power" here means the capacity of people to act in order to achieve objectives even in the face of opposition: the combination of all the various influences and pressures which they can exert. These include both sanctions and the capacity to work together, as well as other influences such as authority.

Wherever one looks at a situation which one group or another regards as a "problem," one encounters an actual or a perceived inequitable distribution of power. These groups may include, for example: exploited economic classes, harassed religious minorities, populations of attacked or occupied countries, the victims of attempts at genocide, suppressed peoples under domestic dictators, nations under colonial empires, despised ethnic or racial groups, and a large number of others. In all such cases the problem exists because one group has the power to impose its will on a weak group. "For the tyrant has the power to inflict only that which we lack the strength to resist," as Krishnalal Shridharani wrote.[1] The maldistribution of power makes such problems possible.

Therefore, if we are concerned not only with correcting a specific problem, but also with preventing the emergence in its wake of other potentially more grave ones, the distribution of power must be fundamentally altered.

Our society seems to be moving toward both increased concentration of effective power in the State and certain institutions, and toward increased power for certain groups which traditionally have had little power. Clearly, there are opposing trends. On the one hand, for example, workers can organize, strike, and boycott, Afro-Americans can demonstrate and use their votes, and women are beginning to throw off their mantle of oppression, challenging stereotypes, and establishing new social patterns. As a result of such action, these and other groups now possess relatively more power than they did a few decades ago. On the other hand, however, much of the thrust of change in our society has been in the opposite direction, especially in our economic and political life. The overall trend has been toward larger institutions, increased centralization, and stronger elite controls. Furthermore, as discussed in several previous chapters, on the world level this century has seen a growth of dictatorships, often in more severe forms, the growth and permeation of violence throughout society, a failure to create a society with both economic well-being and political freedom, increased capacity for genocide, disrespect for human life and dignity, efforts to control human minds, and the multiplication of military weaponry and destructive capacity. Most people feel powerless to reverse these developments.

PAST REMEDIES INADEQUATE

Over the decades and centuries, people have become more aware of their responsibility to alleviate the shortcomings of society in meeting human needs, and they have advocated and instituted a variety of changes toward those ends. Often these have been emergency measures — to provide food during famines, shelter following floods and bombings, and clothing to protect against the cold. These measures are still important, and must be evaluated in terms of their capacity to relieve emergency needs. But programs which are instead intended to meet human needs in the long term, on a regular basis, require more rigorous standards of evaluation.

From this perspective, many programs, both past and present, have proven inadequate. First, existing programs and policies frequently ignore certain psychological, social, and "political" needs. Second, a program or policy may, for a variety of reasons, fail to accomplish the intended objective. Third, the effort may provide only temporary or limited relief from the most pressing consequences of the problem, while leaving the problem itself unresolved. At times, focus is shifted away from required fundamental changes. Fourth, even a well-designed program may be so mangled in application as to be ineffective; the substance of the program may be sacrificed to other considerations, such as powerful interest groups or incompatible political objectives.

In some cases, the present approaches to meet human needs suffer from more fundamental inadequacies. Probably the gravest of these is the failure of most programs and policies to empower people so that they gain positive control over their own lives and society. In fact, whatever else existing "remedies" may do, most of them contribute in the long run to the further disempowering of people.

PROBLEMS WITH RELIANCE ON THE STATE APPARATUS

Many people who want to resolve human problems and meet human needs more adequately assume that the basic way to act is to secure the intervention of some higher level of government. This may take a variety of forms: executive orders, a new law, a constitutional change, a government-financed and administered policy, State ownership, or other means. The common aim is to provide the proper corrective action by doing something *for* people. This approach stands in sharp contrast to one which would actively involve people themselves in dealing independently and directly with their own problems.

State action of various types has differed in its effectiveness in dealing with the original specific problem or need. Even when such government programs are reasonably successful in meeting the particular immediate need — hunger, housing, and the like — it is the result of the power of the State or the institution responsible, while the people who have benefited remain themselves at least as powerless as before. They are at best the beneficiaries of the decisions and actions of others; they have not themselves reshaped their lives and society by their own efforts. The causal maldistribution of power has not been corrected, but often exacerbated. The result may be new, more severe, problems.

In contrast, changes resulting from their own efforts could have contributed significantly to increased self-respect, capacity to work together to provide their own needs, and ability to defend themselves — in short the ability to wield effective power to control their own lives and society. Empowering change is likely to help people to deal with other problems in the future, and to ensure that the gains they make will not be reversed unless they choose to do so.

On the other hand, reliance on other groups and higher levels of government, executive orders, legislation, court decisions, and the like to make desired changes suffers from a very serious disadvantage: that which is thus given may be as easily, and even more quickly, taken away. At some time in the future when the mood of the country shifts, new problems take precedence, or new forces gain control of the legislature, courts, or executive, the policy may in the same manner be reversed. The State apparatus may be removed as the provider and protector. It may even be turned against those who had earlier benefited from the newly-abandoned policy.

THE GROWTH OF STATE POWER

It may be no accident that the problems of dictatorship, genocide, war, systems of social oppression, and popular powerlessness have grown in severity during the same time frame that our political, economic, and even many social institutions have increased in size, have come more severely under elite control, and become highly centralized. The centralization in these institutions is often extreme and has widespread serious consequences. These centralizing tendencies are even more marked in the particular institution of the State. The most elemental view of twentieth century politics should reveal that it is precisely the concentration of power and expansion of control by the State which is a major source of the *capacity* to inflict the problems which have devastated so many people and societies. Rethinking politics and developing realistic measures to deal with our most grave problems require that we reconsider and reevaluate the expansion of the State to meet the various legitimate needs of people and society.

The growth of the State is continuing in most parts of the world, with only limited counter-tendencies. The State, of course, is not the same as the society as a whole. The State is a particular institution, a particular structure of government — there are other possible ones — which includes as parts of the system of political control a permanent bureaucracy to administer its programs and measures, a permanent police and penal system to punish antisocial persons and often dissidents, and a permanent military system to threaten and fight against foreign enemies and domestic uprisings. All these are under the command of the person or group which occupies the position of "ruler" at the head of the State.

This growth of the State, and of other institutions, in absolute and relative size, elite control, and centralization, has taken a variety of forms, and is the result of diverse influences. It has often been in response to pressing needs, and to weaknesses and inadequacies of earlier less centralist institutions. At other times, the growth of central controls by ever larger institutions has come without conscious choice, and in response to other changes.

The scale, technology, and severity of modern wars, combined with the requirements of an effective military system, have contributed very significantly to the growth of political centralization. The need for effective command, control of resources, transportation, manpower, and military secrets is among the significant factors which have operated to produce that result. In the United States the Civil War clearly contributed to political centralization, which was later greatly accelerated by the First World War and the Second

World War. Two other major factors which have contributed to the general concentration of power and growth of centralized institutions are the large-scale technologies which have been chosen for development over smaller-scale technologies, and also the types of energy which have been selected for use in place of decentralized alternatives. Both of these have contributed to the massive growth of centralized, large-scale economic institutions, variously controlled by the elites of national and multinational corporations, or by heads of bureaus, Party leaders, and State officials. Commonly, when the growth of centralization and State power has occurred as a result of these various factors, the factors themselves, and sometimes even the process of centralization, have gone unnoticed, or have been seen as necessary. Hence, the resulting growth of centralism and State power has aroused little opposition.

Much expansion of the power of the State itself and weakening of the effective power of the populace has also resulted from ignoble motives and deliberate efforts by rulers to establish or perpetuate their domination. Also, the State often becomes interlocked with other institutions in controlling the society. When noticed, such expansion of the State is often seen as threatening and, when the populace is capable of resisting this expansion of State controls and the agencies of regimentation and repression, this growth of State power may arouse oppostion in the name of freedom or justice.

STATE POWER FOR SOCIAL CHANGE

In contrast to those situations, much of the growth of the State apparatus has often occurred as a result of noble, and even humane, motives. Many people who have sought social change have viewed the single institution which combined a permanent bureaucracy with legitimated capacity for political violence as very useful to them — if only they could gain control of it and use it for their own ends. The State has therefore been used in order to meet more adequately various physical human needs, and often to control large-scale economic institutions, or oppressive practices of one section of the society against another. When reformers and revolutionaries have sought to impose controls over powerful economic groups, classes, or institutions, they have usually done so by establishing State regulations over them or by transferring actual ownership of the economy to the State.

When the expansion of State controls and the State itself is instead carried out for humane purposes by a political democracy, and even by authoritarian systems, significant opposition may not develop. The expansion is often then intended, or perceived as aimed, to improve the lives of people; few persons will then wish to be, or be seen to be, supporters of past injustices and opponents of new social and economic services. The expansion may, therefore, meet very little opposition — except from adversely affected vested interests, and from persons more opposed to "big government" than to past injustices and deprivations. However, this is far from the whole story.

At times the advocates of social change by State action have relied upon liberal democratic processes. These reformers have accepted liberal constitutional democracy, with its procedures, restrictions, and individual rights. These people assume that political freedom and use of the State to effect social change are compatible. It is consequently common in American society and many others to assume that if we have a problem we must seek the intervention or take-over of an ever higher level of government which possesses the machinery of control, the legal apparatus, the financial resources, and the police and military systems, to utilize for that good cause.

More extreme advocates of change have resorted to coup d'état or guerrilla warfare to seize the State. Once they have gained control of the State, these advocates of social change have rarely been willing to exercise restraint in using the capacities of the State and to respect democratic procedures and the rights of those who disagree with them. To the contrary, generally no procedures, limitations, or calendars have been permitted to interfere with their perceived mission: to achieve total change by full use of State power.

Highly important differences exist in the consequences of these two approaches; those must not be minimized. However, both approaches contribute to the growth of State power — neither contributes to empowerment of the populace. A major factor underlying the inadequacies of both approaches is the failure to appreciate sufficiently the importance of all of the human needs presented earlier in this chapter, not only the physical needs of food, shelter, clothing, and protection from the elements. Sometimes — not always — in terms of meeting human physical needs, the services and changes provided by State intervention have been significantly improved in quantity and quality as compared to earlier arrangements. That cannot be ignored. Nor should we be satisfied with poverty, injustice, and inadequate provision of the material needs of people. The point instead is that even when a plan to deal with such problems by State action succeeds in correcting the outward effects of the specific problems, something else very serious happens which is not intended: one more step is taken in shifting effective power from the people themselves and from the nongovernmental institutions of the society to the State apparatus. Thereby, the people who were already too weak — the problem itself is evidence of this — become even weaker than they were, and the non-State institutions which were capable of limiting the power of the ruler become enfeebled without the compensating strengthening of other *loci* of power.

The strategy of relying upon the State to make needed social and economic changes, instead of using some other means of action and different institutions, not only does not empower the people who are already weak; that strategy actively contributes to increasing the concentration of effective power in the State. As discussed in Chapter Two, "Social Power and Political Freedom," this may strongly facilitate the development of dictatorships. Nor has State action contributed to democratization even within the economic institutions. While elite controls and the absence of participation by workers and consumers were characteristics of large corporations for many decades, and have been accentuated in multinational corporations, these are not corrected by State intervention. State regulation and ownership of economic institutions have reduced neither their size, the degree of centralization, nor elite controls within them. Instead, State intervention has increased all three of these within the specific enterprises and in the economy generally. The "solution" applied to genuine social and economic needs has resulted in consolidation, increased centralization, and yet another level of management, taking control still further from workers, consumers, and specialists. These people become less and less participants in those institutions, and more and more the "workers," "staff," "consumers," and "clients" of those who are "in charge" — those who "know" what should be done.

On the political level, the extension of this centralization and elite control has been widely associated with a real or perceived reduction in the extent, quality, and effectiveness of popular participation and control of political institutions and public policies. This has often been accompanied by the denigration of localism, and outright dissolution of small-scale institutions and services — even schools, rail transportation, health facilities, and post offices. The growth of State controls over the economy has resulted in a major expansion of the size of the State itself, a growth of the scale of our institutions, enhancement of elite controls, centralization of decision-making, growth of bureaucratization, increases in the areas of society under State control or absorbed by the State, and an increasing powerless dependency of the people. The theory and slogans of democratic control are, however, often still espoused.

DANGERS FOR POLITICAL FREEDOM

That strategy is dangerous for political freedom, as well as for the ability to meet adequately the several human needs beyond basic physical requirements for life. In that strategy the *loci* of power come increasingly under centralized State control, or are outright destroyed. As a direct consequence, the rest of the society becomes weak in comparison to the State apparatus. This process can be a continuing and circular one. As the weakening of the independent institutions of the society and the lower levels of government continues, the concentration of effective power in the hands of the central State grows. The institutionalized capacity of the State for political violence and the bureaucracy also usually expand. The result is that the relative and absolute strength of the population declines. The population becomes increasingly powerless and subject to manipulation and control by those in command of the State apparatus. Without new influences to reverse the process, the increase in the maldistribution of effective power continues to grow cumulatively. The power of the State grows, while the capacity of people to act to save themselves continues to lessen.

When this has occurred, whoever can control the State apparatus is likely to have little trouble in controlling the society for their own purposes. This happens even when those purposes are very different ones from those of the earlier social reformers and revolutionaries who used the centralized State simply to meet human needs more adequately and to build a better society. A State apparatus which is strong enough to free us is also strong enough to enslave us.

Once the society's *loci* of power are weakened or destroyed, the bureaucracies are established and expanded, and the population is reduced to dependency on the State for its material needs, once the police systems are centralized and enlarged, and the military system is expanded as a separate institution from the rest of society which can be turned against the country's own people, then the State machinery is prepared for potential effective use by tyrants. At this point, the State may be used for different objectives, and with greater ruthlessness, than originally intended, and may be applied to oppress the population which it claimed to serve. That political machine may also be seized from democratically chosen rulers by usurpers. In the wrong hands this State can be highly dangerous, for it can impose tyranny, wage wars, establish or defend social oppression, control people's minds, and commit genocide. It is this machinery which makes modern tyranny possible. Bertrand de Jouvenel, a prominent French political philosopher, has perceived this more sharply than most of us:

> Had Hitler succeeded Maria Theresa on the throne, does anyone suppose that it would have been possible for him to forge so many up-to-date weapons of tyranny? Is it not clear that he must have found them ready prepared? The more we think on these lines, the better we can appreciate the problem which faces our Western world. [2]

It is possible, of course, that such developments may not occur; the State may not be shifted to autocratic purposes. Constitutional barriers, legal limitations, and traditions may be respected. No facilitating crisis may occur, and no would-be political savior, power-hungry leader, or messianic party may arise. The factors which prevent the shift to tyranny are highly important, and must not be neglected or go unappreciated. They must not, however, be permitted to comfort us into neglecting the problem.

The ways in which the State is operated and controlled vary widely. Liberal constitutional procedures may be very precise about provisions to allow popular participation in the selection of those who will make the decisions and issue the instructions in the name of the State. Such constitutions and laws may also set boundaries against the intrusion of the State into certain activities or aspects of individual or social life, and issue guarantees of personal liberties against State interference. Other systems in control of the State apparatus not only may not have such procedures, restrictions, and guarantees, they may repudiate all such limits to full pursuit of the ruler's objectives. Those may include extension of the power and profit of the system, restructuring of the institutions of the society, extermination of an unwanted group, pursuit of a foreign enemy, or even remaking the nature of human beings. The differences between the systems which significantly limit the effective control by the State and those which reject such limits are highly important.

The growth of State power and the increase in centralization of power and controls throughout the world have occurred to a significant degree even in the United States. This is true in spite of the fact that its original political system was deliberately designed to be decentralized with a very weak State apparatus. The American political system was once an extreme example of a multilayered federalism with a relatively weak federal government. This was structured so as to maximize democratic qualities and to avoid the dangers of tyranny which were perceived to be intrinsic to highly centralized government which possessed the capacity for violent repression of the populace.

Even if the most severe dangers from the weakening of the society and strengthening of the State do not occur, that political society is not, to say the least, a vital practicing democracy. The people remain passive recipients of the benefactions of the administrators, without the vitality and participation of running their own lives and their own society.

VULNERABLE DEMOCRATIC CONSTITUTIONS

When the society is weak and the State is strong traditional liberal democratic legal and constitutional measures are inadequate to prevent destruction of the constitution. There can be no guarantee against such attempts. It is not enough to establish electoral and governmental procedures of fair play, nor to seek to persuade all political bodies to adhere to democratic principles and practices. Laws and constitutional restrictions are insufficient barriers to those who are willing to violate the laws and to destroy the constitution.

The Watergate activities of the Nixon administration demonstrated that high American officials were willing deliberately to disobey existing laws, and to claim the right to do so, in order to implement their will, and even to usurp the established electoral procedures. The proposal, therefore, of disturbed Congressmen and Senators to enact new laws to prohibit such activities demonstrated their failure even to understand the nature and gravity of the problem: how to prevent usurpation by those *willing deliberately to disobey* both statutes and the constitution and to manipulate elections, in order to remain in office. Something more than a new law is obviously required to do that.

It must be made *impossible* for those who wish to become tyrants and who are willing to sweep aside democratic institutions and humane considerations to seize and to maintain effective control of the State apparatus, and by means of that of the society as a whole.

Among the ways in which this expanded State apparatus may be shifted to imposition of tyranny are these: First, no abrupt shift may occur, but instead the governmental apparatus and the society may gradually be brought under progressively more thorough and severe elite control, and step by step the constitution altered in practice to become an increasingly authoritarian system. Second, persons chosen for executive positions by constitutional means, as a president, prime minister, or chancellor, may deliberately exceed or expand the constitutional boundaries. With or without a declaration of emergency, enabling legislation, or constitutional amendment, he or she may carry out an executive usurpation. Under certain conditions, this could be done in the United States by an elected president — perhaps a more ruthless and intelligent "Richard Nixon" — who wished to be free of constitutional barriers and to remain in office without the possibility of removal. Third, a political party, military group, police or intelligence body, or combination of these, with or without foreign assistance, may conduct a coup d'état, ousting the old ruler and establishing themselves in control of the State apparatus. Fourth, successful foreign military invaders may either establish themselves or their puppets at the head of the State in the occupied country, and use it for their own objectives.

The combination of bureaucracy, police, prisons, and military forces, all under a single command, makes possible the turning of that combined State power from serving the members of the society to control, repression, and on occasion, war, against its own population. In modern times, the State is always stronger than any other single institution of the society. Where those societies have been weakened because of neglect, attrition, or deliberate attacks, or even because of a well-intentioned extension of controls over the society, the economy, and lower levels of government, those who have seized control of the State apparatus are likely thereby to gain the power to retain it. They can then use the State for their own ends. The only alternatives available for blocking their success seem to be the will and capacity to wage either a bloody civil war or a massive noncooperation struggle. Seizure of the State is an obvious and permanent danger to anything which might be called democracy, liberty, and freedom. A weak society facing a strong State apparatus commanded by a power-hungry ruler is in a most dangerous situation.

The long-term costs to a society of meeting its needs and correcting its ills by expansion of the State apparatus may therefore be extremely high: reduced democratic qualities, growth of alienation, an increased sense of powerlessness, greater vulnerability to further extension of elite domination, and even political usurpation. Advocates of social change therefore need to reverse the perpetual strategy of enlisting the State apparatus to provide human needs, to right wrongs, and to build a new society.

EMPOWERMENT FOR ACCEPTABLE CHANGE

In the light of the tragedies of recent decades, and the dangers in the future, we have at least three fundamental responsibilities which we need to fulfill if we are to meet human needs more adequately: (1) to right wrongs, lift oppression, and achieve positive conditions for human life; (2) to help ourselves to become empowered in order to achieve internal and societal self-liberation, and, (3) to remove from human society political violence which not only harms and kills people but also, as discussed in the previous chapter, provides the institutionalized capacity which is the prerequisite for some of our most serious problems. If we are to fulfill those responsibilities adequately, we can no longer repeat the programs of the past, but instead must seek new ways to meet the needs of people today, and those of tomorrow's societies.

We need to understand why a maldistribution of power has harmful effects on society which violate the ideals which most people in our society espouse. We also need to understand what produces this maldistribution of power. Without understanding the causes which produce these effects, we are unlikely to be able to correct them. Similarly, if we are to have the capacity to achieve a more equitable distribution of power in our society, we need to examine more closely what components are involved in the distribution of effective power among people and institutions.

A seriously inequitable distribution of power may result from a variety of factors. Two such, closely interrelated, factors, are: which types of groups wield the power, and what kind of power it is. To a greater degree than has usually been thought, the type of power may at times strongly influence, or even determine, which types of groups wield that power. We shall explore this more fully later in this chapter. Both the types of power and which groups wield it are related to the type of ultimate sanction which is applied as a source of power. Therefore, the subject of sanctions requires major attention in any consideration of how to achieve acceptable social change, and of how to implement more fully our ideals in social and political life.

SANCTIONS AND SOCIETY

The provisions of the formal constitution concerning the selection of members of the ruling group and the right to individual liberties are not the ultimate determinants of the distribution of effective power in the political system, much less in the political society as a whole, as we saw in Chapter Two, "Social Power and Political Freedom." Nor, important as they are, do the number and vitality of the society's *loci* of power alone determine that distribution. The type of ultimate sanction relied upon also, to a high degree, helps to determine the distribution of effective power in the society.

Sanctions are clearly one of the important sources of political power.[3] Because that is so, and because the sanctions of institutionalized political violence are prerequisites for such grave problems as dictatorships, genocide, war, and systems of social oppression, we must give adequate attention to the possible impacts of different types of sanctions on the distribution of effective power in the social and political system. Our past failure to do so may explain to a significant degree our inability to solve our gravest problems.

All societies require sanctions of some type.* Sanctions here mean punishments, pressures, and means of action used to penalize, thwart, and alter the behavior of other persons, groups, institutions, or States. Internally, sanctions are used to maintain stability and order in face of hostile and injurious behavior, to keep a subordinate group in subjection, to resist challenge to the established system, to conduct acute internal conflicts, and to achieve conformity to socially determined minimally acceptable behavior, especially when normative constraints have broken down. Externally, sanctions are used to achieve goals against an unwilling opponent, and to ward off external intimidation and attacks. That is, sanctions are applied as the final means of action to wield power in acute conflicts, either defensively or offensively, which have not been otherwise resolved under acceptable terms and conditions. People and institutions use sanctions to apply pressure and to wage conflict. Sanctions may be violent or nonviolent in form.

SYSTEMIC CONSEQUENCES OF DIFFERENT SANCTIONS

Generally, sanctions have not been perceived as having social and political impact beyond their immediate influence on individuals, social conditions, and the objectives at issue. The nature of the ultimate sanction relied upon by the society — whether violent or nonviolent — has not been seen as a significant factor shaping the lasting character of the society itself, including its institutions and its internal distribution of effective power. Occasionally the influence of military systems and wars on political centralization has been noted, or even their impacts on the creation and growth of the State as a unique institution. Most people have usually assumed, however, that since violence was believed to be the only effective ultimate sanction, the best one could do in face of such influences was to apply ameliorative measures to limit, adjust, or regulate the use of such violence, as by legal and constitutional procedures and prohibitions. The political consequences of reliance on violent sanctions or the possibility of

*See the discussions on sanctions in Chapter Ten, "Seeking a Solution to the Problem of War," and Chapter Eleven, "The Societal Imperative."

effective alternatives to them have not usually been explored much further than this.

Increasingly, however, the widespread confidence in violent sanctions has been challenged by claims that they themselves create or aggravate several serious problems. For example, it is at times argued by a variety of people that: (1) the destructive capacity of violent sanctions has reached unacceptable levels; (2) satisfactory ways to deal with certain types of political violence — as terrorism, genocide, and nuclear weapons — have not been found; (3) reliance on violence to struggle against an opponent with continued superior capacity for violence tends to force one's own group into submission, self-destruction, or struggle by attrition of both sides; and (4) undesirable long-term structural consequences of political violence as the society's ultimate sanction appear to exist. These contentions are only illustrative of others which merit investigation.

To a degree hitherto unrecognized, the nature of the ultimate sanction used by a society may determine the nature of that society. Obviously, the sanctions will not be the only influential factors, and the degree to which they will shape the society and political system will differ from case to case. The nature of those sanctions, however, may be far more important in shaping the society than any other single factor, including both ideals and economics.

Violent sanctions and nonviolent sanctions appear to have very different consequences in shaping the nature of the society, the distribution of effective power within it, and the forms and character of its political system. Institutionalized violent sanctions appear to contribute causally to increased centralization of effective power. This occurs in the form of increased centralization in decision-making, in the structure of the political system, and in the control of the capacity to apply the sanctions themselves. On the other hand, nonviolent sanctions appear to contribute causally to decentralization and diffusion of effective power. This occurs in the form of decentralization in decision-making, in the structure of the society as a whole as well as the political system, and in the control of the capacity to apply the sanctions — even by members of the society who have long perceived themselves to be powerless. If this is true, the choice of violent or nonviolent sanctions will have profound long-term consequences for that society.

However, for most people the question of choosing between two types of ultimate sanctions has never arisen. It has been assumed that the most serious and effective sanctions can only be violent. The ultimate sanction has been perceived, almost by definition, to be violent, both for the State apparatus and also for the people and revolutionaries, for whom it was believed to be the *ultima ratio populi,* the ultimate resource of the people. We have rarely even noticed the widespread existence of alternative nonviolent sanctions, nor examined whether they might be instrumentally effective for meeting the need of sanctions for objectives which benefit human beings, as distinct from those which harm or oppress them. As a result of these assumptions and this perception of political reality, the question has rarely been asked as to whether violent sanctions and nonviolent sanctions may have different consequences for the structure and character of the society as a whole.

PROBLEMS OF LIBERATION BY VIOLENCE

In earlier centuries, faced with an oppressive ruler, the population armed with the weapons of violence had a fair chance of winning by waging a violent mass revolution or civil war, using fairly conventional strategies. Karl Mannheim, a German political sociologist, argued that the nature of those weapons prior to the developments of the twentieth century effectively diffused power in the society, and that this was at the heart of the development of political democracy:

> The secret of the democratization which took place in the eighteenth and nineteenth centuries lay in the simple fact that one man means one gun, the resistance of one thousand individuals one thousand guns.[4]

> The guarantee of the general democratization of the preceding century lay not only in industrialization but also in the fact of universal conscription which, especially after a lost war, could become the means of general insurrection.[5]

The capacity of the subjects to deal with internal rulers who had outraged the citizens, or with foreign invaders, was therefore considerable. The right of each man to be armed with the weapons of war was seen to be significantly related to the preservation of freedom and to popular control of the ruler. For example, the Swiss have the strong tradition of each home having a rifle above the hearth, and the colonial and newly-independent Americans insisted on the right of the citizens to "bear arms."

In the intervening decades significant changes took place in the weaponry of violent conflict, in the technology of transportation and communication, and in political organization. The capacity to wield military power become concentrated in the hands of the ruler. This tended to restore the distribution of power to a condition similar to that of certain societies before the period of democratization described above. In some earlier social orders, wrote Mannheim, where minorities could gain control of the instruments of military power, they could monopolize effective power in the society. That earlier possibility under certain circumstances, with the changes in weaponry, technology, and political organization, now became almost universal, he argued. It was not the number of people willing to fight in a mass violent uprising or civil war, or in a war against an invader which was then most important. It was the weapons which were available. These were normally effectively concentrated under the control of the ruler. Therefore, Mannheim argued in 1949: "In the decisive political conflicts of the near future...the greatest significance must be attached to the *concentration of the instruments of military power*."[6] This meant that the traditional means of violent rebellion to achieve liberation became remnants of responses to an earlier stage of military technology and political organization, remnants which had little to do with current military and political realities.

> [T]he techniques of revolution lag far behind the techniques of Government. Barricades, the symbols of revolution, are relics of an age when they were built up against cavalry.[7]

Understandably, in response to this situation groups wishing to remove entrenched unpopular rulers have shifted to other means of doing so in place of mass violent revolution and civil war with relatively conventional strategies. These alternatives which have developed to a significantly greater degree than previously, in both use and sophistication, are coup d'état, guerrilla war, and nonviolent struggle. Before their fuller development, Mannhein had predicted that the concentration of military power would "be followed by a new kind of revolutionary strategy...."[8] Interest and practice of these objectives has grown for a variety of political objectives. This is especially true of coup d'état and guerrilla war. Both revolutionary groups and established governments, including those of both the Soviet Union and the United States, have been actively interested in both techniques to advance their foreign policy objectives. Users of the coup d'état have accepted the concentration of weaponry, but sought to seize control of it quickly along with the rest of the State. Guerrilla warriors, on the other hand, have combined a political struggle for the loyalty and cooperation of the population with unorthodox military strategies. (These strategies are at least used at the initial stages of a struggle, until the guerrillas amass sufficient military weaponry and disciplined troops to shift to conventional frontal warfare.)

LIMITATIONS OF COUPS D'ETAT

As a quick seizure of the State from the previous ruling group, the coup d'état[9] appears to have certain advantages. It avoids protracted struggle and immense casualties. Once control of the State is consolidated, that apparatus with its bureaucratic, police, and military branches can be actively applied to maintain control over the population and society. Not only active supporters of the coup but also all those persons who simply wish to avoid protracted internal civil war are likely to submit to the new regime. Only a relatively small number of active conspirators and military or para-military units, along with widespread passive submission of government employees, minor officials, and the general population are required for success. The coup d'état, however, is not an instrument of popular empowerment.

When successful, a coup d'état will establish a new person or group in the position of ruler in command of the State apparatus. This ruler may or may not exercise that power with more self-restraint or for different ends than did the earlier ruler. The coup may or may not accompany or follow expressions of popular discontent with the previous ruler. The coup may even take place against popular wishes and establish a more autocratic regime. A regime brought to power by a coup would clearly continue to depend upon institutionalized political violence for its existence and as its ultimate sanction. The coup maintains, and at times even furthers, the concentration of effective political and military power, rather than diffusing power throughout the society. This technique possesses no characteristics which operate intrinsically in the short or long run to increase popular control over the ruler or to empower the population. To the contrary, the strong tendency is for continuation of the concentration of effective power in the hands of those occupying the position of ruler.

CENTRALIZING EFFECTS OF GUERRILLA WARFARE

Guerrilla warfare[10] is different in many ways from coups d'état, and within the former are considerable variations. Guerrilla warfare requires considerable support among the civilian population, and in its early stages commonly involves small bands of guerrilla fighters using hit-and-run tactics in an apparently highly decentralized way. It is therefore thought by some persons that guerrilla warfare contributes to empowering people and to decentralizing effective power in the society. This effect may occur in early stages, although it is easy to exaggerate it even at that point.

The long-term results clearly concentrate effective power in the hands of the regime. If the guerrilla struggle fails, the old regime will have been forced to become increasingly autocratic and regimented in the military struggle against the attackers. If the guerrillas succeed, then in the later stages of the military struggle, the rebels' own military capacity grows significantly in numbers, weaponry, and centralized organization; it is transformed into conventional military forces able to fight positional war and to conquer and hold territory and cities. Mao Zedong (Mao Tse-tung) wrote of "the great strategic task of developing guerrilla warfare into mobile warfare."

> Guerrilla warfare [he wrote] will not remain the same throughout this long and cruel war, but will rise to a higher level and develop into mobile warfare. Thus the strategic role of guerrilla warfare is twofold, to support regular warfare and to transform itself into regular warfare.[11]

The final stage of a successful guerrilla war is conventional frontal war, as occurred in Vietnam. This requires the development and expansion of organized and disciplined military institutions. These continue after the success against the enemy, even if in reconstituted forms. That means the creation of a powerful lasting military system, powerful especially in relation to the other institutions of the society and other branches of the political system. They become a part of the new order's institutionalized capacity for political violence to advance its objectives and to defend itself against internal and external attackers. Hence, the military establishment would be capable of exerting effective pressures, controls, and even of seizing the State in a coup after victory.

One result of a successful guerrilla war is almost inevitable: a far more powerful military establishment relative to the society's civil institutions will exist after the revolution than the former oppressor wielded. As discussed in the previous chapter, the recently institutionalized political violence can be shifted to new purposes which it was never originally intended to serve. These may include repression of the population in service to either the new revolutionary regime or to a group which has seized or manipulated control of the State. In any case, the capacity for effective struggle is now concentrated in an institution of the State, rather than diffused among the population generally. Another guerrilla struggle against oppression by the new regime would at best take much time and — as in most guerrilla wars — involve immense casualties and social destruction. In addition, as long as the population accepts the belief that power derives from violence, the population will perceive itself to be powerless vis-à-vis the new State with its enhanced institutionalized capacity for political violence. Thus, guerrilla war cannot be described as contributing in the long run to increased popular empowerment, much less to reduced reliance on institutionalized political violence.

Therefore, both coup d'état and guerrilla war are types of political violence which become institutionalized and which, in the long run, concentrate effective power in the hands of whatever ruler can gain command of the State apparatus. Aldous Huxley argued:

> A violent revolution does not result in any fundamental change in human relations; it results merely in a confirmation of the old, bad relations of oppressor and oppressed, or irresponsible tyranny and irresponsible passive obedience. In de Ligt's own phrase, "the more violence, the less revolution."[12]

When coup d'état or guerrilla warfare succeed in removing a particular despot, that is all that has happened; those techniques are not capable of abolishing despotism itself, or of establishing lasting controls over the power of rulers. To do so would require changes in the underlying social condition, the diffusion of effective power throughout the society, and increased ability of the population to control their rulers and any elite by possession of sanctions and means of struggle, and capacity to use them, to defend and advance themselves, their principles, and their institutions.

CONSEQUENCES OF INSTITUTIONALIZED
POLITICAL VIOLENCE

The failure of violent sanctions to empower people generally and to remove the capacity for central domination and dictatorship appears to be rooted in the nature of those sanctions as such, especially in their institutionalized forms. Only atomistic violence by isolated individuals, perpetrated for whatever reason, can be said to decentralize power and to empower individuals, and even then only those individuals who commit it. That empowerment is very limited, however, for the only power which accrues to those particular individuals is the power to kill and destroy, not to create or construct.

When violent sanctions are intended to enforce the established system, to oust an existing regime, to attack internal or foreign opponents, or to defend against attacks, that violence cannot be spontaneous, haphazard, atomized, or decentralized. It cannot be the spontaneous expression of frustration and hostility. It cannot even be directed by diverse political wills. To succeed for such objectives, that violence must be organized and coordinated, and possess a command system. Such violence must be institutionalized. Advance preparations, a structure, and a command system are required not only to avoid chaos of numerous uncoordinated acts of small-scale violence; they are also required to produce the maximum instrumental effectiveness.

The institutions for applying political violence are unique in the society, precisely because only they are constantly equipped to apply their violence against the other institutions and the population of the society, that is, they can be turned to attack and suppress the rest of the society. Political violence, therefore, is not a neutral technique — as has usually been assumed — which can be used for any and all causes without having special side-effects which help to shape the society which uses it, as well as the group or society against which it is used.

Institutionalized political violence in the State helps to determine who rules and who is ruled. That is to say, that capacity to apply violent sanctions helps to determine stratification by political class.* The consequences of the society's ultimate sanction on the distribution of effective power in the society therefore have profound significance for those persons and groups which wish to end oppression and enhance freedom and social justice.

Significant reasons exist which explain why the institutionalized capacity for political violence tends to structure the society toward elitist domination, toward centralized structures in society, economics, and especially politics, and toward the impotence and helplessness of the population. The pressure for centralization and the potential for internal oppression are produced by that institutionalization of political violence which can be shifted to other purposes than originally intended, as discussed in the previous chapter, by the command system and other requirements of those institutions (particularly in crises), and by the disproportionately large effective power capacity of those institutions vis-à-vis the civilian ones. (The last factor can be altered if the civilians do not accept violence as the ultimate source of power and if they learn to transform their power potential into effective power by organization and effective use of nonviolent forms of sanctions, such as economic and political noncooperation.)

The requirements of institutionalized political violence for effectiveness contribute directly and indirectly to wider centralization and regimentation. For example, during actual war the demands for military weaponry, manpower, efficiency, central decision-making, secrecy, economic controls, silencing of opposition, and clear lines of action regardless of legal provisions produce especially powerful centralizing influences. For the defeated side, the results may be more blatant in the form of a military government imposed by the victor. But even for the winning side similar effects are produced on the society and political system. Certain political sociologists and

---

*Attention must also be paid to social class and economic class dynamics and relationships, and their roles in politics. Stratification is, however, not only social and economic but also political, and it is valid to speak of "political class" in addition to other forms. (See Gaetano Mosca, *The Ruling Class* [New York and London: McGraw Hill, 1939], and Ralf Dahrendorf, *Class and Class Conflict in Industrial Society* [Stanford: Stanford University Press, 1959].)

anthropologists, such as Bronislaw Malinowski, have pointed to the apparent causal interrelationships between war and dictatorships, to the tendency for dictatorships often to be expansionist and belliger-ent, and, conversely, for war to erode or corrupt democratic proc-esses and to increase the dictatorial characteristics of that society.[13] The developments in the technologies of modern military weaponry, transportation, communication, computers, police methods, and other fields continue to aggravate this problem. They combine to increase the capacity of institutionalized political violence to over-whelm, dominate, and suppress the rest of the society.

Countervailing forces to the centralizing impact of institutional-ized political violence may exist which modify or restrain the tenden-cies toward centralization and expansion of the command system. These forces may even prevent the more extreme consequences of the institutionalized capacity for violence. The potential for internal violent action against the rest of the society, or even against the established government itself may not be utilized in a given situation. However, the potential and the pressures are there; they always exist when the society relies on institutionalized political violence to pro-vide its ultimate sanction. Favorable conditions will increase the chances that that potential and those pressures will prevail. Those conditions exist when the independent institutions (*loci* of power) of the society are weak, when their capacity for resistance by other sanctions is negligible, when the crisis facing the society is severe, and when the scale and intensity of the political violence are extreme. When these all occur simultaneously the dangers of the growth of centralization and the expansion of the command system will be great. These may then overwhelm the rest of the society, and signifi-cantly modify the character of the society as a whole.

The danger becomes very real when those in command of the institutions of violence are unwilling to abide by established proce-dures and standards of legitimacy. Most of the coups d'état which have occurred in recent decades have been actively carried out by certain military units, while others acquiesced to the take-over.

In other contexts, too, the side effects of the use and expansion of institutionalized political violence have scarred the original objec-tives. In the Soviet Union, for example, efforts to achieve justice through the path of political dictatorship *for* the proletariat com-manded by the elite of an elite Party, relying in part upon the army, political police, prisons, camps, and executions, resulted in a tyranny and political terror under Josef Stalin which was far more extreme than any tsar had ever been capable of imposing. It included the deaths of millions of people in the 1930s in the collectivization and other programs, the creation of one of the world's largest military establishments, and a continuing elite control and regimentation of the economy and political system.

SUBMISSIVENESS AND THE DOCTRINE OF VIOLENCE

In addition to structural consequences, reliance on institutionalized political violence has other serious results for the society. These are psychological — really political-psychological. They affect the attitudes and feelings of people whose resulting behavior may have profound political effects. If the population believes that the "real" power derives from violence, that it "comes out of the barrel of a gun," then whoever has the guns will find it much easier to control the population. Those who wield the guns are then seen to be nearly omnipotent by those persons without guns — or at least with fewer guns, smaller ones, guns not wielded by professional troops or not backed by the technology and means of combined modern police, prison, and military systems. It is true that the power *potential* of the people without guns may be very great, and that under appropriate conditions they could mobilize that potential into effective power capacity by noncooperation and defiance to destroy a well-equipped dictatorship. Nevertheless, as long as the people *believe* in the omnipotence of those wielding superior violence, they will be unlikely to mobilize their own power potential. The doctrine that "power comes out of the barrel of a gun" therefore leads to the submission of the people to violent rulers.

The psychological effect on the perpetrator of violence caused by submission of the population to that violence is also extremely important. Submission to violence teaches the perpetrator of that violence to use it again next time. This may have severe political consequences, contributing to the expansion and increasing severity of violence by those who want their own way. Both Mohandas K. Gandhi and B. F. Skinner have pointed to this effect. On the other hand, both of them have insisted that the withholding of both counterviolence and submission to the will of the attacker will tend to reduce future attacks. This response teaches the attacker that the desired objectives cannot be gained by violent means.* Unless this happens, however, the continued application of violence, submission to it, and renewed application of the successful pattern of violence to gain one's objectives will in turn contribute to the centralizing institutional effects which we have discussed above.

The structural tendencies of institutionalized violence in the hands of the State being what they are, whoever uses the State's full capacities with the intent of developing an equalitarian society will fail. At the very least, if the *quantum* of institutionalized political violence remains approximately the same as before, the forces producing centralization, class rule, elitist controls, and the capacity to dominate the population which derive from this source will remain. If the *quantum* of institutionalized political violence is increased — as for such reasons as the use of significant violence to seize control of the State or to maintain that control, or expansion of police or military systems to deal with domestic or foreign crises — and if the society's *loci* of power have been weakened while effective power has been shifted to the State, then the distribution of effective power in the society resulting from the use of the State apparatus is likely to be more inequitable than under the previous system. The capacity of the State — whoever controls it — to impose domination on the populace will have grown, even under a new political flag which once symbolized the will of the people. Clearly, reliance on violence to empower the people does not work.

It is therefore especially ironic and tragic that the doctrine that "power comes out of the barrel of a gun" — which is compatible with an oppressive elitist system — was adopted by various groups which sought revolution against oppression in the name of the people. That doctrine is so crude a reflection of the nature of political power that not even Adolph Hitler subscribed to it. That doctrine ignores the diverse sources of power and the different kinds of power. It also ignores the very important question of who shall wield power, and the consequences of the doctrine on the society and political system. It leads directly to the expansion of institutionalized political violence and of State power, which can be applied to bring about dictatorship, genocide, war, and social oppression. That doctrine, when acted upon in politics, intrinsically leads to establishment of an elite in

*See Appendix C, "Skinner and Gandhi on Defeating Violence."

command of the institutionalized capacity for political violence. For all of the beautiful phrases about "the people" which sometimes accompany that doctrine, the nature of violent political sanctions, when institutionalized as required for effectiveness, actually excludes the general populace from actively exercising power.

By selecting the doctrine that power derives from violence, the so-called revolutionaries have chosen the distillation of the worst characteristics of the social system they denounced as inhuman, and which they wished to destroy, to be the foundation on which to build their new order. It need not, therefore, be wondered that the resulting political system resembles the old one so closely, only in more extreme forms. It is a shattering, but usually unnoticed, fact that in every country in which an avowed social revolution has occurred by means of violent struggle or political dictatorship, there exists a military establishment and system, and a police and prison system, which are more powerful absolutely in weaponry, combat strength, and in surveillance and control abilities, than were those of the *ancien régime*. The new institutionalized capacity for political violence is also relatively more powerful in comparison to the civil institutions of the society and other branches of the political system than was the case under the old order. That produces a society very like the old one, only more so.

In any society institutionalized political violence is intrinsically dangerous to free institutions and democracy. At the very minimum, extreme care must be taken with it. If one wishes to create a society in which people really do rule, and in which oppression is impossible, then one ought to explore alternative ways to meet the society's basic need for sanctions.

Pointing the finger at violence as a main culprit in the genesis of our serious problems is not a naive individualist approach derived from ignorance about politics and from romanticism. Quite the opposite: it puts the finger on a key to an explanation of why our society is the way it is despite our ideals, and may provide the key to discovery of how it can be changed to implement our ideals more adequately.

REQUIREMENTS OF LASTING LIBERATION

"[V]iolence may destroy one or more bad rulers," Gandhi wrote, "but...others will pop up in their places, for the root lies elsewhere."[14] Real and lasting liberation requires changes in the internal power relationships within the society. These cannot be produced by violence, which will actually impede them. Exponents of liberation who ignore the likely long-term effects of their technique of struggle upon the society they seek to free can only be regarded as shortsighted and irresponsible.

It is also exceptionally important to be clear about whose task it is to liberate people from oppression, of whatever type. So long as the old regime or system is changed or abolished, we often assume that the means make relatively little difference. However, important differences in results tend to follow from alternative answers to that question. Without the direct participation of the population itself in the effort to change, no real changes in the relative power positions between the population and whoever occupies the position of ruler are likely to occur. At most, a new group will replace the old one as ruler. The new one may or may not behave with greater restraint and concern about the welfare and liberties of the people *at its own discretion.* The liberation of oppressed people must, therefore, if it is to happen, be essentially self-liberation by means which are compatible with a lasting capacity of people to govern themselves and to shape their own society. Otherwise they face the likelihood of a new, even more, oppressive ruler waving a different flag.

The great Indian Gandhian socialist Rammanohar Lohia once wrote that he was tired of hearing only of the need to change the hearts of the oppressors. That was fine, but far more important was the effort to change the hearts of the oppressed, so that they would become unwilling to continue accepting their oppression, and become determined to build a better society. It is weakness in people's determination and ability to act which makes possible their continued oppression and submission. Change that, and they can never again be oppressed. Such self-liberation can only be done through the strengthening of the subordinates by their own efforts.*

---

*In contrast to Lenin's confidence in the small elite Party of "professional revolutionaries," Rosa Luxemburg and Karl Liebknecht argued: "Social revolution and reconstruction cannot be undertaken and realized except by the masses themselves.... The proletarian masses are called on to build Socialism stone by stone by their own efforts. Free, self-government [can only be achieved by]...the work of the toilers themselves, not by the acts of despair of a minority." (Quoted by Barthélemy de Ligt, *The Conquest of Violence* [New York: E. P. Dutton, 1938, and London: Geo. Routledge & Sons, 1937, and New York: Garland Publishing, 1972]).

According to our understanding of the nature of all political power, people have immense *power potential* because ultimately their attitudes, behavior, and cooperation supply the sources of power to all rulers and hierarchical systems. Power potential is not always, however, tranformed into *effective power*. What is required for this to happen? Once the subordinates wish to make changes, and once they are willing to act to do so, they require some type of sanctions. They then need a technique of action through which they can maintain and strengthen their existing independent institutions, create and defend new ones, and, very importantly, resist, confront, and undermine the power of the ruler. Such a technique should preferably also be one which will in the long run, with repetition, give the subjects a lasting capacity to control any ruler or usurper, and to defend their capacity to rule themselves. The choice of the ultimate sanction to maintain and to change a society is highly important in shaping the resulting society. In contrast to the centralizing effects of violent sanctions, which in the long run disempower the populace, nonviolent sanctions tend strongly to diffuse and devolve power in the society, and particularly help to empower the oppressed and powerless. Let us, therefore, examine some of the structural consequences of nonviolent sanctions.

UNCERTAIN SOURCES OF POWER

An understanding of the nature of nonviolent sanctions is required at this point, although it cannot be repeated here.* These sanctions have major impacts on the distribution of effective power in political societies because of two major factors: (1) the nature of the power of all hierarchical systems and rulers which makes them vulnerable to nonviolent sanctions, and (2) the impact of nonviolent struggle, especially when successful, on the capacities of persons and groups which have waged it. The combined effect of these two factors on the distribution of effective power establishes without question the interrelationships between political power and nonviolent sanctions.

*See the brief discussions of the technique of nonviolent action in Chapter Nine, " 'The Political Equivalent of War' — Civilian-based Defense," and Chapter Eleven, "The Societal Imperative," and the extensive examination in my previous work *The Politics of Nonviolent Action* (Boston: Porter Sargent Publisher, 1973).

The power which rulers wield, their capacity to act, do great or terrible deeds, implement policies and punish, conquer and plunder, serve, dominate, and oppress, is not their power. It does not come from their persons. Nor does the ruler's power come from guns. Rather, it comes from sources in the society which can be located. They include: authority, human resources, skills and knowledge, intangible factors, material resources, and sanctions. These sources are all rooted in the society itself, in its institutions, and ultimately in its people. People must accept the legitimacy of the power-wielder, and cooperate in providing the needed sources of power. They must also submit to orders and even to repression intended to intimidate the populace into obedience if the ruler is to maintain his or her control.

The sources of the ruler's power are derived from people who believe that they should submit because they are morally bound to do so, or because they believe themselves to be too weak to resist, from the people who provide economic resources, pay their taxes, and become the experts, administrators and aids, as well as from the people who staff the armies, courts, and prisons. All these people, and many others, provide the sources of power of all rulers, both beneficent and malevolent.

Hence, the most crucial problem for all rulers: people do not always do what they are told or are expected to do. If people reject the ruler's legitimacy, his or her authority is gone. If people withdraw their cooperation by disobedience, economic noncooperation, denial of needed knowledge and expertise, refusal to operate the bureaucracy, and to cooperate with the administration, then all those sources of power are weakened or removed.

If people are willing to defy both threats and the infliction of repression as the price of change, if police and soldiers become disturbed at their own deeds in repression and come to doubt the legitimacy of the regime already weakened by massive defiance, and, finally, if they then refuse further orders to punish or kill the defiant populace, then the regime is at its end. The people must continue to persist and defy, even in face of repression, until the sources of power are dried up, and therefore the regime is fatally weakened and disintegrated.

Without bestowed authority and ideological legitimacy, without aides and henchmen, without administrators, bureaucrats and a myriad of helpers, without wealth and economic resources, without institutional backing and administration, without police, prisons, and armies, without obedient subjects, even the most autocratic ruler or ruthless tyrant becomes politically impotent.

Such a dissolution of the ruler's power by withdrawal of its sources demonstrates that the power of rulers, dominating elites, and oppressing classes is not theirs, but rather comes from the very people they would control. The power of rulers is therefore intrinsically fragile. This insight alone opens the way for a conscious choice by people whether to obey and cooperate, and awareness of such a choice prepares the way for a drastic change in power relationships. All the sources of political power are thereby directly vulnerable to nonviolent sanctions.

DECENTRALIZING EFFECTS OF
NONVIOLENT SANCTIONS

Nonviolent sanctions often use the refusal by people to do their usual jobs and to behave in the expected ways, and their insistence on behaving in forbidden and unexpected ways, as weapons. These means of action frequently use people's usual roles and positions in society as power bases, and their accustomed functions as power levers. This type of weaponry can, under appropriate conditions, be far more effective than guns because it strikes directly at the sources of power of institutions and rulers. Nonviolent struggle is therefore primarily a power-wielding technique and set of sanctions, capable both of controlling the political power of others and of wielding power in its own right. Oppressors and tyrants fear the spread of this insight into the nature of all political power.

Nonviolent sanctions have several characteristics which contribute actively to decentralization and the diffusion of effective power capacity in the society. These characteristics are related to five main factors:

- the nature of leadership in applications of nonviolent sanctions;
- the qualities of specific nonviolent methods or "weapons";
- changes in the self-perception and attitudes of members of the nonviolent struggle group;

- increased self-reliance of those who wield nonviolent sanctions; and
- the growth of the non-State institutions of the society.

As compared to leadership in violent conflicts, leaders in movements applying nonviolent sanctions generally are less likely to have used violence to control their own group, if such means were available and otherwise acceptable. This factor is not only likely to influence the current conflict, but may also carry over into the poststruggle society because of its association with greater genuine commitment to humanitarian goals and principles. Also such leaders are less likely later to use violent sanctions autocratically to maintain and extend their power position, even if they then hold positions in the State apparatus. Some earlier nonviolent leaders — such as Jawaharlal Nehru, Kwame Nkrumah and Kenneth Kaunda — have accepted positions as prime minister or president and used violent sanctions, while others — such as Mohandas K. Gandhi and Jayaprakash Narayan — have refused or not sought such positions.

In nonviolent struggle movements the leadership is intrinsically unstable, and tends to diffuse downward hierarchically, moving among increasing numbers of people. This occurs because under most such conditions the leadership is deliberately placed "in the front lines" in the struggle and is seized by arrest and imprisonment, or other repressive means. As this occurs, and as communications and transportation may be restricted, new layers of leaders are required, and more leaders are needed since they must operate more locally. This both produces new personnel in leadership positions and multiplies their numbers. Where the struggle movement is strong and repression is severe, as these larger numbers of leaders are seized, the diffusion of leadership may extend to such a degree that the movement becomes effectively "leaderless." This experience may have important long-term consequences for the society, increasing decentralized self-reliance and reducing the perception that centralized leadership is always necessary. (This factor is not present, of course, in cases where the nonviolent sanctions are both initiated and applied by central State decision and orders, such as in international economic embargoes.)

In contrast to that which often occurs in the application of violent sanctions in both civil and international wars, the sanctions which the nonviolent leadership may apply against the members of their own group to maintain solidarity and to discourage defection to the opponent should be, and are more likely to be, nonviolent ones. Also, since violent sanctions are not used in the struggle against the opponent, no additional capacity to apply them will be developed to be carried over into the postconflict period for possible use for other objectives. For both of these reasons, even the nonviolent leaders who step into, or continue to hold, positions of State authority will not have at their disposal an *increased* capacity to apply violent sanctions which has accrued during the conflict. They may still use the regularly available State capacity for violent sanctions; that will, however, be more limited than it would have been following a violent struggle. That limitation will set certain restraints on internal repression.

Following violent struggles the new regime may aim to prevent unwanted challenges by taking possession of weapons and controlling the supply of weapons and ammunition. In these circumstances, with the population's faith placed in the efficacy of violent sanctions, even the most severe excesses of the regime are likely to go unchallenged by action of types which cannot be ignored. In the case of nonviolent sanctions, however, the weapons are not physical ones which can be seized, controlled by regulation of supply, or made inoperative by restriction of ammunition. Knowledge of various nonviolent weapons — nearly two hundred at least exist — once gained is not as easily controlled as physical weapons and ammunition. Previous experience in their application also operates as "training in battle." This will contribute significantly both to their actual ability to conduct such struggles in the future, and to their confidence in their ability to do so. Both of these may be very important in determining the distribution of effective power following that particular conflict. People who have, and know that they have, the capacity for independent effective struggle are more likely to be treated with some respect by governing elites than people who are in crises politically impotent. Experience in the application of nonviolent sanctions, especially when successful, arms the population with an ability to do so again should the need arise, as when the new ruler alienates the support of the majority of the subjects on matters of extreme importance.

When nonviolent sanctions are applied successfully, the people using them are likely to experience an enhanced perception of their own qualities and capacities which reflect actual changes in them. Before subordinates in the relationship can begin to use nonviolent sanctions they must change their prior attitudes of submissiveness and acceptance of inferiority. The group very probably has previously been passive and believed itself to be helpless in face of perceived wrongs. When they then begin to act to correct their grievance they are likely to experience a liberation from that sense of powerlessness. This change is likely to grow as their movement continues and gains strength. At the beginning of the conflict, the actionists may need consciously to control their fear of the opponent's sanctions, but later they may discover that they are no longer afraid. This change is not only important for individuals; it is important politically, for it undermines hierarchical systems which have depended on fear of violent punishments to keep the subordinates "in place." Their own willingness to act and to persist in the face of dangers, and the recognition by the opponent and others of their new power are likely to contribute to an increase of the group's self-esteem. The group will see their qualities and capabilities to be more significant than they previously perceived. Knowledge that they possess genuine strength even vis-à-vis the power of the State is likely to nurture a new spirit and arouse a new hope that they can help shape their own future.

Somewhat less certainly, the nonviolent actionists may become more respectful of the life and person of others, even their opponents in extreme conflicts. The actionists may also become more able to think through problems for themselves, reach their own decisions, and adhere to them even in difficult circumstances. While these are highly personal qualities, to the degree that they develop they will in the long run indirectly affect the distribution of effective power in the society.

Effective nonviolent sanctions are likely to strengthen the group using them, both absolutely and in comparison to the opponent group. Internal group solidarity and ability to work together are likely to grow. Increased internal cooperation is both a requirement in many cases for effective use of nonviolent sanctions, and also the result of such action. Internal cooperation is needed to apply the nonviolent sanctions effectively, and also to provide those needs formerly met by the opponent with whom cooperation has been withdrawn. The latter may include alternative ways to maintain social order even in the midst of conflict, as well as various social, economic, and political needs. To provide these, members of the group will need to increase their self-reliance and self-help, which will contribute further to self-empowerment. Existing institutions may be strengthened, they may be modified to meet needs more adequately, or changed in their internal operation. New institutions may also be created. These are constructive counterparts of noncooperation with the opponent. They can help to change existing power relations very quickly during an on-going conflict. The result could be lasting structural changes.

Sometimes this balance of noncooperation with cooperation is consciously planned and organized, while at other times it happens spontaneously and rapidly without plans or preparations. When the institutional changes are only temporary, they will contribute to changes in the power relationships between the contending groups while the struggle continues. When the institutional changes survive beyond the immediate conflict, they can have profound structural consequences contributing to the diffusion of effective power in both its institutional and its sanction forms.

One further factor may indirectly have long-term consequences for the power distribution of the society. The use of nonviolent sanctions will reduce the tendency for the struggle group to become themselves brutalized as a consequence of the struggle itself. Violent sanctions in a liberation struggle, revolution, or continuing defense effort mean a constantly increasing round of brutalities, retaliation, and counter-retaliation. The human personality becomes coarsened and hardened, until finally the human sensitivity and ability to react to human suffering wither, and all but die. The person who once struggled against inhumanities now pursues with ardent zeal the methods which when used by the opponent were once deplored, toward a goal the heart of which has been forgotten. This development is unlikely to occur in nonviolent struggles, which provide other sanctions which require abstinence from acts of violence and brutalities. This difference may have very important effects on the nature of the poststruggle society and political order.

Associated with this brutalization is one other factor important to the future society but probably not very consequential for the distribution of politically-significant power. Espousal of some type of political violence as the ultimate sanction of the society, and demonstrations of its practice in the legitimated forms of police shootings, executions, and war, are likely to instruct individual members of the society, including antisocial and emotionally unstable ones, that violence is indeed the ultimate sanction. It is highly doubtful that our efforts to restrict its use to certain institutions of the State — and then only for designated purposes, and when authorized by established procedures — can be effective as long as certain people, rightly or wrongly, feel that their own objective is valid and can also only be gained by violence. Legitimated acts of violence on behalf of the system may therefore unintentionally contribute to nonlegitimated acts of violence by individuals and groups with their own problems and objectives. The use of nonviolent sanctions on behalf of the system would not have that effect; it might instead contribute to the use of nonviolent sanctions by individuals and groups acting on their own, even against the standards and principles of the rest of the society. That might not be ideal, but it would be a considerable improvement over the multiplication of individual and group violence.

As a consequence of the effects of nonviolent struggle on the opponent's own power capacity and also on the power capacity of the group applying nonviolent sanctions, a fundamental alteration in power relationships will occur under appropriate conditions. This differs fundamentally from the power situation following the institution of changes by other peaceful means, including conciliation, legislation, court decision, or executive decree. In those cases, unless power changes have been made independently by other forces, the relative distribution of power after the specific change will remain approximately the same as it was before. Nothing will have occurred to change it, and people will not have gained increased abilities to restrict the power of their opponent, nor to wield sanctions themselves. Even when a major limited demand or objective has been thus granted, the people themselves would still be no more capable of achieving their will against the opponent or ruler who is unwilling to grant their wishes. Similarly, the immediate item which has been granted may, when the occasion suits, be as easily withdrawn. That which is given, and not earned, can as easily as it was received be taken away. That which is earned by work and struggle has durability, and is capable of both defense and further development by the people who have become empowered during its achievement.

SHAPING A SOCIETY'S "POLITICAL CONDITION"

The structural influences of violent and nonviolent sanctions play a significant role in determining the political condition of the society as a whole. The "political condition" of a society can be defined as the configuration of three main factors: (1) the way in which the political system operates; (2) what it does; and (3) what it cannot do. A political condition includes such specific elements as: the degree of concentration or diffusion of effective power; the society's ideals and goals; the system's humane characteristics and accomplishments; its capacity to impose a dictatorship, commit genocide, wage wars, and impose or support social oppression, and the likelihood of its doing any of these; conversely, its capacity to nurture and support freedom, democracy, social justice, and peaceful relationships internally and externally; the degree to which the society serves human beings or stultifies and harms them; and the extent to which it meets (or allows to be met) the diverse human needs outlined earlier in this chapter. Political conditions clearly differ widely, both within a single society from one time to another, and also between different societies.

These factors are not isolated and unrelated specific characteristics, but are interrelated in a variety of ways. On the basis of analyses in this and earlier chapters, it appears that the political condition of a society is closely associated with: (1) the actual distribution of effective power in the society (as distinct from the legal or constitutional allocation of decision-making authority); and (2) the type of ultimate sanction relied upon by the society and the extent to which it is developed into institutionalized capacities. Further attention is needed to the interrelationships between these two factors.

In Chapter Two, "Social Power and Political Freedom," it was argued that different types of institutional distribution of effective decision-making power, associated with the number and strength of the *loci* of power, supersede in importance the formal constitutional allocation of authority. The actual distribution of power in the political society and the actual practices of that society may differ from, or even be incongruous to, the formal constitution or the espoused ideals and doctrines of the society. Both of those are important, but are clearly secondary to the ways the society actually operates. Strong *loci* of power may impose actual limits on even a theoretically omnipotent autocrat. Conversely, weak or negligible *loci* of power will permit the ruler of a State with a formal democratic constitution to rule autocratically, or even to scrap the constitution, essentially at will.

In Chapter Eleven, "The Societal Imperative," it was also argued that the institutionalized capacity for political violence, once established for any purpose, can be shifted to other purposes not originally intended, and that this shift can be made essentially at the will of the persons in command of those institutions (unless other forces intervene). Hence, dictatorship, genocide, war, and systems of social oppression were viewed as closely interrelated, for they were four applications of institutionalized political violence; without that capacity they could not occur. Institutionalized political violence was seen to be the necessary, but not sufficient, condition for the development of those four phenomena. The absence of such institutionalized capacity, on the other hand, should allow more positive conditions to develop. In addition, the decentralizing and empowering effects of nonviolent sanctions, as discussed in this chapter, will tend to produce new conditions and characteristics of the political society which will exceed those which we have termed freedom, respect for life, peace, and social justice.

Both institutions and sanctions are, therefore, seen to be highly important in shaping the political condition of a given society at all times, and they are interrelated. For example, in a society with strong *loci* of power people will be more able to use nonviolent sanctions effectively as they will have organizational bases for group struggle. These *loci* are likely to be especially important when they control sources of political power. On the other hand, the *loci* of power are likely to be strengthened and people's capacity to organize is likely to increase during significant nonviolent struggles, especially when they are strong enough to succeed.

In the following discussion we are primarily concerned with influences of the distribution of effective power and sanctions on the political condition of the society. As a key element in any power capacity, sanctions will be discussed as a separate phenomenon, and we will narrow the remainder of the elements of effective power down to "institutional distribution of effective decision-making capacity."

A SOCIETAL FORMULA

The basic hypothesis to be explored here is that the interaction between the institutional distribution of effective decision-making capacity and the society's sanctions — including their type, capacity, and practice — are the central factors which over time will tend to produce the society's "political condition." As the two factors will vary from time to time, and on occasion change significantly, so as a result the political condition will also change. We are referring to the situation of both factors in the political society as a whole — including the general populace, the independent organizations and institutions (the *loci* of power), and the governmental bodies (including the State). While it is most difficult or impossible to measure each factor with precision, that is not necessary for our purposes; we are dealing with the major characteristics of the distribution of decision-making and the sanctions used. It may help to express this relationship as a formula:

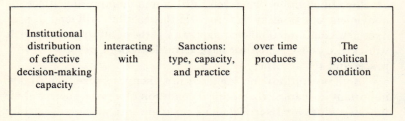

| Institutional distribution of effective decision-making capacity | interacting with | Sanctions: type, capacity, and practice | over time produces | The political condition |

In the long run, the political condition is created and modified by the interaction of the relative institutional distribution of effective decision-making capacity and the type of sanctions relied upon, including their capacity and practice. Other factors may also operate on the political condition, but these two are seen to be dominant.

The operation of this formula may be illustrated by showing the influence of particular combinations of institutional distributions of decision-making and sanctions, in cases in which these are relatively clear. We will present this for five different conditions which, although analytical models, approximate actual political conditions.

Condition One: In this type of situation, the *loci* of power are extremely weak, or have been systematically undermined and destroyed. Effective decision-making has been very highly centralized in the hands of a very small elite in command of the State apparatus, which also controls any other significant institutions which are present. The sanctions of the political society are overwhelmingly violent ones. A highly developed institutionalized capacity for such violent sanctions has been developed in both police and military forms. Violent sanctions are widely applied by threat or practice for internal control and in international relations.

When that combination of types of decision-making and sanctions exists in the political society the resulting political condition will be a type of dictatorship capable of oppressing society, waging war, and inflicting genocide if the ruler of the system wishes to do so. This would be true even if the ideals espoused and the ultimate goals of the system were humane, and even if a written constitution still nominally in force established very different procedures and practices. In the latter case, the ruler could easily abolish the formal constitution and bring the official structure in line with the actual political system. Condition One can be illustrated by this diagram:

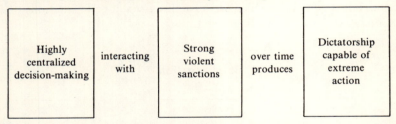

Condition Two: In this type of situation the *loci* of power are very strong in comparison to the State structure and are capable of independent decision-making even in opposition to the ruler in command of the State apparatus. The sanctions of the State are violent ones, and the sanctions of the *loci* of power include nonviolent sanctions in their internal operations and most relationships with each other. However, the *loci* of power for extreme crises also rely upon violent sanctions. The resulting political condition will tend to be unstable.

The unstable political condition will include a high degree of freedom and democracy, an absence of systematic social oppression, and the like. However, should a crisis of serious proportions arise, it would result in major expansion of the capacity and practice of violent sanctions. The centralizing effects of such violent sanctions would tend to have institutional effects. As the military requirements for effectiveness necessitate, and as the institutionalized capacity for political violence in the hands of the State is expanded and applied, the relative strength of the *loci* of power in comparison to the State is likely to decline. This is likely even if the violent struggle, as against an invader, is initially waged by guerrilla war; in major struggles the early decentralist stages of guerrilla warfare are in later stages supplanted by increasing centralization and transition to conventional military forces and combat.

On the other hand, given the initial unstable situation, if in a major crisis nonviolent sanctions are relied upon instead to combat the danger, with a resulting expansion of their capacity and practice, the effects on the political condition are likely to differ significantly from those following violent sanctions. Instead, assuming success, the decentralist institutional characteristics of the society are likely not only to be preserved but even to be expanded, thereby avoiding various consequences of violent sanctions and introducing those of nonviolent sanctions which we have discussed. These situations of Condition Two can be diagramed:

Basic situation

Decentralized decision-making among *loci*	interacting with	Violent State sanctions, limited nonviolent but mainly violent sanctions by *loci*	over time produces	Unstable condition

Alternative A

Unstable condition	affected by	Major expansion of violent sanctions	over time produces	Weakening of *loci* and expansion of State

Alternative B

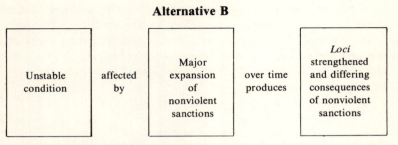

| Unstable condition | affected by | Major expansion of nonviolent sanctions | over time produces | *Loci* strengthened and differing consequences of nonviolent sanctions |

Condition Three: In this type of situation the institutional structure of the society is highly centralized, with *loci* of power few or weak, and decision-making concentrated in a small elite in command of the State apparatus. The State has in the past relied upon institutionalized violent sanctions, but this has ceased to be the case and nonviolent sanctions have become more important due to particular circumstances and responses. This situation is unstable.

The probable outcome of this unstable condition will vary with a number of factors, including the reasons for the shift to nonviolent sanctions and the thoroughness and permanence of the change. The shift might have resulted from a major policy change by those in command of the State apparatus because of the perception that against an impending attack by an overwhelmingly militarily superior enemy, military resistance was suicidal. Or, the shift might have occurred because of a successful nonviolent revolution against the previous system. In the former case, rapid planned or unplanned devolution of decision-making from the centralized State would be necessary for effective resilient nonviolent struggle against the attacker. In the latter case, the devolution of decision-making is likely already to have occurred; either existing independent institutions have become democratized and assumed for themselves significant decision-making authority, or new *loci* of power with decision-making capacity have been created prior to or during the revolution.

The longer-term effects of the shift to nonviolent sanctions on the political condition are then likely to be determined by the degree to which the changes are lasting. If the changes are temporary, and violent sanctions are reinstituted and again become the overwhelmingly predominant ultimate sanctions of the society, then the centralized structure dominated by a small elite is again likely to emerge. On the other hand, if the change to nonviolent sanctions is lasting, and they become the predominant sanctions of the political society instead of violent sanctions, then the resulting political condition is likely to be one of enhanced popular empowerment, more adequately meeting human needs, and avoidance of the consequences of institutionalized political violence. These situations of Condition Three can be diagramed:

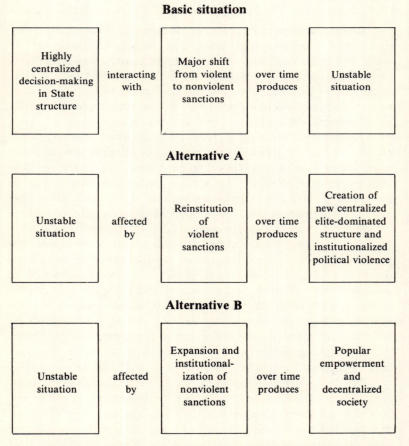

Basic situation

| Highly centralized decision-making in State structure | interacting with | Major shift from violent to nonviolent sanctions | over time produces | Unstable situation |

Alternative A

| Unstable situation | affected by | Reinstitution of violent sanctions | over time produces | Creation of new centralized elite-dominated structure and institutionalized political violence |

Alternative B

| Unstable situation | affected by | Expansion and institutional-ization of nonviolent sanctions | over time produces | Popular empowerment and decentralized society |

Condition Four: In this type of situation the decision-making capacity is highly diffused among strong *loci* of power with the central State apparatus weak. Nonviolent sanctions have been systematically adopted and institutionalized in place of violent sanctions, and are highly developed with strong capacity to function when needed as reserve or applied sanctions. The resulting political condition is likely to be relatively stable, with high popular empowerment, without the dangers of institutionalized political violence, and with strong contributions to freedom, democracy, respect for life, domestic and international peace, and social justice. The situation of Condition Four may be diagramed:

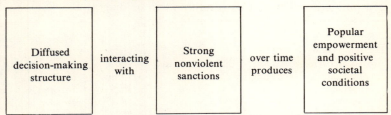

Unless completely new factors are introduced, the above Conditions One and Four are relatively stable, so that when one knows the distribution of decision-making and the type of sanctions one can predict fairly accurately their consequent political conditions. On the other hand, Conditions Two and Three are highly unstable. In those cases until the type of distribution of effective decision-making and the choice and development of ultimate sanctions are both settled, it is impossible to predict with any accuracy the ensuing political conditions.

Condition Five: The above four conditions involve either the strong reliance on one of the types of sanctions or a period of uncertainty in which the society hovers between reliance on one type or the other. In a fifth condition effective institutional decision-making is shared, in various possible proportions, between the State and the *loci* of power. The development and use of nonviolent sanctions are extremely limited or negligible; at the same time, however, the violent ones, although accepted as the society's ultimate sanction, are weak and relatively undeveloped. This can occur when perceived dangers and threats requiring strong sanctions of any kind are absent or weak. The resulting political condition is likely to be one of a moderate but significant degree of freedom, respect for life, without extreme social oppression, and few major violent conflicts and wars, if any. Pressures to decentralize and devolve power which come from nonviolent sanctions will be absent, although such pressures could come from other sources, such as beliefs, philosophies, and institutional needs.

This political condition is likely to remain stable only so long as no crises arise which produce a major need for sanctions. If such crises occur, the capacity for violent sanctions is likely to be expanded quickly. Their development and large-scale use will exert pressures toward increased centralization of decision-making and institutional controls, and toward other consequences of large-scale institutionalized political violence. This condition can be diagramed:

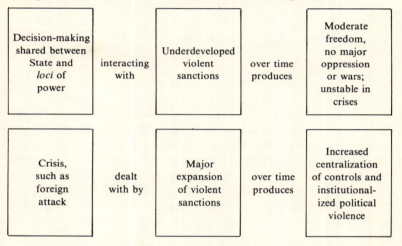

| Decision-making shared between State and *loci* of power | interacting with | Underdeveloped violent sanctions | over time produces | Moderate freedom, no major oppression or wars; unstable in crises |
| Crisis, such as foreign attack | dealt with by | Major expansion of violent sanctions | over time produces | Increased centralization of controls and institutionalized political violence |

Critical examination of this theory about the roles of the types of distribution of decision-making and of sanctions in shaping the political condition of a society is required. If the theory is valid, however, it will have fundamental ramifications for development of new grand strategies of social change which are more adequate than those of the past.

DEVELOPING STRATEGIES OF EMPOWERMENT

Many people readily accept that it is possible to change our political institutions to a significant degree by conscious choice. The capacity to make these choices to reshape our political societies also applies to the selection of the type of sanctions relied upon by our society and to a decision as to whether our political systems are to be highly centralized or instead possess a diffused decision-making system. Analyses in earlier chapters have suggested that the existing ways to meet necessary functions of a society are not the only possible ones. If effective alternative ways can be found or developed they can replace the present ways as functional substitutes.* This insight, Robert K. Merton wrote, "unfreezes the identity of the existent and the inevitable."[15] With this emphasis on the possibility of functional substitutes that type of analysis becomes a key to basic change, rather than a status quo approach as some persons have charged. This approach then becomes an intellectual tool which makes it possible to develop ways to achieve fundamental change, including the resolution of the complex problem of political violence, which has not only not been resolved but has rarely been faced in its fullness.

RECOGNITION OF ALTERNATIVES AS A KEY TO BASIC CHANGE

Our failure to resolve the problems of institutionalized political violence, and various sub-problems such as war, has been largely rooted in our failure to perceive that violent sanctions are not the only possible ones, and that we can explore the potential of alternative nonviolent sanctions. This failure has been one of perception of both persons who strongly support Western liberal democracy and capitalism and also those who oppose them and support instead one of the socialist systems.

This type of analysis, however, points the way to examination of functional alternatives, or functional substitutes, which, if instrumentally effective, might do the needed jobs instead of the way they are presently done. This may be the key to basic change in our political sanctions. As we have seen in this and earlier chapters, nonviolent sanctions have been used in place of violent sanctions in many situations in the past in highly diverse societies. Alternative nonviolent sanctions therefore do exist. This opens the way for basic change to the extent that they are substituted for violent sanctions. If they are or can be made effective, and if they are adopted in a series of

*See Chapter Nine, " 'The Political Equivalent of War' — Civilian-based Defense," and Chapter Ten, "Seeking a Solution to the Problem of War."

specific substitutions as discussed in the previous chapter, then the violent sanctions can be abandoned as unneeded. A series of such substitutions would contribute to systemic change involving increasing popular empowerment and institutional democratization.

This analysis of substitute ways to meet societal needs is not limited in its application only to sanctions, however. It can be applied also to our centralized large-scale institutions with their elitist decision-making processes and their disempowerment of the people affected or controlled by those institutions. These include both large-scale economic institutions and the State apparatus. To the degree that we can, step by step, vitalize, expand, and even create important substitute non-State institutions and lower levels of participatory government to meet the social, economic, and political needs of the society, we can reverse the extraordinary gravitation of effective power to the large corporations and the central State apparatus.

As we contemplate the problems of our society and the growth of centralized State power, we need to do more than to conserve those aspects of our society which originated in the past which remain valid and important today, and more than to make changes to right particular wrongs. We must deliberately act in ways which strengthen the non-State institutions of our society, and consciously refrain from increasing the concentration of effective power in the State.

Simple denunciation of the dangers of strong central government, the insensitivity of bureaucracies, or the high tax rates can produce no lasting solution to the problem of elite control, centralization of power, and constant expansion of the size and prerogatives of massive corporations and the State apparatus. Institutional change is required. One way to do this is to develop alternative institutions to meet those desirable and necessary functions now provided by the large centralized institutions.

Some tasks now carried out by the central State apparatus are not really needed, or are even inappropriate to a society which speaks so often of freedom and democracy. Those functions, and those parts of the State apparatus which are involved in them could simply be abolished to the advantage and welfare of the society. However, most general functions which are (or are supposed to be) carried out by the central State apparatus, and many proposed additional ones, are seen by most people to be desirable and necessary. The State's involvement in meeting those needs will not be drastically reduced or terminated until and unless those functions are being otherwise successfully performed by other bodies. Consequently, if one wishes to halt further expansion of the central State apparatus, one needs to develop alternative ways to meet neglected genuine social, economic, and political needs which reformers propose can be remedied by State action. Expansion of the State into the society and economy cannot be blocked by abdication of social responsibility or by neglect. Nor can it be done by leaving everything to the huge centralized national and multinational corporations. Unless alternative institutions and solutions are developed, progressive expansion of the State apparatus still further into the society is inevitable.

In order to reduce progressively the size of the existing central State apparatus, and thereby its dangers, it will be necessary to create or strengthen smaller-scale institutions (*loci* of power) with decentralized decision-making to provide genuine needs, and then gradually to shift to them tasks now carried out by the State. We need to aim toward a much larger number of institutions, each individually operating on a smaller scale with high democratic participation, cooperating where needed with others on projects of regional and national concern.

None of this is meant to imply that small-scale organizations, institutions, and lower levels of government are always idyllic cases of humanity and participatory democracy. But, at their worst, smaller institutions can do less harm than large ones. With smaller bodies it is easier for their participants and constituents, acting directly, to correct problems. Smaller institutions make possible greater participation and control by those directly concerned than do large ones.

On the governmental level, despite or even because of the developments in politics during the past century, we need to consider carefully various ways to increase democratic control and participation. Hannah Arendt's ideas, discussed in Chapter Six, "Freedom and Revolution," merit particular consideration. Where organs of direct democracy have survived even in mangled forms — such as the New England town meetings or Midwestern farmers' organizations — we need to explore how to preserve them and bring new vitality and responsibilities to them. Where they do not exist, we may need to explore how to initiate responsible experiments in introducing them to deal, initially, with limited but significant matters.

The combination of the gradual development and adoption of

both substitute nonviolent sanctions, and of independent smaller-scale institutions in a stage-by-stage program of responsible change, would help to develop a political condition which implements to a far higher degree than at present the ideals which our society espouses.

NONVIOLENT LIBERATION STRUGGLES

The long-term structural consequences of both violent sanctions and nonviolent sanctions have strong implications for liberation struggles against various types of oppression. Two points are clear:

1. Liberation must be primarily self-liberation; and

2. Only liberation by means which strengthen the subordinate group can contribute to long-term changes in power relationships, and thereby prevent future oppression.

These are not comforting prospects. It would be much easier if one could find some "liberator" who would overthrow the oppression single-handed, without effort or costs being required from the oppressed. Although belief in that prospect is widespread, it is dangerous. That belief is based upon a failure to distinguish between a particular oppressor and a general condition of oppression. In that condition the populace is constantly vulnerable, because of weakness, to whoever might gain the position of ruler and use it to oppress them. In that condition, one oppressor may simply be replaced by another. "Liberation" which is given by the oppressor in a fit of magnanimity or for ulterior motives, or "liberation" which is delivered to the oppressed without major effort on their part by a third party which has intervened and defeated the old oppressor, does not strengthen the subordinates and their institutions, and can be taken away as easily as it was received. On the other hand, liberation which is won by the oppressed themselves, as a result of self-strengthening efforts and the waging of noncooperation and defiance, replaces the condition of oppression with a condition of self-reliant societal strength and therefore cannot easily be taken away. This latter condition will have far more beneficial and lasting long-term consequences.

As long as people are able to think for themselves and maintain their self-respect, they will struggle to achieve, preserve, and extend their freedom. Yet it happens that in many countries and under various systems the power of the ruler and the economic elite is so extensive and uncontrolled that the condition suffered by the general population can only be described as oppression. The particular type of system may vary. It may be the remnants of colonial rule, foreign occupation, economic exploitation, social domination (as of women and untouchables), racist systems, internal dictatorship, or have some other name. When people seek to throw off oppression, to establish popular control over political power, over social domination, and over elites of various kinds, they are struggling for liberation.

The problem of liberation has, therefore, not disappeared simply because most of the old European colonial regimes have been replaced by indigenous regimes. Freedom — in a wide social, economic, and political sense — still remains a goal imperfectly achieved at best, and in many cases blatantly violated in extreme ways under various systems and flags.

The important questions therefore become *how* the oppressed shall wage their struggle and achieve the change, whether they will succeed, what the costs will be, and whether a substantially better society will result in the long run, one which approximates freedom.

The question of how to struggle is often answered by the emotions derived from the pain of past oppression. Struggles for liberation of any kind always contain emotional and highly subjective elements. In any revolutionary situation something intangible is present which is difficult to analyze objectively. It is even more difficult to produce this intangible element by careful analysis and rational decision.

It is a spirit of a people rising against conditions which they can no longer tolerate and at the same time remain true to themselves, their beliefs, and their dreams of the future. It is the willingness at a given moment to stake all against odds which cannot be calculated, lest the intellect decree against the heart which is fundamentally the creator of revolutions. It is the courage to strike the first blow for freedom while others stand waiting for a sign. It is the willingness to go on, knowing, if one counts the odds, that one cannot win. It is a person willing to die for a future that only others will see.

While the emotional element is therefore strong in all types of social change movements, the avowed goal is not simple satisfaction of one's personal psychological needs but to produce change. Especially in major liberation and revolutionary movements, if one allows oneself to be guided solely by emotions, one may make serious errors in the choice of instruments — both sanctions and institutions — for achieving one's objectives. If one has a sense of responsibility for the results actually achieved, which will affect many people now living as well as future generations, one needs to consider carefully how to achieve one's goals instrumentally, as well as how to meet one's personal emotional needs.

This choice is not simply between the ways which appear easy and difficult. Often ease and difficulty in means are hard to predict, and if one is seeking basic change, there often is no easy way. Nor can one calculate solely on the basis of anticipated differences in suffering between the use of violent sanctions and nonviolent sanctions. Those differences must be considered, and it appears that nonviolent sanctions produce far less suffering and far fewer casualties than do violent sanctions. That is important, but cannot be the single factor considered. Whether one chooses to struggle or to do nothing, the victims of oppression will suffer.

In all cases of oppression, the most important single problem of liberation movements is how to act by means which will change the situation, end the unjust conditions, and establish lasting control by people over their own lives and society. The extent of the change required, whether minor or fundamental, will strongly affect the type and extremity of such action. In revolutionary situations, the problem is simply more severe, but it is essentially the same problem.* The problem is strategic: how to act so as to achieve maximum effectiveness to end the immediate oppression and to establish an alternative system with greater justice, popular control, and freedom. This problem requires the attention of all who would combat oppression and build a better society.

---

*Barthélemy de Ligt wrote: "The great problem of revolutionary action by the masses lies in this: how to find the methods of struggle which are worthy of men and which at the same time even the most heavily armed of reactionary powers will be unable to withstand." (Barthélemy de Ligt, *The Conquest of Violence: An Essay on War and Revolution* [New York: E. P. Dutton, 1938, and London: Geo. Routledge & Sons, 1937, and New York: Garland Publishing, 1972], p. 163.)

KEY FACTORS IN NONVIOLENT LIBERATION

These are a few of the significant factors which must be considered by persons and groups which wish to achieve liberation by nonviolent struggle:

1. They will need to understand as fully as possible the nature of the opponent and system, and of the wider situation in which both the opponent and the group which is struggling will operate. Lack of understanding, or errors in perception, may lead to serious strategic or tactical mistakes. Accurate and fuller understanding of the opponent and society may make possible the choice of the most effective courses of action.

2. The type of sanctions — the technique of action — to be used in the struggle needs to be consciously chosen with consideration of both short-term and long-term consequences, the strengths and weaknesses of the struggle group and of the opponent, and the wider context in which the conflict occurs. This choice should not be left to chance, the decision of small groups, the fruits of bitterness, or unexamined assumptions about power.

In the past, very often the type of sanctions has not been chosen consciously, and too often the rebels have relied upon political violence which their opponent was better equipped to use. That choice has often been immediately disadvantageous, and has contributed in the long run to a different type of society than desired, as discussed above.

3. Nonviolent sanctions — the methods of the technique of nonviolent action — need to be thoroughly understood. This includes the technique's theory of power, methods, dynamics, and mechanisms of change, requirements, conditions for effectiveness, principles of strategy, responses to repression, and alternative means of concluding individual conflicts.

4. Broad knowledge of the grand strategy of struggle and of the nature and requirements of nonviolent sanctions needs to be spread widely in the society. That will enable the general population to act in harmony with them, whatever may be the points of their action and level of participation.

5. Individual strategies, with supporting tactics, are needed for each particular situation, to be developed with the background of the above, and additional, factors.

6. As large a group of people as possible needs to be developed with a dedication to the cause of liberation, a thorough understanding of nonviolent sanctions, and a willingness to use them in a disciplined manner.

7. Constant attention to the condition of the struggle movement in the constantly changing conflict situation will be required. Efforts will be needed to remedy its weaknesses. Particular campaigns will need to be evaluated for lessons.

8. Where a struggle has broken out spontaneously, it may be strengthened by intuitive and intellectual understanding of the technique which is already being used, and also by initiatives developed during the struggle by persons with greater understanding of this type of sanctions.

9. In a major struggle, to the degree that it is compatible with nonviolent discipline, militant initiatives and strategies of conflict are required, along with accurate perceptions that the nonviolent sanctions are being instrumentally effective. If these do not happen, demoralization or a shift to violence may develop, with harmful consequences.

10. Assuming sufficient strength, the nonviolent struggle movement must persist in the face of repression and intimidation, and refuse to submit. Leaders must set an example in this for all participants: they must not allow the opponent to make it appear that they have accepted reduced punishment in return for reduced resistance. Such behavior contributes to demoralization or to a shift to political violence; it can only be corrected by rejection of those leaders and by launching more militant nonviolent initiatives.

11. Unless the populace and *loci* of power are extraordinarily strong in comparison to the State apparatus, liberation cannot usually be achieved by a single brief struggle. Instead, it is likely to occur in phases. During these phases the subjects' strength increases, their ability to apply nonviolent sanctions grows, their social groups and institutions (*loci* of power) develop and strengthen, while the opponent's sources of power are restricted or severed, and while third parties have time to shift their loyalties and support. At certain points, dissension and weaknesses may appear within the opponent group. On the other hand, the nonviolent struggle group may increase its effective power capacity to achieve its objectives.

12. It is essential to remember that this type of liberation struggle is one of constant development and change, with nothing remaining static permanently. At times rapid changes may occur.

13. The forms of final victory also vary, from a graceful negotiated agreement to a complete collapse of the opponent's position and power as the extreme possibilities.

Attention to such factors as these will ensure that attention is paid both to institutions and to sanctions in the course of the conflict in order that the type of society they will tend to produce is compatible with the ideals espoused by those who sought change in the first place.

NONVIOLENT SANCTIONS FOR "UNJUST" PURPOSES?

Nonviolent sanctions have been used for purposes which many people would call unjust, and on occasion nonviolent challenges to the established elite have been met with counter nonviolent sanctions or with other responses that did not involve violent repression. These developments have disturbed some people, especially persons who hold that only people who believe in an ethical or religious system enjoining moral nonviolence should or can use nonviolent action. Demonstrably, others *can* and have used nonviolent sanctions, often with initial effectiveness. Whether persons pursuing "unjust" causes, or persons and groups seeking to defeat a challenge by nonviolent action, *should* use nonviolent sanctions to that end is a more complicated question than might first appear. Our answers to these questions will affect the proposal made in this book to develop systematic substitutions of nonviolent sanctions for violent ones.

The first preference of the group engaged in nonviolent struggle would, of course, be that groups pursuing "unjust" causes, or seeking to defeat a nonviolent struggle movement, should adopt the aims espoused by the nonviolent group. Those types of nonviolent action which seek to convert the individual members of the opponent group, as distinct from those which seek settlements by accommodation or nonviolent coercion, are intended to achieve that end. However, not all people using nonviolent action can or should pursue change solely by the conversion mechanism. In any case, it is naive to expect that every group which is challenged by nonviolent means will easily abandon their long-standing beliefs, practices, and goals. At times, it is even undesirable that they should do so. For example, the nonviolent group may be in the eyes of many on the "wrong" side of the issue; after all, at a certain point the Nazis organized economic boycotts of Jews, and advocates of integration in the Deep South were at times subjected to social and economic boycotts by segregationists. Even when the nonviolent group is on the "right" side, something more may be required than quick changes in the opponent's beliefs. Changes in power relationships may be required, for example, and these take time and effort to achieve.

It is a fact that persons, groups, powerful elites, and classes are going to continue to hold beliefs, persist in practices, and pursue goals which many of us would reject as "unjust," regardless of their being challenged by nonviolent sanctions. It is also a fact that when these bodies are challenged by nonviolent means those groups will usually refuse to capitulate and will react with application of sanctions. That is a basic "given" factor of the conflict situation which cannot be wished away by those who would prefer it to be otherwise.

It is in this context that the question of such groups using nonviolent sanctions must be viewed. Given their beliefs and situation, they will use sanctions of some type: the only question is *which* type. Does one prefer that such groups use violence? Since ultimate sanctions are of two types, violent sanctions and nonviolent sanctions, one or the other will be used. No third option is available. Therefore, within the constraints of the situation, one must ask whether it is "better" — by whatever standards of measurement — that the sanctions used are violent or are nonviolent.

When the groups and institutions which are backing "unjust" causes abandon violent sanctions to achieve their ends and substitute nonviolent sanctions, those bodies will still be "a problem." It would be far better, for example, if their outlooks, such as racism, which motivate their actions could be replaced by views and beliefs which recognize the human dignity of all people. When that does not happen, however, it is much to be preferred for the society as a whole, and for the group against which they vent their hostility, that the groups shift from violent sanctions to nonviolent sanctions to pursue their objectives. For example, if a "white" racist group is willing, in support of its beliefs, to march under strict nonviolent discipline under all conditions during that organized demonstration and in the future, that can be a major advance in humanizing the way in which extreme conflicts are fought out in a racist society. That event must be compared not only with the ideal in which racism is abolished, but also with the earlier methods of racist groups, including lynchings, beatings, bombings, and other acts of physical violence to harm, kill, and intimidate people.

Occasionally when people realize for the first time the possibility that nonviolent sanctions not only can be powerful but can be adopted by racist and other groups whose outlooks and policies they detest, they ask: "What if Hitler had used nonviolent action to achieve his goals?" Had Adolph Hitler and his Nazi cohorts shifted from violent means to only nonviolent ones, they would still have been a serious threat but the whole nature of Nazism would have been changed. Racism, anti-Semitism, and elitism would still have been present and would have required vigorous countermeasures from those people and groups who rejected them and who wished to remove their influence. However, without violence the Nazis could never have established concentration camps, tortured and executed political opponents, exterminated Gypsies, Jews, Eastern Europeans, and others, or invaded or bombed other countries. Had the Nazis restricted themselves only to economic boycotts, marches, and hunger strikes, for example, they could in the atmosphere of that time still have done much harm, but there would have been no Holocaust and no war. The issues of racism, anti-Semitism, elitism, and the leadership principle could have been the direct objects of attack by the opponents of Nazism — in contrast to what actually happened during the Second World War. The adoption of nonviolent sanctions and abandonment of violent sanctions by groups whose views and objectives we regard as unjust is a change to be welcomed as a very limited but significant step toward the needed more fundamental changes.

It is far better that nonviolent sanctions be used for "unjust" causes, and that they be applied against a movement for change which is itself using nonviolent action than that those same groups use violent sanctions for the same purposes. This is because the individual and societal consequences of even this use of nonviolent sanctions are preferable to those of violent sanctions.

CONSEQUENCES OF NONVIOLENT SANCTIONS

Nonviolent sanctions, as compared to violent ones, will tend to:
* result in significantly less physical suffering, injury, and death;
* be psychologically far less injurious to the participants (Franz Fanon documented psychological damage to users of violence for revolutionary purposes,[16] and such injuries among United States soldiers in Vietnam are well known);
* affect profoundly the course of the conflict, reducing escalating physical and social destruction, and introduce very different dynamics with less harmful and even beneficial results;
* help to maintain the focus on the issues at stake in the conflict, rather than shifting it to other matters, thereby opening the way for a lasting resolution of those issues;
* contribute to major shifts in power relationships toward diffusion of power and popular empowerment; and
* contribute to the development of a new stage in the application of sanctions in political societies in which unresolved acute conflicts are fought out by use of nonviolent sanctions on both sides, instead of by violence and counterviolence.

This last factor is likely to lead to refinement of nonviolent sanctions in a variety of ways. These will include increased consideration of the factors contributing to success, of human factors involved in the conflict, and of the need for improved mutual understanding. Perhaps most importantly, the uses of nonviolent sanctions for "unjust" purposes and as countersanctions to challenges by nonviolent struggle will contribute to the break from the old pattern of violent sanctions against violent sanctions with its consequent centralization of effective power, great concentrations of institutionalized political violence, and potential for grave consequences.

REVERSING DIRECTION

Present policies intended to deal with our major problems give few grounds for encouragement, and are not easy or free of risks. If something new does not begin to reverse our present direction, the path toward our future is dim. The tools at the disposal of modern States for operating dictatorships, conducting genocide, waging war, and supporting social oppression continue to be refined and continue to grow. It is our societal imperative that we reverse that direction.

We need not only ways to topple a particular dictatorship. We need to develop the capacity to prevent the development of any dictatorship. We need not merely bewail past genocide. The greatest honor to the victims of the Holocaust, the dead Armenians, and many others, would be to learn how to prevent genocide from ever occurring again. Our need is not only for policies which will enable us to survive or limit a war. We need to prevent wars by adopting a different means of combat and developing a capacity to deny future attackers their objectives. We do not need the types of opposition to social oppression or those programs for liberation which result in continuing powerlessness of people, or, worse, a new system of political enslavement in the name of the people. Instead, we need to restructure human institutions and facilitate self-empowerment so that no one can ever oppress us again.

The analyses in this volume have pointed toward a broad framework for changes to deal with these problems and to meet human needs more adequately, requiring both changes in institutions and in the type of sanctions on which we rely. We need now to develop these as key components of a comprehensive program for acceptable change:

1. A constructive program[17] to build new institutions and renovate and revitalize existing ones to meet human needs more adequately; and

2. Development of capacitites to apply nonviolent sanctions in place of violent ones for meeting particular needs in a progressive series of substitutions.

These main components of a grand political strategy of work, resolution, and renovation rely upon means which intrinsically diffuse, rather than centralize, decision-making and effective power, strengthen the independent institutions of the society, and stimulate self-reliance. Since empowerment of people is an essential part of ending oppression, these means are likely to be, in the long run, more effective to that end than either open political violence or reliance on central State action, whether by legislation, executive orders, or judical decision. Experience in both types of activities is also likely to increase people's ability to tackle for themselves other problems which beset them and to resolve self-reliantly the difficulties of the future.

A CONSTRUCTIVE PROGRAM

A constructive program consists of a variety of activities to remedy social problems and meet human needs more adequately. It does this by changing attitudes, social practices, and institutions by means of voluntary organized action, including the building of new institutions and sometimes the renovation of existing ones. The constructive program has been described as the scaffolding upon which the structure of the new society will be built. The various aspects of a constructive program are conceived as an intermeshed program of social reconstruction, in which the autonomous activities of a variety of organizations and groups contribute to an integrated, but flexible, program for constructive development and change.

Examination of the potential of this possible contribution to change is merited, as an alternative to both existing situations and to continued expansion of State action to remedy social ills and meet human needs. The development of an encompassing constructive program requires major efforts of a variety of people and groups with diverse experiences, analytical abilities, expertise, and skills. Appropriate broad fields of work would include social, cultural, educational, political, economic, and environmental problems, issues, and alternatives. Specific areas of work and tasks to implement them need to be selected under such broad fields, depending on the needs of the individual society. These tasks would then be implemented by a combination of individual, group, and institutional action, independent of both massive corporations and the State apparatus, in order both to deal with the specific need and simultaneously to strengthen the society as a whole.

EXPLORING NONVIOLENT ALTERNATIVES

The second key component of a comprehensive program of acceptable change is development of capacities to substitute nonviolent sanctions for violent ones to meet a wide range of social and political needs for sanctions. This includes serious exploration of the potential of nonviolent sanctions, and, where they are or can be made to be feasible, development and implementation of plans to substitute them to meet particular needs for which people have generally relied upon violent sanctions. This component will at times precede the constructive program and at times operate parallel to it. The exploration and adoption of nonviolent sanctions need not, and ought not, wait until institutional change is at an advanced stage.

Our responsibilities here include three tasks: (1) to survey the resources upon which we can draw, that is, to learn more about the nature, effectiveness, and potential of nonviolent sanctions; (2) to determine what at any given point are the extent and means by which they can be substituted for violent sanctions; and (3) to take those steps as part of a series of specific substitutions. In each of these tasks the active involvement of many people is needed in the investigation, education, thought, planning, work, and action. There is, therefore, a task and a responsibility for each of us.

The first of these tasks includes, among other parts, education about the nature of nonviolent alternative sanctions and noncentralist institutions. This education includes both that offered within our formal educational institutions and that which in more diffused and less institutionalized ways is offered to members of the general public. Let us discuss each of these.

Educational institutions must never become vehicles of indoctrination or distortion by a biased selection of subject matter. However, it is not only legitimate but imperative to correct the selective biases of the past in the choice of subject matter. These biases may have derived from the preconceptions people have held and from the views of special groups. Various topics and fields have been belittled, slanted, or excluded in the fields of study. These biases need to be corrected by the inclusion of important additional subject matter and knowledge. For example, a series of additions to our history courses and texts is required. The field of history is especially important, for on the basis of our understanding of what has happened in the past, we shape our perception of what can happen now and what are the options among which we can choose for shaping our society in the future. Consequently, the primary focus of so many of our text books and courses on wars and the actions of powerful kings, emperors, and presidents, to the neglect or deprecation of major nonviolent struggles, of popular self-government, non-State forms of government, and small political units, of the movements of people to correct the social evils of their day and to build a better society, is extremely serious and indeed politically dangerous. A whole series of additions to our histories is required to balance the record. Comparable additions are required in courses in other fields.

There will also often be a need for special courses. These include ones which help students to learn how to make group decisions, how to develop the skills for effective group participation, how to resolve conflicts, how to analyze and resolve problems, and others. Courses specifically on nonviolent action are urgently required in our educational institutions on all levels from primary schools through graduate studies in universities.*

The general public remains largely ignorant of how this nonviolent technique operates, its history, its requirements, how to apply it to achieve maximum effectiveness, and its consequences. It is possible to correct past neglect, and to bring to nonviolent sanctions a variety of tools to increase our knowledge of them. This knowledge and various viewpoints about nonviolent alternatives can then be offered to the public through several means, including adult education courses, newspapers, magazines, radio, television, and books. These means can also be used to encourage critical discussion and evaluation of these options. This spread of knowledge of nonviolent sanctions will enable people to consider them intelligently. To the degree that people find merit and potential in these options, they are likely to become more sympathetic to serious exploration and adoption of nonviolent sanctions in place of violent ones. This would be a necessity, for example, prior to and during any serious consideration of the potential of a civilian-based defense policy, or any other official shift to substitute nonviolent sanctions.

With or without the opportunity for public and official consideration of the possible merits of shifting to nonviolent sanctions, increased public knowledge of them is likely to have significant effects on the distribution of effective power in the political society. Knowledge of the nature and use of nonviolent struggle is power potential. With new knowledge of this option and confidence in its capacity, people in situations in which they otherwise would passively submit, be crushed, or use violence, will more likely apply alternative nonviolent sanctions. This will both help them to deal with the serious and genuine conflicts of our age by their actions, and simultaneously avoid the destructiveness and pitfalls of political violence.

*See Appendix B, "Twenty Steps in the Development and Evaluation of Nonviolent Sanctions."

Knowledge of how to act, how to organize, and how skillfully to transform one's power potential into effective power in nonviolent struggle enables even otherwise disfranchised people, to whom the doors of participation in the institutions which affect their lives have been shut or never opened, to wield effective power and to participate in the determination of their own lives and society. When blockages are placed in development and operation of parts of the constructive program, people will be able to act peacefully to remove them in order to resume work to resolve present problems and build democratic institutions.

SUBSTITUTING NONVIOLENT SANCTIONS

Effectiveness in this type of sanctions is not the result simply of spirit or the will to change. In addition to emotional components, an almost technical element exists in how to apply nonviolent sanctions with maximum effectiveness. This includes such questions as organization, strategy and tactics, choice of specific leverages, group discipline, and responses to the sanctions of the opponent. In these and other aspects we can learn how to utilize them more skillfully. We can develop resources, make preparations, and develop training programs for the efficient application of nonviolent sanctions for diverse purposes in place of violent ones. These various steps are important in the substitution of nonviolent for violent sanctions.

As discussed earlier, nonviolent sanctions have already been substituted for violent sanctions in many situations. These substitutions are therefore, in principle, possible.* With the foundation of the recommended research, policy studies, training, and preparations, further deliberate substitutions should be possible. These include both those which are noninstitutionalized initially (as struggles for changes in the society and political system), and those which are from the beginning institutionalized (as deliberate shifts to nonviolent sanctions to operate and maintain the system). These substitutions may begin slowly and with considered deliberation in some situations. They may develop rapidly in other cases.

---

*See Chapter Nine, " 'The Political Equivalent of War' — Civilian-based Defense," and Chapter Eleven, "The Societal Imperative." For fuller treatment, see Sharp, *The Politics of Nonviolent Action.*

With the emergence of effective substitute nonviolent sanctions a new path for the resolution of the problem of political violence would open. People would not then have to choose between use of political violence and acceptance of political irrelevancy. They will have the option of effective nonviolent sanctions. These alternative sanctions would break the cycle of presumed necessity that each side in a conflict use violence against the violence of the opponent. It would no longer be necessary to postpone removal of violence from politics until the arrival of some distant condition of political *nirvana,* or vainly to attempt to gain massive numbers of converts to moral doctrines prohibiting all violence. It would become possible to begin specific important changes in this highly imperfect and dangerous world by developing and substituting nonviolent sanctions for violent ones.

Some of the general needs for which substitute nonviolent sanctions might replace violent sanctions are:

- enforcement of minimal standards of acceptable social behavior;
- conducting conflicts in which both sides believe they cannot compromise without violating their principles;
- righting wrongs against particular groups;
- defense of basic liberties;
- liberation and revolution against oppression;
- defense of the constitutional system against internal usurpations (as coup d'état); and
- national defense against foreign invasions and occupations.

Several of these are discussed in earlier chapters.

Two important questions arise from this: Could nonviolent sanctions be effective for meeting these specific needs for sanctions in each particular situation? Could the substitutions be successfully achieved, and if so how? Those questions will require major attention in each instance in which a substitution is contemplated.

The change in sanctions therefore would *not* be a sweeping adoption of a new way of life by the whole population, nor a sudden sweeping transformation of the whole society. It would instead be a phased comprehensive attempt over some years or decades to develop and substitute nonviolent sanctions for violent ones, moving from one particular substitution to another, for those functions for which our society legitimately requires effective sanctions and today relies upon political violence. At times more than one such changeover might take place simultaneously. As these specific changes proceeded, a demonstrated viability of the substitute nonviolent sanctions for one purpose could facilitate consideration of similar substitutions for other purposes. However, specific adaptations and preparations would be required for each specific changeover where the shift was to be institutionalized in the system. Thereby, the changes would by stages reduce the overall reliance on institutionalized political violence and on noninstitutionalized political violence for all purposes. The consequences of this, as discussed in the previous chapter, would be profound.

POPULAR EMPOWERMENT

The substitution of nonviolent sanctions for violent ones on a major scale will likely have far-reaching and fundamental ramifications for the society. These will extend beyond meeting the particular need for sanctions and beyond short-term effectiveness for the nonviolent sanctions on the particular issue and occasion. The decentralizing effects on the structure of the political society have already been discussed earlier in this chapter. Nonviolent sanctions will also contribute significantly to the more equitable distribution of power by empowering the people as a whole who learn how to apply them. The combination of these two consequences of nonviolent sanctions can have profound results. This offers an important "handle" for getting a hold on the problem of how to move our society closer to the ideals which it espouses.

People "armed" both with the ability to organize and work together to achieve positive goals in aspects of the constructive program and also with the ability to apply the technique of nonviolent action will not need to seek "someone" to save them — "the government," "the Party," or the most recent political "leader." They will instead be capable of saving themselves, even in extreme situations. Richard Gregg pointed to this consequence of nonviolent action in the 1930s when he wrote:

> Reforms will come to stay only if the masses acquire and retain the ability to make a firm veto by mass nonviolent resistance .... Hence, reformers would be wise to lay less stress upon advo-

cacy of their special changes and concentrate on the teaching of
nonviolent resistance. Once that tool is mastered, we can make all
sorts of permanent reforms.[18]

Popular empowerment will enable people to revitalize freedom,
to make it more durable and genuine. It will make it possible for them
to end social oppression by direct popular efforts which turn helpless
victims into masters of their own destinies. This capacity can also
empower potential victims of genocide and others to resist successfully any future attempts at extermination. Popular empowerment
will also help people to cast off, and remain free from, internal and
foreign elite domination, by defeating attempted internal take-overs
and international aggression by civilian modes of struggle. Because
these sanctions build on the basic nature of all social and political
power, when bolstered by training and preparations, they provide the
capacity to make quickly major acceptable changes in political societies which people have commonly thought would not be possible
except in the very distant future.

This type of social change cannot be implemented *for* the people,
by whatever means, no matter who makes the attempt — "good
people," "true conservatives," "the Party," "real liberals," or "genuine
radicals." Instead, this exercise in rethinking politics points toward a
process which the general population, consisting of people of diverse
talents working through many institutions, may initiate and implement on a long-term basis. It is a process in which people are acting to
shape the present, and simultaneously are increasing their ability to
act to determine their future.

The conception of acceptable change as presented in this volume
can offer no panaceas, no easy path, no guaranteed safety, no assurances of success in every respect and on each occasion. However, the
possibility exists that we can deliberately contribute to the development of a new stage of human history. We can resolve the acute
problems with which we have been confronted for so long. We can be
on the verge of a new departure of human capacities, which we can
develop if we wish, in order that people can regain, or perhaps for
many achieve for the first time, the capacity to control their own
destinies.

NOTES

1. Krishnalal Shridharani, **War Without Violence: A Study of Gandhi's Method and Its Accomplishments** (New York: Harcourt, Brace, 1939, and reprint New York and London: Garland Publishing, 1972), p. 260.
2. Bertrand de Jouvenel, **On Power: Its Nature and the History of Its Growth** (Boston: Beacon Press, 1962 [1948]), pp. 12-13.
3. See Gene Sharp, **The Politics of Nonviolent Action** (Boston: Porter Sargent Publisher, 1973), pp. 10-11.
4. Karl Mannheim, **Man and Society in an Age of Reconstruction: Studies in Modern Social Structure** (New York: Harcourt, Brace, and London: Routledge & Kegan Paul, 1949), p. 48.
5. Ibid.
6. Ibid. Italics are Mannheim's.
7. Karl Mannheim, **Diagnosis of Our Time: Wartime Essays of a Sociologist** (London: Routledge, 1966 [1943]), p. 10. For earlier discussions of the difficulties of violent liberation struggles under modern conditions, see also Aldous Huxley, **Ends and Means: An Inquiry into the Nature of Ideals and into the Methods Employed for their Realization** (London: Chatto & Windus, 1938), and Barthélemy de Ligt, **The Conquest of Violence: An Essay on War and Revolution** (New York: E. P. Dutton, 1938, and London: Geo. Routledge & Sons, 1937, and New York: Garland Publishing, 1972), pp. 70-85.
8. Mannheim, **Man and Society in an Age of Reconstruction**, p. 49, n. 2.
9. On the coup d'état, see D. J. Goodspeed, **The Conspirators: A Study in the Coup d'Etat** (Toronto: Macmillan, 1962), William Andrews and Uri Ra'anan, **The Politics of the Coup d'Etat: Five Case Studies** (New York: Van Nostrand Reinhold, 1969); S. E. Finer, **The Man on Horseback: The Role of the Military in Politics** (Harmondsworth, Middlesex, and Baltimore, Maryland: Penguin Books, 1976 [1962]); Edward Luttwak, **Coup d'Etat: A Practical Handbook** (New York: Alfred A. Knopf, 1969); Ruth First, **Power in Africa: Political Power in Africa and the Coup d'Etat** (New York: Pantheon Books, 1970); and Eric A. Nordlinger, **Soldiers in Politics: Military Coups and Governments** (Englewood Cliffs, N.J.: Prentice-Hall, 1977).
10. On guerrilla warfare, see Franklin Mark Osanka, ed., **Modern Guerrilla Warfare** (New York: Free Press of Glencoe, 1962); Mao Tse-tung, **Selected Military Writings of Mao Tse-tung** (Peking: Foreign Languages Press, 1966); John Gerassi, ed., **Venceremos! The Speeches and Writings of Ernesto Che Guevara** (New York: Macmillan Co., 1968), Chapters 2, 7, 9, 21, 23, 31, and 35; Charles W. Theyer, **Guerrilla** (New York: Harper & Row, 1963); George K. Tanham, **Communist Revolutionary Warfare: The Vietminh in Indochina** (London: Methuen, 1962); and Peter Paret and John W. Shy, **Guerrillas in the 1960's** (Rev. ed.; New York: Frederick A. Praeger for the Center of International Studies, Princeton University, 1962).
11. Mao Tse-tung, "On Protracted War," in **Selected Military Writings of Mao Tse-tung**, p. 246. See also pp. 210-217 and p. 247.
12. Aldous Huxley, "Introduction" to Barthélemy de Ligt, **The Conquest of Violence**, p. x.

13. See Quincy Wright, **A Study of War** (Chicago: University of Chicago Press, 1942), vol. I, pp. 232-242, 302, and esp. 311; Bronislaw Malinowski, "An Anthropological Analysis of War," **American Journal of Sociology,** vol. XLVI, no. 4, esp. p. 545; and B. Malinowski, **Freedom and Civilization** (New York: Roy Publishers, 1944), esp. pp. 265 and 305.

14. **Harijan,** 21 September 1934, p. 250; quoted in Gopi Nath Dhawan, **The Political Philosophy of Mahatma Gandhi** (Third rev. ed.; Ahmedabad: Navajivan, 1962 [1957]), p. 276.

15. Robert K. Merton, **Social Theory and Social Structure** (Glencoe, Ill.: Free Press, 1949), p. 52.

16. Franz Fanon, **Wretched of the Earth** (trans. by Constance Farrington; New York: Grove Press, Evergreen Black Cat Edition, 1968), "Colonial War and Mental Disorders," pp. 249-310.

17. On the theory and components of Gandhi's constructive program, see Gene Sharp, **Gandhi as a Political Strategist, with Essays on Ethics and Politics** (Boston: Porter Sargent Publishers, 1979), Chapter Five, "The Theory of Gandhi's Constructive Program," pp. 77-86.

18. Richard Gregg, **The Power of Non-violence** (Second rev. ed.; New York: Schocken, 1966, and London: James Clarke, 1960), p. 146.

Appendix A

Doctrinal Responses to the Choice of Sanctions

Violence in politics has rarely been perceived as a general problem, except by small doctrinally-oriented pacifist groups. Only specific types of violence, or violence used for particular purposes, have been perceived as problems. However, the analysis in Chapter Eleven, "The Societal Imperative," does identify institutionalized political violence in general as a serious problem. This would appear to make the solution to the four individual problems (dictatorship, genocide, war, and systems of social oppression) discussed in that chapter beautifully simple: only the renunciation and abandonment of violence as the pacifists have urged us would appear to be required. The answer, however, may not be so simple. Doctrinal approaches of any kind are not of much help to us in this situation.

Both "nonviolence" and "violence" have been the objects of strong doctrines. Believers in these doctrines have asserted "nonviolence" and "violence" to be good or evil, to be the imperative or instrument of God or of History, or to be acts of defiance of either. "Nonviolence" and "violence" have been declared to be natural or unnatural behavior, required of or prohibited to responsible human beings, and to be necessary for or destructive of a decent society.

Doctrinal approaches, whether to "nonviolence" or to "violence," are unable to help us in developing the answer which is required in the situation we face. In fact, these approaches most often stultify exploratory analysis and distract attention from indispensable elements of the situation which must be faced. Therefore it is necessary to examine these doctrines.

For many centuries individuals and groups have developed, advocated, and sought to live by doctrines which repudiate violence.* Some of these doctrines have viewed efforts to change society as a

*For a fuller presentation of the types of principled nonviolence and their positions on sanctions, see Gene Sharp, *Gandhi as a Political Strategist, with Essays*

whole as doomed to failure, or perceived them to be completely irrelevant to the diagnosed needs. Some doctrines have presented the world as beyond redemption; therefore, the duty of the individual is to live more purely, and to avoid being contaminated, while preparing for eternal life. Other doctrines of "nonviolence" have expected that the world would be saved by some divine intervention or by a spontaneous social upheaval — both beyond purposive human control. Still others have anticipated that the gradual transformation of the world would occur as a result of the rebirth of individuals, the spread of certain beliefs, and the infusion into social and political relationships of a new spirit and attitude. Many of these doctrines have also emphasized human responsibility to carry out acts of mercy, kindness, and relief of suffering. Often they have viewed not only violence but also struggle, contention, and conflict as evil. Nonviolent struggle has often been rejected by believers in certain of these doctrines, especially when it is waged by nonbelievers and when practiced with attitudes of hostility rather than with efforts to convert the opponent.

Where efforts have been made by these believers to change society, major emphasis has often been placed on "witnessing," setting examples, changing the "values" of others, asserting the "truth," accepting or developing a "way of life," and repudiating "violence." "Violence" and "nonviolence" (if the word is used) are usually seen dualistically, with little or nothing in between them. Their very definitions are usually made on the basis of moral judgments and approximations of accepted norms, rather than on the basis of observations of behavior and practice. Believers in these doctrines of "nonviolence" generally assume that we already know most or all that we need to know about "nonviolence." Therefore, the enjoined responsibilities are to share convictions, live according to them, and gain converts.

These approaches constitute no solution to the problem as diagnosed in Chapter Eleven. Moral appeals to renounce violence in politics have always been heeded only by a very small minority; there are no signs that any significant reversal of that fate will occur. These appeals to repudiate violence may fly in the face of social and political

---

on Ethics and Politics (Boston: Porter Sargent Publishers, 1979), Chapter Ten, "Types of Principled Nonviolence," and Chapter Twelve, "Morality, Politics, and Political Technique."

needs. Such appeals leave people to compare the moral sentiments they hear espoused to the political reality they know. Faced with a choice between words expressing unrealized beautiful sentiments and concrete strong action by violence, with which they are familiar and for which their society is equipped, most people have no real choice. To them, under these conditions, the present political facts are all that exist. Therefore they must hold to political violence as the means of last resort. Under these conditions it will never be possible to remove violent sanctions.*

These doctrines of "nonviolence" have their counterparts in the doctrines of "violence." The latter are espoused far more widely than are the doctrines of "nonviolence." Many individuals and groups which accept the personal, social, and political necessity of using violence in serious conflicts adhere to these doctrines. The widespread belief in them makes these doctrines even more stultifying than are the doctrines of "nonviolence" in the effort to resolve the problem of institutionalized political violence. Believers in the doctrines of "violence" claim that they describe reality. They do so, however, with highly incomplete and selective data, ignoring or assertively denying contradictory evidence. These doctrines may include the belief that violence is inevitable because of "human nature," our genetic make-up, or our propensity for "aggressiveness." Violence is believed to be the sole alternative to weakness. It is seen as the instrument for restoring "manhood" to the oppressed and the wronged. Violence is axiomatically believed to be the most effective possible means of action, and the ultimate source of power in politics. Exponents of these doctrines *believe* that violence "works," while other means of action and struggle are by definition milder, and less effectual. Violence is assumed to be an essentially neutral technique, with little or no structurally determined consequences, equally capable of advancing both freedom and tyranny. Though untested and without critical examination of contrary evidence, these doctrines of violence widely pass as obvious truth and support the unfounded belief that violence is universally effective.

Adherents of the doctrines of violence commonly reject alternatives to violence without critical examination. Such alternatives are assumed to be passive, and impotent in the face of extreme opponents. The exponents of these doctrines of violence consider the

*For this analysis, see Chapter Ten, "Seeking a Solution to the Problem of War."

arguments for such nonviolent alternatives to be morally arrogant or politically naive. They believe significant cases of nonviolent struggle to be historically rare, except in unusual situations or when led by persons believed to be "unique personalities" such as Gandhi and King.

Both the exponents of the doctrines of "nonviolence" and of the doctrines of "violence" treat the issues and substance with which they deal as matters of axiomatic or obvious truth, rather than as questions, problems, phenomena about which our knowledge, understanding, and even conceptualization are limited, and about which we could, if we tried, extend our understanding, judgement, and skill.

Both of these types of doctrines possess very serious weaknesses. Believers in both doctrines do not examine possible causal links between sanctions and political structures, and between institutionalized political violence and the four grave problems which we are considering.

Most doctrines of "nonviolence" do not address the problem of sanctions, and the need for effective means of struggle, nor do they propose ways to remove reliance on institutionalized political violence as part of the structure of society, not even substitute nonviolent sanctions. The doctrines of "violence" on the other hand, are equally rigid, and do not allow even for rational examination of possible alternative paths to solve these problems. Neither of these doctrinal approaches is adequate to resolve the problem we are confronting. We therefore need to continue our search for its resolution.

Twenty Steps in Development and Evaluation of Nonviolent Sanctions

The adoption of nonviolent sanctions depends upon whether they are, or can be made to be, adequate to meet our needs in place of violent sanctions. A multifaceted program of research, policy development, action, education, decision-making, and implementation is required in order to develop and adapt nonviolent sanctions as such substitutes. Our capacity to evaluate them intelligently will also be enhanced by this exploration. Such a program would include at least the following five areas, divided into twenty components.

A. RESEARCH AND POLICY DEVELOPMENT

1. Basic research on nonviolent sanctions and related phenomena.

We need basic research using the tools of several academic disciplines to gain increased knowledge of the nature of nonviolent sanctions, their history, dynamics, requirements, capacities, limitations and consequences. Basic research will also be required on other phenomena, such as the strengths and weaknesses of dictatorships, political and military violence, genocide, and relationships between social and political structures and sanctions.

2. Problem-solving research on nonviolent options.

Special research is required to determine whether difficulties encountered or anticipated in certain applications of nonviolent sanctions can be resolved. For example, can deliberate efforts enhance the population's capacity to persist in nonviolent resistance despite extreme repression, and if so how? What, if anything, can increase the resisters' capacity to continue struggle despite removal of their leaders? Could people learn how to use nonviolent struggle for new objectives for which precedents do not exist? Could deliberate efforts limit the willingness of troops or police to inflict brutal repression, and if so how? How can problems of organization and communication for resistance be handled in extreme situations?

3. Policy development for substitution of the nonviolent sanctions.

Special policy studies are required on possible specific substitutions of nonviolent sanctions, especially where these are major departures from present practices. Broad areas of such substitutions include national defense, resistance to coups d'état and executive usurpations, redistribution of power within the society, fundamental structural changes, and the like. Within these and other broad areas a myriad of sub-policies and problems, strategies, counterpolicies, and countermeausures would require exploration and examination.

4. Feasibility studies for specific substitutions.

Feasibility studies will be required to examine the practicality and adequacy of specific proposed substitutions of nonviolent sanctions for institutionalized political violence to meet specific needs of particular countries. These could include examination of alternative scenarios of future conflicts, attack, defense by nonviolent sanctions, and possible courses of the struggles. Attention may also be given to alternative possible plans to prepare and train the population for civilian-based defense and for other policies. The feasibility of alternative plans for introducing new uses of nonviolent sanctions, and for expanding their roles, would also require examination.

5. Analyses of other components in social change.

Other elements of social change beyond those closely tied to the nature of the society's ultimate sanction also require careful attention in the context of this program. Such explorations should not follow automatically the assumptions and perspectives of past analyses, doctrines, and policies. Among the particular topics which will need study are power and social structure, attitudes and beliefs, means of decision-making, and alternative technologies.

6. Funding and institutional arrangements for research and policy studies.

In order to conduct the needed research and policy studies, and to develop educational resources, it will be necessary to establish centers or institutes for this work, often attached to quality universities. This inevitably will be expensive, and major funding will be required. Initially, even very modest sums can be extremely important, but in due course vast quantities of funding and several institutions will be necessary.

One possible model for this research would begin with a ten year program of research and policy studies with private and public funding. This would be initiated by studies on the scale of ten million dollars a year for the first five years, and followed by doubled efforts for the second five years. Assuming that the results demonstrated substance to the policy potential of nonviolent sanctions, this could be followed by an expanded ten year research and policy development program funded by the equivalent of one percent of the military budget.

B. NONVIOLENT ACTION AGAINST EXISTING SOCIAL AND POLITICAL GRIEVANCES

7. Popular nonviolent action on social issues and liberties.

Thoughtful, quality, and (ideally) successful practice of nonviolent action by people to deal with their own problems may be useful in several ways. It could contribute to the resolution of significant problems, help the population to accept responsibility and to gain increased self-confidence, and also help to train the participants and educate observers in the use of nonviolent sanctions.

8. Training and organization programs and centers for nonviolent action.

Such centers may help to initiate, organize, and train people to conduct such nonviolent action skillfully against grievances and to achieve or defend liberties.

9. "How-to" handbooks on nonviolent action.

Development, publication, and distribution of quality handbooks and guides of various types for groups considering how to act in a conflict, or how to use nonviolent sanctions, may provide information useful in making that decision, and when such action is used, help to raise its quality, increase its effectiveness, and reduce possible undersirable results.

C. EDUCATION ABOUT NONVIOLENT ALTERNATIVES

10. General public education on nonviolent alternatives.

A broad public education program on the nature of nonviolent action as an alternative to political violence may contribute to improved understanding of this option and help to correct popular misconceptions. This educational program could include such means as books, newspaper articles, fiction, historical novels, adult education courses, study group guides, television drama series, radio programs, and magazine features.

11. New publications on nonviolent struggle and contemporary problems.

The publication of several series of books about nonviolent sanctions and the problems of dictatorship, genocide, war, and systems of social oppression and their solutions would be a natural product of the research and policy studies. These would provide not only educational materials, but also important background for the policy and feasibility studies and for evaluation of proposed new policies utilizing nonviolent sanctions.

12. Curricula development for educational institutions.

Development of new curricula resources, alternative curricula, and effective educational methods would greatly facilitate the adoption and operation of courses focused on nonviolent alternatives in formal educational settings from grade schools through graduate schools. Here the basic research, especially in history and the social sciences, will be very important in the preparation of new textbooks and other educational aids. This is a major task.

13. Faculty training for education in nonviolent alternatives.

Development of highly qualified faculty for this field of study for all levels of the educational process may be assisted by summer schools, workshops, on-the-job training programs, and specialized courses and programs in colleges, universities, schools of education, and graduate schools. Such courses and programs would need to give major attention to both content and improved pedagogy.

14. Elementary and secondary education about nonviolent sanctions.

Specific efforts are required in elementary and secondary education to correct the long neglect of nonviolent forms of struggle. This should *not* take the form of indoctrination. Instead, the approach should be to provide information and understanding of the nonviolent technique to balance the frequent overemphasis on wars and the view that human "aggression" makes violence inevitable.

15. College and university education about nonviolent options.

Curriculum developments are especially needed in colleges and universities to compensate for the neglect of nonviolent sanctions in our educational systems and academic studies. These changes may involve adding new subject matter to existing courses, and utilizing text books which incorporate information about nonviolent sanctions along with more traditional subject matter.

These changes will also require the introduction of new courses about nonviolent struggle and related areas on both introductory and advanced levels. These courses may be given both within existing departments — history, sociology, psychology, political science, philosophy, international relations, and the like — and on occasion in special new departments or programs. Such special efforts — as in the case of "black studies" and "women's studies" — may at times be required temporarily as measures to correct the extreme past academic neglect of this field and because the revamping of a multitude of courses in several departments to correct that neglect could take considerable time.

University level courses may range from basic introductions to a variety of specialized courses and seminars. The specialized ones may focus on historical cases, psychological and socio-political dynamics, power theory, relationships to social structures, and other specific topics. Even when such studies are offered in a special department or major, they are likely to be most effective when students gain simultaneously a quality training in one or more regular disciplines or in rigorous interdisciplinary research.

16. New faculty positions and chairs.

New positions for faculty with expertise in both nonviolent sanctions and other fields of study are needed. This is the case, in part, precisely because budget austerities cause regular departments to restrict hiring to those who teach standard subjects. Privately endowed chairs for this field are necessary under present conditions to ensure sufficient educational attention to this field, and to facilitate initiation of research and policy studies within the university framework.

17. University graduate studies in nonviolent alternatives.

A high quality program of graduate studies in nonviolent sanctions, conducted in cooperation with departments with exceptional standards in regular academic disciplines and multidisciplinary training, is urgently required. This graduate program would contribute to the training of future faculty, researchers, policy analysts, and leadership for this field.

D. PUBLIC EVALUATION AND DECISION-MAKING FOR REPLACING VIOLENT SANCTIONS

18. Public evaluation and discussion of specific proposed adoptions of nonviolent sanctions.

At appropriate times, in-depth and widespread public discussion and consideration of the policy problems and potentialities of proposed specific adoptions of alternative nonviolent sanctions will be needed. When this should take place will vary with the state of research and policy studies and the problems and condition of the society. In some cases this could come much earlier than in others. The specific substitution under discussion at any given time will vary, but may include preparations to defeat internal take-overs as well as other types of civilian-based defense.

19. Official evaluation and decision-making by responsible bodies.

At appropriate times, again varying with the state of research, policy studies, and the problems and condition of the society, official evaluations will be required by governmental bodies and nongovernmental institutions of the feasibility and desirability of substituting nonviolent sanctions for violent ones for specific tasks, including national defense.

Official consideration would doubtless begin with initial research, policy examination, feasibility studies, and committee examination. These efforts would focus on potentialities, problems, and effectiveness, as well as the possibility of combining both violent and nonviolent sanctions. They would also examine ways to handle the changeover period. Finally, legislative and administrative action might be taken for the first steps in adoption and implementation.

E. INITIAL CHANGEOVER PREPARATIONS

20. First steps in changeover for particular tasks.

The official decision to introduce preparations and training for nonviolent sanctions will be, in all likelihood, for a single specific purpose only. This purpose will vary with the particular country, the evaluations of the limitations and potential of the usual violent means, estimates of particular threats to the society, and evaluations of the capacity of the substitute nonviolent sanctions for meeting that situation.

For example, in certain countries preparation to defeat a possible internal coup d'état or executive usurpation, for which military means are recognized as rather unsuited, may be the first such specific purpose. In other countries, which may retain regular military forces and alliances, civilian-based defense might be adopted for emergency use in case of the obvious futility of military resistance, or in case of the failure of military means to keep out a foreign invader. Other countries may explore more complete changeovers. Quite different scenarios are possible for the official adoption of nonviolent sanctions for a particular internal use, depending in part on the particular type.

Such first steps in a changeover would build particularly on the policy and feasibility studies, as well as on basic and problem-solving research. The extent and effectiveness of the various types of education about nonviolent alternatives would also be influential. Once the decision toward specific adoption was officially made, implementation would begin of the chosen plans for preparations and training. Preparations would include selected ways to provide resistance organization, leadership, communication, and choice of strategies for specific contingencies and needs.

ACHIEVABLE STEPS

These five broad areas and twenty specific steps require, of course, refinement and development. However, they are all feasible. Each of them is small enough, and sufficiently concrete, that at the appropriate stage specific means to achieve each one can be developed and can succeed. Most of these components will not seem to most people to be excessively radical or threatening, and are unlikely at the point at which they are appropriate to arouse enough hostility to block their implementation.

These are all tasks which we are now, or could soon be, capable of undertaking. It is crucial that each component be implemented with the utmost care and be of the highest quality. The content must not be diluted by doctrines pressed by any group which has its own, very different, agenda.

Certain of the twenty components in this program would build on others, and would assist additional components as the program developed. Some components can, and often should, operate institutionally independently of others. Some components may form natural groupings. Most — except the final two groups — could proceed side by side. In these cases they can be initiated without waiting for the successful completion of other components of the overall program. Thus, the harmonious participation of a variety of persons, institutions, and talents will be possible.

If the broad analysis which has been presented in Chapter Eleven of the role of institutionalized political violence in dictatorship, genocide, war, and systems of social oppression is even approximately valid, then these twenty components become significant steps toward fundamental change. These steps would progressively contribute to replacing political violence as the ultimate sanction of the society with refined and developed nonviolent sanctions. The cumulative results may be profound.

Appendix C

Skinner and Gandhi on Defeating Violence

Both the important behavioral psychologist B. F. Skinner and the prominent nonviolent strategist M. K. Gandhi have argued that a more effective way exists to end violent attacks for some purpose than either to resist them with counter-violence or to submit to them and grant the attacker's objective. This other way is simultaneously to withhold both counter-violence and also submission, refusing to provide that which the attacker wants. Let us look first at the views of Skinner and then at the remarkably similar ones of Gandhi.

Speaking of "the threat of force" to control behavior, Skinner, in his novel *Walden Two* through the character T. E. Frazier, said that although retribution and revenge are natural, "...in the long run the man we strike is no less likely to repeat his act."

> He'll still *tend* to repeat it. He'll *want* to repeat it. We haven't really altered his potential behavior at all.

Whereas "the earlier forms of government" were based on punishment, Frazier continued, they were in their new system developing instead "a great change to positive reinforcement" of acceptable behavior instead. It also involved refusal to punish as a means in the long run to *"control the stronger man...."*[1]

This clearly did *not* mean, however, giving in to those who engaged in antisocial behavior in order to stop the violent attacks or keep the peace. The action which reinforces certain behavior may not be intended to do so, but may nevertheless lead the person deliberately to repeat the behavior because the results initially obtained were satisfying.[2]

"The relation between the controller and the controlled is reciprocal," Skinner continued. "Reciprocal control is not necessarily intentional in either direction, but it becomes so when the consequences make themselves felt." The slave driver may whip the slave in order to induce him or her to work. The slave may learn that working will prevent whipping. However, when the slave works because of that, the slave driver is taught that the next time he wishes work, he should whip or threaten to whip the slave because that action produces the result he wants. Similarly, Skinner illustrated the point: the mother learns to pick up and carry her baby to stop the crying, and even that doing so first will often prevent the crying from beginning. However, the baby may also learn that when he or she wishes to be carried, the best way to get the result is to start crying.[3] "When a bit of behavior is followed by a certain kind of consequence, it is more likely to occur again, and a consequence having this effect is called a reinforcer."[4] Some people may treat others adversely because such treatment by their experience gets the results they want. Other examples include a parent nagging a child until the child performs a certain task, the victim paying the blackmailer to avoid exposure, the student paying attention when threatened with corporal punishment by the teacher. In each case the compliance of the attacked or threatened person, whatever else it may do, reinforces that same behavior for the dominant person, and makes it more likely that such attacks or threats will be repeated against the same person and others.[5]

Compliance with threats and attacks, along with not punishing the attacker, therefore is clearly no way to halt such attacks. If one submits in face of overwhelming violence, one simply confirms the attacker's confidence in violence and makes repeated attacks more likely because the attacker was given the desired submission. If one counterattacks the attacker by violence and defeats him in the particular case, this not only builds up long-term resentment and desire to repeat the behavior. It also teaches the attacker that violence really is the most powerful means of getting one's way, and that he simply at the moment did not have enough capacity for violence or was not sufficiently ruthless. Both could be corrected in the future.

A way exists to deal with this situation differently, however, Skinner argued. "Another possibility is to break up the contingencies under which punished behavior is reinforced...aggressive behavior is attenuated by making sure that nothing is gained by it...."[6] In other words, without either violent punishment or violent counterattack, the attacker must be refused the goals of the attack or other desirable results. This may help to answer the "great problem" of how "to arrange effective counter-control and hence to bring some impor-

tant consequences to bear on the behavior of the controller."[7]
Gandhi made essentially the same points:

> Violence always thrived on counter-violence. The aggressor had always a purpose behind his attack; he wanted something to be done, some object to be surrendered by the defenders. Now, if the defender steeled his heart and was determined not to surrender even one inch, and at the same time to resist the temptation of matching the violence of the aggressor by violence, the latter could be made to realize in a short while that it would not be paying to punish the other party and his will could not be imposed in that way. This would involve suffering. It was this unalloyed self-suffering which was the truest form of self-defence which knew no surrender.[8]

> ...[A]t the back of the policy of terrorism is the assumption that terrorism if applied in a sufficient measure will produce the desired result, namely, bend the adversary to the tyrant's will. But supposing a people make up their mind that they will never bend to the tyrant's will, nor retaliate with the tyrant's own methods, the tyrant will not find it worth his while to go on with his terrorism.[9]

> A warrior lives on his wars whether offensive or defensive. He suffers a collapse, if he finds that his warring capacity is unwanted.[10]

Against a demand backed by violence, Gandhi insisted, the nonviolent person not convinced of the justice of the demand should refuse to submit to it. "He was not to return violence by violence but neutralize it by withholding one's hand and, at the same time, refusing to submit to the demand."[11]

Nonviolent noncooperation may, therefore, teach the opponent by experience that violent sanctions are not always successful and that by using them he may still be denied his objective, without, however, either building up the continued desire to use violence or a confidence that renewed or enlarged violence would get the desired objective next time. This may provide the means of "control which does not have aversive consequences at any time," as Skinner phrased it.[12] The congruity of the views of these very different persons is of great potential significance.

NOTES

1. B. F. Skinner, **Walden Two** (New York: Macmillan, Paperbacks Edition, 1972), pp. 260-261.
2. B. F. Skinner, **Beyond Freedom and Dignity** (New York: Bantam Books, 1972), pp. 102-103.
3. Ibid., pp. 161-162.
4. Ibid., p. 25.
5. Ibid., pp. 25-26.
6. Ibid., p. 61.
7. Ibid., p. 163.
8. Quoted in Gene Sharp, **Gandhi as a Political Strategist, with Essays on Ethics and Politics** (Boston: Porter Sargent Publishers, 1979), pp. 148-149.
9. Ibid., p. 149.
10. Ibid., p. 151.
11. M. K. Gandhi, **Non-violence in Peace and War** (2 vols. Ahmedabad: Navajivan, 1948–1949), vol. II, p. 234.
12. Skinner, **Beyond Freedom and Dignity**, p. 38.

Appendix D

Nonviolent Sanctions
and Ethics

The term "nonviolent" in nonviolent sanctions and in the technique of nonviolent action is not restricted to those forms of action which meet the highest ethical and moral standards. Throughout this book "nonviolent" is descriptive of *actual behavior* regardless of motives or attitudes. Marching as protest, distributing leaflets, refusing to work, unwillingness to purchase certain products, disobedience of orders, sit-ins, and even creation of a parallel government, need not involve the use or threat of physical violence. They apply other influences as levers, and abstention from violence is required to maximize their impacts. They can also be applied in ways which raise or create ethical problems.

Within nonviolent action vast differences exist in the type and amount of pressure exerted, the scale of the action, attitudes to the opponent and third parties, motivations, the operative mechanism of change (conversion, accommodation, or nonviolent coercion), and other factors. While some of the most serious ethical problems in politics are directly derived from the use of political violence,[1] other ethical problems arise in applications of nonviolent sanctions. Some believers in types of "principled nonviolence" therefore argue that it is necessary for people to adopt a full belief in nonviolence as an ethic or norm.[2] That may be fine if it occurs, but that simple repeated assertion ignores the social reality within which we must operate: as long as people perceive violent sanctions to be the only possible ones or the most effective ones, violence cannot be removed from political societies by witnessing against it or denouncing it on moral grounds.

Therefore, if one disapproves of that violence for whatever reason, one must decide what is one's primary concern. Is it to dissociate one's self individually from all such violence and to declare to others its immoral qualities, while the political society goes on much as it has? Or, is it instead to change the society in ways that reduce, and eventually replace, violent sanctions with nonviolent ones? The adherents of various religious pacifist traditions and certain other beliefs have primarily chosen the former one of dissociation and witnessing. The approach recommended here is the latter one of finding ways to act responsibly in a highly imperfect world by changing it through substitution of nonviolent sanctions. This is necessary in order to lift dependency on political violence as the ultimate sanction in order both to implement more fully our espoused ideals, and also to remove those grave problems directly associated with institutionalized political violence.

If one wishes to resolve the major ethical problems in politics, the first major step becomes examination and adoption of alternative nonviolent sanctions in place of violent ones for meeting specific needs, as I have discussed elsewhere, for the problems of political ethics associated with violence are the most grave ones. This shift to nonviolent sanctions must be primarily on the basis that they are or can be at least as effective as the violent ones for socially desirable objectives.

Once that major changeover has been completed, or is well under way, serious problems of political ethics will still remain, but they will be of a different character than is true of those associated with violent sanctions. Only at this stage will most people be able to consider and deal with the finer ethical problems which arise in the application of nonviolent sanctions and with refinements in their practice.

NOTES

1. See Gene Sharp, **Gandhi as a Political Strategist, with Essays on Ethics and Politics** (Boston: Porter Sargent Publishers, 1979), Chapter Eleven, "Ethics and Responsibility in Politics: A Critique of the Present Adequacy of Max Weber's Classification of Political Ethics," and Chapter Twelve, "Morality, Politics, and Political Technique."
2. See ibid., Chapter Ten, "The Types of Principled Nonviolence."

Appendix E

Education for Self-reliance

The quality and results of our educational systems are very uneven. In them is much which is beneficial and praiseworthy, and many educators at all levels are committed to their tasks and deeply concerned with assisting their pupils and students. Unfortunately, that is not the whole story. Serious inadequacies exist. Some of these have strong negative effects on the capacities, and even the desires, of people to exercise greater self-reliance and power. The inadequacies are primarily rooted in the basic approach to education, and to a lesser degree in the subject matter.

Many of our educational systems are becoming increasingly larger and larger, and more centralized, as smaller schools are absorbed into consolidated units, and as the numbers of students in them at all levels grow. Expansion is often seen as almost a "good" in and of itself. However, the human consequences of this and its effect on education can be harmful. The child, youth, or adult in those systems is rarely deeply integrated into the educational experience itself. He or she often feels like simply a body occupying a chair, or a number, rather than an active participant in the development of his or her capacities and potential. Continuous individual attention by persons who know the student well is often not available. Students become alienated — even hostile to education. It is no accident that youths often vandalize or burn school buildings.

Given the assumptions on which much of education is based, and the pressures for economic efficiency, the style of education, "necessarily" it often seems, becomes more like the production line of a factory. Students are put through a series of production steps in which others act *upon* them to make them "educated." If they survive, at the end of the series of timed steps, they emerge with certification that they have completed the requirements.

Commonly during the process, the "teachers" are perceived to be the only active agents, and the students to be the passive recipients of an "education." The students are taught to learn what they are told, to memorize, to repeat what is in the books or what the teacher said. Thinking for one's self, and asking perceptive questions are not often encouraged; they are even widely discouraged and penalized. This is an important contributing factor in the common condition of students in our educational institutions: they have very low self-esteem, see themselves as stupid, are uninterested in learning, have little ability to understand or use ideas, are unable to think critically and creatively, and are lacking in desire to change any of this.

These results of a passive role for students follow from the assumption that the primary aim of education should be to impart facts, very specific skills, and the appearance of expertise in the students. While facts, skills, and expertise are very important, they must be secondary to the primary responsibility of developing .he students' intellectual capacities. With that goal the orientation of education shifts fundamentally to the task of facilitating and stimulating the students in the growth of their abilities to use their minds, to think, to solve problems, and to seek new knowledge and understanding. For this a participatory pedagogy is required in which the students come to accept responsibility for their own educations and become active participants in the process of developing their intellectual capacities.

In many ways our educational systems are highly influenced by basic assumptions of our society generally, and are the victims of forces and conditions outside of the control of educators. That is not the whole story, however. In the fields of educational approach and content of studies, educational systems can, to a high degree, control themselves, in association with local boards of education, and the prerogatives of independent schools. People in our society and in our educational systems can change the educational approach of our schools and correct the biases in the subject matter if we wish. This would help to advance the objectives of education and simultaneously would assist our society in fulfilling its espoused ideals.

A different type of education is required if our society's ideals are to be more than the clichés of a bygone era, and certainly if our society is to become vitalized in institutions and action in the ways which have been discussed in Chapter Twelve. Smaller-scale, more personal educational experiences, combining a participatory approach with academic rigor, which can stimulate and cultivate the minds of the students are required.

If freedom is to become a reality, students need to learn how to think for themselves, to reason, to seek fresh solutions to problems, to challenge with reason their "teachers" and text books, to learn from the knowledge, experience, and authority of others, but also to be willing and able to go beyond established knowledge and authority when needed to seek greater knowledge and understanding. All this implies willingness to work cooperatively together with others and to help each other.

Education with the general type of approach presented here, and with additions to the curriculum, will facilitate the changes in institutions and sanctions discussed in this volume. This can occur by improving people's abilities to think, reason, and develop new solutions to problems, and also by providing them with knowledge and understanding useful in facing new situations. For individual students the results of such education are likely to include an enhanced and earned self-esteem and self-confidence, resulting from hard work, and proving to themselves that they have good minds and can think for themselves. These students are likely to have improved abilities to participate constructively in the institutions of which they are members. They are likely to be able to perceive when those persons in positions of authority in government and other institutions have exceeded their legitimated authority, and when sanctions must be applied to bring them back to democratic heel.

An educated public with a rich background of knowledge and understanding, the capacity to think for themselves, and the skills of democratic group action is more likely to succeed in developing and operating more participatory democratic institutions, and in applying nonviolent sanctions instead of relying on institutionalized political violence, than one without these capacities. A society made up of such people would be unpalatable both to would-be internal tyrants and to foreign conquerors.

Appendix F

Economics and Technology

Most of this book has been primarily focused on politics rather than economics, and generally the economic ramifications of these analyses have been left to exploration by those with greater expertise in that field. However, as was suggested in the discussion of socialist approaches,* basic rethinking of ways to rebuild our society economically as well as politically is required. The old approaches accept too many assumptions axiomatically which are probably invalid. Often those assumptions are closely related to politics, or the results of their application include political consequences. The following points are offered to stimulate some of the needed rethinking in this area.

Efforts to solve economic problems ought not to utilize means and policies which increase the centralization or power in society, expand the controls and means of manipulation in the hands of whoever possesses the State apparatus, and perpetuate or increase the disempowerment of the population. Past efforts to use the State to solve economic problems have had those negative effects on the distribution of power.

If politics is to be used to reshape the economic structure of the society, extreme care is required to prevent the use of approaches which increase the concentration of power, weaken the society's *loci* of power, enlarge the State, and increase the *quantum* of institutionalized political violence. The discussion in Chapter Two, "Social Power and Political Freedom," is highly relevant at this point. Exploratory thinking, analysis, and policy development are required to determine how politics might be utilized to assist economic change without actively making our political situation worse.

Those political problems of economic change can to a large degree be by-passed if purely *economic* means — as distinct from political means — can be utilized to resolve economic problems and to restructure economic institutions. More attention to these alternatives is merited. They include the building of new economic institu-

*See Chapter Eight, "The Problem of Political Technique in Radical Politics."

tions at all levels of activity, the restructuring of existing ones, and the utilization of economic sanctions of diverse types. These could replace State take-overs, State regulation, and dependence on legal prosecutions and court-imposed fines and imprisonments for violations of laws and regulations.

Steps which could be taken, which are both ends and means, include: expansion of both consumers' and workers' ownership and control; establishment of new firms to provide alternatives to existing ones whose size and practices are viewed as undesirable; maintenance of the independence of small privately-owned firms from take-overs by massive corporations; changing specific practices and products of existing firms when they are deemed to be of poor quality or otherwise harmful; and promotion of economic decentralization to enhance the population's economic well-being, independence, and ability to withstand crises. To the degree that a society transarms from military means of defense to civilian-based defense,* the freeing from military use of resources, production capacity, labor, and expertise for civilian needs could have highly beneficial economic results.

People need to have a sense of participation and control in the running of their own economic lives, that they will not be determined by some distant board of directors, government decision, or impersonal forces perceived variously as beneficent or malevolent. This requires exploration of new very different ways to structure and own our economic institutions. We need to bypass both the models of massive investor-owned corporations and of State ownership, and instead explore seriously and experiment with different forms of ownership and management. These include ownership and management by consumers, workers, and technicians, and by small-scale private incorporated groups or individuals. For example, could not some combination of consumers, workers, technicians, and perhaps others, establish jointly-owned democratically-operated nonprofit companies to build newly designed quality vehicles developed from the first conception to be safe, lasting, and fuel efficient, and do so on a smaller scale than present companies, and with internal democracy and social responsibility? The impact of success with such a venture might exceed all of the government regulations ever issued in that

---

*See Chapter Nine, " 'The Political Equivalent of War' — Civilian-based Defense."

field. Unless alternative means of ownership and control are developed in most fields of production and distribution, we are likely to face continued massive growth of uncontrolled huge corporations, and, in response, State ownership.

So basic a factor as the production and distribution of food requires major reconsideration and restructuring from present practices and trends if power is to become diffused and people are to become empowered. A similar situation exists in the supplies of fuels and other forms of energy, and potentially even of food and water. Where the sources are geographically distant, and the control of production, transportation, and distribution is in the hands of corporations, States, officials, or bureaucrats which may place their own political or economic objectives above the welfare of the population, serious structural problems exist.

In extreme crises the supply of these necessities may be severed without effective means of recourse by the population. Such crises may include major natural disasters, strikes and breakdowns of the transportation systems, foreign military attacks, terrorist attacks on transportation or distribution centers, and deliberate political controls to force submission of the population resisting a foreign occupation, internal usurpation, or domestic tyranny. Such a situation is structurally inimical to freedom. Genuine empowerment of people and more adequate provision of human needs both require major changes in the production and distribution of food, water, and energy.

The objective of popular empowerment in our society also requires that we give fresh attention to the type of technology on which we depend, and to the question of size in economics, society, and politics. For some time in the United States it has been assumed that everything should be on as large a scale as possible. Much of the rest of the world has adopted that assumption and Western technology, which has been largely based upon it. While there may be certain advantages to largeness and centralization, they are most often highly exaggerated, and their disadvantages neglected. We need to abandon the assumption that big is always better, and instead examine critically the alternatives and consequences of small, medium, and large-scale technologies for specific needs and situations.* The type of

---

*See E. F. Schumacher, *Small is Beautiful: Economics as if People Mattered* (New York: Harper & Row, Perennial Library, 1975).

technology which can multiply the efficiency of production and manufacturing does not necessarily have to be on an ever increasing scale of size, with the corollary of increasing centralization of control which goes with larger and larger size. Major development of intermediate level and of small-scale technology is required, especially that which could use locally available materials and sources of energy, and supply local needs. This type of technology appears to be actively conducive to diffusion of power and popular empowerment.

Appendix G

Recommendations for Course Usage

This book as a whole, or individual chapters, may be used, in conjunction with other resources, in a variety of college and university courses, as well as in courses for advanced high school students, and in adult study groups and continuing education courses. For the following subjects, the chapters listed under each heading are especially recommended for consideration by the instructor or coordinator. In courses focusing on major contemporary problems or on the political potential of nonviolent action, the whole book may be relevant.

ARMS CONTROL AND DISARMAMENT

Four   Facing Dictatorships with Confidence
Nine   "The Political Equivalent of War" — Civilian-based Defense
Ten   Seeking a Solution to the Problem of War

CIVILIAN-BASED DEFENSE*

Nine   "The Political Equivalent of War" — Civilian-based Defense
Ten   Seeking a Solution to the Problem of War

DECENTRALIZATION

Two   Social Power and Political Freedom
Six   Freedom and Revolution
Eight   The Problem of Political Technique in Radical Politics
Twelve   Popular Empowerment

*A national defense policy of prepared nonviolent noncooperation and defiance against foreign occupations and coups d'état.

DEMOCRATIC THEORY AND PRACTICE

DICTATORSHIPS

GENOCIDE

INTERNATIONAL RELATIONS

LAW

RESISTANCE AND REVOLUTION

SANCTIONS

SOCIAL AND POLITICAL THEORY

SOCIAL CHANGE

SOCIAL CONFLICT

SOCIAL MOVEMENTS

SOCIAL PROBLEMS

THE STATE

STRATEGY

STRATIFICATION

VIOLENCE

WAR AND PEACE

Appendix H

Origins of
the Chapters

Four of the present volume's chapters have been written especially for this book, sometimes drawing upon lectures delivered at several universities and institutions. Eight have been edited or revised from essays and chapters which have appeared in a variety of publications in the United States, England, India, Sweden, and Norway. All of these have been reworked to some degree, and some have undergone major changes. Several appear here under new titles.

Chapter One, "Rethinking Politics," has been written especially for this book, but parts of it draw upon a lecture given to a student organization at Cambridge University in 1963 or early 1964.

Chapter Two, "Social Power and Political Freedom," in an earlier version, was originally published in K. P. Misra and Rajendra Avasthi, eds., *Politics of Persuasion: Essays Written in Memory of Dr. G. N. Dhawan* (Bombay: Manaktalas, 1967), pp. 58-86. That chapter was based upon a second part of the power analysis in the unpublished 1963 draft of the manuscript which eventually became *The Politics of Nonviolent Action* (Boston: Porter Sargent Publisher, 1973). This second part of the power analysis was not included in that book. The chapter here has been revised significantly from the 1967 published chapter.

Chapter Three, "The Lesson of Eichmann: A Review-Essay on Hannah Arendt's *Eichmann in Jerusalem"* is largely based upon a review of that book which was published as "Another Eichmann: How Many Would Help?" in *Peace News* (London), no. 1424, 11 October 1963. Approximately the last quarter of the chapter, discussing the Holocaust and the Second World War, has been written especially for this book.

Chapter Four, "Facing Dictatorships with Confidence," is written especially for this book, and is based upon work done while in residence for doctoral studies at Oxford University, 1961–64.

Chapter Five, "Civil Disobedience in a Democracy," was originally published as a *Peace News* (no. 1391) Supplement, 22 February 1963. A condensed version was published in J. S. Mathur and P. C. Sharma, eds., *Facets of Gandhian Thought* (Ahmedabad: Navajivan Publishing House, 1975), pp. 38-56. This chapter includes a new introduction and significant additions to the original text.

Chapter Six, "Freedom and Revolution. A Review of Hannah Arendt's *On Revolution*," was originally published in *Peace News*, no. 1442, 14 February 1964. This chapter includes a new introduction and significant revisions.

Chapter Seven, "What Is Required to Uproot Oppression? Strategic Problems of the South African Resistance," was originally published in *Peace News*, nos. 1408, 1409, 1410, and 1426, 21 June, 28 June, 5 July, and 25 October 1963, under the titles, "Can Non-violence Work in South Africa?", "Problems of Violent and Non-violent Struggle," "Strategic Problems of South African Resistance," and "How Do You Get Rid of Oppression?" This chapter includes a new introduction, editing, and biographical notes on Albert Luthuli and Robert Sobukwe. The strategic situation faced by the resistance groups discussed here is still basically that of 1963, which also raises many of the basic issues in resistance and liberation movements at other times and in other places.

Chapter Eight, "The Problem of Political Technique in Radical Politics," was originally published as "The Problem of Political Method in Radical Politics," in *Mankind* (Hyderabad), vol. IV, no. 8 (March 1960), pp. 6-17. It appears here with minor revisions.

Chapter Nine, " 'The Political Equivalent of War' — Civilian-based Defense," was originally published by the Carnegie Endowment for International Peace as the whole number of their publication *International Conciliation*, no. 555, November 1965, 67 pp. It has been also published in translations: Danish (1966), German (1968), and (in a condensed version) Dutch (1979). A section of it was reprinted as "Control of Political Power and Conduct of Open Struggle," in Mark E. Smith III and Claude J. Johns, Jr., eds., *American Defense Policy* (Second Edition; Baltimore: Johns Hopkins Press, 1970), pp.

526–537. The chapter here is largely identical with the original 1965 publication, except that a section on Czechoslovakia 1968–69 has been added, some of the discussions of nonviolent action and civilian-based defense have been revised, and the term "civilian-based defense" has been substituted for "civilian defense," as explained in the note on the first page of the chapter.

Chapter Ten, "Seeking a Solution to the Problem of War," was originally a paper presented to a meeting of the American Association for the Advancement of Science, December 1972, in Washington, D.C., and was first published under the title, "An Examination of the Significance of Domestic Nonviolent Action for Development of a Substitute for International War," in Joseph Ben-Dak, ed., *The Future of Collective Violence: Societal and International Perspectives* (Lund, Sweden: Studentlitteratur, 1974), pp. 165–181. A shortened version was published as "Nonviolent Action as a Substitute for International War," in the *Bulletin of Peace Proposals* (Oslo), vol. 9, no. 4, 1978, pp. 321–328. The full original chapter was published under the title, "The Significance of Domestic Nonviolent Action As a Substitute for International War," in Severyn T. Bruyn and Paula M. Rayman, eds., *Nonviolent Action and Social Change* (New York: Irvington Publishers, 1979), pp. 233–253. The chapter here has been revised editorially.

Chapter Eleven, "The Societal Imperative," has been written for this book. It is a development of a theme which was presented in several different lectures. These are: "Transarmament: A Concept of System Change," at a conference at Fordham University, 6 March 1976 sponsored by The Center for Global Community Education and The Institute for World Order; "The Societal Imperative: A Program for Prevention of War and Oppression," Inaugural Lecture of the Louis M. Brown Peace Studies Lecture Series, Manhattan College, 30 September 1976; "Perpetual Dissent or Fundamental Change? Thoughts on the Occasion of the Anniversary of the Slayings at Kent State University," Lectureship in Peaceful Change, Kent State University, 3 May 1977; "Facing War, Genocide, Dictatorship, and Systems of Social Oppression," Peace and Justice Symposium, Newport College, Salve Regina, 8 March 1978; "A Post-Doctrinal Approach to Nonviolent Struggle," Martin Luther King, Jr. Lecture Series, Harvard University, 18 April 1978; "Politics and Nonviolent

Action," Seattle University, sponsored by the University Friends Meeting and the World Without War Council of Greater Seattle, 7 May 1978; and "Confronting the Violence and Oppression of Our Age," Southeastern Massachusetts University, 18 October 1979.

Chapter Twelve, "Popular Empowerment," has been written for this book. In part it draws upon ideas presented in lectures presented at sessions of Annual Institutes on Nonviolence held in Atlanta and sponsored by the Martin Luther King, Jr., Center for Social Change with the cooperation of the National Education Association, "Nonviolent Strategies for Reform in the '70s," 29 July 1976, "Nonviolent Social Change: Preparing for the Future," 5 August 1977, and "The Path of Nonviolence: Meeting Basic Human Needs," 2 August 1978. The Chapter also draws upon ideas in unpublished parts of the 1963 draft of *The Politics of Nonviolent Action* and new analysis.

Appendix A, "Doctrinal Responses to the Choice of Sanctions," is based upon a section of my lecture, "A Post-Doctrinal Approach to Nonviolent Struggle," Martin Luther King, Jr., Lecture Series, Harvard University, 18 April 1978.

Appendix B, "Twenty Steps in Development and Evaluation of Nonviolent Sanctions," has been edited from a section of my lecture, "Perpetual Dissent or Fundamental Change? Thoughts on the Occasion of the Anniversary of the Slayings at Kent State University," Lectureship in Peaceful Change, Kent State University, 3 May 1977.

Appendix C, "Skinner and Gandhi on Defeating Violence," has been written for this book, originally as part of a draft of Chapter Twelve, "Popular Empowerment." Notes for this piece were, however, made several years previously for an intended independent article.

Appendix D, "Nonviolent Sanctions and Ethics," has been written for this book, originally as part of a draft of Chapter Eleven, "The Societal Imperative."

Appendix E, "Education for Self-reliance," and **Appendix F, "Economics and Technology,"** have been written for this book, originally as parts of a draft of Chapter Twelve, "Popular Empowerment."

Appendix G, "Recommendations for Course Usage, and **Appendices H and I,** have of course been prepared for this book.

Appendix I

Copyright Acknowledgements

Appreciation is gratefully acknowledged to the authors and publishers whose works are quoted in this volume. Complete publication details are provided in the notes.

Arendt, Hannah, **Eichmann in Jerusalem.** Copyright © 1963, 1964 by Hannah Arendt. Reprinted by permission of Viking Penguin, Inc.

───────── , **On Revolution.** Copyright © 1963, 1965 by Hannah Arendt. Reprinted by permission of Viking Penguin, Inc.

Bull, Hedley, **The Control of the Arms Race: Disarmament and Arms Control in the Missile Age.** Copyright © 1961, 1965 by The Institute for Strategic Studies. Permission courtesy of Weidenfeld and Nicolson.

Dallin, Alexander, **German Rule in Russia 1941–1945.** Copyright © 1957. Permission courtesy of St. Martin's Press, Inc., and Macmillan & Co., Ltd.

Deutsch, Karl W., "Cracks in the Monolith: Possibilities and Patterns of Disintegration in Totalitarian Systems," in Friedrich, Carl J., ed., **Totalitarianism.** Copyright © 1954 by the President and Fellows of Harvard College. Reprinted by permission of Harvard University Press.

Hilberg, Raul, **The Destruction of the European Jews.** Copyright © 1961 by Quadrangle Books, Inc. Permission courtesy of Raul Hilberg.

Jouvenel, Bertrand de, **Power: Its Nature and the History of its Growth.** Copyright © 1948 by The Viking Press, Inc. Permission courtesy of Beacon Press.

───────── , **Sovereignty: An Enquiry into the Public Good.** Copyright © 1957 by Bertrand de Jouvenel. Permission courtesy of The University of Chicago Press.

Kennan, George F., **Russia, the Atom and the West.** Copyright © 1958 by George Kennan. Permission courtesy of Harper & Row, Publishers, Inc.

Lippmann, Walter. "The Political Equivalent of War," **Atlantic Monthly,** August 1928, vol. 142, pp. 181-182. Copyright © 1928 by The Atlantic Monthly Co. Used with the permission of the President and Fellows of Harvard College.

Lochner, Louis P., ed., **The Goebbels Diaries.** Copyright © 1948 by The Fireside Press, Inc. Reprinted by permission of Doubleday & Co., Inc.

Mannheim, Karl, **Man and Society in an Age of Reconstruction.** Permission courtesy of Harcourt Brace Jovanovich, Inc.

Merton, Robert K., **Social Theory and Social Structure.** Copyright © 1957 by The Free Press. Permission courtesy of The Free Press, Macmillan Publishing Co., Inc.

Montesquieu, Baron de, **The Spirit of the Laws.** Translated by Thomas Nugent. Introduction by Franz Neumann. Copyright © 1949 by Hafner Publishing Co. Permission courtesy of Hafner Press, Macmillan Publishing Co., Inc.

Morgenthau, Hans J., **Politics Among Nations: The Struggle for Power and Peace.** Copyright © 1948, 1954 by Alfred A. Knopf. Permission courtesy of Alfred A. Knopf, Inc.

Mosca, Gaetano, **The Ruling Class.** Translated by Hannah D. Kahn. Edited and revised with an Introduction by Arthur Livingston. Copyright © 1939 by McGraw-Hill. Permission courtesy of McGraw-Hill Book Co.

Reitlinger, Gerald, **The Final Solution: The Attempt to Exterminate the Jews of Europe 1939-1945.** Copyright © 1961 by Gerald Reitlinger. Permission courtesy of A.S. Barnes & Co., Inc.

Simmel, Georg, **The Sociology of Georg Simmel.** Translated, edited, and with an Introduction by Kurt H. Wolff. Copyright © 1950 by The Free Press. Permission courtesy of The Free Press, Macmillan Publishing Co., Inc.

Skinner, B.F., **Beyond Freedom and Dignity.** Copyright © 1971 by B.F. Skinner. Permission courtesy of Alfred A. Knopf, Inc.

Venturi, Franco, **Roots of Revolution.** Copyright © 1952 by Giulio Einaudi Editore. English translation copyright © 1960 by George Weidenfeld and Nicolson, Ltd. Permission courtesy of Giulio Einaudi and Weidenfeld and Nicolson.

Index

Accommodation (mechanism of change), 103, 222, 301, 365, 395
Africa, 114, 192
African National Congress, South Africa, 164, 174
Africans, 286
Afrikaner Nationalists, South Africa, 163, 173
Agents provocateurs, 107, 165, 245
Alegranza, Helen, 114
Algeria, 115, 121, 168
Algerian Revolution, 163, 166
Algiers coup d'état of 1961, 115, 121
America, 152; colonial, 145, 146, 150, 152, 153, 200; colonial struggles, 94, 221. *See also* United States of America
American Indians. *See* Native Americans
American Revolution. *See* War of Independence
Anarchism, 145, 155, 181, 182
Ancien régime, 33, 34, 36, 37, 338
Anti-Semitism, 72, 80, 367
Anweiler, Oskar, 156
Apartheid, 162, 166, 171, 175, 177
Apathy, 4
Ardrey, Robert, 281
Arendt, Hannah, 20, 359; on cooperation with the Holocaust, 75-76, 78-79; on totalitarianism, 82; on relationship of freedom and peace, 143-144; on violence, 144, 147-148; on liberation and freedom, 144-146, 147; on failure of revolutions, 147-151; on authority, 149-150; on government, 151; on "council-based" government, 155-157; on power, 158-159
Argentina, 72, 115
Armenians, 2, 286, 369
Arms control, 197, 201, 207
Assassination, 17n, 121, 130, 291, 294
Assistance: power depends on, of people, 23; withdrawal of, 26. *See also* Consent; Cooperation; Obedience
Asylum, 79
Atomization: in society, 38, 40, 41,

119, 243, 248; under totalitarianism, 40; prevention of, 107
Auschwitz, 74, 89
Austin, John: on power of government, 213
Austria, 279
Authoritarian controls: as a response to terror, 15
Authority, 149, 341-342; defined, 23, 149; uses, 27; limits to, 33; types of, 34, 149, 399; loss of by citizens, 45; source of, 150; and freedom, 149-150; and power, 211, 212, 341. *See also* Legitimated violence; Power and political power

Baden, Germany, 75
Barcelona, Spain: bus boycotts, 192
Barry, Stephanie, xiv
Belgium: resistance to Nazis, 79, 221, 222
Bengal, India, 2
Bengalis, 286
Bennett, John, 204, 267
Berlin, Germany, 78, 85, 88, 92, 215; and Jewish resistance, 225; and Kapp *Putsch,* 229-230
Between a Rock and a Hard Place (Mark O. Hatfield), viii
Bigotry, 2, 290
Blacklist: by Communist regimes, 41
Brophy, Agnes, xiv
Boëtie, Etienne de la: on the power of tyrants, 213
Bolsheviks, 155
Bonaparte. *See* Napoleon Bonaparte
Bondurant, Joan V., 159; on substitute nonviolent sanctions, 305
Bonnet, Georges, 72
Boulding, Kenneth, 281
Boycott, 313; international, 164; in South Africa, 166, 170, 176; in Indian independence struggles, 192; in Montgomery, Alabama, 192; in Barcelona and Madrid, Spain, 192; as a type of nonviolent action, 193; of political institutions, 219; of events, 248; as nonviolent resistance, 249. *See also* Economic boycott; Economic

419

Strikes
Nonlegitimated violence, 288n, 347.
See also Force; Legitimated violence; Political violence; Violence
Nonrecognition of new organizations,
248
Nonresistance, 169
Nonviolence, viii, 164; and violence,
167-168; in Montgomery, Alabama, bus boycott, 223; and political jiu-jitsu, 246; moral nonviolence and nonviolent action, 365;
doctrines of, 379, 380-381, 382;
inadequacies of doctrinal approaches to, 379, 381, 382; as
ethical norm, 395. See also Nonviolent action/sanctions/struggle;
Nonviolent alternatives; Nonviolent resistance; Pacifism; Pacifists
Nonviolent action/sanctions/struggle,
26, 57, 61, 81, 83, 109, 114, 143,
167, 276, 299, 301, 302, 357, 382,
385, 386; defined, 218; general
characteristics of, 61, 102, 103,
170, 219, 246, 274, 300, 302, 340-
342; as a technique of struggle,
25-26, 163, 192, 222; as alternative sanction to replace violence,
19, 57, 62, 163-164, 177, 273-275,
279-280, 300, 329, 342, 347, 357,
360, 370, 371, 373-375, 385, 399;
combined with violent sanctions,
168, 245, 351, 353, 355, 388; use
of, by loci of power, 61, 349, 351;
and power, 25-26, 27, 80, 103, 158,
169, 192, 218, 274, 301, 334, 342;
effects of distribution of power on,
60-62, 80, 167, 219-220, 225, 273,
327, 340, 342-347, 349, 355, 375;
consequences of, 173, 307, 347,
367-368, 375-376; and control of
rulers, 60, 62; creates no institutionalized repression, 61; to replace existing political means,
192-194; and ethics, 395-396; not
pacifism, 219, 274; education
about, 308, 371-373, 385-387; public evaluation of, 387-388; increase
effectiveness of, 232, 302, 303, 306,
307; adapting for new objectives,
383; program for change-over,
306-308, 385, 388-389; needs research and preparations, 105-109,
175, 220, 277, 307-308, 369, 383-
385; changes achieved by, 62, 340;
mechanisms of change in, 103,
222, 275, 301, 365, 395; inadeqa-
cies of, 169-172; failures of, 164;

against oppression/for liberation,
102, 174, 360-365; for revolution,
46, 158, 190, 192, 374; against
dictatorships, 102-105, 109-111,
275; for "unjust" purposes, 365-
368; repression of, 165, 167, 170,
212, 213, 220, 226, 228, 301, 341,
364; and brutalization, 346; and
suffering, 167-168, 170, 246, 362;
and militant initiatives, 364; and
council system of government,
158; and new politics, 193, 194;
for civilian-based defense, 230,
232-233, 275, 280-281, 304; international relevance of, 248-254,
277-279; aims in social policy, 193,
305; specific substitutions of, 304;
vs. violent opponent, 226, 227;
and political jiu-jitsu, 167, 227-
228, 246; openness in, 107, 175;
and cooperation, 345; strategy in,
175-178; and submission, 107, 172,
212, 218, 226, 240, 300, 345, 391;
leadership in, 60-61, 106, 171,
228, 238, 276, 342, 383, 389;
capacity to defend changes, 62;
and political condition, 348, 352,
353, 355; categories of, 218-219;
examples of, 103-104, 192, 221-
222, 279; in U.S.A. history, 299;
case in Montgomery, Alabama,
222-223; case in Vorkuta,
U.S.S.R., 224; case in Berlin,
Germany, 1920, 229-230; case in
Berlin, Germany, 1943, 225; case
in Norway, 226-227; case in South
Africa, 164, 169-170, 192; case in
Czechoslovakia, 230-231, 277-278;
case in Ruhr, 230, 278. See also
America; Belgium; Bulgaria;
China; Civilian-based defense;
Denmark; Effective power; Germany; India; Italy; Jews; Loci of
power; Netherlands; Noncooper-
ation; Nonviolent resistance; Nor-
way; Power and political power;
Resistance; Sanctions
Nonviolent alternatives, viii, 382
Nonviolent Blitzkrieg: in civilian-based
defense, 242, 243
Nonviolent coercion (mechanism of
change), 103, 220, 222, 301, 365,
395
Nonviolent defiance: as nonviolent
sanction, 300. See also Defiance
Nonviolent discipline, 61, 114, 301,
366; and militant initiatives, 364
Nonviolent intervention, 26, 219, 224,

on the war and extermination, 85;
on Nazi extermination program to
September 1939, 86; on Nazi extermination program to October
1941, 88; on connection of genocide and Second World War, 88
Religious opposition, 229; to Nazis,
76, 104
Repression, 8, 100, 108, 162, 277, 322,
344; to force cooperation and
obedience, 99, 107, 108, 213, 341;
against nonviolent struggle, 167,
170, 220, 300, 301; violence brings,
165; State's means of, 185, 188,
193, 289, 294, 317, 323; of dictatorships, 97; may fail to produce
submission, 101, 167, 173, 176,
212, 226, 245, 249, 341, 364; may
produce political *jiu-jitsu*, 167,
210, 228; nonviolent resistance to,
strengthens *loci* of power, 61;
need to eliminate State's means
of, 189; disobedience of agents of,
98, 109; following guerrilla war,
332; and leadership in nonviolent
struggle, 60, 61, 343, 344, 364;
minimizing, 242, 383. *See also*
Effective power; Institutionalized
political violence; Nonviolent ac-
tion/sanctions/struggle; Power
and political power; Sanctions
Resettlement, 77, 80
Resignation of officials, 79, 228
Resistance, 10, 162, 163, 235; spirit
of, 33, 226, 241; right of, 34, 150;
to ruler, 43, 50; to usurpation,
49, 110; to dictatorship, 77, 81-82,
99, 102, 105-110; to Nazis, 77, 80,
81, 103, 104; of Jews, 79, 80; nonmilitary types, 209, 272; as nonviolent action, 218, 277; increased
by repression, 226, 249; to Communism by West, 235; initiating,
in civilian-based defense, 238; selective and total, 242-244; capacity
for future, 243, 249; to the establishment of civilian-based defense,
251; by violent action, 277. *See
also* Civil disobedience; Disobedience; Noncooperation; Nonviolent action/sanctions/struggle;
Nonviolent resistance; Revolution
Resources, human. *See* Human resources
Rethinking politics. *See* Politics
Revolution, 8, 11, 12, 54, 141, 142,
143, 145, 148n, 172, 277, 294; and
destruction of respect for rulers,

33, 149, 158; of peasants, 36; leads
to concentration of power, 37, 38;
Lenin's theory of, 58; right of,
against tyranny, 142, 303; does
not produce freedom, 143, 144,
145, 146-147; and war, 144; spirit
of, 145; "permanent," 146; and
violence, 144, 147-148, 158;
reasons for failure of, 147-151; and
direct democracy, 152, 158; as
seizure of power, 154; possible
without violence, 159; not identical
with peace, 265; may increase military system, 270n; techniques of,
329. *See also* Coup d'état; Guerrilla war; Nonviolent revolt; Nonviolent revolution
The Revolution, 149, 186, 187, 188
Revolutionary violence: as a technique
of struggle, 163. *See also* Nonviolent revolution; Political violence; Revolution; Violent revolution; Violent struggle
Rhodesia, 86
Ribbentrop, Joachim von, 72, 87
Riesman, David: on limits to power of
dictatorships, 97-98, 101
Rioting, 17n, 121, 166, 231, 291; and
substitute sanctions, 305
Riotous Assemblies Act (South
Africa), 171
Roberts, Archbishop T. O., S. J., 115,
126
Robespierre, Maximilien: on constitutional government, 147, 154
Roosevelt, Franklin D., 281
Rosenberg, Alfred, 89
Rousseau, Jean Jacques, 213
Ruhr, Germany: resistance to Franco-
Belgian occupation, 1923, 221,
230, 278
Ruler, 45, 54, 291, 312, 329; defined,
23, 316; traditional means to control, 22, 328; constitution inadequate to control, 39, 47-50, 51,
146, 351; selection of, vs. control
of, 47, 52-55; self-restraint by, 21,
25, 31, 50, 53; unwilling to accept
limits, 23, 26, 30, 48, 53; requirements for effective control of, 25,
46, 47, 328, 332, 340; controlling,
by withholding cooperation, 25-
26, 29, 39, 102, 212, 214, 218, 245,
301; authority and collapse of
authority of, 23, 33, 149, 211, 341;
control depends on internal social
strength, 44; sanctions and control
of, 57; nonviolent action and con-